Expertise and Architecture in the Modern Islamic World

Expertise and Architecture in the Modern Islamic World
A Critical Anthology

Edited by Peter H. Christensen

intellect Bristol, UK / Chicago, USA

Expertise and Architecture in the Modern Islamic World is part of the Critical Studies in Architecture of the Middle East series. The series is edited by Mohammad Gharipour (Morgan State University, Baltimore) and Christiane Gruber (University of Michigan, Ann Arbor).

Critical Studies in Architecture of the Middle East is devoted to the most recent scholarship concerning historic and contemporary architecture, landscape, and urban design of the Middle East and of regions shaped by diasporic communities more globally. The series invites interdisciplinary studies from diverse perspectives that address the visual characteristics of the built environment, ranging from architectural case studies to urban analysis.

First published in the UK in 2018 by
Intellect, The Mill, Parnall Road, Fishponds, Bristol, BS16 3JG, UK

First published in the USA in 2018 by
Intellect, The University of Chicago Press, 1427 E. 60th Street,
Chicago, IL 60637, USA

Copyright © 2018 Intellect Ltd

All rights reserved. No part of this publication may be reproduced, stored in a retrieval system, or transmitted, in any form or by any means, electronic, mechanical, photocopying, recording, or otherwise, without written permission.

A catalogue record for this book is available from the British Library.

Series: Critical Studies in Architecture of the Middle East
Series ISSN: 2059-3562
Contents editor: Kıvanç Kılınç
Copy editor: MPS Technologies
Cover designer: Holly Rose
Production manager: Katie Evans
Typesetting: Contentra Technologies

Print ISBN: 978-1-78320-928-6
ePDF ISBN: 978-1-78320-930-9
ePUB ISBN: 978-1-78320-929-3

Printed and bound by Gomer, UK

This is a peer-reviewed publication.

Contents

Acknowledgements	vii
Introduction Peter H. Christensen	1
Chapter 1: 'I don't want orange trees, I want something that others don't have': Ottoman Head-Gardeners after Mahmud II Deniz Türker	21
Chapter 2: A Nineteenth-Century Architectural Archive: Syed Ahmad Khan's *Āṣār-us-Ṣanādīd* Mrinalini Rajagopalan	51
Chapter 3: The Balyan Family and the *Linguistic Culture* of a Parisian Education Alyson Wharton	85
Chapter 4: Drawing Knowledge, (Re-)Constructing History: Pascal Coste in Egypt Eva-Maria Troelenberg	123
Chapter 5: A Bourguibist Mural in the New Monastir? Zoubeïr Turki's Play on Knowledge, Power, and Audience Perception Jessica Gerschultz	151
Chapter 6: Expertise in the Name of Diplomacy: The Israeli Plan for Rebuilding the Qazvin Region, Iran Neta Feniger and Rachel Kallus	179
Chapter 7: Industrial Complexes, Foreign Expertise, and the Imagining of a New Levant Dan Handel and Alona Nitzan-Shiftan	213
Chapter 8: Mobilities of Architecture in the Global Cold War: From Socialist Poland to Kuwait and Back Łukasz Stanek	237

Chapter 9:	Form Follows Faith: Swedish Architects, Expertise, and New Religious Spaces in the Stockholm Suburbs Jennifer Mack	271
Notes on Contributors		287
Index		291

Acknowledgements

Several of the essays in this volume were first published in the *International Journal of Islamic Architecture* (IJIA), volume 4.2 (2015). The contributors and I wish to thank Kıvanç Kılınç for his editorial insight and advice during the preparation of that issue. I am grateful to Mohammad Gharipour and Christiane Gruber for their invitation to produce this expanded volume. Yasser Tabbaa provided thoughtful criticisms on the Introduction. Katie Evans at Intellect proved invaluable in the production of all aspects of this expanded volume. Additionally, I am grateful to the Department of Art and Art History at the University of Rochester for supporting the costs associated with indexing this volume. Finally, I thank the contributors for their rigorous and original contributions.

Peter H. Christensen
Editor

Introduction

Peter H. Christensen

Islamic Architecture after 1800

Paradigmatic turns in the study of culture are a constant, and the field of Islamic architecture is no exception. A panorama of literature and conferences on the topic from the last decade suggests that we have been in a turn toward historiography and that this period of self-reflection is gradually ending. This historiographic turn has grown in steady proportion to a cross-cultural turn, the latter of which continues to grow. Such turns proffer the double-edged spectre of elemental change to the way in which history is written and the more fleeting trends of fashion.

Yet despite the paradigmatic shifts, some structural concepts persist, and the notion that the intrinsic meaning of architecture in the Islamic world decreased with the advent of European imperialism and colonialism lingers in much of the literature today, even when this notion has been challenged by several scholars, such as Esra Akcan, Sibel Bozdoğan, Zeynep Çelik, and Yasser Elsheshtawy, among others.[1] The imperial and colonial eras were not mere harbingers of erosion, ridding the arts of Islam of their supposed purity and clarity, but were also times of immense synthesis, with the roles of actors in the construction of the built environment, both internal and external to the religious sphere of Islam, changing in dynamic ways. This volume shines a spotlight on these dynamics through new research, bringing historiographic critique together with primary research.

It is easy to understand why the cross-cultural literature has tacitly favoured the periods prior to European imperialism. An environment devoid of vastly imbalanced external political pressure, the erosion of state sovereignty, and couched within the distance of pre-modern space carries with it 'pure' forms of interactional dynamics, equanimity, affinity, and agency as opposed to the sealed and sullying processes of hegemony, subjugation, and force. This edited collection asserts that this contrast of context, and the periodization which results from it, is artificial and neglects the continuous nature of time and the constancy of change; and it serves to remind us how important the inclusion of the nineteenth, twentieth, and twenty-first centuries is to the study of Islamic architecture in its broadest sense.

The chapters in this volume, organized around the specific leitmotif of expertise, demonstrate the thematic importance and specific utility of expertise in the processes that have shaped the construction and form of architecture in the Islamic world from c.1800, where many traditional histories of Islamic architecture end, to the present. The embedded nature of expertise in all issues related to the creation of architecture is salient, too, because it allows the scholarship built around the topic to eschew present and future turns and instead to give expertise the inherent role it deserves as an important lens of analysis in the field.

Architecture, Transmutation, Technicalism

Nasser Rabbat has described the erosion of the arts of Islam as an acceptance of 'incongruity' between Islamic architecture and modernism hinged around a moment when modernism eclipsed Islamic architecture and 'took its place'. 'Consequently,' he argues, 'the architecture built under colonialism and after independence was not considered "Islamic"; it was seen as either modern or culturally hybrid. Studying it was thus the domain of the modernist or the area specialist.'[2]

Modernists and area specialists have typically had few instances to come together at the same table and this is why looking to global history, and particularly its early seminal texts, is useful. Marshall Hodgson's historical portrayal of this Modernist shift centres on the concept of transmutation, which has a number of morphological implications for the study of architecture. Hodgson introduces the concept of transmutation in his exegesis on the 'Generation of 1789', where he defines the ways in which specific economic, social, and intellectual transformations in the Occident fractured the Afro-Eurasian ecumenical world and subsequently facilitated a European hegemony in the nineteenth century.[3] He supplants heroic and local accounts of early modern and Enlightenment era transformation by placing a unique European metamorphosis into a global historical framework that focuses on process rather than product, and mechanics rather than a preordained notion of progress.

As actors, not victors, nineteenth-century Occidentals shifted their allegiances from 'custom and continuity' to 'calculation and innovation', in ways which were more tactical than strategic. Having supposedly manifested its 'greatest' florescence prior to Europe's, Islamic culture had already established institutions of 'independent calculation' and 'personal initiative' and had tactically acclimated its cultural production to accommodate religion. The transmutation, as such, was less a transformation of life than of what Hodgson terms 'technicalism',[4] broadly defined as the primacy of specialized technical considerations over all others. It was this transformation, not religion or culture per se, which facilitated ascendancy and European hegemony, with unique and discrete effects:[5]

> In that special form [of technicalism] [...] the shift went to unprecedented lengths, so that the results set new conditions for all historical life. It was not that the human mind as such was suddenly emancipated, as if by some mutation, and could therefore begin freely to explore all calculable possibilities where, before, new paths could be opened only by chance and despite the weight of customary bias. Rather, concrete new sorts of opportunity for social investment, hitherto impractical even for the most emancipated mind, became practicable, attracting even minds that still, by and large, resisted any deviation from intellectual habit. And then the resistance was gradually reduced.[6]

Introduction

The transmutation and this gradual reduction of resistance to change were global and dependent on the world at large for their actualization. Technicalism trumped the boundaries and challenges posed by artificial limits like state borders, language barriers, and 'hard to exploit markets' because that was its modus operandi.[7] Within the Islamic world, the transmutation and its technicalist grasp introduced specific conflicts and anxieties, including a conflict with agrarian societal organization, which caused significant moral and psychological duress. Yet the transmutation was normalized by the second half of the nineteenth century, partly because technicalism was embraced by Islamic culture and partly because much of the Islamic world came to be ruled by Occidental states that gave it no clear alternative.

The new imperative of technicalism subjected virtually the entire Islamic world to both political and psychological pressures that altered the economies and nature of expertise in that world.[8] In the twentieth and twenty-first centuries, such transformations are more widely described under the rubric of 'globalization', a system where access to expertise is open to so many and so readily that its structure merely mimics capitalist culture writ large with its tendencies toward designification, mimesis, kitsch, and ubiquity.[9] The short-lived but rich Critical Regionalism movement, and to a lesser degree postmodernism, wrestled with these phenomena and yet the void in the literature concerning expertise is plainly evident.

Architecture and Expertise

Although 'expert' and 'expertise' are commonly used to describe the processes of architectural production, both terms are markedly devoid of a critical perspective. Defined as comprehensive and authoritative knowledge of, or skill in, a particular area, the notion of expertise is clearly tethered to the entanglement of power and knowledge at the core of postcolonial studies. Yet, its inherent association with applied 'real-world' design matters has exempted it from the scrutiny directed toward other economies of knowledge in the last three decades.

Owen Jones's *Grammar of Ornament*, for example, is commonly understood as a document that simultaneously constructed knowledge and represented – and in turn perhaps even dominated – much of the non-Western world.[10] But what of the technical expertise of the chromolithographers who made possible the tome's impressive colour reproductions and dispersal to a wide audience? Are they implicated in the process of British hegemony, or does the nature of their technical expertise (as well as their technicalism) make them innocent? Is the question one of innocence in the first place?

One way to think through these questions is to examine the ways in which adjacent fields are rethinking the very rudiments of what constitutes expertise. Thinkers from other humanistic fields have suggested a new sociological paradigm of 'interactional' expertise that generates knowledge through transactional and multilateral engagement.[11]

The flagship example of 'interactional' expertise involves the use of language. Collins and Evans explain:

> […] in France everyone can speak French, 'even the little children', and it is not thought of as an expertise. On the other hand, in Britain a person who is fluent in French is thought of as an expert and can, for example, command a salary as a translator or teacher. It's the opposite way round in France, where it is speaking English that counts as the useful expertise. In a purely relational theory, the expertise involved in speaking French and English is no more nor less than that attributed to speakers of the languages in their respective countries. In a realist/substantive analysis, on the other hand, the degree of expertise in speaking a language remains the same in whichever country the language is spoken.[12]

The fissure this example poses between the 'relational' model and the 'realist/substantive' model could just as easily be seen in the technical skills that aggregate to form Hodgson's notion of technicalism. Like commanding a salary in Britain for expertise in French, commanding a currency of power for expertise in railway engineering, irrigation technology or building construction in places from which those particular forms of expertise did not originate is only expertise when the skill is juxtaposed with the place where it is both not intrinsic and being deployed. If the assumption that a juxtaposition must be made is dropped, the realist model will emancipate us from the notion that the economy of expertise is, in the positivist sense, a system with intrinsic value.

Others have theorized expertise as a system of knowledge management, contending that 'expert' knowledge has no single source (such as a monolithic 'West').[13] Particular to this theorem are the productive aspects that come from the limitations of human cognition. Hinds and Pfeffer note:

> One set of limitations on sharing expertise is cognitive, that is, the way experts store and process information may make it difficult for them to share that expertise with others regardless of whether or not they are motivated to do so. The cognitive limitations faced by experts come partly from the way that they mentally represent the task. As expertise increases, mental representations become more abstract and simplified.[14]

In this model, the ability to represent one's expertise, be it that of an artisan in a guild or of a university graduate, is inversely proportional to the depth of that expertise. 'Western' experts who are contracted to apply their expertise abroad are, by their very selection, top-notch experts and thus, according to the knowledge management model, the least able to transfer their expertise as their knowledge is the most internalized. But as we know, in the Islamic world and elsewhere, the transfer of expertise and technology occurred, often with spectacular effects that went well beyond contract work. The knowledge management model insists that this only occurs when a management system is in place, one in which experts act both as experts – whether as stonemasons or hydroengineers – and also as managers who iteratively communicate and 'represent' their expertise to others in order to execute a project with the optimal balance of context and innovation.

The questions that the new forms of 'interactional' and knowledge-management expertise pose for the study of the Islamic world's architecture are wide-ranging. How, for example, were the dynamics of competition between associations of craftsmen in medieval and early modern Islamic cities reconfigured after 1800, and how were the key urban spaces where information was exchanged – the storehouse, the market, and the university – reshaped or transmuted in the process? With the Islamic world's rapidly increasing contact with Europe, and also with Africa, East Asia, and later North America, how did conceptions of expertise shift in light of the crafts and skills of previously unknown populations? To what extent has technology (perceived as originating outside the Islamic world) from the nineteenth century to the present reinforced the stereotype of an expert 'West', and to what extent has such technology facilitated new forms of autonomous creative production in the Islamic world? What are the promises and the pitfalls of the contemporary free market economy's ability to import foreign expertise to develop local built environments?

Modern Heuristics

As much as the nature of expertise in architecture transformed through the erosion of guilds and empires, the transformation did not have a one-to-one relationship with state sovereignty. The German–Ottoman relationship, which blossomed around the midpoint of this volume's chronological scope and existed within the ambiguous context that comes with a semi-colonial condition, is a useful heuristic for understanding the full range of transmutations that followed the relatively static pre-nineteenth-century model of expertise.

While we can see a clear Ottoman desire for German technological and economic expertise in the construction of their railways (constructed between 1868 and 1919), there are also thousands of construction sites, large and small, where German plans were executed through the expertise of Ottoman labourers and craftsmen, under varying degrees of German supervision – providing an exemplar of what Faroqhi describes as an informal system of artisanal 'input' in the wake of the traditional guild system's demise.[15]

The very ambiguity of the input between Germans and Ottomans is splendidly evident in a single artefact: the German Fountain, centrally located in Istanbul's historic Hippodrome. This German Fountain (*Alman Çeşmesi*) is the most potent symbol of the German–Ottoman partnership, and its provenance clearly illustrates the process of transmutation. In 1898, Kaiser Wilhelm summoned the architect Max Spitta and apparently quickly sketched a fountain to be given as a memento to the Sultan, asking Spitta to develop and execute the fountain.

Apparently, Wilhelm had been intrigued by the fountain's double function in Islamic society as both a benevolent civic provision and a facilitator of the customs of worship. At some point thereafter, the emperor and Spitta enlisted the service of the former Ottoman ambassador to Berlin and then Minister of Foreign Affairs, Ahmet Tevfik Pasha, who, equipped with perfect German, relayed Spitta's plans for the fountain to the sultan through verbal descriptions of its form, an iteration of interactional expertise.

Spitta's designs went through several trials before Wilhelm found them satisfactory. The first design was a covered octagonal pavilion constructed of medium-sized ashlar, with stout Byzantine-style columns of black marble and thickly framed, rounded arches. Beneath a decorative band, two faces depict the *Bundesadler*, the symbol of imperial Germany in the form of an eagle, and a third depicts the *tuğra*, the sultan's imperial emblem. Upon close inspection, one notices a large pencilled 'X' drawn across the centre of the fountain's image [Figure 0.1]. The intersection of the 'X' appears virtually on top of the central *Bundesadler*. This mark, most certainly made by the emperor, indicates a rejection of Spitta's scheme and, perhaps,

Figure 0.1: *Max Spitta, design for a fountain in Constantinople, elevation, iteration 1, 1899.* Architekturmuseum der Technischen Universität Berlin.

of the figurative *Bundesadler* in particular. Does this indicate Kaiser Wilhelm's cognizance of the supposed prohibition of figural motifs in Islamic art? Wilhelm was, as we know from his diaries and numerous other accounts, an amateur student of the Orient and Islam and their customs. Regardless, the *Bundesadler*, which now emerges as the locus of visible versus invisible extraterritorial ambition, would not appear in subsequent iterations. Spitta went through four more iterations of the design before completing the fifth and final rendition.

Up close, the fountain bears even more symbols and inscriptions. These include two epistolary works, one in German and one in Ottoman Turkish. The Ottoman text is an eight-couplet poem with epigraphy by Hattat İzzet Efendi (1841–1903), reproduced by the Berlin mosaic artist August Oetken (1868–1951) as a band undulating over the eight archways within the interior of the dome.[16] The text, presumably edited with Abdülhamid's blessing, is a typical hagiographic epigram, identifying Wilhelm as a 'well-informed' and 'able' soldier, a 'compassionate' visitor to the Holy Land, a ruler 'honoured with respect of Islam', and the builder of the fountain. The word used for 'fountain', *selsebil*, actually refers to a mythical fountain in paradise providing sweet water.

While German archives reveal certain tensions in the morphology of Spitta's design, Ottoman records speak to tensions around the fountain's siting. In the summer of 1899, the General Protocols Office reported that the Sultan, upon hearing of the Kaiser's intention to give the fountain as a gift, noted that the suburb of Nişantaşı would be an ideal location.[17] With a great deal of polite flourishes, an official named Tahsin reported Wilhelm's apparent objection to siting the fountain in the suburbs, preferring instead to situate it in a place where the Kaiser's 'obedience' to the Porte would be seen by more people.[18] And so it was resolved to site the fountain in its ultimate, extremely prominent location. Tacitly, this shows the sultan's expertise in handling the Kaiser's unwanted demands, and it also implicates him as the expert on the fountain's proper siting. Viewed from an alternate direction, it may show, instead, that Wilhelm, with his rudimentary knowledge of the Orient, was able to 'play' the sultan.

After being inaugurated in January 1901, the fountain provided a stream of headaches for its beneficiaries. Within weeks, vandals had stripped the fountain of all of its faucets and a number of its most precious mosaic stones.[19] To make matters worse, the vandalism forced a protracted debate between the Ministry of the Interior, the Ministry of Foreign Affairs, the Ministry of Public Works, and the Grand Vizier himself over who, precisely, was the expert responsible for the fountain's well-being.[20] The debate essentially hinged on whether the fountain was considered primarily a diplomatic symbol or a waterwork.

The onus for the fountain's upkeep ultimately fell upon the Ministry of the Interior, indicating that its delegation as a diplomatic symbol trumped that of a fountain.[21] It also indicates that the authorities were loath to call upon Spitta himself for the replacement parts for fear of embarrassment over their custodial neglect. When the faucets were again stolen, within three weeks, it became clear that the reason was not a perceived value of German faucets as manufactured objects but rather a general public disregard for the fountain's status as a site for ablutions.[22] The Minister of the Interior was both baffled and irritated by the recurring faucet disappearances and, after replacing them a second time and building a wrought iron fence around the structure to the tune of 140,300 piasters, he delegated the fountain's security to the Constantinople police sergeant Arif, who appointed full-time guards for its protection.[23] Expertise, as became clear in the case of this small monument, required the collective insight and talents of the kaiser, the sultan, a diplomat, an architect, a poet, an epigrapher, a mosaicist, and two policemen, a multi-level and multi-national admixture that became more the norm than the exception in the modern period.

A more widely known project, Hassan Fathy's New Gourna Village in Upper Egypt, offers insight into how expertise factors into the canon of the modern architecture of the Islamic world, to the extent such a canon exists. In 1945, Fathy was enlisted by the Egyptian government to author and execute a master plan for the inhabitants of the village community of Old Gourna. Effectively, the Egyptian government was seeking to use planning and architecture as a means of terminating the villagers' longstanding livelihood of looting antiquities from nearby pharaonic tombs, in turn 'civilizing' the population and settling them in established communities that emphasized mainstream economics and civic values.

Fathy, born into an upper-class family of Ottoman Turkish origin, trained at King Fuad University in Cairo and quickly gained a reputation as a skilled planner and architect who distinguished himself from his Western colleagues, many of whom were receiving major commissions for the construction of new towns and cities in the post-World War II order.[24] Fathy's plan for New Gourna comprised a close adherence to the Nubian mud brick tradition, classical pharaonic architectural elements including freestanding vaults and arches, and a spatial ethos that upheld the Islamic tradition of a clear delineation between public and private spheres through the design of courtyards, privacy planes, and a constellation of prominent public facilities including a central square, a khan, a mosque, a theatre, and town hall, among others [Figure 0.2]. New Gourna was partially realized but left incomplete in 1952 due to an array of bureaucratic hurdles, disagreements with villagers, and financial problems.[25] Nevertheless, the project was extoled by numerous Western critics and visitors, many citing the ways in which Fathy applied a modernist design sensibility in conjunction with a sensitivity to the climate, materiality, and anthropology of those for whom he was designing. It was for many a harbinger of the so-called Critical Regionalism movement, whose promise lay in its ability to reconcile certain 'universal' humanistic aspects of modernism with local cultures and contexts. In fact, just such a sentiment remains the main lens through which a number of institutions have viewed Fathy's project and his life work more generally. Among them is the World Monuments Fund, which said the following of the project in a 2011 Executive Report concerning the conservation of the project:

> At New Gourna, Fathy pedestaled his vision of vernacular building traditions and promoted precise forms and materials he had seen and utilized in rural Egypt. Intended as a model public housing project and perhaps the codification of a national style, the mud brick, domed dwellings gained international attention and are today considered early experiments with appropriate technology and sustainable architectural systems.[26]

Introduction

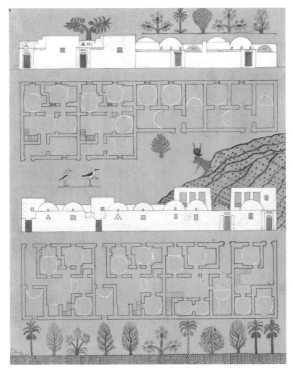

Figure 0.2: *Hassan Fathy, representational scheme of New Gourna, 1945.* Aga Khan Trust for Culture, Geneva, Switzerland.

As Hana Taragan has shown, however, Fathy's utopian vision for New Gourna was far from successful, certainly programmatically but perhaps also conceptually. For starters, the villagers did not wish to give up the lucrative looting practices on which generations rested, and they were provided with few economic alternatives by the Egyptian government.[27] Architecturally too some issues proved problematic: the Egyptian writer and journalist Fathi Ghanim highlighted the confusion and scepticism surrounding Fathy's extensive use of the dome in his 1959 novela entitled *al-Jabal* in which the narrator and his wife echo the villagers' befuddlement over the use of the dome as a sort of cellular unit because they understood domes in Nubian architecture to be synonymous primarily with tombs and tombs alone.[28]

The most intractable aspect of Fathy's project at New Gourna, however, is neither political nor architectural but rather centred in the philosophical strictures through which Fathy himself asserted and projected expertise. Fathy's position as an educated, upper-class Egyptian who was well connected with the government afforded him a rarely duplicated authorial and representative platform to describe what it meant to be both modern, particularly in terms of welfare and comfort, and Egyptian. What complicates this platform is that Fathy's philosophical rhetoric, most notably in his 1969 treatise *Architecture for the Poor*, a book that details Fathy's thinking in New Gourna, is essentially philanthropic rather than ideological. He commonly describes the New Gourna villagers in ambivalent terms like 'poor', 'ignorant', 'shrewd', 'loyal', 'genial', and 'simple' that make it at once difficult to dispute his design expertise but also challenging to understand the motives for which he deploys it. Taragan has gone so far as to suggest that the New Gourna project was a vehicle for Fathy to propel his ego and his career at the expense of what was best for the villagers.[29]

But when one returns to the question of expertise, one must reckon with a more ambiguous reality, one Taragan overlooks despite the rich excerpts explicitly addressing the topic in *Architecture for the Poor*. Early on his exegesis, Fathy describes expertise in unequivocal terms:

> The modern advance in technology which has given us new materials and methods in building has also necessitated the intrusion of the professional architect, a specialist who has been taught the science of working in these materials. The architect with his expertise has taken all the pleasure of house building away from his client, who is unable to catch up with the rapidly advancing techniques. Now, instead of the unhurried, appreciative discussions with the craftsmen as the house is being built, the owner has the opportunity to exercise his choice over marks on a plan in the architect's office. He doesn't understand the idiom of architectural drawing nor the architect's jargon, so the architect despises him and browbeats him or else deceives him into accepting what the architect wants by adding specious trees and motorcars.[30]

Architectural expertise qua architectural expertise is for Fathy the imprimatur of systemic oppression on which knowledge is weaponized to disempower the poor and conform them to a way of life that they may not need, want, or know how to perform. Indeed, expertise is an explicitly socio-economic topic, as he exclaims shortly thereafter:

> And the architect? If he has no time to spend in individual consultation, if he is not offered enough money to make the job worth his while, then the job is not for him. Let him go and hawk his expertise to people who will pay for it, and leave the poor to design their own houses. To take the other alternative, to design one house and multiply it by a thousand, as a road engineer designs a section of road and unreels it for any number of miles, is to betray his profession, to sacrifice the artistic nature of house to money, and to abandon his own integrity.[31]

Remarkably, what Fathy suggests in his disavowal of architectural expertise is the promotion of the architect to embody and exercise alternative forms of expertise, that of the anthropologist or the sociologist, in inherently imbuing them with the ability to evaluate and diagnose what is or is not suitable (be it motorcars or mud brick) for their clients.

It is not until later in his text that Fathy contends with the intricacies of expertise as it relates to the governmental network with which he himself was so entangled.

> There is in every village a traditional and very reasonable tendency to look upon 'the government' as a kind of heathen god, to be feared, propitiated, prayed to, and from which unexpected blessings may descend, but it seldom occurs to the villager that the government is something you may cooperate with, something with which you may even conclude a reasonable agreement on tackling a problem [...] The cost of everything – architects, engineers, machines, masons and clerks – had to come out of that [government] money. If the villagers availed themselves of our expertise, then they could have good houses very cheaply, but only if they contributed the unskilled labor and much of the transport themselves for nothing.[32]

So while Fathy reminds us that architectural expertise is a loaded socio-economic mechanism that can be used for control and subjugation, he nevertheless also suggests that the poor might consider swallowing a certain amount of pride when it comes to accepting such expertise for the financial stakes and potential gains, which for New Gourna were enormous. Herein Fathy weaves an unusual and interrelated web of expertise contingent on the relations between a primary triad of actors: the government, the architect, and the common man. In so doing, Fathy suggests that expertise is a sort of bartering economy in the modern era, one in which the advantages of what are often Western notions of welfare and comfort are weighed against individual sovereignty and integrity. The biggest ramifications of such a triangulation are indeed those of the architect: the architect's expertise as a designer is ostensibly 'devalued' in direct proportion to his ability to act as anthropologist and sociologist.

Fathy's tactical argument that the expertise of the architect is largely embedded in anthropology would seem to foreshadow the intellectual landscape today. Anthropology today may indeed be the great bastion of expertise discourse when it comes to architecture, which is perhaps why architectural historians have to a large degree overlooked what it is saying. One of the very best examples of such work is Trevor Marchand's work on the masonry traditions of Djenné [Figure 0.3].

Marchand's study rests on the author's extensive fieldwork in Mali, where he lived and worked alongside mud brick masons as they built a large residential vacation complex for a Dutch client. Located on the Bani River in Mali, Djenné has been a lively settlement for more than two millennia, situated at the crossroads of numerous historical trade and pilgrimage routes extending across Africa to both its east and west and north and south. Djenné is particularly renowned for its mud brick architecture, which are most commonly associated with the large central mosque and the residences of important merchant-traders. The masons hesitantly take Marchand on as an apprentice on the project and from there the reader follows him on his journey to become a skilled craftsman. Marchand's insights

Figure 0.3: *View of a mason at work in Djenné.* Trevor H. J. Marchand.

into the masons' lives reveal, among other things, a string of dualities. These include the tension between their relatively low economic status and a certain working-class valour that is bestowed upon them within the community and the non-verbal yet profoundly coded means of communicating both knowledge and logistics at the building site.

The second point is particularly important to the theme of expertise, which is for all intents and purposes the central theme to Marchand's study. Early in his apprenticeship, Marchand makes the following observation:

> Not surprisingly, much work-related communication between craftspeople is nonverbal, commonly relying on an intercourse of gesturing and deictic pointing, as well as other sources of visual, auditory, and somatic information exchanged between acting bodies. Daily immersion in this environment heightened my attentiveness to a multitude of stimuli that impact the making of both builders and buildings.[33]

Such observations of the non-verbal communication of expertise typify the knowledge management theory of expertise, where knowledge, and eventually the mastery of it in the form of expertise, is performed not in the traditional teacher-student condition but rather in a nexus of collaborative work that renders it difficult to articulate in more conventional forms of transmission. Relational theory is also at play, primarily as the result of the slow but steady changes in traditional masonry in Djenné that began with French colonialism and continue with globalization. The organic crenellations of the buildings grow sharper and geometric when the masons began to use French spades made of metal. The shape of the bricks themselves changed from cylindrical to rectangular, streamlining the facades and creating sharper edges. And, as is plainly evident, in Marchand's own construction site, the sheer scale of the buildings began to grow as UNESCO and foreign tourists and investors turned their attention to the ostensibly separate but intrinsically intertwined missions of preserving and developing the city.

Marchand makes plain the ways in which masonry expertise in Djenné is tied not only to a knowledge management model but to a distinct social and cultural status that carries with it its own political economy:

> A Mason's knowledge is embodied in his activities and is therefore conceived as interiorized and individually possessed. Like the secret knowledge of *bey-bibi* and *bey-koray*, trade knowledge should be carefully managed and selectively revealed. It is coveted as a precious resource that differentiates craftspeople from others, and its accumulation in the form of skilled practice and secret incantations promotes a public recognition of expertise and status.[34]

From the Gardens of Istanbul to the Suburbs of Stockholm

This volume is arranged in rough chronological order and opens with '"I don't want orange trees, I want something that others don't have": Ottoman Head-Gardeners after Mahmud II' by Deniz Türker. Türker's study of the Bavarian gardener Christian Sester and his design for the groves at Çırağan Palace demonstrate how Ottoman Tanzimat reforms, long associated with modernization based on European models, impacted the highly symbolic, yet sorely understudied, culture around gardening. Sester's position as the inaugural 'Head-Gardener', it turns out, was actually a role shaped largely from a desire to extend the pre-Tanzimat tradition of foreign horticultural expertise. The significant change in the Ottoman imperial relationship to gardening was, Türker demonstrates, more a cross-cultural conjugation of Sester's training in post-Enlightenment principles than a simple desire on behalf of the Ottomans to Europeanize.

In 'A Nineteenth-Century Architectural Archive: Syed Ahmad Khan's *Āṣār-us-Ṣanādīd*' Mrinalini Rajagopalan explores how the establishment of British colonialism in the nineteenth-century India cannot be separated from European projects that surveyed and classified the objects, peoples, and practices of the subcontinent. She demonstrates how Indian and European curiosity about architectural monuments took on a special significance at this time as historic buildings were seen as purveyors of 'factual' historical information.

This chapter, rooted in the *Āṣār-us-Ṣanādīd* (Traces of Noblemen, first ed. 1847), a 600-page comprehensive survey of Delhi's monuments written in Urdu by the Indian intellectual Syed Ahmad Khan, examines the visual, chronological, and comparative methodologies used in the *Āṣār-us-Ṣanādīd* and argues that Syed Ahmad created a thoroughly modern archive of Delhi's historic architecture and shaped the idea of the monument itself.

In her chapter 'The Balyan Family and the *Linguistic Culture* of a Parisian Education' Alyson Wharton documents the education of two Armenian–Ottoman architects in Paris in the middle of the nineteenth century. Following Nigoğos and Serkis Balyan to the Collège Sainte-Barbe, the Ecole Centrale, and the Ecole des Beaux-Arts, it traces aspects of the education they were exposed to. The chapter then moves on to investigate where the impact of this education can be seen in specific architectural works. Showing how these architects manipulated their Parisian education to express an Ottoman renaissance, the chapter stresses how these Ottoman subjects were not creating imitative works but were creative actors in their own right, 'linguistically' engaging in an original way with what they had learnt, and refashioning it in a pragmatic way to their Istanbul setting.

Eva-Maria Troelenberg's 'Drawing Knowledge, (Re-)Constructing History: Pascal Coste in Egypt' explores the nature of expertise in Pascal Coste's work for Muhammad Ali, Khedive of Egypt and Sudan, through the medium of the drawing. This chapter revisits Coste's work as an engineer and as an historian of architecture and highlights drawing as a medium that articulated cross-cultural knowledge both tied to and divergent from conventional notions of expertise as they were formed in Europe. Troelenberg's careful assessment of Coste's portfolio provides a fresh perspective on the role of the Muslim Middle East and related notions of tradition within the narrative formulated in France of a larger modern Mediterranean.

Jessica Gerschultz's 'A Bourguibist Mural in the New Monastir? Zoubeïr Turki's Play on Knowledge, Power, and Audience Perception' tackles the issue of expertise through a close examination of *La Procession des Mourabtines*, a mural by Zoubeïr Turki, a prominent artist of the École de Tunis. Gerschultz places us in the lobby of the Hôtel Ribat in Monastir, the site of the mural, a single vantage point from which we observe how the complex issues of iconography, patronage, and position in Monastir's postcolonial architectural landscape unfold and elucidate the contentious and hierarchical relationships of power underwriting the art and tourism industries during the decade of Tunisian socialism. The artist's dual reference to Tunisia's Islamic history and Habib Bourguiba's burgeoning cult of personality testify to his engagement with claims to religious expertise in a contested political economy.

A trio of articles, focusing on Israel, Iran, and Kuwait, brings us to the 1970s and 1980s, two decades that witnessed nation building as much as they did the commodification and redefinition of expertise on a truly international scale. Dan Handel and Alona Nitzan-Shiftan's 'Industrial Complexes, Foreign Expertise, and the Imagining of a New Levant' explores the linguistic codification of expertise in the loaded geographical term 'Levant'. Handel and Nitzan-Shiftan show how, while still in circulation well after World War II, the term came to acquire an anachronistic and derogatory aura as the Middle East was realigned with the interests of new world powers, geared toward the potential of oil fields in the Persian Gulf.

The capacity of 'Levant' to act as a meaningful term received a surprising reinforcement from Israeli industrialist Stef Wertheimer, who advanced a series of experimental industrial complexes, known as the Tefen Model, which were facilitated by the work of American organizations, planning, and architecture experts and the legacy of the Marshall Plan. While the Tefen model began as a contained regional project, focusing on the contested Israeli Galilee region, it gradually scaled up its regionalist argument, anchored in both the proto-neoliberalism of its founder and the knowledge of the experts he employed, to redefine a *New Levant* according to the terms of free economy and, possibly, to galvanize an industrial-based form of neo-imperialism in the Cold War period.

Tracing the surprising aftermath of the September 1962 earthquake in the Qazvin region of Iran, Neta Feniger and Rachel Kallus detail the story of a group of Israeli experts sent to assist Iranian relief efforts. A small project, the reconstruction of one village, led to a larger project initiated by the United Nations, in which a team of experts from Israel were sent to survey and plan the region devastated by the quake. Israeli assistance to Iran was also intended to reinforce bilateral relations between the countries. The disaster offered an opportunity for demonstrating Israeli expertise in a range of fields including architecture, and to consolidate Israel's international image as an agent for development. This chapter examines transnational exchange via professional expertise, using the participation of Israeli architects in the rebuilding of Qazvin as a case study, to demonstrate that architects were agents of Israel's diplomatic goals. The architects had professional objectives, namely the creation of a modern plan for the region and its villages. At the same time, these objectives were intertwined with the Shah of Iran's national modernization plan, and with Israel's desire to become Iran's ally in this drive for change and modernization, in the hope of promoting a different Middle East.

Addressing the issue of the Iron Curtain from a different purview, Łukasz Stanek takes us to Kuwait in his chapter 'Mobilities of Architecture in the Global Cold War: From Socialist Poland to Kuwait and Back' to explore the little-known economies of expertise surrounding a circle of architects from socialist countries who worked in that country. Stanek demonstrates how transfers between Eastern Europe and the Gulf expedited a shift in transnational architectural culture, with architects from socialist countries learning in Kuwait at least as much as they brought with them. During their work in the Gulf, they responded to the disenchantment with post-oil urbanization in the region, expressed by the widespread turn toward images, ways of use, and patterns of mobility associated with 'traditional' urbanism and reinforced by postmodernism as the new mainstream in architectural discourse and practice. Yet rather than considering this shift as an architectural 'mediation' between 'global' technology and 'local' culture, Stanek shows how it was facilitated by re-contextualized expert systems, such as construction technologies and computer-aided design (CAD) software, but also by the specific portable 'profile' of experts from socialist countries.

The final chapter, 'Form Follows Faith: Swedish Architects, Expertise, and New Religious Spaces in the Stockholm Suburbs', examines the contemporary role played by architects in Western and Northern Europe as they design mosques and other religious buildings in staunchly secular contexts. Jennifer Mack's particular case study of the northern suburbs of Stockholm is fascinating, posing, and tentatively answering, a number of important questions: What happens when clients request Islamic ornament or completely separate internal spaces for men and women, moves which are anathema to Swedish convention? How has bureaucratic expertise in these projects become an asset that trumps the design knowledge, which a more seasoned mosque architect – either from abroad or from within the community – might bring? Why does the city's bureaucracy seek to restrain the formal and social aspirations of those who wish to invest in what is nonetheless an expensive icon of a 'New Swedish' architecture?

Taken together, these chapters address how the processes of empire building, modernization, statecraft, and diplomacy – some of the most common themes of architecture in the nineteenth, twentieth, and twenty-first centuries – have been contingent on a web of expertise defined by a rich and varied array of authors and contexts. These studies demonstrate that while European and later North American agents and paradigms of expertise left a strong, often forceful, imprint on the architecture of the Islamic world, a number of dynamic forces internal to Islamic tradition, from the practices of gardening to mosque design, from the mural to the master plan, consistently inflected these imprints, turning our attention away from a sweeping obsession with agency toward the vicissitudes of historical and cultural context.

Notes

1 See, for example, Esra Akcan, *Architecture in Translation: Germany, Turkey, and the Modern House* (Durham, NC: Duke University Press, 2012); Sibel Bozdoğan, *Modernism and Nation Building: Turkish Architectural Culture in the Early Republic* (Seattle: University of Washington Press, 2002); Zeynep Çelik, *Empire, Architecture, and the City: French-Ottoman Encounters, 1830–1914* (Seattle: University of Washington Press, 2008); Yasser Elsheshtawy, *The Evolving Arab City: Tradition, Modernity and Urban Development* (London: Routledge, 2011).
2 Nasser Rabbat, 'What Is Islamic Art Anyway?', *Journal of Art Historiography* 6 (June 2012): 3, http://arthistoriography.files.wordpress.com/2012/05/rabbat1.pdf.
3 Hodgson, *Venture of Islam* (Chicago: University of Chicago Press, 1977), 177.
4 Ibid.
5 See Ziya Gokalp's distinction between culture (*hars*) and civilization (*medeniyet*), which are indebted to the thinking of Émile Durkheim. Niyazi Berkes, trans., *Turkish Nationalism and Western Civilization: Selected Essays* (London: Allen & Unwin, 1959).
6 Ibid., 182–83.
7 Ibid., 201.
8 See, for example, Arnold Pacey's comparison of the British and American 'railroad empires' with those of India, Turkey, and Japan in *Technology in World Civilization* (Cambridge, MA: MIT Press, 1990), 131–67.
9 Perceptions of these effects were also important in galvanizing the critical regionalist movement, which paid considerable attention to the effects of globalization on the Islamic

world. See Liane Lefaivre and Alexander Tzonis, *Critical Regionalism: Architecture and Identity in a Globalised World* (London: Prestel, 2003).
10 Carol Hrvol Flores, *Owen Jones: Design, Ornament, Architecture & Theory in an Age of Transition* (New York: Rizzoli, 2006).
11 Harry Collins and Robert Evans, *Rethinking Expertise* (Chicago: University of Chicago Press, 2007), 77–90; primarily a sociological study.
12 Ibid., 3.
13 Mark Ackerman, Volkmar Pipek, and Volker Wulf, eds, *Sharing Expertise: Beyond Knowledge Management* (Cambridge, MA: MIT Press, 2003), 77–158; a business and management study.
14 Pamela J. Hinds and Jeffrey Pfeffer, 'Why Organizations Don't "Know What They Know": Cognitive and Motivational Factors Affecting the Transfer of Expertise', in *Sharing Expertise*, eds Ackerman, Pipek, and Wulf, 5.
15 Suraiya Faroqhi, *Artisans of Empire: Crafts and Craftspeople Under the Ottomans* (London and New York: I.B. Tauris, 2009), 186–207.
16 Başbakanlık Osmanlı Arşivi (BOA), Y.PRK.MF 4 40; Y.PRK.HR 27 32.
17 BOA, Y.PRK.EŞA 35 39.
18 Ibid.
19 BOA, ZB 379 59.
20 BOA, DH.MKT 2391 44.
21 BOA, ZB 45 95.
22 BOA, ZB 55 62; ZB 374 112.
23 BOA, ZB 379 59; DH.MKT 2520 41.
24 See 'Fathy, Hassan 1900–1989', in *Encyclopedia of 20th-Century Architecture Volume 1 A–F*, ed. R. Stephen Sennott (New York and London: Taylor & Francis, 2004), 838–41.
25 Hana Taragan, 'Architecture in Fact and Fiction: The Case of the New Gourna Village in Upper Egypt', *Muqarnas: An Annual on the Visual Culture of the Islamic World* 16 (1999): 169–78.
26 World Monuments Fund, 'New Gourna Villages: Conservation and Community', (report issued March 2011), accessed October 15, 2017, https://www.wmf.org/sites/default/files/article/pdfs/New%20Gourna%20Report%20Final%2015%20Meg.pdf.
27 Taragan, 'Architecture in Fact and Fiction', 169.
28 Fathi Ghanim, *al-Jabal* (The Mountain) (Cairo: Dar al-Hilal, 1965); first published in serial form in the weekly *Ruz-al-Yusuf* in 1958, then as a book in 1959.
29 Taragan, 'Architecture in Fact and Fiction', 175.
30 Hassan Fathy, *Architecture for the Poor: An Experiment in Rural Egypt* (Chicago: University of Chicago Press, 1973), 14. The book was originally published in Cairo in 1969 as *Gourna: A Tale of Two Villages*; see also *Construire avec le people: histoire d'un village d'Égypte, Gourna* (Paris: Sindbad, 1970).
31 Fathy, *Architecture for the Poor*, 16.
32 Ibid., 66.
33 Trevor H.J. Marchand, *The Masons of Djenné* (Bloomington: Indiana University Press, 2009), 9.
34 Ibid., 97.

Chapter 1

'I don't want orange trees, I want something that others don't have': Ottoman Head-Gardeners after Mahmud II

Deniz Türker

The reform-minded sultans Mahmud II (*r*.1808–36) and his son Abdülmecid (*r*.1836–61) eagerly sought out advisors to help transform their environments to befit the enlightened, politically engaged, public role they cast for themselves. The sites they chose for their new residences on the shores of the Bosphorus would naturally become emblematic of this imperial refashioning. Çırağan Palace's vast and hilly backdrop, which would later become Yıldız Palace's ten-hectare park, would constitute the principal experimental ground for this image quest. The site's makers were the trained recruits of a Bavarian gardener called Christian Sester (1804–66). Leading labourers predominantly from Albania and the Black sea, Sester, his assistants, and his successors would institute a predominantly German gardening dynasty in the Ottoman court – a new kind of gardening corps crafted from a long-established imperial institution. The work of Sester's team would only be disrupted at the turn of the century, when the court began to value different modes of horticultural expertise, and turned its attention to France. If, in very broad strokes, the nineteenth-century Ottoman garden history is characterized by grand landscaping projects modelled on Yıldız, the twentieth century marked an obsessive turn to cultivation and acclimation of plants inside the most technically advanced greenhouses and palm houses.[1] Ultimately, these changes of interest were not only related to matters of taste, but also tinged with the competitive spirit of shifting diplomatic alliances, as well as national and international political networks.

Until Mahmud's overhaul of the Janissary corps in 1826, the Ottoman imperial gardens, from aspects of their design to the agricultural production derived from them, were tied to one of its most prominent branches: the *bostancı ocağı* (gardeners' corps).[2] Only a few months after the Janissaries were violently disbanded, the gardeners' corps was completely and, much more peaceably, restructured under a military charter (*nizamname*) on August 5, 1826.[3] The eldest members were forced to retire with lifetime pensions (*kayd-ı hayat*), while the able-bodied were redeployed to train with Mahmud's new army, the *asakir-i mansure-i Muhammediye*, and serve as officers (*zabit*) in the gates, barracks, and police offices on the Dolmabahçe-Ortaköy shoreline, where the court now resided full-time.[4] A decade later, Mahmud's ambassador to Vienna came back with an idea that would fill the void for the upkeep of the many imperial gardens: a foreign garden-director – a professional with knowledge of the latest in landscape design, botany, and horticulture – would restore the vacant post of the palace's *bostancıbaşı* (translatable to head-gardener) to its erstwhile garden-centred metier. This practice would continue until the First World War at Yıldız, the longest serving imperial palace of the nineteenth century, transformed in half a century into the corps' operational headquarters.

In the gardeners' corps' earliest incarnation under Mehmed II (r.1444–46, 1451–81), its members attended to the palace gardens and royal retreats, while their superior *bostancıbaşı*, the only court official allowed to grow a beard, held the privileged position of helming the sultan's boat during the latter's seafaring trips along the Bosphorus [Figure 1.1].[5] The structure of this corps would undergo drastic transformations, and shed the fifteenth-century horticultural requisites of the young Janissary conscripts that gave their group its name. Especially with the emergence of Janissary unrest in the seventeenth-century, the corps started to represent the personal security force of the imperial household.[6] By the time Marie-Gabriel-Florent-Auguste de Choiseul-Gouffier (d.1817), the French ambassador to the court of Abdülhamid I (r.1774–1889) and dilettante-antiquarian of ancient Greek artefacts, published his *Voyage pittoresque en Grèce* (1782), the head-gardener had become '*la police intérieure du sérail*' (interior police of the palace), who presided over the Bosphorus in an austere waterfront building in Kuruçeşme, allocated to his office and in the immediate vicinity of the sultan's summer retreat in Beşiktaş

Figure 1.1: *Le Bostandji-Bachi, J.M. Moreau (le jeune) in Marie-Gabriel-Auguste-Florent Choiseul-Gouffier,* Voyage pittoresque de la Grèce *(1782–[1824])*. Harvard University Fine Arts Library Collection.

'I don't want orange trees, I want something that others don't have'

Figure 1.2: *Vue du kiosque du Bostandji-Bachi á Kourou-Tchechmé, Marie-Gabriel-Florent-Auguste de Choiseul-Gouffier,* Voyage pittoresque en Grèce *(1782–[1824])*. Harvard University Fine Arts Library Collection.

[Figure 1.2].[7] Later, the first recruits of Selim III's new model army, the ill-fated *nizam-ı cedid*, wore the red-felt *barata* headgear of the ruler's *bostancı*-bodyguards as a symbolic gesture of the trust established between the ruler and his protectors.[8]

Foreign Head-Gardeners in the Ottoman Court

In fact, it was during Selim III's reign that the court first experimented with a foreign head-gardener to redesign its imperial gardens in the capital. Later on, Mahmud II's restoration of a majority of the novel offices that Selim had instituted would also extend to the reactivation of this post. Baron von Herbert, the Austrian *internuncio* to Selim's court, had imported a gardener from Rastatt by the name of Jacob Ensle (*d*.1832) in 1794, who was fortunate enough to be residing with his stepbrother, the distinguished naturalist Franz Boos (1753–1832), botanical gardener and menagerie director of the Schönbrunn Palace in Vienna, during von Herbert's recruitment efforts. Ensle, who appears to have led many a late-eighteenth century European traveller through the doors of the Topkapı's new sections, while maintaining relative anonymity as 'M. Jacques from Rastadt' in their accounts, himself left a narrative of his time in the Ottoman court.⁹ In it, he boasts that 'through the skilful leveraging of a connection [he] managed to achieve an assignment as the chief-gardener of the Bostandji [*der Obergärtners der Bostandgi's*] in the palace,' and notes that Selim III's mild regime allowed a Christian to fill this post.¹⁰ This work is also traceable in the detailed map that Antoine Ignace Melling (1763–1831) provides in his *Voyage pittoresque de Constantinople et de rives du Bosphore* (1819), and the eyewitness account that the Austrian Orientalist Joseph von Hammer-Purgstall (1774–1856) provides in his *Constantinopolis und der Bosporos* (1822), but Ensle also contributed to the gardens in Selim's Beşiktaş Palace and Eyüp.¹¹ At Topkapı, he worked on a set of terraced spaces reserved for Selim and for the women's quarters, and as per the sultan's request, instituted the 'French and Dutch conventions [*Sitte*]' rather than the picturesque landscapes that Europeans had begun to install in their own estates.¹² If Napoleon hadn't conquered Egypt in 1798, Ensle's work in the gardens of Topkapı and other summer dwellings of the court would have had a chance to flourish. Not wanting to remain in an environment suddenly hostile to foreigners and volatile due to ceaseless uprisings against Selim's reforms, he left for his fatherland in 1802.

The subsequent decades pitted a young Mahmud II (r.1808–39) against influential viziers, powerful provincial rulers, Balkan insurgencies, Russian advances, and, most significantly, insubordinate janissaries. These disruptive events also made crossing through the Balkans, which Ensle undertook, geographically impossible for even the most adventurous Westerner.

Figure 1.3: *The Summer Palace at Beglier-Bey, W. H. Bartlett in Julia Pardoe,* The Beauties of the Bosphorus *(1839)*. Harvard University Widener Library Collection.

Besides a few European renegades, expatriates were hard to come by in an increasingly unstable Istanbul.[13] After a beleaguered but resolute Mahmud restored a semblance of order in his empire through a complete overhaul of the military and political bodies, the multilingual Ottoman bureaucrats of his newfangled administration began the hunt for foreign experts to furnish the backdrops of their homes. The English travel writer Julia Pardoe (1806–62) identifies the beginnings of this practice by remarking on the foreign gardeners of varying European nationalities attending to each of the terraces of Mahmud II's garden in the Beylerbeyi Palace in 1836 [Figure 1.3].[14]

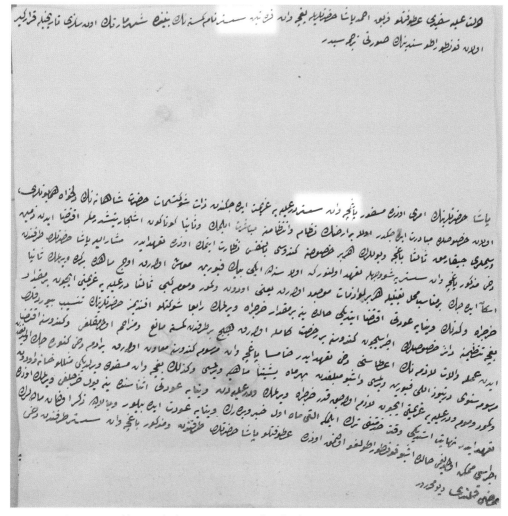

Figure 1.4: *Contract signed between 'Bahçıvan Kretyen Sester', and Fethi Paşa, BOA D. DRB. I 2/12.* Başbakanlık Osmanlı Arşivi (BOA), Istanbul.

While serving as an ambassador to Austria, Ahmed Fethi Pasha (*d*.1858), Mahmud's anglophile son-in-law, an enterprising industrialist of glass factories, and long-time marshal (*müşir*) of the Tophane armoury, signed a contract with Sester [Figure 1.4]. According to the loosely worded agreement, once the 31-year-old landscape gardener arrived in Istanbul, he would begin ordering the grounds allotted for the Sultan's imperial gardens, draw out the plans appropriate for growing multifarious trees, and closely supervise all aspects related to gardens and their walkways himself.[15] Promised a generous annual stipend of two thousand florins, comfortable lodgings, candlewax, coal and firewood, protection from any hindrances to his work, and an option to quit with a six-month notice, Sester arrived in Istanbul in 1835 along with an assistant (*muavin*). He was given – or, rightfully borrowing from his European precedents, requested for himself – the lofty title of Imperial Garden Director (*großherrlicher Gartendirektor*).[16] Until his death in 1868, Sester would remain in the service of three out of the four nineteenth-century sultans – Mahmud II, Abdülmecid, and Abdülaziz – and transform most of the imperial gardens of the period in Istanbul.

Christian Sester and the English Landscape Garden in the Ottoman Capital

The Bavarian parvenu's *résumé* played a significant role in his selection to the Ottoman post. Born and raised in Aschaffenburg, Sester came from a family of gardeners employed in the upkeep of the picturesque park of Schönbusch Palace, then belonging to Karl Theodor von Dalberg (*d*.1817), the Prince-primate of a confederation of Rhenish states that, in alliance with Napoleon I, had declared their independence from the Holy Roman Empire. At a very young age, Sester abandoned his training in Latin in order to completely devote himself to 'the noble art of gardening'.[17] He grew up in a world of affluent provincial patrons and their German garden experts who travelled around Europe to master the various branches of the practice.[18] His obituary, published in a local Aschaffenburg newspaper, would later mention Sester's hereditary calling for the garden arts from a very young age as follows: 'The seed that slept in him, suddenly awoke to unfold itself into a blossom, which shone forth as alone in its kind.'[19] With this familial predisposition, he was first apprenticed in his hometown under Schönbusch's head-gardener, Christian Ludwig Bode (*fl*.1801–24). Under his supervision, Sester honed his skills 'as a gardener in general, and as a landscape gardener [*landschaftsgärtner*] in particular'.[20] Soon after that, young Sester initiated his scholastic Grand Tour (often referred to as the gardener's 'journeyman years')[21] with a visit to the Nymphenburg botanical gardens in Munich, which were conceptualized by Schönbusch's first landscape gardener, Carl Ludwig von Sckell (*d*.1828) as extensions to the baroque summer palace of the Bavarian rulers.[22] Bode was a disciple of Sckell, and was entrusted with the creation of English gardens with a German bent – a complete turn to nature, and a sparse, economical use of garden structures – which he must have imparted to his apprentice while at Schönbusch. Following his training in Munich, Sester was appointed head-gardener to Dalberg's smaller country estate in Bohemia – his first venture into the Habsburg domains –

and then returned to Bavaria in 1832 when he was tasked with the supervision of the gardens of Frauendorf's horticultural society.[23] He had only recently been hired as a head-gardener (*obergärtner*)[24] by Prince von Dietrichstein to lay out the gardens of his new Viennese summer residence, when his eastern adventure beckoned. Dietrichstein had recommended him to Sultan Mahmud II.

Although a drawing or plan from Sester's own hand of the Ottoman gardens he created has yet to be identified, he left behind a short ekphrasis from 1832, which appeared in the newspaper *Frauendorfer Blätter* on July 3, 1845, on how he envisioned the gardens while he served as a head-gardener. Borrowing from the hackneyed European convention of describing the Tanzimat courts of Mahmud II and Abdülmecid as stalwartly progressive, Sester's erstwhile hosts in Frauendorf heralded him in this news item as the artistic counterpart to these two reform-oriented sultans, and republished the piece in 1845 with a lengthy prologue praising his international success:

> A letter from Constantinople that was printed in the daily newspaper on the 12th of last month emphasised that the young Sultan [Abdülmecid], like his father [Mahmud II], found a great deal of pleasure in everything new and better. For example, when setting up his palaces, the Sultan expressly ordered, on numerous occasions, that he no longer wanted the Old, but rather the New according to better European taste. Thusly, the garden at Tscheragan [sic] Palace, which was installed some six years ago by one of our countrymen, Herr Sester of Aschaffenburg, pleased the Sultan so extraordinarily that while he was recently moving from his palace to Beylerbeyi, he ordered that Tscheragan should be outfitted for the next winter so that he could spend Fall and also the Winter there. We are pleased by this news all the more because we have not heard from our old friend Herr Sester for quite some time. What a wonderful direction human fate can take! In 1832, Herr Sester was still helping to install the gardens in Frauendorf. While this garden was later destroyed by high winds and hail, we can take solace in the fact that the spirit of progress managed to transplant a refined taste for gardens in Turkey in the form of Herr Sester, placing him at the summit of that country's artistic reform.[25]

In Sester's ekphrasis, titled 'On the Cliff Bench in Frauendorf, May 8, 1832', and appended to this flattering introduction, the gardener describes his walk through the garden of his own creation much in the way of a musical composition. The sentimental tone of the narrative, which the gardener intends to evoke with his garden, is in dialogue with his literary companion Hirschfeld, and with Pückler-Muskau, whose treatise reads like a real-time walk in his own gardens, where each view brings about different sets of emotions. From a vast and stage-like clearing, Sester enters a steep and narrow path lined with a thick mass of conifers with only a 'handrail made of bark-stripped branches' to hold onto, having been seduced by the violets under the shade of a spruce tree down below.[26] As he descends, he reveals his horticultural knowledge by pairing up plants that share a symbiotic relationship – cherry trees against the pine, hardy berries with delicate dayflowers, primrose entwined about the pear tree – but the experience is so immersive and natural that the environment belies the human hand that put it together. At some point, he comes across a bench, where he sits to listen to the sounds (of starlings, blackbirds, and the rushing creek) and contemplates the moss-covered precipice and all that is beyond it. As night descends and nature's sublimity takes over, Sester reveals his philosophical inspiration: Johan Gottfried Herder (1744–1803)'s short work of prose titled *Kalligenia: Die Mutter der Schönheit* (1803) that inquired into the aesthetic qualities of nature and its laws, and the happy convergences between an artist and scientist's findings when studying them.[27] The gardener, who crafted himself from facets of both of these professions, writes: 'The philosopher should hurry to this spot, disdaining the trinkets of the masses, and devote serious contemplation to the purpose of man; and celebrated goddess will come to him, as Kalligenia did to Kallia, in the dreams of Herder.'[28]

The *Frauendorfer Blätter*'s push to connect the English landscape garden with liberal rule might not be too much of a stretch and may be, in fact, a reflection on a common sentiment of the era. German writers of garden treatises, who were Sester's contemporaries and sources, believed in the close correlation between an enlightened, benevolent ruler, and the manner in which he laid out his estate. One of the most widely read among these figures, a member of the landed nobility from the north and an obsessive landscape designer himself, Prince Hermann Ludwig von Pückler-Muskau (*d*.1871) propounded that the best garden model for an estate-owner was the English one, because with all of its philosophical connotations it offered the best contrast to Le Nôtre's Versailles and Vaux-le-Vicomte, which had become the paragons of French autocratic rule alongside the structures they circumscribed.[29] By deliberately including the working lands of the ruler – a hint of a peasant's cottage here, a farm there – with untouched nature, the English landscape garden was for Pückler-Muskau a 'microcosm of the civilised world'.[30] So, if Mahmud II and later on Abdülmecid strove to make distinctive visual claims about transformations to their rule as reform-oriented sovereigns eager to instate a completely new administrative and judiciary system with a new set of cultural offerings for their public, it is not unlikely that they selected a similar aesthetic schema to the benevolent German gentry for their surroundings, as it would fit their newfangled, reinvented image.

It is not surprising that Sester was acquainted with the writings of German philosophers. Excerpts from their most popular texts were printed and circulated even in the monthly gardener's almanacs of Frankfurt. Herder's *Kalligenia*, written close to his death, was one of the short and evocative narratives that also made its way into the homes of the working classes.[31] Starting with Kant, figures like Herder, Goethe, and Schiller included garden art among the highest plastic arts of their time. For them, and for Christian Cay Lorenz Hirschfeld (1742–92), their minstrel in all things related to landscape art, who penned the popular multi-volume garden treatise *Theorie der Gartenkunst* originally published as a series between 1779 and 1785, a gardener was equal to if not more privileged than a landscape painter, in his command over space, light, and sound.[32] These philosophers of aesthetics not only gave the gardening profession incredible agency in shaping nature; they fuelled the garden artist's creative powers with the German proto-national ideas of freedom of the mind and creative expression. Rustic, seemingly untouched landscapes were the perfect backdrop for their fiery ideas as well as their best visual representations. Sester was also geographically close to these members of the *Sturm und Drang* movement of arts and letters, preoccupied with the shackles of Enlightenment rationalism, and was certainly spurred on by the romantic fervour of their aesthetic inclinations. If Goethe's novella *Elective Affinities* (*Die Wahlverwandtschaften*) of 1809 is any indication, the patrons of garden estates were also deeply involved in the landscape projects alongside their gardeners.[33] Dalberg, who was Sester's first patron and his family's benefactor, was a close friend, intellectual equal, and travel companion to Herder – they journeyed together in the Tyrolean Alps and Italy – who would find gainful employment for this ubiquitous theologian, because as a powerful political figure Dalberg (later the Archbishop of Regensburg) also held great sway in ecclesiastical appointments.[34] Therefore, Schönbusch afforded a young garden artist both the practical and intellectual stage to develop his creative inklings.

His obituary also enacts Sester's first interactions with Mahmud II, who, unlike Selim III, did not want orange trees in his gardens – an eighteenth-century fad, now too commonplace – and instead desired something that 'others didn't have'.[35] In their four-year collaboration, Sester installed a spacious portico on the side of Mahmud's wooden Dolmabahçe Palace. Under this section, and protected from the 'icy winds the Pontus not so seldomly sends, a fantastical artwork [*fantasiereiches Kunstwerk*] arose, whose painting we encounter only in the *Thousand and One Nights*'.[36] He installed waterfalls with alcoves moulded out of grottoes, and planted flowering evergreens – azaleas, rhododendrons, and only recently acclimatized dryandra, native to Oceania – alongside his beloved exotic conifers, the araucaria.[37] The gardener's undertakings did not end with simple gardening; he won a building commission, over the costly proposition of the unidentified imperial architect, for a garden house.

However, Sester's biggest contribution to the capital's landscapes was his gradual two-step conversion of the ravine-bisected hills behind Mahmud II's marble colonnaded Çırağan Palace, a residence that cupped the shoreline between Beşiktaş and Ortaköy, into a sprawling romantic landscape. Under Mahmud, Sester had to work within the bounds of the traditional terraced aesthetic imposed upon the hilly topography by earlier generations, but he naturalized these spaces as much as he could by turning the large flower parterres into uneven lawns and adding multiple bodies of water with undulating borders. An undated, gouache-tinted engraving from Dolmabahçe Palace's object collection that offers up a view from this hillside garden looking onto the back of the crenellated palace, the delicate footbridge that connects it to the garden, and the walled elevation of the terraced parterres, captures the early phase of Sester's work: the swelling ha-has that hold up the two ponds, a white classical temple-like folly, which must have been one of his architectural commissions, and mounds of soil removed to open up the pools, occupying the foreground

Figure 1.5: *Çırağan Palace, unknown artist, gouache on engraving, 52x70 cm., undated.* Milli Saraylar Resim ve Heykel Müzesi, 12/2838.

[Figure 1.5]. On the flatter ground, right behind the palace's administrative structure (*mabeyn*), the painting reveals a fragment of a garden developed for private use with similar pools. Pardoe, who had likened the horticultural activity in the terraced, climbing gardens of Beylerbeyi to a tower of Babel of foreign gardeners, was also witness to the frenzied activity behind Çırağan. Sester and his assistant must have started on the projects within months of their arrival since the travel account was published in 1836, only a year after his contract signing. Her description of what Sester pursued behind Çırağan animates the content of the undated painting, as well as the engraving corresponding to the traveller's account [Figure 1.6]:

> The gardens of the palace are extensive, but will require time to make them worthy of description; at present, a great portion of the hill-side, behind the building, is left in its original state, boasting for all ornament, sweeps of fine cypresses, and here and there a tuft of almond trees, a group of acacias, or a majestic maple; while the white tents of the Bulgarian workmen employed upon the walls, give to the scene the *picturesque* and cheerful appearance of a summer encampment.[38]

Sester's obituary further expands upon his accomplishments in this 'great compound of Ortaköi'.[39] Under his supervision, 'mounds had to be removed, rocks blown up, and basins filled in', in order to properly realize 'the conceits of painterly garden scenes, and to faithfully imitate the images of nature'.[40]

Foreign visitors, privileged enough to visit the site with the imperial gardener in tow, stress its terrain's aridness and provide insight into the multiple stages of its fecundation

Figure 1.6: *Scene from Above the New Palace of Beshik-tash*, W. H. Bartlett in Julia Pardoe, The Beauties of the Bosphorus *(1839)*. Harvard University Widener Library Collection.

process under his command. Before Sester had begun the second phase of forestation for Abdülmecid, and only seven years into his directorship, Countess Ida von Hahn-Hahn (d.1880), novelist to the German aristocrats and a pen friend to Prince Hermann von Pückler-Muskau, met Sester by chance at the lodgings of the Pera proprietress Madame Balbiani in the fall of 1845. The gardener, a frequent guest of the Balbiani boarding house, offered to take his compatriot on a tour of Mahmud's Çırağan. In a letter to her mother, after providing a lengthy description of the palace interiors, from its porcelain collection to its sundry mirrors and clocks, the Countess gives a description of the garden that was being developed:

> The garden of this palace is quite new, situated on the steep and totally bare side of a hill, where as yet, nothing is to be seen that would give us the idea of a garden – no flowers, no shade, no verdure, no water, nothing but the heavenly view of the Bosphorus; perhaps in ten or twelve years it may be transformed into a garden.[41]

Prince Leopold, Duke of Brabant (and the future king of Belgium), who was hosted by Abdülmecid in 1860, took a guided tour of the garden with Sester and recorded its transformation in his travel diary on April 13.[42]

> After lunch, we went down the Bosphorus by boat to the gardens and kiosks of Tschéragan [sic]. This garden, drawn by a German, is large and handsomely created. One sees

Constantinople, the Bosphorus, and even a bit of the Sea of Marmara. The soil, rocky here, is not overly favourable for vegetation and the garden provides no shade. Near here, in the lower part of the garden, is another kiosk of the Sultan, all in white marble and richly adorned, but in bad taste.[43]

Both the Countess and Duke's observations of the garden's barrenness and lack of shade find their representation on the lid of an Ottoman writing box. Executed in oil by the Armenian artist and marquetry specialist Mıgırdıç Melkon (*fl.*mid-nineteenth century), the painting is not only a rare local depiction of Mahmud's version of Çırağan, but also the single mid-century visual proof of Sester's output [Figure 1.7].[44] Melkon's painting shows the full span of the garden, reaching all the way up to a second, larger, green-painted kiosk that has the same billowy roof resting on thin columns as the tent (*çadır*) kiosk once perched right besides Sa'dabad's canal. This structure is likely the earliest incarnation of the brick and stone neoclassical pavilion that would later replace it during Abdülaziz's additions to the garden, but continue to maintain its original shape-derived designation, a common documentary practice of preserving names of structures in the Ottoman visual and archival records [Figure 1.8]. The artist's depiction of Sester's winding paths and burgeoning saplings presents a sharp contrast with the even more arid hilltops to the garden's right, and the urban sprawl to its left. A curious dune-coloured wall behind the southern wing of the palace appears to support a greenhouse, whose glass panels are visible next to the temple-like garden folly – the same structure from the undated oil painting in Dolmabahçe's collection.

What the painting does not show is how Sester filled up the arid valley sandwiched between the Valides' walled-in, hilltop residence and the thicket of cypresses surrounding the saintly precinct of Yahya Efendi's tomb, nestled on the northeast corner of the Çırağan grounds. This was the second phase of his expansion, commissioned under Abdülmecid. Although no paintings like the two previously mentioned have survived of what would first become the forested extension of the Çırağan gardens with lakes and waterfalls, and later the centrepiece of Abdülhamid II's Yıldız Palace, there are seventy-five, single-page expense accounts spanning weekly work, starting on February 5, 1849, that indicate intense gardening activity in the area. Each of these expense accounts only sparsely fills a single page and lists the day labourers' rates (*rençber yevmiyesi*) and unfortunately none provides a detailed plan of Sester's overall undertaking. However, they all bear his Ottoman seal, which identifies his position in Abdülmecid's court as the chief-gardener of the Çırağan waterfront palace (*Çeragan sahilsaray serbagçıvanı Sester*) [Figure 1.9].[45] These ledgers also provide a general overview of the landscaping project by describing it as the levelling (*tesviye*) of the new garden between Çırağan, its mountains and Yıldız pavilion, as well as the construction of the gardener's home adjacent to the Ortaköy side of the new garden.[46] Levelling most likely meant the knocking down of walls that divided the shoreline palace's garden with the barren site next to it and the Yıldız estate, once intact and outlined on Melkon's writing box. Finally, some of these accounts document the aggregate cost of multiple weeks' worth of

'I don't want orange trees, I want something that others don't have'

Figure 1.7: *Writing box with an image of the Beşiktaş Palace, Mıgırdıç Melkon, oil and papier-mâché, 60x90cm, undated, CY 454.* Topkapı Saray Müzesi, Istanbul.

Figure 1.8: *Çadır Pavilion in the Imperial Park of Yıldız, photographer unknown, 1880–1893, Abdul Hamid II Collection, LC Lot 95, no. 14.* The Library of Congress Prints and Photographs Division (LC), Washington, DC.

Figure 1.9: *Sester's Ottoman seal, 'head-gardener of the waterfront palace of Çırağan', BOA, HH. d. 18928.* Başbakanlık Osmanlı Arşivi (BOA), Istanbul.

work: for example, under the oversight of Selim Efendi, the head-chamberlain of the sultan, the treasury disburses Sester over two million *guruş* from the 50th to 130th week.[47]

The Austrian Jewish writer and ethnomusicologist Ludwig August von Frankl (*d*.1894), who followed the recommendation of the Ottoman ambassador of Naples and met with Sester in Istanbul on his journey to Jerusalem in 1856, had the opportunity to spend time in this one-storey stone house, perched close to the imperial gardens, which contained 'a large hall, the windows of which framed the low-lying Bosphorus, offering a huge picture'.[48] He emphasizes the fact that a house made of stone reflected a certain kind of privilege 'in Constantinople, where conflagrations are a regular feature', and adds that the beautiful house 'had been constructed by the Sultan for Sester, whom he loves and holds in high esteem'.[49] It was in this intimate space that the Austrian traveller was able to observe the gardener, in full Oriental garb, convalescing from an unidentified, 'jealous' underling's poisoning attempt. In a seated position, Sester entertained his guests, along with his Armenian-Catholic wife Rosa (birth name Askerian).[50] Frankl describes him as 'a man with a serious demeanour, a demeanour that exudes an Oriental calm that is pleasant, as it is not caused by thoughtlessness'.[51] Almost two decades into his service as a gardener at the time of Frankl's visit, Sester seems to have created a familial environment inside his home that combined native practices with touches from his homeland: 'We were presented with food and drink in an Oriental fashion; yet we were also given the opportunity to think about our German homeland, thanks to an extremely fine wine from the Rhineland.'[52]

Overall, Sester experienced better luck at integrating with the Ottoman court than his predecessor Ensle. The gardener from Bavaria cultivated a deeply personal relationship with Mahmud and Abdülmecid in the more forbearing atmosphere of the empire's period of reform. A foreign member of the court, he still yielded considerable power over a large group of workers. A short memo passed between the office of the Grand Vizier and the Ministry of Superintendence in 1852 reports that an unruly gardener, a Croatian by the name of Zeynel, was brought over to the head-gardener, accompanied by the city's police force.[53] Sester's obituary adds that while working on his ambitious Ortaköy project he had already grown powerful in the Turkish language, so he must have been able to communicate directly with his staff.[54]

The Stolpe map of the Ottoman capital drawn out between the years 1855 and 1863 (and later expanded in 1882) labels Sester's gardening feat on the slopes of Çırağan as the '*Grossherrlischer Lustgarten*' – sandwiched between the neighbourhoods of Beşiktaş and Ortaköy – and delineates his adjacent residence on the garden complex's northeast as the imperial garden directorate [Figure 1.10]. While most other expatriate court officials like Sester's contemporary Giuseppe Donizetti (1788–1856), the instructor-general of the Office of Ottoman Imperial Music, chose to reside in Pera, the garden-director combined his office and family home in the privileged zone around the palace.[55] Sester and his gardeners likely kept the no-longer-extant plans and drawings here, and the head-gardener maintained control of his gardeners in a militaristic manner by arranging them into squadrons, all in accordance with their posting among the various imperial gardens of the capital. This practice would be sustained into the twentieth century, evidenced in the salary registers of the gardeners, all referred to as privates (*nefer*) kept by the Ottoman imperial treasury.[56]

Sester's reputation, at least in the imperial neighbourhood of Beşiktaş, survived posthumously. Two maps of Ortaköy undertaken by members of the imperial army under Abdülhamid II identified the site of the garden directorate as belonging to the former head-gardener Sester [Figure 1.11].[57] These maps were drawn between 1899 and 1900 at the sultan's behest under the plan to expand Yıldız's gardens into Ortaköy by absorbing the gardens of the Feriye Palaces and the small plots of land owned by the neighbourhood's tradesmen, in order to create a palatial extension replete with a new imperial mansion to host and entertain diplomatic guests as well as a porcelain factory and a completely new, picturesque garden. While one of the maps details the lodgings for Abdülhamid's trusted

Figure 1.10: *Plan von Constantinopel mit den Vorstädten, dem Hafen, und einem Theile des Bosporus (1856), C. Stolpe, expanded and reprinted by Lorentz & Keill, Istanbul, 1882.* Harvard University Map Collection.

Albanian *zouave* regiments, the other one focuses on the immediate surroundings of Sester's house and pinpoints its commanding location in a small town's square with a fountain in the middle and the house of the head-gardener's assistant (*bagçıvan kalfa*) sandwiched between the head-gardener's residence and that of the caretaker (*türbedar*) of the Yahya Efendi lodge. The mansion that was built over Sester's residence under Abdülhamid would continue to be known among the palace officials as the head-gardener's pavilion well into the reign of Mehmed V (r.1909–18) [Figure 1.12]. When Mehmed V chose to make Yıldız his palace after a brief and unpleasant stint inhabiting the drafty Dolmabahçe, his sons would host banquets for the palace officials in this mansion.[58] Twice in his hefty memoirs, Mehmed's head-scribe Halid Ziya (1866–1945) talks about the new building's function as a place for banquets, and how it retained the name of the site's famous former inhabitant. In his first recollection, Halid Ziya ponders why the name '*Bahçıvanbaşı Sesvter* [sic] köşkü' was adopted, but later on, having found out the back-story, yet still unsure of the foreigner's name, he describes it as 'a pavilion that was built for the head-gardener Chester [sic] on the clearing in the

'I don't want orange trees, I want something that others don't have'

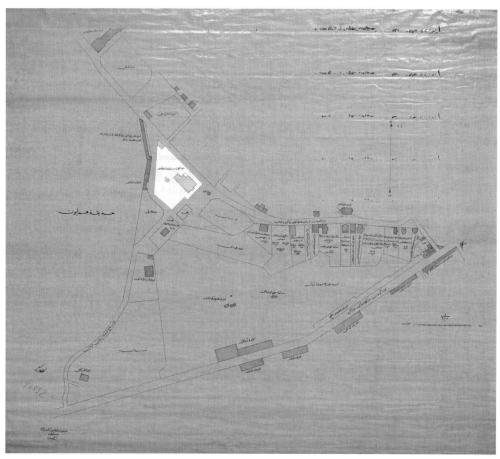

Figure 1.11: *Sketch map of the Ortaköy section of Yıldız's gardens with Sester's garden and residence highlighted, 1867?, 93332.* İstanbul Üniversitesi Nadir Eserler Koleksiyonu.

forest cascading from Yıldız to Ortaköy, and these days referred to as the world-exhibiting [*Cihannüma*] pavilion', for its resplendent views of the Bosphorus.[59]

Istanbul's Germanic Networks and Imperial Gardeners after Sester

In the empire's new century, at a time when renegades and émigrés could acquire privileged posts, Sester fashioned himself an aristocrat, through his professional title as a garden-director of the Ottoman court, at the very least among the foreign populations in the capital. Frankl describes a salon-like gathering in the gardener's home, where the government's reforms were discussed among a diverse group including the doctor of the German hospital

Figure 1.12: *The new Yıldız Pavilion that replaced Sester's residence, photographer unknown, 1902?, 90552.* İstanbul Üniversitesi Nadir Eserler Koleksiyonu.

in Istanbul, a Dr Stolle, and his entourage and the gardener's wife and niece. Taking advantage of the gardener's access to Mahmud II and Abdülmecid, the Austrian ambassador to Constantinople, Anton Graf Prokesch von Osten (*d.*1876), seems to have employed Sester as a palace informant during his time in the diplomatic service, from 1855 to Sester's death in 1866. Jotting the gardener down as *Hofgärtner* in his diaries, Prokesch von Osten encouraged Sester to visit him regularly to share his views of the newly appointed sultan, Abdülaziz. The gardener must not have been in the new ruler's good graces, or was disappointed over the fact that he was not permitted the same courtly intimacy that he had shared with the two preceding sultans. In 1863, Sester would describe Abdülaziz to Prokesch as 'ignorant, fickle, heartless, and spiteful'.[60] A counter-claim by a confidante of the new sultan would characterize the gardener to Prokesch in much the same terms.[61] Prokesch feared that Abdülaziz would thwart reform efforts to allow more rights for the Christian populations in the empire, a topic continually occupying the competitive agenda of the Austrians and the Russians. According to Prokesch's diary, Abdülmecid seems to have forewarned his gardener in dramatic fashion soon before his death that his chosen successor was against granting privileges to Christians. The state of the empire's religious minorities also affected the gardener's life personally. As a Catholic Armenian, his wife and her family must have experienced the often-violent repercussions of the schism between and among the empire's Apostolic, Catholic and Protestant Armenian populations in the early half of the century with respect to rightful representation, and the involvement of external bodies (Rome and the European protectorate) over local ones (Sultan, Patriarch, Mekhitarists, and the wealthy and influential Catholic *amira* families like the Balyans and Bezjians who were members of the Armenian National Council).[62]

Sester might have relied on Austrian protection for his foreigner's rights, but in his private hours, he worked for the German community in Istanbul. For example, in May 1855, he petitioned to the German Federal Assembly (*Bundesversammlung*) to advocate the purchase of a hospital building in the Ottoman capital that would be financed by the German mutual aid societies of the different German federal governments (*höhe deutsche Bundesregierungen*).[63] His petition won the German Hospital, founded in 1846 but without a building of its own, a permanent site through the aid of the German federal charity funds. In the aftermath of the Hungarian uprising against the Habsburgs of 1848–49 and the influx of émigrés into the Ottoman lands, Sester also provided gardening employment in Çırağan's expanded grounds for six defectors of the Hungarian army, who were all German volunteers from Baden and Württemberg fighting for the *Magyar* cause.[64] Eventually, hundreds of soldiers of the Hungarian army found their way into the colony-like club run by a young Hungarian baron called Balázs Orbán (*fl*.1848–80), who would find jobs for them in the capital.[65] Similarly, for the German-affiliates the Teutonia Club, which was established in 1847, fostered a lively community of Germans, Austrians, and Swiss, where the proactive head-gardener likely presided over the convivial pan-German brand of diasporic personalities.[66]

The French newspaper *La Turquie* announced Sester's passing a day after he died from an 'attack of apoplexy' on December 17, 1866.[67] This was an undifferentiated diagnosis given to all sudden deaths at that time. He was interred in a marble tomb in the catacombs of the Catholic St. Esprit Cathedral in Pangaltı in 1867, and shares a central aisle with the empire's eminent Levantine families, consuls, dragomans, and with Donizetti [Figure 1.13].[68] This small, neoclassical church had served as the main ecclesiastical site for the city's Catholics, and was built by the Swiss architect Giuseppe Fossati (1822–91) in 1846. From its inception, the sultan's gardener donated generous sums to the upkeep of this church.[69] There he also maintained a family chapel that was attended to by the chaplain Nicholas Perpignani from the Aegean island of Tinos, who was summoned to Istanbul by the British admiralty to provide 'spiritual services' to the British hospital in Tarabya during the Crimean War.[70] The family chapel would have had special significance for his wife, because for a long time Catholic Armenians had no churches of their own and had to use sites designated by the state for the Catholic Levantine communities.

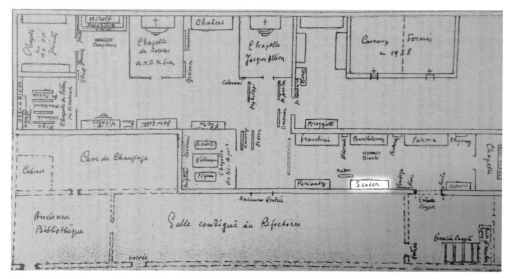

Figure 1.13: *The layout of the St. Esprit Cathedral catacomb with the location of Sester's family tomb highlighted, reproduced in Sac. Ph. Victor Del Giorno,* Chroniques de La Basilique Cathedrale du Saint-Esprit, *2 vols (Ankara: 1983), vol. 1. Deniz Türker.*

Rosa was buried next to her spouse in 1896 – Sester appears to have received the interrment permissions required to make it a family tomb during his lifetime, and with the help of the then-grand vizier, and one of the pre-eminent Tanzimat bureaucrats, Mehmed Emin Âli Pasha (d.1871). Cholera outbreaks and the often-refractory protocols of the Vatican made burial processes in prestigious catacombs, especially in foreign lands, difficult.[71] Another indication that a lot of planning went into the tomb's making is evidenced in its sculptural marble reliefs. These stand apart from their more austere neighbours. A knight's helmet, a stand-in for invulnerability and protection, and four swans, representing grace, wisdom, and harmony, furnish the prominent baroque crest of the tomb [Figure 1.14]. The eminent garden-director created it for his family: the knight for himself and four swans for his wife and three children. The larger swan is perched on top of the knight as a devotional gesture towards Rosa's role in the family. Below the crest, the tomb's two roundels preserve the Victorian reliefs of the husband with his stately moustache and the wife in a creased blouse, both bearing expressions of a hard-earned life. They face each other in the fashion of a marriage portrait under the flowering branches of holly, the heraldic symbol of truth. They are festooned with the literal fruits of their service to the court: apricots, apples, figs, and poppies hang from garlands around the couple. The centralized placement of the poppies among the bouquet of fruit is intriguing. In this extremely autobiographical iconographic scheme, Sester may very well be alluding to the fact that he cultivated these opiates to relieve himself of the debilitating pain caused by arsenic.

'I don't want orange trees, I want something that others don't have'

Soon after his death, Sester's post was taken up by his assistant Steffel, who had come along with him to Istanbul in 1835.[72] Amidst scant archival evidence, we come across Steffel's wife's plea following his passing in 1870 to recover the amount promised to him from the imperial treasury for the construction of his ill-fated Ortaköy residence. Steffel had designed and built this structure close to Sester's and in the vicinity of the imperial gardens of Çırağan, which was later deemed too intrusive in its proximity to the palace by a decree issued from Abdülaziz's scribal office, and its second floor completely demolished.[73] After Sester and Steffel, the post of the head-gardener and his assistant became a well-oiled system in the palace's roster of employees. Much as he took in German defectors after the Hungarian Revolution of 1848, Sester brought in a steady stream of his compatriot experts to expand his royal horticultural team, most likely to be able to adequately service the expanded gardens of Çırağan under Abdülmecid. For a brief period, a certain Fritz Wentzel became Sester's secretary, after the head-gardener was introduced to him while the former was convalescing from rheumatism at the German hospital, the very institution that the latter had helped fund.[74] An anonymous reporter of the weekly journal *Gartenwelt* would happen upon a few of Sester's pupils including Wentzel in Istanbul in 1907, and find out about the legacy of their tutor, their professional lives in Istanbul, and the state of gardening

Figure 1.14: *The Sester family tomb, St. Esprit Cathedral, Istanbul.* Deniz Türker.

Figure 1.15: *Announcement of Adam Schlerff's passing in* Die Woche, *9.5, 1907.*

43

in the Ottoman capital. In the same neighbourhood where Sester's residence was located, both Wentzel and the reporter's second German informant, an old German gardener by the name of J. D. H. Koch from Darmstadt, had opened nurseries (*Baumschulen*), which served the ever-increasing gardening enthusiasts of the city. Among the many foreign *kalfa*s that joined Sester's team along the way, Adam Schlerff (*d*.1834–1907) of Frankfurt who had entered into service as a foreman in 1857, would take the helm as the garden-director after Steffel and Wentzel [Figure 1.15].[75] Like Sester before him, Schlerff would also be given a home in Ortaköy's green valley, in the vicinity of the Armenian-Catholic church and Greek cemetery, and not far from Koch's residence and nursery.[76] Schlerff's Ottoman seal marks a register of gardeners employed in the imperial sites in 1883.[77] This document lists only the 252 Muslim members of the corps, but most intriguing is the fact that the recruits were either from the central Black Sea province of Kastamonu or Shkodër in Albania's northwest.

Through the insights his two seasoned informants provide, *Gartenwelt*'s patriotic reporter lamented the demise of the more than half a century long, far-reaching German influence on the gardens and parks of Istanbul's ruling elite. Charles Henry (*fl*.1895–1914), a French greenhouse expert who was initially brought to the imperial gardens to operate a greenhouse built with a hot-water system, intended to replace the pre-existing, inefficient versions heated by dry canalization, soon supplanted the septuagenarian Schlerff in rank and file.[78] *Gartenwelt*'s reporter, disheartened as he was by the German fall from grace in the garden arts, still admitted to Henry's superior ability in rearing exemplary plant cultures in Yıldız's forcing houses [Figure 1.16].[79] Although the old Germans stayed on without a salary reduction they became *kalfa*s under Henry, the last Ottoman head-gardener.[80]

In conclusion, the influence that these figures wielded during their lifetime as foreign garden experts over Istanbul's landowners incited a frenzied bourgeois interest and competition in botany, horticulture, and their many accessories.[81] Among the Ottomans, garden arts became an almost academic preoccupation, and therefore, continued to provide employment to these foreign expatriate experts as well as their trained personnel. If some of the Germans remained in the city as successful nursery owners, Albanian and Black Sea migrants of the Ottoman imperial gardens dominated the gardening profession in the city's many market gardens.[82] Throughout the nineteenth and early-twentieth centuries, affluent Ottomans presided over the delicate contents of their own greenhouses, collected gardening books for their private libraries, imported rare seeds from around the world, converted their overgrown groves into picturesque parks, and dotted them with ambitious rockery and miniature pavilions. Although this hobby had transformed into a competitive consumer's trend, each of these sites reflected the patron's discretionary taste, which negotiated with its designer's training and creative prowess. Neither one ended up looking like the other. Ultimately however, Yıldız, first as the grove and gardens of the shoreline palace of Çırağan, and through to its final incarnation as the last Ottoman palace complex, remained at the centre stage of the city's overall fascination with the picturesque and a rediscovery of Bosphorus's topography.

'I don't want orange trees, I want something that others don't have'

Figure 1.16: *View of a palm-house from the new additions to the Châlet Pavilion in the imperial gardens of Yıldız, undated, 90552.* İstanbul Üniversitesi Nadir Eserler Koleksiyonu.

Notes

1 Charles Henry, 'Les jardins de Yildiz au temps d'Abdul-Hamid', *Revue Horticole* 84 (Paris: Audot, 1912). Unfortunately, very little has been written on the shift in Ottoman gardening practices at the turn of the century. However, the photographic evidence in the Abdülhamid Albums of not just imperial gardens but the gardens of Hamidian bureaucrats, and the last caliph Abdülmecid's garden-centric archives and library collection in Dolmabahçe Palace Museum's collection, are evidentiary starters of amateur horticulturalism among the urban elite.

2 İsmail Hakkı Uzunçarşılı, *Osmanlı Devletinin Saray Teşkilâtı* (Ankara: Türk Tarih Kurumu Basımevi, 1988), 465–87; on the corps' employees responsible for the upkeep of the imperial gardens, and referred to as *gilman, usta* or *üstad* and their organizational composition, see

specifically, 467–68. For an overview of the Ottoman gardens and their varied typologies in the capital, see Gülru Necipoğlu, 'The Suburban Landscape of Sixteenth-Century Istanbul as a Mirror of Classical Ottoman Garden Culture', in *Theory and Design of Gardens in the Time of the Great Muslim Empires*, ed. Attilio Petruccioli (Leiden: E.J. Brill, 1997), 32–71.

3 Ahmed Lûtfî Efendi, *Vak'anüvîs Ahmed Lûtfî Efendi Tarihi*, 8 vols (İstanbul: Türkiye Ekonomik ve Toplumsal Tarih Vakfı, YKY, 1999), vol. 1, 146–47.

4 Ibid.

5 Uzunçarşılı, *Osmanlı Devletinin Saray Teşkilâtı*, 475.

6 Mustafa Nuri Paşa, *Netayic ül-Vukuat, Kurumları ve Örgütleriyle Osmanlı Tarihi*, 12 vols (Ankara: Türk Tarih Kurumu Basımevi, 1980), vols 3–4, 122–23. A recent publication has further explored the transformation of the gardeners' corps into the sultan's personal police; see Murat Yıldız, *Bahçıvanlıktan Saray Muhafızlığına Bostancı Ocağı* (İstanbul: Yitik Hazine Yayınları, 2011).

7 Marie-Gabriel-Florent-Auguste de Choiseul-Gouffier, *Voyage pittoresque de la Grèce*, 2 vols (1782– [1824]), vol. 2, 489.

8 Georg Oghulukyan, *Georg Oğulukyan'ın Ruznamesi; 1806–1810 İsyanları. III. Selim, IV. Mustafa, II. Mahmud ve Alemdar Mustafa Paşa*, trans. and notes, Hrand D. Andreasyan (İstanbul: Edebiyat Fakültesi, 1972), 2–3.

9 François Pouqueville, *Travels through the Morea, Albania, and Other Parts of the Ottoman Empire to Constantinople, during the Years 1798, 1799, 1800, and 1801 … By F. C. H. L. Pouqueville* (London: Printed for R. Phillips by Barnard & Sultzer, 1806), 159–69.

10 Franz Gräffer, *Historische Raritäten*, 2 vols (Wien: Tendler und v. Manstein, 1825), vol. 2, 157. For more on Ensle's contributions to the Ottoman court, see Deniz Türker, 'Ottoman Horticulture after the Tulip Era: Botanizing Consuls, Garden Diplomacy, and the First Foreign Head-Gardener', in *The Botany of Empire in the Long Eighteenth Century,* eds. Yota Batsaki, Sarah Burke Cahalan, and Anatole Tchikine (Washington, D.C.: Dumbarton Oaks Research Library and Collection, 2016), 305–36.

11 Antoine Ignace Melling, *Voyage pittoresque de Constantinople et des rives du Bosphore*, ed. Rezan Benatar, trans. Irvin Cemil Schick and Ece Zerman (İstanbul: Denizler Kitapevi, 2011); and, Joseph Freiherr von Hammer-Purgstall, *Constantinopolis und der Bosporos, örtlich und geschichtlich beschrieben,* 2 vols (Pest: Hartleben's Verlag, 1822), vol. 1, 306–21.

12 Gräffer, *Historische Raritäten,* 159.

13 Caroline Finkel, *Osman's Dream, The Story of the Ottoman Empire 1300–1923* (London: John Murray, 2006), 437.

14 Julia Pardoe, *The Beauties of the Bosphorus* (G. Virtue, 1839), 59.

15 Başbakanlık Osmanlı Arşivi (BOA), D. DRB. İ 2/12. The requirements of his appointment are listed in this Ottoman-Turkish contract as follows: '*arzın nizam ve intizamına mübaşeret eylemek, gunagun eşcar yetişdirmeğe iktiza iden zemin ve resimleri çıkarmak, bağçe ve yolların her bir hususuna kendüsi bi'n-nefs nezaret itmek*'.

16 Sester's provisions are outlined in the contract. His girding as a garden director in Vienna is described in his obituary: A.W., 'Ein unterfränkischer Landsmann als Gartendirektor des Sultans', *Erheiterungen, Belletristisches Beiblatt zur Aschaffenburger Zeitung*, December 17, 1867, 1194.

17 A.W., 'Ein unterfränkischer Landsmann', 1194.
18 Ibid. For Schönbusch's garden history, see *Schönbusch bei Aschaffenburg. Amtlicher Führer, herausgegeben von der Verwaltung der staatlichen Schlösser, Gärten und Seen (ehemaliges Krongut)*, ed. Heinrich Kreisel (Aschaffenburg: Verlag der Wailandtschen Druckerei A.G., 1932).
19 '*Allein der Keim, der in ihm schlummerte, erwachte bald, um sich zu einer Blüthe zu entfalten die, ich möchte sagen, als einzig in ihrer Art prangte.*' A.W., 'Ein unterfränkischer Landsmann', 1194. Author's translation from the German original.
20 Ibid.
21 Toby Musgrave, *The Headgardners: Forgotten Heroes of Horticulture* (London: Aurum, 2007), 75–78.
22 Carl Ludwig von Sckell, *Das königliche Lustschloss Nymphenburg und seine Gartenanlagen: Mit einem Plane* (München: In Commission bei George Jaquet [*c.*1837–40]).
23 A.W., 'Ein unterfränkischer Landsmann', 1194.
24 Ibid.
25 'Wohlgefallen des türkischen Kaisers an englischen Gärten', *Frauendorfer Blätter* (July 3, 1845): 202–03. The last sentence of the news report that directly links Sester to the Tanzimat reads in the German original as follows: '*Herr Sester mit großartigen Mitteln an die Spitze der schöpferischen Reform gestellt*'. Author's translation from the German original.
26 Ibid., 203.
27 Johann Gottfried Herder, 'Kalligenia: die Mutter der Schönheit,' in *J.G. v. Herders Sämtliche Werke, zur Schönen Literatur und Kunst*, vol. 6 (Carlsruhe: Im Büreau der Deutschen Klassiker, 1821), 224–34.
28 'Wohlgefallen', 203.
29 Linda B. Parshall, 'Introduction', in *Hints on Landscape Gardening, Together with a Description of Their Practical Application in Muskau by Hermann Prince von Pückler* Muskau, trans. John Hargraves (Basel: Birkhäuser Verlag, 2014), 11.
30 Ibid., 14.
31 'Retrospect of German Literature', *The Monthly Magazine: Or, British Register* 14.2 (1803): 653.
32 C. C. L. Hirschfeld. *Theory of Garden Art*, trans. Linda B. Parshall (Philadelphia, PA: University of Pennsylvania Press, 2001).
33 Johann Wolfgang von Goethe, *Elective Affinities*, trans. with an introduction and notes by David Constantine (Oxford: Oxford University Press, 2008), 46.
34 Robert Thomas Clark, *Herder: His Life and Thought* (Berkeley, CA: University of California, 1955), 233, 245–46, 288, 355–56.
35 In Sester's obituary, Mahmud is personified and declares: 'Ich will keine Orangenbäume, ich will Etwas was Andere keine.' See A. W., 'Ein unterfränkischer Landsmann', 1195.
36 Ibid.
37 Ibid., 1194.
38 Pardoe, *The Beauties*, 18.
39 A. W., 'Ein unterfränkischer Landsmann', 1195.

40 Ibid.
41 Gräfin Ida Hahn-Hahn, *Letters from the Holy Land* (London: J. & D. A. Darling, 1849), 246.
42 Léopold II, *Voyage à Constantinople, 1860* (Bruxelles: Editions Complexe, 1997), 56–57.
43 Ibid. Author's translation from the French original.
44 For Mıgırdıç Melkon, see Garo Kürkman, *Armenian Painters in the Ottoman Empire, 1600–1923*, 2 vols (İstanbul: Matüsalem Publications, 2004), vol. 2, 619–31.
45 The 75 notebooks begin with BOA, HH. d. 18928, and end with 22266. Often there are jumps in the numbering, and some notebooks are missing, so 18940 follows, for example, 18937. However, if searched on the archive's index, the combined words 'Çırağan', 'bahçe', and 'tesviye' list all of these short *defter*s. In the seal, the name of the palace is misspelled *Çerağañ* when it should have been *Çerāġān*.
46 The documents refer to the hilltops behind the palace as '*Çırağan dağları*', and the site designated for Sester's lodgings as '*bağcıvanbaşı Mösyö Sestar'ın hanesi*'.
47 BOA, H.H. 22245.
48 Ludwig August Frankl, *Nach Jerusalem!* (Leipzig: Baumgärtner's Buchhandlung, 1858), 173.
49 Ibid., 174.
50 Ibid.
51 Ibid.
52 Ibid.
53 BOA, A.}MKT.NZD. 65/79.
54 A.W., 'Ein unterfränkischer Landsmann', 1196.
55 Emre Aracı, *Donizetti Paşa, Osmanlı Sarayının İtalyan Maestrosu* (İstanbul: Yapı Kredi Yayınları, 2006), 54.
56 Two examples of the military formations implemented for the gardeners installed in various imperial gardens of the capital can be best observed in the Ottoman imperial treasury registries BOA, Y. PRK. SGE. 11/45 from December 20, 1908, as well as, Y. PRK. SGE. 39/19 from the same year.
57 İstanbul Üniversitesi Nadir Eserler Kütüphanesi, Planlar ve Haritalar Kataloğu, 93332 and 93405. The third one is located in the İstanbul Atatürk Kitaplığı, Haritalar Kataloğu, 5908.
58 Halid Ziya Uşaklıgil, *Saray ve Ötesi* (İstanbul: Özgür Yayınları, 2012), 199.
59 Ibid.
60 '[…] unwissend, launisch, herzlos, und boshaft', in Daniel Bertsch, *Anton Prokesch von Ostenein Diplomat Österreichs in Athen und an der Hohen Pforte: Beiträge zur Wahrnehmung des Orients im Europa des 19. Jahrhunderts* (München: Oldenbourg, 2005), 388.
61 Ibid.
62 The most cogent overview of the complicated divisions, disagreements, and religio-political motivations is offered in Charles Frazee, *Catholics and Sultans: The Church and the Ottoman Empire, 1453–1923* (New York: Cambridge University Press, 1983), 256–74. There is a speculative, anecdotal work on the nineteenth-century Armenian community of Istanbul that centres on the Catholic *amira* families; Saro Dadyan, *Osmanlı'da Ermeni Aristokrasisi* (İstanbul: Everest Yayınları, 2011).

63 *Protokolle der Deutschen Bundesversammlung vom Jahre 1856*, Sitzung 1 bis 33 (Frankfurt am Main: Bundespräsidial Druderie), 15.

64 György Csorba, 'Hungarian Emigrants of 1848–49 in the Ottoman Empire', in *The Turks*, ed. Hasan Celal Güzel, Cem Oğuz, and Osman Karatay (Ankara: Yeni Türkiye, 2002), vol. 4, 227–28. On Orbán's club for the Hungarian émigrés, called the Hungarian Society, their activities in Istanbul and social work to support the newcomers' transitions to a completely new life as smooth as possible, see Heléna Tóth, *An Exiled Generation: German and Hungarian Refugees of Revolution, 1848–1871* (New York: Cambridge University Press, 2014), 186–91.

65 Ibid., 228.

66 Stefan Manz, *Constructing a German Diaspora: The Greater German Empire, 1871–1914* (New York, NY: Routledge, 2014), 54–55. Also see Barbara von Radt, *Geschichte der Teutonia: deutsches Vereinsleben in Istanbul 1847–2000* (Istanbul: Würzburg: Ergon, 2001).

67 *La Turquie* 273 (December 9, 1866).

68 Rinaldo Marmara, *Pancaldi, Quartier levantin du XIXe siècle* (Istanbul: Les éditions Isis, 2004), 206.

69 Sac. Ph. Victor Del Giorno, *Chroniques de La Basilique Cathedrale du Saint-Esprit*, 3 vols (Ankara: 1983), vol. 1, 478. I owe the greatest gratitude to the effusive and generous Don Nicola Masedu for taking me down to the catacombs and for sharing the cathedral's chronicles however meager they may have been.

70 Del Giorno, *Chroniques*, vol. 1, 89–90.

71 Ibid., vol. 3, 1378.

72 Unfortunately, Steffel's first name, as well as his age with respect to his director Sester, is currently unknown.

73 BOA, HR. TO., 164/90.

74 C. K. S., 'Vom Goldenen Horn', *Die Gartenwelt* 11 (1907): 604–05.

75 For a detailed account of Schlerff's imperial garden-directorship and description of the corps' work in the palace grounds of Yıldız, see Bernhard Stern, *Der Sultan [Abdul Hamid II] und seine Politik; Erinnerungen und Beobachtungen eines Journalisten* (Leipzig: Verlag von B. Elischer Nachfolger, 1906), 17–26.

76 BOA, Y. PRK. MYD. 2/39.

77 BOA, HH. 17679.

78 A prolific botanist, Henry would contribute articles to French journals such as the *Revue horticole* on plant species he cultivated in the Ottoman imperial gardens in Istanbul, and later as the head-gardener of the khedivial gardens in Cairo. He also leaves behind a travel account of his botanical expedition in Ottoman Bursa and its Alpine environment that he undertook in order to collect samples for an imperial botanical garden project in the capital; see BOA, Y. PRK. SGE. 11/22, and for the travel account's Turkish transcription, see Sinan Çuluk, 'Bahçıvanbaşı Charles Henry'nin Bursa Çevresinde Araştırma Gezisi', in *Arşiv Dünyası Dergisi* 7 (2006): 43–45. He is the last to direct the gardening corps out of Yıldız, and report on its complex demographic and occupational structure (see note 1 for his account). Henry's managerial charge over three hundred gardeners comes to an abrupt end when Abdülhamid's established court order inside Yıldız is disbanded in 1909 to prepare

for Mehmed V's nominal rule under the CUP. A French account of the decaying grounds during Henry's last days in the imperial gardens is provided in Marcelle Tinayre, *Notes d'une voyageuse en Turquie: jours de bataille et de révolution; choses et gens de province; premiers jours d'un nouveau règne; la vie au harem* (Paris: Calmann-Lévy, 1910), 286–91.

79 C. K. S., 'Vom Goldenen Horn', 605. The German praise of Henry's work reads, '*ein ausgezeichneter Leiter der Treibereien und Kulturen*'.

80 BOA, Y. PRK. SGE. 11/54.

81 For the after effects of these figures on landscaping trends in Istanbul, see Deniz Türker, 'Prefabs, Chalets, and Home Making in 19th-Century Istanbul', *Ottoman History Podcast*, December 2016, http://www.ottomanhistorypodcast.com/2017/02/turker.html.

82 For a generational study of the demographic composition of the gardeners in Istanbul's market gardens, and the workers' Black Sea and Albanian origins, see Paul J. Kaldjian, 'Istanbul's Bostans: A Millenium of Market Gardens', in *The Geographical Review* 94 (July 2004): 286, 292.

Chapter 2

A Nineteenth-Century Architectural Archive: Syed Ahmad Khan's
Āṣār-us-Ṣanādīd

Mrinalini Rajagopalan

Introduction

Az naqsh-o-nikār, dar-o-deevār shikastah;
āṣār padīdast ṣanādīd 'ajam ra
(These designs and ornaments, these ruined walls and gates
Reveal the footprints of the noblemen of 'Ajam [Persia])

Syed Ahmad Khan (1847)[1]

Major-General Cunningham, the Director of the Archaeological Survey of India, is now engaged in making a comprehensive history of antiquities, by means of which reliable landmarks of history will become established and more solid information obtained in fixing dates than is at present procurable from native writings, which are more often based on fables and traditions than authenticated facts.

Henry Hardy Cole (1872)[2]

These epigraphs, written a quarter of a century apart, appeared in the frontispieces of two separate urban biographies of Delhi. The first is the opening to an Urdu catalogue of Delhi's monuments authored by the Indian intellectual Syed Ahmad Khan and titled *Āṣār-us-Ṣanādīd* (Traces of Noblemen).[3] The second is in the introduction to *Ancient Delhi*, compiled by Henry Hardy Cole, Superintendent of the Archaeological Survey of North West Provinces of India, to accompany an exhibition of photographs and plaster casts of Indian monuments at the South Kensington Museum, London, in 1872.[4] The latter epigraph also represents colonial perceptions regarding the fundamental difference between European and Indian systems of knowledge – a divide that was cast by Europeans as the chasm between archive and affect. By the mid-nineteenth century a range of European agents, including antiquarians, officers, surveyors, and engineers in the employ of the English East India Company, were committed to creating a stable archive of India's past via a system of rational, empirical, and scientific truths.[5] They believed that such archival knowledge would replace Indian histories they considered affective and emotive, and therefore unreliable.[6] These men fashioned themselves as modern interlocutors of Indian history and culture, justifying the urgency of their work upon the dearth of reliable histories produced by Indians. Yet this fictive dichotomy between scientific European knowledge and unstable Indian mythologies would be subverted by figures such as Syed Ahmad and his scholarly output, which displayed the same rigor of rational analysis and objective documentation considered by European agents to be the sole purview of the European mind. Equally, European histories were not immune from affective overtures, framed as they were by prejudices of racial anxiety or fetishism for Indian material culture.

The twin disciplines of archaeology and architectural history appeared in India in the mid-nineteenth century, coterminous with European colonization of the subcontinent. Institutions such as the Archaeological Society of Delhi (ASD) and the Archaeological Survey of India (ASI), established in 1847 and 1861 respectively, sought to know India through the material culture of its antiquity. Architectural objects acquired considerable purchase in this moment, albeit less for their aesthetic value and more for their utility in revealing through inscriptions and stylistic differences ethnographic information about India's past. In other words, architecture could serve as historical documents for European agents who identified and catalogued them within new matrices of knowledge. The documentation of India's architectural objects unfolded alongside other imperial projects such as the Mysore Survey (1799–1810) and the Great Trigonometrical Survey (1802–84), which collected data about India's terrain, its people, and their cultural and linguistic norms, and arranged such information within strict classificatory schema. It is within this milieu that I submit an analysis of Syed Ahmad's *Āṣār-us-Ṣanādīd* as the first modern survey of Delhi's architecture. Deeply aware of the prevailing European bias against Indian historical writing, Syed Ahmad sought to gain credibility as a scientific thinker and modern historian by using methodologies such as the survey, visual documentation, and comparative analyses in the first compendium of Delhi's architectural heritage. Far from rote mimicry of European methods, Syed Ahmad established key standards with his survey of Delhi's heritage, forwarding early definitions of the architectural monument as well as urban historical change.

In this chapter, I argue that architectural knowledge in the nineteenth-century India cannot be categorized into dichotomies such as European or Indian, or archival vs. affective modalities. Instead, modern architectural histories, whether written by Indians or Europeans, emerged from mutually constituted realms of knowledge where archives were inflected by affective impulses and similarly affective prejudices perpetuated via archival norms of documentation and representation. European and Indian knowledge, perceived as antithetical to one another, were in fact generated via a common dialogue that shaped the discourse of Indian architectural history profoundly. As will be seen in this chapter, while Syed Ahmad sought to establish himself as a legitimate interlocutor within the modern disciplines of archaeology and architectural history, European archaeologists and historians relied on his 'native' abilities of language, cultural memory, and social capital in order to foment their own historical positions regarding India's past.

In what follows I first situate the *Āṣār-us-Ṣanādīd* in its historical and discursive context of the mid-nineteenth century, a moment marked by increased European interest in the built heritage and architectural antiquity of India. As an Indian intervening within a largely European milieu, Syed Ahmad was afforded some opportunities while at the same time having to negotiate several limitations as he composed his catalogue of Delhi's architectural heritage. The three sections that follow, titled 'Image', 'Comparison', and 'Chronology', illustrate the modern methodologies by which Syed Ahmad explored the architectural heritage of Delhi. The sections on 'Image' and 'Comparison' focus on the visual and textual descriptions of the Qutb Minar and its adjoining mosque – a monumental complex begun in the late twelfth century and expanded successively by Islamic rulers through the fourteenth century. The first of these, 'Image', highlights the subtle negotiations that Syed Ahmad made between the tenets of his Islamic faith and a competing impulse for modern objectivity. 'Comparison' focuses on the startlingly similar methods employed by colonial bureaucrat Alexander Cunningham and Syed Ahmad in arriving at different conclusions regarding the origins of the Qutb Minar. The final section, 'Chronology', discusses the tabulation of Delhi's evolution from antiquity to the present as a series of imperial capitals. This classificatory order, which appeared in the second edition of the *Āṣār-us-Ṣanādīd*, created a clear link between imperial power and Delhi's architectural heritage. As an Indian committed to European modernity and its potential for India's advancement, Syed Ahmad essentially created an archive that anticipated European colonial rule as the modern terminus to Delhi's glorious imperial past.[7] In sum, the *Āṣār-us-Ṣanādīd* was a thoroughly modern text that negotiated affect and archive, as well as European and Indian articulations of historical value and the built environment. Most importantly, it was a text that established baseline parameters along which Delhi's architectural heritage would be documented for decades to come.

Delhi's First Modern Architectural Archive

The *Āṣār-us-Ṣanādīd* is a 600-page Urdu catalogue of Delhi's monuments and the city's notable personalities, such as sovereigns, literary elites, and religious leaders. The book was lavishly illustrated with over 100 woodcuts of the monuments and the epigraphic inscriptions found on the structures. Poetry (authored either by Syed Ahmad himself or by well-known poets of Delhi) accompanied the visual and textual descriptions of architecture. The *Āṣār-us-Ṣanādīd* was the first comprehensive survey of the monuments of Delhi and included Hindu, Jain, and Sikh architecture alongside the Islamic heritage of the city.[8] It would only be replaced in 1919 with the publication of the ASI's English-language catalogue on the built heritage of Delhi.[9] When he wrote the first edition in 1847, Syed Ahmed (1817–98) was a 30-year-old employee of the British administration in northern India.[10] It is not clear what his motivations were in producing such a lengthy tome on the historical architecture of Delhi, especially given that his earlier books focused on topics such as the political history of Delhi, imperial genealogies, and an administrative manual.[11] Nevertheless, he set out to complete an ambitious survey of the city's monuments, a task for which he enlisted the help of Maulvi Imam Baksh Sahbaʿī, Head of the Persian Department at Delhi College, and two draftsmen, Faiz Ali Khan and Mirza Shah Rukh Beg.[12]

The primary audience for the *Āṣār-us-Ṣanādīd* was the Asiatic Society (est. 1784), which by the mid-nineteenth century had expanded its attention from textual translations to include discussions of material culture and archaeological evidence. When it was published in 1847, the *Āṣār-us-Ṣanādīd* was well received by some members of the Society, such as Arthur Austin Roberts, who also served as Collector of Delhi. Roberts presented the book to the Society's London chapter in 1848, where his colleagues requested that the text be translated into English. On returning to Delhi, he convinced Syed Ahmad to simplify the elaborate prose of the book and correct the discrepancies of the original before beginning an English translation. Although the translation was never completed the revised manuscript appeared as a second edition in 1854.[13] In order to position the second edition as a truly scientific history of the city's architecture and its cultural development, Syed Ahmad added citations for his textual sources and removed the poems that had originally accompanied the description of several monuments. Also edited from the second edition were the biographies of Delhi's historic personalities as well as some minor monuments, thus making it a less comprehensive survey than the first.[14] The differences in language and content between the first and second editions of the *Āṣār-us-Ṣanādīd* were so radical that some scholars, such as C.M. Naim, have referred to the two editions as separate books that were identically named.[15] Other scholars, such as David Lelyveld, have suggested that the first edition celebrated the living cultures of Delhi, particularly its position as a centre of Urdu literature, while the second edition was created within a more rigid archaeological framework.[16]

Prior to the publication of the *Āṣār-us-Ṣanādīd*, historical accounts of Delhi's architecture appeared in travel literature, or within folios commemorating imperial patrons, or in texts detailing the lifestyles of the nobility and urban elite. Examples of travel writing included an account of eighteenth-century Delhi written by Dargah Quli Khan, the *Muraqqa-e-Delhi*, which portrayed the general ambience of the city and its courtly culture.[17] European accounts of Delhi's history and architecture include William Finch's account of Delhi (1611) and the travel diaries of François Bernier (1656–68), Jean-Baptiste Tavernier (1638–68), and Bishop Heber (1823–26), amongst others.[18] One category of books that proliferated in the eighteenth and nineteenth centuries was lavish architectural folios, such as the *Palais Indiens* (1774), an album of hand-painted drawings that catalogued the monuments of Delhi, Agra, and Faizabad. The drawings, largely produced by Indian artists, were commissioned by Jean-Baptiste Gentil, an officer of the French East India Company, and presented at the court of Louis XVI at Versailles.[19] A text that preceded *Āṣār-us-Ṣanādīd*, and in all probability served as a model for Syed Ahmad, was the *Sair-ul Manazil* (1835). Written by Mirza Sangin Beg in Persian, it featured brief textual descriptions of the primary buildings of the walled city of Delhi.[20] However, the *Āṣār-us-Ṣanādīd* was a significant departure from these earlier models of architectural and urban representation due to its encyclopaedic scope and its combination of illustration and textual description. Syed Ahmad self-consciously presented the built fabric of the city as the empirical basis from which to narrate Delhi's imperial and urban evolution. In his book, architectural objects were not simply the material remains of the past, but rather the primary evidence from which an enduring and complex urban history could be constructed.

The intellectual climate during the mid-nineteenth century was one marked by a special interest in architecture and archaeology. The ASD, composed almost entirely of Europeans who were considered the lettered elite of the city, was established in 1847, the same year that the first edition of *Āṣār-us-Ṣanādīd* was published.[21] Men like Thomas Metcalfe, the British Resident at Delhi, assumed the role of 'experts' of archaeology simply by dint of having lived in the city and claiming a rational vantage point by which to approach Indian history. By contrast, it was quite difficult for an Indian scholar to become a member of the Society, having to be nominated by two existing members and then vetted by the entire board before being granted membership. It was essential, however, for Europeans to employ Indian scholars as well as draftsmen, whom they heavily relied upon for their expertise in Indian languages and cultures.[22] Through his architectural investigations, Syed Ahmad meant to gain credibility with the European members of the ASD who wielded enough cultural capital and political power in mid-nineteenth century Delhi to be recognized as the new patrons of this form of knowledge production. Indeed, by dedicating the first edition of the *Āṣār-us-Ṣanādīd* to Thomas Metcalfe, then President of the ASD, Syed Ahmad hoped to win the favour of his European counterparts and be recognized as a modern scholar and adept translator of Delhi's built heritage. The Society meanwhile, and Metcalfe in particular, maintained an ambivalent stance toward Syed Ahmad and his scholarship, and he was only inducted into the ASD in 1852, two years before the Society disbanded.[23]

Despite the ambivalent relationship between Syed Ahmad and the European members of the ASD, the former was hardly the only Indian intellectual promoting modern theories of Indian architecture and archaeology. For example, in 1834, the Royal Asiatic Society published Ram Raz's *Essay on the Architecture of the Hindus*.[24] Ram Raz had spent close to a decade collating and translating pre-modern Sanskrit texts in order to create a framework for Hindu architecture, urban design, and ornamentation. He was influenced by European models of architectural historicism and sought to illustrate the principles of Hindu architecture according to the same rationalist schema of proportion, structure, and composition offered by contemporary Western texts on architecture.[25] Another contemporary of Syed Ahmad was the archaeologist Rajendralal Mitra, who received a colonial training in archaeology and initially worked very much as an insider in the colonial systems of classification and enumeration. By the 1860s, however, Mitra was committed to recovering an indigenous, if not proto-nationalist, understanding of Indian architecture as emerging from a core set of Hindu principles regarding building and ornamentation.[26]

There is little doubt that Syed Ahmad, Ram Raz, and Mitra were staunch advocates of modern science and history as much as they were committed to their colonial patrons. All three men (and many more of their contemporaries) employed rigorous methods of observation, documentation, translation, and analysis in their interpretations of Indian architecture. The scholarship produced by them was both modern and Indian, derivative as well as original. It should be noted, however, that while Ram Raz and Mitra, both practicing

Hindus, were heavily invested in the idea of Hindu architecture as the foundation of Indian architecture, Syed Ahmad took a more ecumenical approach toward the history of Delhi, even highlighting its mythical Hindu origins and including the few historic Hindu, Jain, and Sikh structures alongside the city's otherwise largely Islamic monuments. In its combination of poetry with textual and visual documentation, the first edition of *Āṣār-us-Ṣanādīd* also stands in contrast to the more rigid presentation in Ram Raz's and Mitra's texts. Nevertheless, these Indian scholars should be considered critical agents in establishing the terms of modern architectural debate alongside their European counterparts.

The *Āṣār-us-Ṣanādīd* was also contemporary to the scholarship of Europeans, such as the architectural historian James Fergusson, and the antiquarian Alexander Cunningham. Fergusson travelled throughout much of India in the 1830s, sketching and making notes on the architecture of the subcontinent. On his return to England, he first published *Picturesque Illustrations of Ancient Architecture in Hindostan* (1848) and the more comprehensive *History of Indian and Eastern Architecture* (1876).[27] The latter proposed a classification of Indian architecture according to racial (e.g., Aryan and Dravidian) as well as religious (Hindu, Buddhist, Jain, Islamic, etc.) types. Fergusson's mapping of India's geography and history according to its architectural objects was paralleled by Cunningham's efforts to establish a central bureaucracy for the documentation and preservation of India's ancient monuments. Cunningham justified the need for such an institution on the basis that Indians had neither the knowledge nor the inclination to care for their own antiquities. His efforts led to the establishment of the ASI in 1861, an institution that quickly calcified the colonial stewardship of Indian heritage and built antiquity.

The art historian Tapati Guha-Thakurta has suggested that by selecting and reproducing particular examples of Indian architecture in his books, Fergusson created the first visual archive of India's architecture. Similarly, she suggests that by excavating those sites of Indian antiquity that were mentioned in newly translated ancient Sanskrit and Pali texts, Cunningham created the first textual archive of Indian archaeology.[28] In comparison, Syed Ahmad's *Āṣār-us-Ṣanādīd* was an archive that included both visual and textual methods of architectural interpretation. It relied on a variety of Persian, Sanskrit, and English records, including: the *Ain-i Akbari*, a sixteenth-century chronicle of the Mughal emperor Akbar's reign; the *Bhagavata Purana*, a life-narrative of the Hindu deity Vishnu and his many incarnations; the *Old Testament*; and the records of the Asiatic Society, to propose a deep and detailed history of Delhi. In terms of creating a visual archive, the first edition of the *Āṣār-us-Ṣanādīd* presented more than 100 views of Delhi's monuments in their contemporary state and in a visual vocabulary that departed considerably from the prevalent aesthetic of the picturesque. One-point perspective and elevations depicted the monuments as faithfully as possible, making the first edition of the *Āṣār-us-Ṣanādīd* one of the richest and most reliable image archives of Delhi's built environment in the early nineteenth century.

Contemporary scholarship has amply illustrated the intimate reliance on their Indian counterparts by early colonial experts, which included surveyors, ethnographers, antiquarians, and archaeologists. In fact, many historians have argued that Indian translators, *pandits*, and scholars worked so closely with European bureaucrats that it is difficult to clearly distinguish the resultant knowledge along the lines of European and Indian.[29] Figures such as Ram Raz, Rajendralal Mitra, and Syed Ahmad comprised a particular category of architectural knowledge-makers who were strategically poised between pre-colonial and colonial understandings of time, place, and culture. Each of these men was heavily invested in the construction of a rational, indisputable regime of truth, where architecture functioned as a means to decode India's past. While Syed Ahmad's expertise was certainly modulated by his European audience and impacted by colonial methods such as the survey, his work should not be seen as mere mimicry of his European contemporaries or rote implementation of their practices. As the following sections will show, the *Āṣār-us-Ṣanādīd* made savvy manoeuvres between modern historical methods and Syed Ahmad's own position as a Muslim intellectual producing knowledge in a climate marked by rising European hegemony.

Image

The 1847 edition of *Āṣār-us-Ṣanādīd* featured over one hundred woodcut illustrations of the majority of the monuments described in the book. Every attempt was made to stay true to the monuments' scales and proportions and often even included faithful reproductions of those parts of the structures that were in disrepair. In order to understand the modes of visual representation that were employed in the *Āṣār-us-Ṣanādīd*, in this section I investigate some of the images produced of the Qutb Minar and the larger complex of the Quwwat-ul Islam mosque.[30] This monumental complex represents the earliest structures of Islamic architecture extant in Delhi. It includes the Quwwat-ul Islam mosque (1192–1316), the Qutb Minar (1202–fourteenth century), the tomb of Iltutmish (1235), a monumental gateway called the Alai Darwaza (1311), the Alai Minar (an additional unfinished minaret intended to be several times larger than the Qutb Minar) (fourteenth century), in addition to several other structures including colleges and tombs [Figure 2.1]. The site of the Quwwat-ul Islam mosque was formerly the garrison fort of the Hindu Chauhan rulers of Delhi. While the earliest layers of the mosque show defacement of non-Islamic building materials and contain inscriptions proclaiming the destruction of 'infidel' temples, these coexist alongside several other examples of careful salvage, re-composition, and display of Hindu and Jain elements in the central courtyard of the mosque. Thus, recent scholarship on the monument has suggested a framework of reuse and appropriation, alongside religious violence, as a means to understand the Quwwat-ul Islam mosque.[31] Meanwhile, the name Quwwat-ul Islam (The Might of Islam) itself is a controversial moniker for the first Friday mosque built by Delhi's Islamic rulers in the thirteenth century. Historians like Sunil Kumar have proven that the name was a corruption of an earlier epithet, Qubba-i Islam (Sanctuary of Islam), used more broadly to refer to the city of Delhi at large.[32] In the fourteenth century, a court-sponsored and orthodox Sunni Islamic ideology appropriated

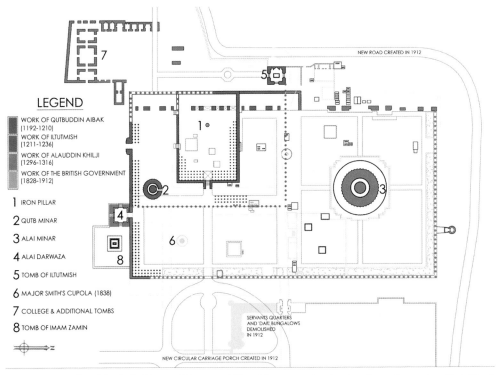

Figure 2.1: *Site plan of the Qutb Minar and Quwwat-ul Islam Mosque complex showing phases of expansion.* Chris Hazel.

the mosque and began referring to it as the Quwwat-ul Islam, mostly to curb the popularity of Sufi leaders who challenged the claim of the Sultan as the sole guardian and defender of Islamic sharia.[33]

In his description of the Quwwat-ul Islam mosque, Syed Ahmad describes the columns as having been sourced from the 'idol-house' (*bhūt khānā*), or the temple that he believed was demolished in order to build the mosque. He praises the level of artisanship and craftsmanship in these original columns, commenting on the intricacy and depth of their carvings. In remarking on their reuse in the central courtyard of the mosque and their defacement, he acknowledges the signs of iconoclasm but does not ascribe this to any particular violence enacted by the incoming Muslim armies or even an imperial order passed by Shahubbudin Ghori or his slave-king Qutbuddin Aibak. Instead, he suggests that the establishment of Muslim rule in Delhi caused such a turn in the 'hearts of men' that they defaced these idols, beheading some and cutting the noses off others, such that the images were rendered impotent.[34] He thus puts forth a reading of the Quwwat-ul Islam mosque as a site of religious and social transformation. In Syed Ahmad's interpretation the defaced statues were less indicative of the violent erasure or abrogation of Hinduism by Islamic conquerors, but rather were the result of the social change brought about by Islam

A Nineteenth-Century Architectural Archive: Syed Ahmad Khan's *Āṣār-us-Ṣanādīd*

in a population that, once converted, found the presence of idols repulsive and therefore mutilated them. Such an interpretation privileged the agency of the subject population over brute imperial force and represented the Quwwat-ul Islam as indicative of a popular embrace of Islamic culture in the subcontinent.

The more vexing issue for Syed Ahmad in the description of this mosque pertained to the visual representation of the defaced columns. After his textual description of their beauty and the history of their defacement, he implied that an image showing the figural nature of the column-carvings was included in the publication. As a devout Muslim, he apologized for reproducing images of humans and beasts in his book, but justified his decision on the basis that it was necessary to make a true documentation of an important aspect of the Quwwat-ul Islam. He ended by asking the reader to look at the images and reflect on the glory of God. The image that followed, however, was an elevation of the mosque's central courtyard, drawn at a scale that rendered the details of the columns invisible to the reader [Figure 2.2]. The particulars of the figural columns did not appear in any other images of the mosque either, leaving the reader to rely only on Syed Ahmad's rich textual descriptions. While this discrepancy between the text and representative image may have been an editing oversight, it is equally possible that Syed Ahmad's hesitation in representing Hindu idols – which were now part of a mosque – would have trumped his need for documentary veracity.[35] Although

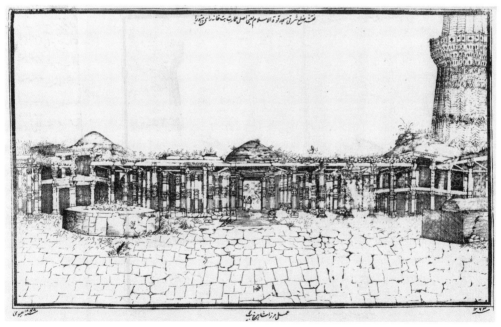

Figure 2.2: *Illustration of the main courtyard of the Quwwat-ul Islam Mosque from the* Āṣār-us-Ṣanādīd *(1847 ed.).* The Bancroft Library.

61

committed to an objective documentation of Delhi's monuments, the presence of human and animal decoration in the Quwwat-ul Islam required Syed Ahmad to use visual strategies that would not violate its integrity as a mosque. In other words, Syed Ahmad modulated the visual archive according to his religious principles while also staying true to the scientific nature of architectural documentation.

The absence of any visual representation of the Hindu imagery on the columns in the Quwwat-ul Islam mosque stands in contrast to the rich reproduction of calligraphic inscription found on the Qutb Minar. The elevation of the minaret showed particular inscriptions from the second to the fifth storey arranged on either side of the tower, wrapping around it as they actually do on the façade of the monument [Figure 2.3]. On the right and left of the fifth storey the inscription acknowledges that Firoz Shah Tughlaq (r.1351–88) rebuilt the fifth and now final storey when lightning damaged it in 770 Hijri (1368–69). The other inscriptions arranged on both sides of the fourth storey credit Iltutmish (r.1211–36) as the patron of the minaret and invoked him as the 'heir to the kingdom of Solomon',[36] while that on the third storey reveals that Muhammad Amir Koh was the superintendent of construction. The epigraph on the second storey again refers to Iltutmish as the patron and builder of the minaret. The inscription reproduced at the bottom of the page, which acts both as a visual border for the image and as a discursive foundation for the image, replicates an epigraph from the top band of the Qutb Minar's first storey. It begins with a well-known verse from a Hadīth that states, 'Whoever builds a mosque for Allah and Allah alone, will be rewarded with a house in paradise', and goes on to read:

> His Majesty the King of Kings, Shamsuddin-wa-duniyā [Iltutmish], who is now deceased and has received God's grace and forgiveness, may his grave be purified and may paradise be his final resting place, built this minaret which was later injured. The damaged minaret was restored during the reign of the illustrious and exalted Emperor Sikandar Shah [r.1489–1526], the son of Bahlol Shah Sultan, may God perpetuate his kingdom and reign and increase his power and prestige. The repairs were carried out under the supervision of Khanzadah Fath Khan the son of Hasnad-i Ali Khawas Khan, who restored the upper stories by filling in cracks and loose joints. These repairs were carried out on the first day of the second Rabia in 909 A.H. [September 23, 1503].[37]

Syed Ahmad consciously chose to only reproduce those epigraphs that provided specific information regarding the patron's names and the time period during which each storey of the minaret was built. He did not, for instance, replicate either in image or text several other Quranic inscriptions that wrap around the Qutb Minar and actually constitute the bulk of the inscriptions on the minaret. Instead, by reproducing only those inscriptions pertaining to the Qutb Minar's builders and patrons, Syed Ahmad presents the minaret as a historical document of Islamic imperial power, where each successive emperor built upon the architectural layers left by his predecessor, creating a pleasing composite whole.

A Nineteenth-Century Architectural Archive: Syed Ahmad Khan's *Āṣār-us-Ṣanādīd*

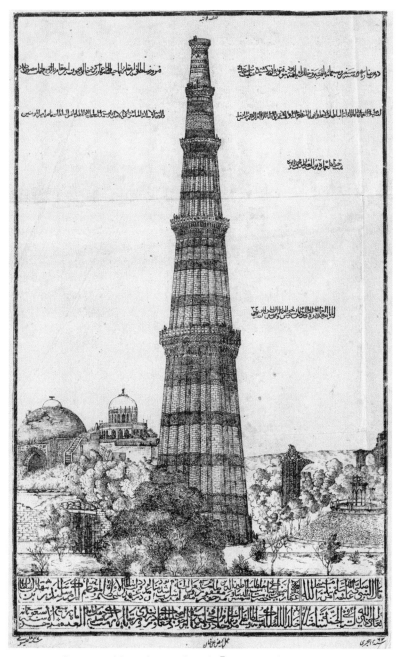

Figure 2.3: *Illustration of the Qutb Minar from the* Āṣār-us-Ṣanādīd *(1847 ed.). The pavilion added by the British in 1828 can be seen towards the bottom right-hand corner of the image.* The Bancroft Library.

In his exegesis on monumental writing on Islamic architecture, Jamal Elias has pointed out that inscriptions often served ornamental as well as didactic purposes for their audiences.[38] This was particularly the case in medieval monuments where only a small percentage of literate persons could comprehend the complex Arabic of Qurʿanic inscriptions. Other factors, such as the intricate calligraphy of the inscriptions, the complexity of the Kufic or Naṣkh script, and the positioning of many inscriptions, meant that epigraphs served as ornamentation rather than purposes of propaganda.[39] In Elias' words:

> The religious epigraphic program of an Islamic building might best be understood in terms of tattooing. Even when the epigraphy is recognized as words, and words are recognized as possessing textual meaning, their affective power is not diminished. They function primarily as visual images with apotropaic powers and as iconically distinct signifiers. Like epigraphy, body tattooing commonly fulfills the dual functions of beautification (and relatedly of drawing attention to the body as a visual object) and of serving as prophylactic armor that wraps or seals the body against misfortune of supernatural or humanly inflicted kinds.[40]

On the one hand, by making visible those inscriptions that were likely difficult for visitors to the Qutb Minar to read from any vantage, Syed Ahmad made historical information from the monument available to readers of the *Āṣār-us-Ṣanādīd*. This was identical to the nature of archaeological and architectural knowledge that Europeans were seeking to establish through new disciplines at the time. Indeed, scholars such as Cunningham and Fergusson sought to gather precisely such epigraphic information and cull accurate details regarding India's past from them. However, by replicating the inscriptions in their original Kufic script and by arranging them on the page so that they simulated the aesthetic of the monument, Syed Ahmad concealed as much as he revealed about the monument. A nineteenth-century reader, especially the Europeans Syed Ahmad spoke to, might have found it difficult to decipher these inscriptions; however, they would have also grasped their affective power quite quickly. Arranged as these inscriptions are, around the minaret and at its base, they attract the reader's attention to the primary image of the monument while also acting as armour that prevents the Qutb Minar from being fully known, especially to the European eye. This image of the Qutb Minar and the preceding illustration of the Quwwat-ul Islam mosque were both faithful representations of the monuments, yet functioned in fundamentally different ways. While the elevation of the Quwwat-ul Islam mosque concealed what was clearly and easily visible to the visitor of the mosque, namely the figural sculptures on the columns, the image of the Qutb Minar revealed that which was difficult to see with the naked eye, the epigraphic information on all four stories of the minaret.

The replication of the Hadīth verse in the image provided a framework to understand the Qutb Minar as a palimpsest of Islamic sovereign rule in Delhi. Four different Muslim emperors – Qutbuddin Aibak, Iltutmish, Firoz Shah Tughlaq, and Sikandar Lodi – had either added to or restored the minaret between the twelfth and sixteenth centuries. Syed Ahmad, however, also inserted the British government into the history of Qutb Minar's building and restoration, for in the accompanying text he talked about the extensive restoration work carried out by colonial engineers. This included clearing the grounds around the structure, building new paths around the minaret and mosque, and fixing the cracks of the minaret; works that cost the British government a sizeable outlay of Rs. 100,000.[41] Syed Ahmad also highlighted a more pointed attempt made by the British to include themselves within the history of the Qutb Minar by the addition of a sixth storey to the top of the minaret in 1828. The pavilion-like final storey was installed by Major Robert Smith of the Royal Engineers, and was meant to replace the original storey that had been knocked down during a storm [Figure 2.4]. Smith's addition, however, was criticized by his British contemporaries who

Figure 2.4: *'Smith's folly': the cupola added to the top of the Qutb Minar by British engineer Robert Smith in 1828 and later dismounted.* Mrinalini Rajagopalan.

found the addition too fanciful (Cunningham berated the addition as incongruous to the rest of the minaret and called it 'a flimsy Mogul pavilion') and ordered that it be taken down.[42] The pavilion was set in a garden close to the minaret and soon acquired the moniker 'Smith's folly', in reference to both its misguided design and the English tradition of small buildings set as curiosities in garden. By including Smith's pavilion in the foreground of his illustration, Syed Ahmad deliberately inserted the British government into the archival record of imperial building represented by the Qutb Minar.

In his exegesis on the archive, Jacques Derrida traces the etymology of the term to the Greek *arkhe*, or commandment. The legitimacy of the archive was deeply linked to the figure of *archon*, a gatekeeper who guarded access to the information housed within the archive and thereby also regulated the interpretation of documents.[43] The archive was thus a repository of knowledge linked to embodied power and the *archon* may be thought of as the personality who determined the terms of debate and commanded authority over documents. In the colonial context, it was invariably Europeans who assumed the role of the *archon*, maintaining access to the contents of the archive and managing its meanings. For example, the ASD functioned as a group of *archons* intent on creating a historical archive of Delhi as well as regulating its interpretation. The *Āṣār-us-Ṣanādīd*, however, interrupted this assumption of colonial hegemony over the archive and the notion that Europeans were its only capable interlocutors. By creating a rich corpus of Delhi's architectural objects, Syed Ahmad fashioned himself as an *archon*, the creator as well as steward of the religious, cultural, and historical meanings of Delhi's architectural heritage. While his archive should in no way be interpreted as a critique of colonial power, for he positions the British government as the modern successors to the Hindu and Islamic empires of Delhi, it should be seen as a shrewd manoeuvre to participate in and shape the fields of archaeology and architectural history that were clearly becoming of interest to Europeans in India.

Comparison

The lasting impact of the *Āṣār-us-Ṣanādīd* can be seen in the way that European experts developed their theories and knowledge of Delhi's past in relation to it. In this section I will discuss the historiography of the Qutb Minar as an argument created in the discursive space between the *Āṣār-us-Ṣanādīd* and the first official reports of the ASI. It should first be noted, however, that the political climate between 1854 (when the second edition of *Āṣār-us-Ṣanādīd* was published) and 1861 (when the ASI was established) was marked by a dramatic change and repositioning of European power in the subcontinent. In 1857, Indians of many ranks (including soldiers in the employ of the British, peasants, merchants, and others) led a mass rebellion against the English East India Company, which the latter was able to extinguish after considerable difficulties and heavy loss of life on both sides. In 1858, Queen Victoria was formally declared sovereign of India and the country became an official dominion of the British Empire. The establishment of various bureaucracies and institutions of governance followed the move from economic imperialism to colonial domination, a shift that is often referred to as the move from Company rule to Crown rule. The establishment of the ASI as a body of cultural management was part of this new regime of power marked by aggressive policies prefaced on the distinction between colonial authorities and Indian subjects.

In the 1847 edition of the *Āṣār-us-Ṣanādīd*, Syed Ahmad attributed the origins of the Qutb Minar to the early Islamic rulers of Delhi. In 1852, however, he read a paper at the ASD in which he claimed that the Qutb Minar was originally a Hindu structure built by the Hindu king Prithviraj Chauhan for his daughter, Bela. Prithviraj Chauhan was the last Hindu ruler of Delhi, whose territories were usurped by the Central Asian ruler Mohammad Ghori in 1192. Syed Ahmad claimed that Ghori's envoy, Qutbuddin Aibak, had appropriated Prithviraj Chauhan's Hindu palace, temples, and minaret, and expanded them into the Quwwat-ul Islam mosque and the Qutb Minar. His changed view of the Qutb Minar's origins appeared in the second edition of *Āṣār-us-Ṣanādīd*, where he submitted five 'scientific' proofs of the Hindu origins of the minaret. These included: the fact that the Qutb Minar was an independent tower, unlike the more common engaged minarets found in mosques; that there was only one minaret whilst most mosques have at least a pair of minarets; that the doorway of the minaret faces north whereas most Islamic monuments have east-facing doorways in order for a worshipper to enter the monument facing West towards Mecca; that the minaret was built without a plinth, a characteristic of Hindu rather than Islamic monuments; and that the ornamentation of the Qutb Minar, especially on the lower story, is heavily 'Hindu', portraying motifs such as bells which are rare in Islamic decoration. With these justifications, Syed Ahmad claimed that the first storey of the Qutb Minar was originally built as a Hindu structure and later added to by Islamic rulers.[44]

A decade later Cunningham would emphatically refute Syed Ahmad's position and make counterclaims regarding the Qutb Minar's origins. In his archaeological reports of northern India (1862–65), Cunningham systematically rebutted the five proofs posited by Syed Ahmad with the following observations.[45] On the issue of the Qutb Minar being a singular minaret built independently of the mosque, Cunningham cited the examples of minarets at Ghazni and Koel to show that early mosques, built between the twelfth and thirteenth century, in Central Asia and northern India had only one minaret and were often disengaged from mosques. As the first Islamic rulers of Delhi were from Central Asia they would have referred to these regional precedents in the construction of the Qutb Minar. In response to the north-facing entrance of the minaret, Cunningham again invoked the example of the Koel Minar and its north-facing entrance. Cunningham also claimed that in his survey of approximately 50 Hindu temples across the subcontinent he had found at least ten with entrances to the West and two to the North, thus refuting Syed Ahmad's claim that most Hindu monuments have north-facing entrances. As counterpoint to the Qutb Minar not having a plinth and therefore being of Hindu origins, Cunningham offered examples of Hindu monuments that had generous plinths, such as the Hindu temples at Khajuraho and the Hindu pillar at Chittor. In addition, he pointed to Islamic minarets built without plinths such as the minaret at Ghazni [Figure 2.5]. Finally, in reference to Hindu motifs such as bells and garlands on the lower story of the minaret, Cunningham posited that since Hindu craftsmen built the Qutb Minar under Islamic direction it was the former's aesthetic that prevailed.[46] Even as

Figure 2.5: *Illustration of the minaret at Ghazni.* James Fergusson, *History of Indian and Eastern Architecture* (London: John Murray, 1876).

Cunningham rejected Syed Ahmad's theory that the Qutb Minar's origins were Hindu, his refutation involved a significant engagement with the *Āṣār-us-Ṣanādīd* and thereby an implicit recognition of the Indian author's expertise. The only other contemporary that Cunningham chose to debate so thoroughly in his reports was the architectural historian James Fergusson. Although Cunningham and Syed Ahmad espoused diametrically opposite positions regarding the origins of the Qutb Minar, and while Cunningham's assessment of its Islamic origins was the more accurate of the two, it appears that European claims to expertise were built on similar historical articulations made by their Indian counterparts.

It is also worthwhile to note the similarity of methodologies employed by both Cunningham and Syed Ahmad. For instance, both men argued their case on the stylistic differences between Hindu and Islamic architecture, such as the ornamentation of bells and garlands or the absence of building plinths. Their expertise thus shared a vocabulary of architectural forms as well as an understanding that Hindu and Islamic art were fundamentally distinct from one another. Secondly, they both used a comparative method to justify their arguments; while Syed Ahmad invoked the more general categories of Hindu temples and Islamic mosques, Cunningham provided specific examples such as the minarets of Ghazni or Koel. In other words, even as Cunningham dismissed Syed Ahmad's claims he did so by mirroring the latter's method and argumentative strategy. After his very measured and objective refutation of Syed Ahmad's claims, however, Cunningham concludes his history of the Qutb Minar on an affective note by stating:

> The object of building this lofty column seems to me to be clear enough. The first Musalman conquerors were an energetic race, whose conceptions were as bold and daring as their actions. When the zealous Muhammadan looked on the great city of Delhi, the metropolis of the princely Tomars and the haughty Chohans, his first wish would have been to humble the pride of the infidel; his second, to exalt the religion of his prophet Muhammad. To attain both of these objects, he built a lofty column, from whose summit the *Muazzin's* call to morning and evening prayer could be heard on all sides by Hindus as well as by Musalmans. The conqueror's pride was soothed by the daily insult and indignity thus offered to the infidel, while his religious feelings were gratified by the erection of a noble monument which towered majestically over the loftiest houses in the city.[47]

In this deeply affective explanation of the origins of the Qutb Minar, Cunningham imagined the motivation of zealous Muslim rulers and their need to insult and mete out indignities to the 'infidel'. While the emotive qualities of this particular passage stood in contrast to the 'objective' analyses that preceded it, it was not the only part in the reports where Cunningham lapsed into impressionistic accounts of the past. Indeed, the archaeological reports of 1862–65 show many instances where he submits theories on subjective interpretations, such as the iconoclastic tendencies of Islamic rulers or the violence that would have necessarily accompanied the Islamic conquest of India. Indeed, the discipline of archaeology served as the scientific conceit for European experts to make claims that had little basis in empirical or historical fact. While European science and rationality had presented itself as the remedy for fanciful Indian histories that were barely distinguishable from myths, it appears that the former too were not immune from affective projections of the historical past.

Following the publication of Cunningham's reports, Syed Ahmad's position as one of the primary interlocutors of Delhi's architectural and urban history quickly faded. By 1872, when Henry Hardy Cole wrote *Ancient Delhi*, he cited Cunningham's archaeological reports as the most reliable source on the subject while the *Āṣār-us-Ṣanādīd* is given only a passing mention. Meanwhile, James Fergusson's *History of Indian and Eastern Architecture* did not cite Syed Ahmad's work at all.[48] Yet the shadow of the debate between Syed Ahmad and Cunningham regarding the Hindu or Islamic origins of the Qutb Minar can be detected in Fergusson's presentation of the Qutb Minar as similar to other types of Islamic minarets such as the one in Ghazni. In the 1927 historical guide to the Qutb Minar and its surrounding monuments, published by the ASI, there is no mention of Syed Ahmad or his *Āṣār-us-Ṣanādīd*, but Cunningham's research on the monuments is cited often.[49] The late nineteenth and early twentieth centuries saw a calcifying archive of the history of Delhi's architecture, mostly written in English by archaeologists working for the colonial government. Cunningham's remarks rose to become the final word on the history of the Qutb Minar and the Quwwat-ul Islam, while it was forgotten that his submissions were formulated through an engagement with and refutation of Syed Ahmad's theories regarding the same. In other words, Cunningham's expertise was divorced from a previously shared realm of Indian and European dialogue and held up as an independent schema of knowledge.

Chronology

Some scholars have described the difference between the two editions of *Āṣār-us-Ṣanādīd* through a framework of loss. For example, Lelyveld has argued that while the first edition was as much a celebration of the Urdu language and culture that prevailed in Delhi, the second edition adopted a more clinical view of the city's monuments with little discussion regarding its contemporary cultures of orality or poetry.[50] In a similar vein, Naim points out that Syed Ahmad himself referred to the first edition as an *ahwal* (an account) and the second edition of the book as a *tarīkh* (history), thereby revealing the changed and more self-conscious posture of the author.[51] While it is true that Syed Ahmad redacted much of the poetic turns and subjective reflections on various monuments in the 1854 edition, he also added a chronology of urban evolution as it related to a series of Hindu and Islamic empires that ruled the city from antiquity to the present in the later edition of the book.[52] In this section I argue that this shift from affective description to chronological precision should be viewed not so much as a loss, but rather as a strategy by which Syed Ahmad formulated a modern taxonomy within which the monuments of Delhi could be arranged.

The narrative of Delhi as a series of imperial capitals can be found in early accounts of the city. In his early reports Cunningham refers to observations made by medieval traveller Ibn Battuta, who alluded to the four cities of Delhi that had melded into one by the time he visited in the fourteenth century and William Finch's remarks on the seven imperial forts and 52 gates of Delhi in the seventeenth century.[53] By the mid-nineteenth century, however, considerable effort was being exerted to move this particular imaginary of the city from the space of travel writing and popular belief into the realm of expertise. In November 1852, the ASD submitted a classification of Delhi's urban evolution, linking the archaeological evidence of the city to a genealogy of empires. Lamenting the incomplete and imperfect nature of the chronology, the members of the Society warned that theirs was only a preliminary attempt to create historical order in the absolute vacuum of such previous knowledge.[54] In the same year Syed Ahmad also published a chronology of Indian empires and rulers titled *Silsilat-al-Muluk* (Genealogy of Kings) for which he had received support from Arthur Austin Roberts.[55] As Roberts became the Vice-President of the ASD around 1852 it is entirely possible that it was he who championed the archaeological co-relation between Delhi's architectural antiquities and former empires. Seemingly in direct response to the ASD's call for a comprehensive mapping of Delhi's material culture remains and their links to previous empires, the 1854 edition of the *Āṣār-us-Ṣanādīd* presents a detailed chronology of Delhi's rulers alongside their architectural products [Figure 2.6]. The table, translated below, lists no less than twenty imperial capitals or forts built by a combination of Hindu and Islamic rulers, stretching from antiquity to the present.

Syed Ahmad's arrangement of Delhi's material culture invokes the structure of a modern survey by creating a matrix of dates, buildings, and historic personalities. By leading with the architectural object and making specific links to its patrons, each of whom represents a distinct era of imperial rule, this classification positioned material culture as the empirical basis from which major historical shifts could be extrapolated. In other words, Syed Ahmad had put forth a new archive for Delhi's history founded on the city's built environment. The provision of precise dates for the cities and forts also allowed Syed Ahmad to submit a chronology of the city's past. However, it is worth pointing out that the scientific presentation of facts and the classificatory order also allowed Syed Ahmad to include cities such as Indrapat and Dehly from the previous era for which no material remains existed and whose dates could only be ascertained by reference to mythological texts or popular traditions. In other words, Syed Ahmad's chronology also calcified as empirical truth the imaginary Delhi that had thus far only circulated in the space of myth or popular belief.

In his exegesis on modern bureaucracies, Timothy Mitchell has argued that epistemological frameworks put in place by colonial bureaucrats, no matter how subjective, quickly acquired an unquestionable authority and created a common belief simply due to the techno-political power through which they were enforced. The racial, biological, and physiological categories created by the natural sciences in the nineteenth century, although socially constructed, were then codified by modern modalities such as the census, the archive, and the survey, which in turn provided them with a veil of scientific objectivity and posited them as inalienable truths.[58] Similarly, and in the context of colonial India, Nicholas Dirks has illustrated how the mechanism of the survey was a product of the Enlightenment, whereby the collection of empirical data and its assortment according to various ideological parameters would reveal universal truths regarding the colonized population.[59] For example, Fergusson acknowledged the contributions of Mackenzie's survey to the study of Indian architecture when he wrote, 'Colin Mackenzie [...] drew everything he found of any architectural importance, and was the most industrious and successful collector of drawings and manuscripts that India has ever known.'[60] Mackenzie's survey thus not only enumerated the architectural monuments of India, but also bestowed them with architectural importance by mere dint of the colonial gaze. In the case of the *Āṣār-us-Ṣanādīd*,

List accompanying the second part of *Āṣār-us-Ṣanādīd*, regarding the building of forts and cities of Delhi.[56]

Number	The name of the fort or the city	Name of the original builder	Year in which built — Hijri (Islamic) date	Year in which built — Christian date	Circumstances/Conditions
1	Indrapat	Judhisthir	–	c.1450 BCE	
2	Dehly	Raja Dehlu	–	c.328 BCE	
3	Purana Qila or Din Panah or Sher Ghadh	Anangpal Toar	57	676	In 940 Hijri/1533 CE Emperor Humayun captured this fort and renamed it Din Panah. Emperor Sher Shah also repaired this fort and renamed it Sher Ghadh.
4	Qila Rai Pithora Qasr Safed	Rai Pithora Qutbuddin Aibak	538 682[57]	1143 1205	The Western gate of this fort is called Ghazni gate. There was a palace in the middle of the fort built by Rai Pithora.
5	Kushak Lal	Ghiyassuddin Balban	664	1265	The fort was built a few years before this date when Balban was still a *vazir* and had not yet become king.
6	Qila Marzghan or Ghiyaspur	Ghiyasuddin Balban	666	1268	The Sufi shrine of Hazrat Nizamuddin is located in this fort.
7	Khilokri or Qasr Maaze	Maghruddin Kaiqubad	685	1286	Emperor Humayun's Tomb is located in this fort.
8	Kushak Lal or New City Kushak Sabz	Jalaluddin Feroze Khilji	688	1289	The Kushak Sabz was a palace inside the fort of Kaushak Lal.
9	Dhilli Alai or Fort Alai or Kushak Siri Qasr-e-Hazaar Sutun	Alauddin Khilji	703	1303	The Hazaar Sutun (Hall of Thousand Pillars) was a palace in the Kushak Siri.
10	Tughlaqabad	Tughlaq Shah	721	1321	
11	Adilabad or Muhammadabad or Monument Hazaar Sutun	Muhammad Tughlaq Shah	728	1327	
12	Jahan Panah Kushak Burj Mandal or Bureeh Manzil	Muhammad Adil Tughlaq Shah	728	1327	Dhilli Alai and Dhilli Kohna (or Qila Rai Pithora) were merged to form Jahan Panah. The Kushak Burj is a domed structure on the exterior of the walls of Jahan Panah.

13	Kushak Feroze Shah or Kotla Feroze Shah City of Ferozabad	Feroze Shah	755	1354	The city was built around the fort of Firozabad.
14	Kushak Jahah Numa Or Kushak Shukr	Feroze Shah	755	1354	
15	Khizrabad	Khizr Khan	821	1418	
16	Mubarakabad	Mubarak Shah	837	1433	
17	Dhilli Sher Shah	Sher Shah	948	1541	The Kabuli Gate of this fort is still standing near the jailhouse.
18	Salimgarh or Nurgarh	Islam Shah	953	1546	The bridge in front of Salimgarh was built during the reign of Emperor Nuruddin Jahangir and the fort was renamed Nurgarh in his honour.
19	Shahjahanabad Fort	Emperor Shahjahan	1048	1638	This fort features European, especially Italian, styles of ornamentation. This fort complex includes the following famous buildings built during the time of Emperor Shahjahan: Delhi Gate Lahori Gate and the Chatta Naqqar Khana Diwan-e-Aam and the Marble Throne Khas Mahal Imtiaz Mahal or Rang Mahal and the inlaid marble image of Orpheus playing the flute Masur Baithak and the Suman Burj Shah Mandal or the Diwan-e-Khas Hammam Moti Mahal Hayat Baksh Garden and the Sawan and Bhadon pavilions Mehtab Gardens
20	City of Shahjahanabad, the surrounding markets, and Faiz Canal	Emperor Shahjahan	1058	1648	This is the city that was built around the fort of Shahjahanabad. It is still extant and will hopefully continue to thrive forever.

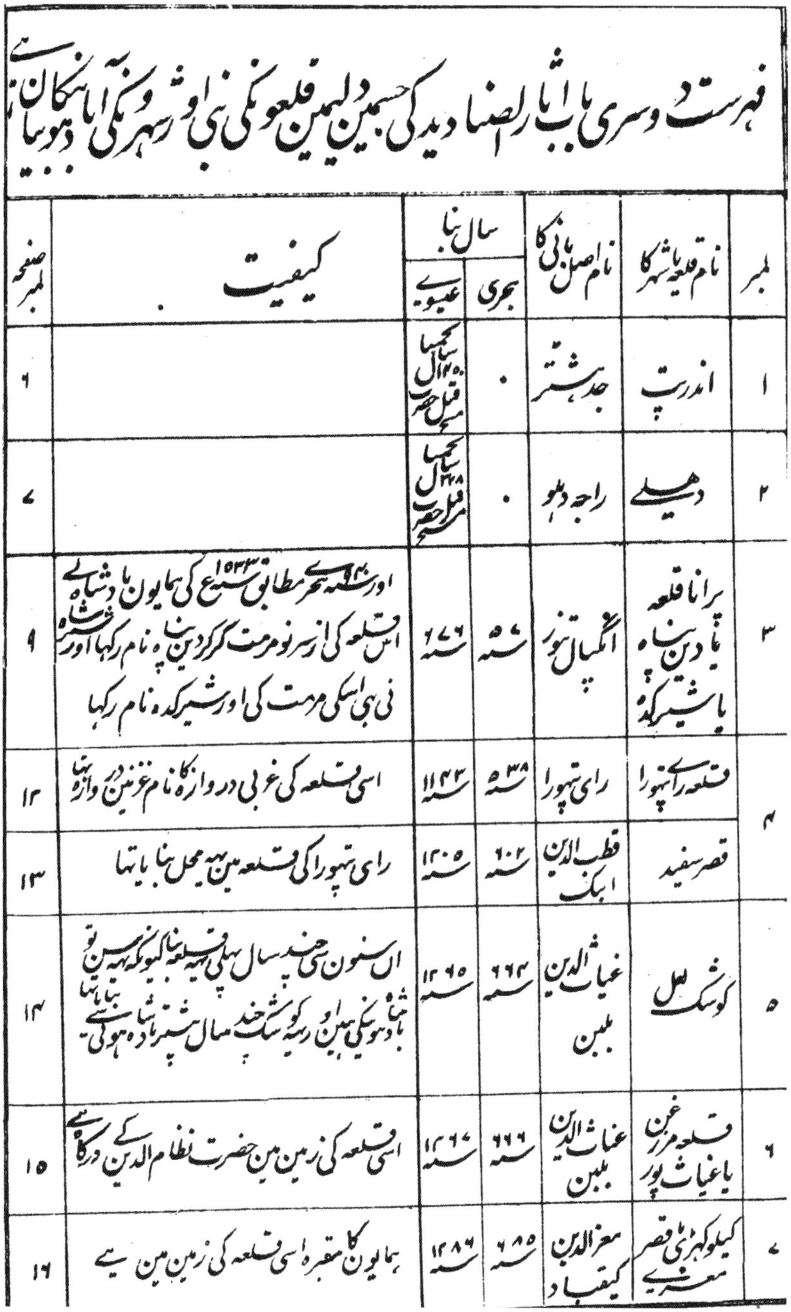

فہرست دوسری باب آثار الصنادید کی جسمین دلیمین قلعونکی بنی اور شہرونکی آباد ہونیکا بیان ہے

نمبر صفحہ	کیفیت	سال بنا عیسوی	سال بنا ہجری	نام اصلی بانی کا	نام قلعہ یا شہر کا	نمبر
۶		سنہ ۳۱۰۱ سال قبل حضرت عیسیٰ	۰	جدہشتر	اندرپت	۱
۷		سنہ ۳۰۸ سال قبل حضرت عیسیٰ	۰	راجہ دہلو	دہلی	۲
۹	اور سنہ ۹۴۰ ہجری مطابق سنہ ۱۵۳۳ع کی ہمایون بادشاہ نے اس قلعہ کی از سر نو مرمت کرکر دین پناہ نام رکہا اور شیر شاہ نی بہی اسکی مرمت کی اور شیرگدہ نام رکہا	سنہ ۶۷۶	سنہ	انگپال تنور	پرانا قلعہ یا دین پناہ یا شیرگدہ	۳
۱۲	اسی قلعہ کی غربی دروازہ کا نام غزنین دروازہ تہا	سنہ ۱۱۴۳	سنہ ۵۳۸	رای پتہورا	قلعہ رای پتہورا	۴
۱۳	رای پتہورا کی قلعہ مین یہہ محل بنایا تہا	سنہ ۱۲۰۵	سنہ ۶۰۲	قطب الدین ایبک	قصر سفید	
۱۴	ان سنون سی چند سال پہلی یہہ قلعہ بنا کیونکہ یہہ سن تو بادشاہ ہونیکی ہین اور یہہ کوشک چند سال شہزادہ ہونیکی بنایا تہا	سنہ ۱۲۶۵	سنہ ۶۶۴	غیاث الدین بلبن	کوشک لال	۵
۱۵	اسی قلعہ کی زمین مین حضرت نظام الدین کی درگاہ ہے	سنہ ۱۲۶۷	سنہ ۶۶۶	غیاث الدین بلبن	قلعہ مرزغن یا غیاث پور	۶
۱۶	ہمایون کا مقبرہ اسی قلعہ کی زمین مین ہے	سنہ ۱۲۸۶	سنہ ۶۸۵	معز الدین کیقباد	کیلوکہری قصر معزی	۷

Figure 2.6: *First page of the urban genealogy of Delhi from the* Āṣār-us-Ṣanādīd *(1854 ed.).* Syed Ahmad Khan, *Āṣār-us-Ṣanādīd* (Delhi: Matb'a Sayyid al-Akhbar, 1854).

A Nineteenth-Century Architectural Archive: Syed Ahmad Khan's *Āṣār-us-Ṣanādīd*

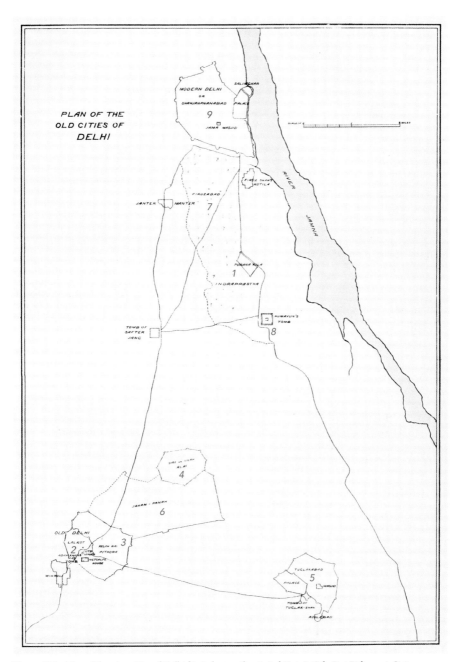

Figure 2.7: *Map of the nine cities of Delhi [1: Indraprastha; 2: Lal Kot; 3: Qila Rai Pithora; 4: Siri; 5: Tughlaqabad; 6: Jahan Panah; 7: Firozabad; 8: Din Panah; 9: Shahjahanabad].* H. H. Cole, *Ancient Delhi* (1872), redrawn by Chris Hazel.

however, the surveying gaze emerged from an Indian subject, albeit one who was heavily influenced by his European counterparts. While the understanding of the survey as an extension of colonial power still stands, it also becomes apparent that Syed Ahmad self-consciously appropriated those modalities of expertise and forms of Enlightenment knowledge that led to the organization of the natural and historical world according to objective parameters and rationales.

Syed Ahmad's chronology of Delhi's historic development would have a lasting impact on the way in which the city's past was represented in the nineteenth and twentieth centuries. In his first archaeological reports, Cunningham included a map of Delhi laying out the major boundaries of the extant cities and forts that Syed Ahmad had pointed out in his chart.[61] In 1872, Cole depicted the landscape of Delhi as a sequence of eight or nine urban settlements, each correlated to a specific Hindu or Islamic empire [Figure 2.7]. The settlements in Cole's map of Delhi are almost identical to those identified by Syed Ahmad in 1854, although Cole disregards those forts and urban sites that are not related to significant historical emperors, such as Kushak Lal, Ghiyaspur, or Khilokri. Syed Ahmad's classification of Delhi's urban development had thus been translated into a cartographic truth – one that would undergird every subsequent historical narrative of Delhi. Indeed, this particular framing of the city's past as a series of seven imperial cities would find renewed purchase in 1911 when the British Empire built New Delhi as a modern addendum to the enduring sequence of the ancient and medieval capitals of Delhi, built by former Hindu and Islamic empires and so neatly organized by Syed Ahmad in the second edition of the *Āṣār-us-Ṣanādīd*.

Colonizing the Archive

> General Cunningham, intends I know, to supplement his archaeological researches with all procurable *facts and illustrations* relating to architecture and ornament. In a few years the efforts of the Indian Government and those of the Science and Art Department will be productive of exhaustive information and of such illustrations and full size facsimiles as will be a valuable addition to architectural studies, and give additional interest to the more sober subject of archaeology.[62]

Cole's words followed those presented in the introduction of this chapter and appeared in his 1874 book *Ancient Delhi*. By emphasizing the scientific nature of European methods, such as thorough documentation and the extraction of factual information from material culture, Cole anticipated a new era of historical and archaeological exploration in India. European agents imagined that colonial institutions such as the Science and Art Department held the capacity, knowledge, and means to articulate India's history and archaeology. Most importantly, the new scientific archive that ensued from such processes of investigation was imagined as immune to affective inflections on the part of the European author. Indian systems of knowledge had already been relegated to the realm of fables and traditions and thus were outside of archival knowledge. However, as I have shown through this chapter, the self-fashioning of the European as the *archon* was neither a fait accompli, nor was the creation of an architectural archive ever outside of affective tendencies and emotive imaginaries. Expertise regarding India's architectural objects and history was a mutually constituted discursive space in the mid-nineteenth century, even if some Europeans such as Thomas Metcalfe were ambivalent about sharing that space with their Indian counterparts, such as Syed Ahmad. Meanwhile, Syed Ahmad's knowledge oscillated between his strong desire to author a modern archive for his beloved city, his religious faith, and cognizance of his audience's prejudices.

The climate of knowledge production changed radically, however, after 1857, bringing more suspicion to Indians who sought intellectual parity with European writers and thinkers. Indeed, by the time Cole wrote *Ancient Delhi* in 1872, Europeans had positioned themselves as the sole interlocutors of India's history. In other words, the parameters of the archive and access to its knowledge were fundamentally reframed by the aggressive assertion of colonial power post-1857. Architecture became simply one more modality in the schema of colonial disciplining alongside others such as religion, ethnicity, and caste. The effect of this new archival regime was seen most starkly in the rigid policies of architectural preservation put in place by the colonial government that attempted to protect Indian monuments from Indians themselves, by regulating the former's uses and managing the latter's bodies. By the early twentieth century, colonial authorities had successfully positioned themselves as the custodians of Indian monuments, as *archons* whose moral duty was to educate Indians about their own built heritage. By casting Indians as ignorant of their own architectural inheritance, colonial cultural policies essentially displaced figures such as Syed Ahmad from the architectural archive. A contemporary recognition of the *Āṣār-us-Ṣanādīd* and an appreciation of the methods used by Syed Ahmad in creating the first comprehensive catalogue of Delhi's monuments serves to dismantle the colonial fictions of the archive as free of affective impulses, and that of European knowledge formed in isolation of its Indian counterpart.

Notes

1. Syed Ahmad Khan, 'Preface', in *Āṣār-us-Ṣanādīd* (Delhi: Matb'a Sayyid al-Akhbār, 1847), n.p.
2. Henry Hardy Cole, *Ancient Delhi: Especially the Buildings Around the Kutb Minar* (London: Arundel Society, 1872), 2.
3. The first edition of this book was published in 1847, with a second edition following in 1854. The Urdu word 'āṣār' from the *Āṣār-us-Ṣanādīd* refers to a variety of concepts that include: footprints, vestiges, tracks, traces, marks, signs, tokens, remains, relics, monuments or memorials, effects, impressions, indications of state or condition, promises, symptoms, sayings or traditions of the Prophet Mohammad, origin, or foundation (of a building).

The word '*ṣanādīd*' translates as: princes, chiefs, lords, noblemen, calamities, misfortunes, dangers, great or formidable events. See John T. Platts, *A Dictionary of Urdu, Classical Hindi and English* (London: Oxford University Press, 1960). Another translation of the text's title is *The Remnant Signs of Ancient Heroes*, found in C. M. Naim, 'Syed Ahmad and His Two Books Called "Asar-al-Sanadid"', *Modern Asian Studies* 45.3 (2011): 669–708.

4   Henry Hardy Cole would later go on to serve as the Curator of Ancient Monuments in India (1880–84) and conduct an extensive survey of the subcontinent's monuments with prescriptions for their preservation.

5   I borrow the definition of archive from Jacques Derrida, who has pointed to its historical origins as a storehouse of legal documents. The word itself comes from the Greek *arkhe*, which translates as commandment, and is underwritten by a sense of situated authority in that it is '*there* where men and gods command, *there* where authority, social order are exercised, *in this place* from which *order* is given'. Jacques Derrida, *Archive Fever: A Freudian Impression* (Chicago: University of Chicago Press, 1996), 9.

6   My definition of affect comes from the cultural theorist Sara Ahmed, who describes it as an economy of sentiments that connects objects, people, and abstract ideas. Ahmed argues that far from being confined to the realm of the intimate, private, or personal, affect is one of the primary modalities through which apparatuses of nation-states, bureaucracies, and legal norms operate. Sara Ahmed, 'Affective Economies', *Social Text* 79 (2004): 117–39.

7   Syed Ahmad Khan's commitment to modernity and his faith in its ability to bring social and intellectual advancement to India was most profoundly borne out in his campaign for Indian educational reforms. In 1877, he established the Mohammadan Anglo-Oriental University in Aligarh (later the Aligarh Muslim University), which sought to modernize Islamic education. Once dismissed as colonial sympathizer and sycophant, recent revisionist histories have portrayed Syed Ahmad as one of the key shapers of modern India. See, for example, Ram Guha, *Makers of Modern India* (Cambridge: Harvard University Press, 2011).

8   In its comprehensive scope and focus on architectural objects, the *Āṣār-us-Ṣanādīd* had few precursors but was nevertheless followed by urban histories of other cities in the late nineteenth century such as *Mumbaiche Varnan* (Description of Mumbai) (1863), written by Govind Narayan in Marathi. Like the *Āṣār-us-Ṣanādīd* it described the city's physical geography and architectural monuments, and also included biographies of Mumbai's most prominent leaders and historical figures. Unlike the *Āṣār-us-Ṣanādīd*, however, it was not illustrated. For an English translation see Murali Ranganathan, trans., *Govind Narayan's Mumbai: An Urban Biography from 1863* (London: Anthem Press, 2009). Two histories of Lahore seem to have drawn direct inspiration from the *Āṣār-us-Ṣanādīd*: *Tahqīqāt Chishtī: Tarīkh-e-Lahor ka Encyclopedia* (Chishti's Inquiries: An Encyclopedia of Lahore's History) (1867) by Noor Ahmad Chishti and Syed Muhammad Latif's *Lahore: Its History, Architectural Remains, and Antiquities, with an Account of Its Modern Institutions, Inhabitants, Their Trade, Custom, etc.* (1892). For a critical analysis on the two urban histories of Lahore see William Glover, *Making Lahore Modern: Constructing and Imagining a Colonial City* (Minneapolis: University of Minnesota Press, 2008), 185–201.

9   Maulvi Zafar Hasan, *Monuments of Delhi: Lasting Splendour of the Great Mughals and Others*, ed. J. A. Page (New Delhi: Aryan Books International, 1919, repr. 2008).

10 Although India would not officially become a colony of the British Empire until 1858, the English East India Company had instituted an elaborate system of revenue extraction, resource management, and military administration that positioned them as the de facto government of a large part of North India. The Mughal Emperor was himself in the pay of the Company and his role had been reduced to that of a mere figurehead. A historical account of this sociopolitical climate can be found in Narayani Gupta, *Delhi Between Two Empires, 1803–1931: Society, Government and Urban Growth* (Delhi: Oxford University Press, 1981).

11 Before writing the *Āṣār-us-Ṣanādīd*, Syed Ahmad had authored six books, the first of which was an imperial history of Delhi. For more on the larger oeuvre of Syed Ahmad and the *Āṣār-us-Ṣanādīd*'s place within his other works, see Naim, 'Syed Ahmad and His Two Books'.

12 Naim has pointed out that the *Āṣār-us-Ṣanādīd* was the first book to contain lithographic illustrations. Lithography altered the vibrant print culture of Delhi by popularizing the book as a medium of communication and also invigorated a public sphere. See Naim, 'Syed Ahmad and His Two Books', 679–80.

13 Fatima Quraishi mentions that although Syed Ahmad had begun working on the English translation of the *Āṣār-us-Ṣanādīd*, the institutionalization of archaeology in the 1860s and the regular publication of preservation and excavation reports made such a translation unnecessary. See Fatima Quraishi, 'Asar-ul-Sanadid: A Nineteenth-Century History of Delhi', *Journal of Art Historiography* 6 (2012): 6/FQ-1. This essay also provides reliable translations of a few key parts of the *Āṣār-us-Ṣanādīd*.

14 Some examples of the types of monuments edited from the second edition of the *Āṣār-us-Ṣanādīd* include: the Sufi shrine of Rasul Numa (Part 1: 232), and the Kalkaji (Part 1: 17–19) and Akash (Part 1: 22–23) temples.

15 Naim, 'Syed Ahmad and His Two Books'.

16 David Lelyveld, '*Sauda Sulaf*: Urdu in the Two Versions of Sayyid Ahmad Khan's *Asaru's-Sanadid*', *The Annual of Urdu Studies* 26 (2011): 21–38.

17 Dargah Quli Khan, *Muraqqa'a-e-Delhi: The Mughal Capital in Muhammad Shah's Time* (Delhi: Deputy Publication, 1989).

18 William Finch, in *India as Seen by William Finch (1608–11)*, ed. R. Nath (Delhi: Heritage Publishers, 1990); François Bernier, *Travels in the Mogul Empire A.D. 1656–1668*, trans. Irving Brock (London: Oxford University Press, 1916); Jean-Baptiste Tavernier, in *Travels in India*, ed. William Crooke (London: Oxford University Press, 1977); Reginald Heber, *Narrative of a Journey through the Upper Provinces of India: From Calcutta to Bombay, 1824–1825* (London: J. Murray, 1843–44). A general treatment of the various travel accounts can be found in Gordon R. Hearn, *The Seven Cities of Delhi* (London: W. Thacker & Co., 1906).

19 A thorough historical analysis of the *Palais Indiens* can be found in Chanchal Dadlani, 'The "Palais Indiens" Collection of 1774', *Ars Orientalis* 39 (2010): 175–97.

20 Mirza Sangin Beg, *Sair-ul Manazil* (New Delhi: Ghalib Institute, 1982).

21 The ASD explained their mandate according to the following primarily goal: 'the investigation, by means of plans, drawings, and elevations, by inscriptional, traditional and historical researches, and, if possible, by publications of the ancient remains, both Hindoo

and Mahomedan, in and around Delhi, *Journal of the Archaeological Society of Delhi* (1850): Appendix: 1.
22 The ASD was deeply suspicious of Indian intellectuals, and during the Society's short-lived tenure (it was disbanded in 1854) only two Indians, Syed Ahmad and Nawab Ziaddun, were granted membership, and this too during the penultimate year of the Society's existence. Both men were considered exceptions as they possessed 'scientific tempers' that were considered scarce amongst other Indians. See *Journal of the Archaeological Society of Delhi* (1853): 24.
23 Christian Troll has argued that Syed Ahmad was only inducted into the ASD when his supporter, Arthur Austin Roberts, took over as Vice-President in 1852 and made a strong case on his behalf. Christian W. Troll, 'A Note on an Early Topographical Work of Sayyid Ahmad Khan: *Āṣār al-Ṣanādīd*', *The Journal of the Royal Asiatic Society* 2 (1972): 135–46.
24 Ram Raz, *Essay on the Architecture of the Hindus* (London: Royal Asiatic Society, 1834).
25 Madhuri Desai, 'Interpreting an Architectural Past: Ram Raz and the Treatise in South Asia', *Journal of the Society of Architectural Historians* 71.4 (2012): 462–87.
26 The contributions of Ram Raz and Mitra to the fields of architectural history and archaeology has been more thoroughly explored in Tapati Guha-Thakurta, *Monuments, Objects, Histories: Institutions of Art in Colonial and Postcolonial India* (New York: Columbia University Press, 2004) and Upinder Singh, The *Discovery of Ancient India: Early Archaeologists and the Beginnings of Archaeology* (New Delhi: Permanent Black, 2004).
27 James Fergusson, *Picturesque Illustrations of Ancient Architecture of Hindostan* (London: J. Hogarth, 1848) and *History of Indian and Eastern Architecture* (London: John Murray, 1876).
28 Guha-Thakurta has argued that Fergusson chose the monuments to include in his *Picturesque Illustrations of Hindostan* on the basis of those that displayed picturesque qualities of the 'Indian ruin'. Since the book was collated after Fergusson returned to England, the archive of Indian architecture was also formed out of the limited set of images he had access to. Similarly, Cunningham's archive of India's archaeological sites was limited by the Sanskrit texts translated by the time of his research. See Guha-Thakurta, *Monuments, Objects, Histories*, 22–31. Thomas Trautmann and Carla Sinopoli have argued that while Cunningham's interest in establishing the ASI was to divert more attention and resources to the study of India's material evidence rather than the translation of ancient Sanskrit texts, he himself was seduced by textual accounts which then created the primary framework for his archaeological research. They say, 'Cunningham's archaeology was limited and limiting by today's standards. It remained dependent on the written word to provide the main outline for the past'. Thomas R. Trautmann and Carla M. Sinopoli, 'In the Beginning Was the Word: Excavating the Relations between History and Archaeology in South Asia', *Journal of the Economic and Social History of the Orient* 45.4 (2002): 500.
29 The two key texts on the history of knowledge production in colonial South Asia remain: Christopher Bayly, *Empire and Information: Intelligence Gathering and Social Communication in India, 1780–1870* (Cambridge: Cambridge University Press, 1999) and Bernard Cohn, *Colonialism and Its Forms of Knowledge: The British in India* (Princeton: Princeton University Press, 1996). Other studies that have looked at the substantial role of Indian

intellectuals in the creation of this so-called 'colonial' knowledge include: Nicholas Dirks, 'Guiltless Spoliations: Picturesque Beauty, Colonial Knowledge, and Colin Mackenzie's Survey of India', in *Perceptions of South Asia's Visual Past*, eds Catherine B. Asher and Thomas R. Metcalf (New Delhi: Oxford and IBH Publishing Co, 1994), 211–32; Thomas Richards, 'Archive and Utopia', *Representations* 37 (1992): 104–35; Rama Sundari Mantena, *The Origins of Modern Historiography in India: Antiquarianism and Philology, 1780–1880* (New York: Palgrave Macmillan, 2014).

30 Syed Ahmad, *Āsār-us-Ṣanādīd*, 1st ed. (1847), Part 1, 127.

31 There are several studies that provide a historical analysis of the Quwwat-ul Islam mosque and the reuse of Hindu and or Jain building fragments in its construction. See Barry Flood, 'Appropriation as Inscription: Making History in the First Friday Mosque of Delhi', in *Reuse Value: Spolia and Appropriation in Art and Architecture from Constantine to Sherrie Levine*, eds Richard Brilliant and Dale Kinney (Surrey: Ashgate Publishing, 2011), 121–47; Alka Patel, 'The Historiography of Reuse in South Asia', *Archives of Asian Art* 59 (2009): 1–5; Richard M. Eaton, 'Temple Desecration and Indo-Muslim States', in *Beyond Turk and Hindu: Rethinking Religious Identity in Islamicate South Asia*, eds David Gilmartin and Bruce Lawrence (Gainesville: University Press of Florida, 2000), 246–80.

32 Sunil Kumar, 'Qutb and Modern Memory', in *The Present in Delhi's Pasts* (New Delhi: Three Essays Press, 2002), 140–82.

33 In recent years the name Quwwat-ul Islam has also found purchase with Hindu nationalists in India who perpetuate narratives regarding the violence of medieval Muslim armies toward Hindu polities and the desecration of Hindu temples under Islamic empires in India. I have chosen to retain Quwwat-ul Islam here for the pragmatic reason that it is how Syed Ahmad identifies the mosque in the *Āsār-us-Ṣanādīd*. It is also the name used by the ASI and international bodies, such as UNESCO, for the mosque.

34 Syed Ahmad, *Āsār-us-Ṣanādīd* (1847), Part 1, 127.

35 In the first edition of the *Āsār-us-Ṣanādīd* Hindu idols were shown in the depictions of temples such as Akash Mandir (Part 1: 22–23) and Kalkaji (Part 1: 17–19). Syed Ahmad's reluctance to show Hindu iconography in the Quwwat-ul Islam mosque may have had to do with their presence within the larger context of a mosque rather than a simple taboo against reproducing figural images.

36 Here Syed Ahmad (Part 1: 128–29) credits Sultan Iltutmish with laying the foundation of the Qutb Minar and for building its first, second, and third storeys. This information was based on the epigraphic sources available to Syed Ahmad at the time. It has now been proven that Qutbuddin Aibak (r.1192–1210), the vassal left behind by Mohammad Ghori after his conquest of Delhi in 1192 and after the latter had returned to Central Asia, started the minaret's construction and established its first storey. Iltutmish and other later rulers of Delhi added more storeys and/or repaired the Qutb Minar well into the sixteenth century.

37 Syed Ahmad, *Āsār-us-Ṣanādīd* (1847), Part 1, 133.

38 Jamal Elias, *Aisha's Cushion: Religious Art, Perception, and Practice in Islam* (Cambridge: Harvard University Press, 2012), 264–83.

39 In their analysis of the epigraphy of the Qutb Minar and the Quwwat-ul Islam mosque, Welch et al. have argued a different position than Elias, maintaining that different parts of

the mosque stressed various points of Islamic conduct and offered historical perspectives of Islamic imperial power in the subcontinent. It is their opinion that the inscriptions of the mosque functioned as a tectonic book of sorts, encouraging pious Islamic visitors to make connections between Islamic doctrine and local history. Anthony Welch et al., 'Epigraphs, Scripture, and Architecture in the Early Delhi Sultanate', *Muqarnas* 19 (2002): 12–43.

40 Elias, *Aisha's Cushion*, 268.
41 Syed Ahmad, *Āṣār-us-Ṣanādīd* (1847), Part 1, 123.
42 Alexander Cunningham, 'Four Reports Made During the Years 1862–63–64–65', *Archaeological Survey of India* (Varanasi: 1862–65), 198.
43 Derrida, *Archive Fever*, 1–4.
44 It is difficult to know what may have prompted such a *volte-face* in terms of Syed Ahmad's position on the Qutb Minar. One reason may be that having gained the attention of the ASD with his other archaeological studies and propositions, such as a paper delivered in 1853 where he excavated various types of bricks in and around Delhi in order to create his chronology for *Silsilat-ul-Muluk* (Genealogy of Kings), he felt empowered to use the same archaeological methodology for other ancient buildings in Delhi. The paper that Syed Ahmad read pertaining to ancient bricks of Delhi and their correlation to different strata of imperial rule was published in the *Journal of the Archaeological Society of Delhi* (1853). Another reason Syed Ahmad perpetuated the Hindu origins of the Qutb Minar might have had to do with Thomas Metcalfe's belief regarding the same. Cunningham points out that Metcalfe was taken with this particular narrative of the monument and Syed Ahmad may have forwarded such an argument to forge a professional connection with Metcalfe. See Cunningham, 'Four Reports', 189.
45 The five points of the counter-argument made against Syed Ahmad by Cunningham can be found in ibid., 190–94.
46 Ibid., 194.
47 Ibid., 195.
48 Fergusson's oversight of the *Āṣār-us-Ṣanādīd* may have had to do with the fact that he left India around 1847 and therefore did not have a chance to know about Syed Ahmad's work. Nevertheless, given Fergusson's later public and very visceral dismissal of the work of Indian archaeologist Rajendralal Mitra, it is safe to assume that had he known of the *Āṣār-us-Ṣanādīd* he might have been similarly supercilious of it. For more on the debate between Fergusson and Mitra on Indian archaeology, see Singh, *Discovery of Ancient India*, 322–44.
49 J. A. Page, *A Guide to the Qutb, Delhi* (Calcutta: Government of India, Central Publication Branch, 1927).
50 Lelyveld, *Sauda Sulaf*.
51 Naim, 'Syed Ahmad and His Two Books'.
52 The first edition of *Āṣār-us-Ṣanādīd* did not carry any similar classification of Delhi's physical or political history. Instead, after a brief introduction that contained praises of the Prophet and a lengthy dedication to Thomas Metcalfe, Syed Ahmad launched directly into descriptions of the monuments and historic personalities of Delhi.
53 Cunningham, 'Four Reports', 132–33.

54 *Journal of the Archaeological Society of Delhi* (Delhi: 1853): 56.
55 Troll, 'Work of Sayyid Ahmad Khan', 137.
56 Syed Ahmad Khan, *Āṣār-us-Ṣanādīd,* 2nd ed. (Delhi: Indian Standard Press, 1854). This table appears between pages 64 and 66 of the 2nd edition. In this translation I have not included the column that appears on the extreme left in the original, which refers to the page numbers that reference these buildings or settlements.
57 This appears to be an error in the original as the Islamic and the Christian dates do not agree.
58 Timothy Mitchell, *Rule of Experts: Egypt, Techno-politics, Modernity* (Berkeley: University of California Press, 2002), 1–15.
59 Dirks, 'Guiltless Spoliations', 220.
60 James Fergusson cited in ibid., 215.
61 Cunningham, 'Four Reports', Plate XXXV.
62 Cole, *Ancient Delhi*, 2–3 (emphasis added).

Chapter 3

The Balyan Family and the *Linguistic Culture* of a Parisian Education

Alyson Wharton

Karapet Balyan (1800–66) and his sons Nigoğos (1826–58), Serkis (1831–99), and Agop (1837–75) dominated the construction of imperial works under Abdülmecid (r.1831–61) and Abdülaziz (r.1861–76). They built Dolmabahçe Palace (1856), Ortaköy Mosque (1854–55), Ihlamur Kiosk (1853), schools such as Cemaran Mektebi (1838) and government buildings such as the Naval Ministry (1865–69). Nigoğos, Serkis, and Agop were among the earliest Ottoman architects educated in Paris. Rahip Yeprem Boğosyan,[1] Pars Tuğlacı,[2] and Kevork Pamukciyan[3] have used Armenian periodicals to document their stays. However, Aygül Ağır has drawn attention to the fact that these were not official sources and has questioned the nature of the Balyans' enrolment.[4]

This chapter clarifies Nigoğos and Serkis' educational status using fresh archival documentation. Reading a Parisian education as interactional expertise, it offers a reinterpretation of the Balyans' architecture as an adaptation of the *linguistic culture* of Paris to Ottoman building traditions and imperatives for displaying imperial power.[5] Charting their assimilation of approaches to architectural communication from the institutions that they attended (the Collège Sainte-Barbe, the Ecole Centrale, and the Ecole des Beaux-Arts), I show how these approaches were adapted to the Ottoman context. The Balyans were not agents of change responsible for the desertion of Ottoman forms, nor were they 'men of practice' who were not engaged in the debates of their time. Instead, they were fully immersed in the communicative methods, or *linguistic culture,* of these institutions, including their intellectual underpinnings. In the end, however, none of the Paris-educated Balyans graduated, and the aspects of their education that they implemented took the form of communication on the surface of their buildings. Thus their expertise can be considered a mixture of formal and informal – or interactional – proficiency, rather than as a straightforward transition to Western-style professionalization.

Texts produced in the late Ottoman period narrated the development of Ottoman architecture in formalist terms. Celal Esad Arseven portrayed the eighteenth and early nineteenth centuries as the 'Baroque Age' and the 'Empire Age', developing into a European mode (*Avrupa karı*) under Abdülaziz, a shift that Arseven hailed as *İntibah Devri* (Age of Awakening). During this period, a mixed and adulterated style appeared (*karışık ve mahlut bir üslup*), exemplified by the Pertevniyal Valide Sultan Mosque in Aksaray (1872) and the Çırağan Palace (1871), both of which were Balyan works. Arseven described their role in general terms, stating that 'Armenian architects educated in Europe continued to bring buildings in a baroque and renaissance style into existence'.[6] Arseven viewed a text produced for the 1873 Vienna Exposition, *Usul-u Mimari-i Osmani* (the Rules of Ottoman Architecture), as the beginning of a scientific approach.[7]

As Sibel Bozdoğan has shown, the views of Arseven dominated the republican perspective of Ottoman architecture.[8] There was a desire to present Ottoman architecture as distinct from Orientalist conflations of Arab, Indian, Iranian, and Turkish styles.[9] The question of why the *Usul* and Arseven praised the Valide Mosque and Çırağan Palace as an 'awakening' or an 'Ottoman Renaissance',[10] when these works blended Islamic and non-Islamic traditions, has never been explained satisfactorily. Ahmet Ersoy ascribed it to the *Usul*'s role as 'an officially prescribed agenda of Ottoman modernization'.[11] Ersoy, at the time, did not see any connection between the circle responsible for the *Usul* and the Balyans.[12] Aside from Boğosyan, Pamukciyan, and Tuğlacı's biographical accounts, it was only a recent exhibition catalogue that began to observe the Balyans as creative actors. One contribution by Ersoy translated a proposal that Serkis wrote for a school of arts and industry, focusing on his technical education as a reflection of the professionalization of the Ottoman builder (*kalfa*).[13]

This chapter argues that, through their exposure to a Parisian education, Nigoğos and Serkis gained linguistic socialization and took on aspects of the prevailing *linguistic culture*, a concept that Harold F. Schiffman has defined as:

> [...] the set of behaviours, assumptions, cultural forms, prejudices, folk belief systems, attitudes, stereotypes, ways of thinking about language, and religio-historical circumstances associated with a particular language.[14]

In other words, *linguistic culture* is an aspect of acculturation. It is a way of communicating, or a 'degree of commonality in the understandings of how language is to be used to get certain things done'.[15]

As the examination here will indicate, the Balyans assimilated methods of (architectural) communication taught in Paris. These were accommodated within works that retained an Ottoman framework, floor plans, and messages (relating to the power of the sultan and his territorial sovereignty).[16] Therefore, the Balyans' own points of reference and experience as Ottoman subjects were equally important to shaping the new works. This picture contrasts with views on Ottoman development that stress 'translations' or 'purchase' and claim that an indigenous tradition in science and industry failed to develop.[17]

Because none of the Paris-trained Balyans graduated from the institutions that they attended, their education can be considered a prototypical form of interactional expertise. This is a realm of knowledge that resides between the formal and the informal, 'the ability to converse expertly about a practical skill or expertise, but without being able to practice it, learned through linguistic socialization among the practitioners'.[18] There is typically an opposition between these two types of knowledge (formal and informal).[19] In the history of art, this is seen in the difference between medieval, practice-based master builders and architects of the Renaissance who theorized their works. In the Ottoman Empire, there is the related development from *kalfa* (master builder) to architectural professionalization in the nineteenth century. However, such a division underestimates the blend of master builder and architect that figures like the Balyans represented.

Interactional expertise includes the subject becoming 'immersed, not in the entire form of life of some domain but only in the language-world of those who were immersed in the form of life proper'.[20] Through linguistic socialization, tacit skills are gained, but a full practical training is not. The engagement of the Balyans in the language of Parisian practitioners is seen in several aspects explored here: first, Nigoğos' intellectual transformation through exposure to the Sainte-Barbe and the language of romanticism; second, Serkis' adoption of the pragmatic approach of the Centrale; and third, the revivalist ornament that Serkis used, following ideas propounded at the Beaux-Arts.

The Balyans' Parisian education demonstrates interactional expertise over and above other forms of expertise, including 'contributory' or 'full'.[21] This is because they became linguistically socialized through mixing with students in ateliers and participating in project work, rituals, and ceremonies that encouraged fraternity amongst alumni. On a formal level, the pedagogy encouraged a particular mode of architectural communication. Nigoğos and Serkis connected with this world through their imagination and empathy: they participated in the intellectual movements prevalent at these institutions, most notably that of romanticism, and they used this engagement to rethink their approach to Ottoman architecture.[22] They assimilated what was taught and adapted it. However, they never became full practitioners: new expertise was implemented in conjunction with traditional plans and messages. Thus their 'material form of life and distinct contributory experiences' (in the sense of their background in Ottoman traditions of building and architectural expression as well as their attachment to Ottoman and Armenian identity) remained strong in the Balyans' output.[23]

The Language of the Sainte-Barbe: Nigoğos' Romantic Transformation

Armenian sources state that Nigoğos, Serkis, and Agop all attended the Collège Sainte-Barbe.[24] Student registers of the Ecole Préparatoire show that a 'Ballian' was present in the 1848–49 school year.[25] This must have been Serkis, who travelled to Paris in 1848 (Nigoğos had returned to the Ottoman capital in 1846).[26] The Sainte-Barbe was an important institution for elite education in the nineteenth century. Henri Labrouste (1801–75) and Théodore Labrouste (1799–1885) met Léon Vaudoyer (1803–72) at Sainte-Barbe.[27] From the 1840s onwards, the school held a pivotal role in the education of Ottomans, including Armenians, who became diplomats, such as Artin Dadian (1825–1901),[28] and intellectuals, such as İstepan Oskanyan (1825–1901).[29] In the time that Serkis Balyan attended, illustrious classmates included, in 1848–49, an unspecified Labrouste, and in 1850–51, Gustave Eiffel (1832–1923). It is possible that Eiffel and Balyan would have known each other, as they both progressed to the Centrale, and it may be significant that the design of the Konak Pier in Izmir may have been connected to Eiffel.[30]

Such networks could become useful for professional operations. When employed to build the residence of the banker Mıgırdiç Cezayirliyan (1805–61), the Armenian architect 'Jacob Mélick' (b.1817), who attended Sainte-Barbe and the Beaux-Arts, brought with him Pierre Victor Galland (1822–92) and Charles Séchan (1803–74).[31] Léon Parvillée (1830–85), a French architect, decorator, and ceramicist, was another member of the team. Several of these individuals later worked on the Dolmabahçe Palace.[32]

The networks of Sainte-Barbe's drawing teachers also show the potential for making connections.[33] Drawing teachers at the time of the Balyans' studies included Jules Ernest Panis (1827–95), who exhibited at the salons of 1850 and 1874. His connections are particularly rich: Tournachon Nadar (1820–1910) was a friend, and (Ingres' student) Henri Lehmann (1814–82) was Panis' teacher. We can suggest that the Balyans may have had some contact with this world through their drawing teacher. Panis' other students included Jean-Baptiste-Camille Corot (1796–1875), indicating that he was an inspiring teacher himself. There is evidence that the rich social setting of the Sainte-Barbe – a centre for the intellectuals of the time – was reflected in the Balyans' own networks. A dossier concerning Nigoğos' son Léon (b.1855) lists his guardian as 'M. Donon', a relative of the poet, writer, and critic Théophile Gautier (1811–72), showing that the Balyans indeed had connections to the highest level of the Parisian cultural elite.[34]

The head of the Sainte-Barbe was Alexandre Labrouste (1796–1866). His brother, Henri, was part of the Romantic movement that distanced itself from the traditional methods of the Beaux-Arts and espoused the view that architecture should not copy ideal models but rather reflect society.[35] These architects, as Van Zanten has written, 'understood polychromy as a clothing of a structural skeleton with objects, inscriptions, and scenes communicating the building's social function and history'.[36]

Armenian sources suggest that Nigoğos Balyan had a special connection with the Labroustes. Krikor Odian (1834–87), a close friend of Nigoğos who wrote his obituary in the newspaper *Meğu*, states that Nigoğos was the best-loved student of 'Baron Labrouste, Headmaster of the School'.[37] The newspaper *Masis* describes how Nigoğos learnt architecture in the classes of 'Baron Labrouste, director of the "Imperial School of Fine Arts"'.[38] Through the social environment of the Sainte-Barbe, Nigoğos Balyan imbibed the romanticism that Labrouste championed. Odian states:

> As a follower of the architectural school of revival/renaissance, he [Nigoğos] fortunately got rid of artificial rules and superstitions. He brought a very clear horizon where his beautiful imagination could fly freely.[39]

Odian adds that: 'This was a freedom, which was based on Rationalism that was introduced into the philosophy of Descartes and, in literature, by Victor Hugo, and which he encouraged to be introduced into our literature.'[40]

Romantics promoted an understanding of the genius as a man endowed with 'semidivine forces of creation, thaumaturgical in his miraculous yield'.[41] Ledoux portrayed the architect as an inspired genius who 'on his imaginary journey, entered a trance-like state'.[42] Odian emphasized Nigoğos' 'imagination set free', his works' immortality and their being 'condemned to obscurity'. Antoine-Laurent-Thomas Vaudoyer (1756–1846) explained how architecture expressed sensations inspired by nature through imitation.[43] Odian evoked how Nigoğos crafted his architecture on the banks of the Bosphorus in collaboration 'with the beauties of nature' and shaped them through his intelligence, talent for artistic beauty, and fecund imagination.[44]

Nigoğos' participation in Romantic tropes is underlined by Gautier's description of the Dolmabahçe Palace.[45] Gautier described its ornament as 'not Greek, nor Roman, nor Gothic, nor Saracen, nor Arab, not yet Turkish' and likened it to the masterpieces of Venice, to the Plateresque, and to Gothic cathedrals. Foreshadowing Ruskin's obsession with the blue of the lagoon and the white of the Doge's Palace, Gautier referred to the contrast between the marble of Dolmabahçe and the azure of the sea. In an echo of Odian, Gautier added that Dolmabahçe was 'built for immortality'.[46]

Nigoğos learned Parisian techniques for architectural communication through the Sainte-Barbe's *cours de dessin*. It is also likely that he attended the atelier of Henri Labrouste. In these settings, Nigoğos would have been exposed to the methods of the Romantic rationalists (using inscriptions and scenes to communicate a building's function and meaning). Nigoğos' adaptation of this to Ottoman traditions can be seen in the Dolmabahçe Palace.

The Dolmabahçe Palace was completed in 1856 during the reign of Abdülmecid [Figure 3.1]. This period saw the Tanzimat reforms, which modernized Ottoman institutions and subjecthood along egalitarian lines.[47] The move from the Topkapı Palace to the Bosphorus allied Abdülmecid with the consulates and the social and commercial life of Pera (the area on the European side of Istanbul now known as Beyoğlu). Abdülmecid's palace was also built to coincide with Ottoman entry into the Concert of Europe. Dolmabahçe was thus crafted to communicate resurgent Ottoman identity.

Armenian sources state that although Karapet Balyan was architect of the Dolmabahçe, Nigoğos was responsible for some features, namely, the Treasury Gate and the Audience Hall.[48] These parts are characterized by expressive ornament, showing the input of the *linguistic culture* of the Sainte-Barbe.

The Treasury Gate [Figure 3.2] was the ceremonial entrance to Dolmabahçe. Its fusion of modes of architectural communication taught in Paris with an Ottoman message of sovereignty set the tone for the rest of the palace. Although entrance portals topped by an inscription and sultan's monogram (*tuğra*) were a traditional feature of Ottoman mosques and the Topkapı Palace, the Treasury Gate at Dolmabahçe took the shape of a triumphal arch. This choice presented the Ottomans as heirs not only to the Romans, but also of Napoleon's Arc de Triomphe (1806–36) and Arc du Carrousel (1806–08).

Ottoman architecture communicated according to a competitive discourse with other traditions. Kritovoulos of Imbros' description of Mehmed II's building activities sheds light on this mentality: 'For he was constructing great edifices which were to be worth seeing and should in every respect vie with the greatest and the best of the past.'[49] In its use of a

Figure 3.1: *Dolmabahçe Palace (1856), view from Bosphorus.* Alyson Wharton.

Figure 3.2: *Dolmabahçe Palace (1856), Treasury Gate.* Alyson Wharton.

triumphal arch, the Treasury Gate announced the Ottomans as the foremost empire of the nineteenth century.

On a pragmatic level, the triumphal arch was a reflection of Parisian educational practice. Jacques-François Blondel's (1705–74) textbook instructed architects on techniques for evoking the sovereignty of the ruler, including triumphal gates.[50] Despite this assimilation of Parisian architectural communication, details of the Treasury Gate were adapted to express its local relevance. First, the arch was crowned by an inscription and *tuğra*, following Ottoman traditions. Second, the carved decoration amplified this message of Ottoman power.

The carved ornament in the Dolmabahçe was a departure from Ottoman traditions, which had been governed by a system of decorum, wherein ornament highlighted elements of the structure. Although in the eighteenth century relief carving became more widespread, the ornamental overlay seen at Dolmabahçe shows the input of the *linguistic culture* of the Romantics. As Gautier noted, Dolmabahçe 'makes the façade of a building resemble a gigantic piece of goldsmith's work' [Figure 3.3]; '[i]t is a palace, which might be the work of an ornamentist'.[51] Carved ornament was a Romantic preoccupation: in *La Comédie de la mort*, Gautier depicted architecture that was composed of *feston* (scallop) and *dentelle* (lacework), and he engaged in 'embroidering his construction' to the extent that 'he calls the very notion of function into question' through his purposely self-indulgent form.[52]

But despite its novelty and French resonances, the ornamental overlay of Dolmabahçe communicated a distinctly Ottoman message. The motifs depicted – Corinthian capitals, neoclassical friezes, baroque urns, shells, S-scrolls, brooches, cross hatching, and neo-Renaissance garlands – were symbols of power (dynastic brooches), or evoked plenty (fruit,

Figure 3.3: *Dolmabahçe Palace (1856), ornament on seaside façade.* Alyson Wharton.

Figure 3.4: *Dolmabahçe Palace (1856), detail of Treasury Gate.* Alyson Wharton.

flowers, shells, urns). The American traveller Harriet Trowbridge Allen (1841–77) noted: 'The whole of Europe had been laid under tribute to complete this Oriental palace.'[53] The inscription of the gate [Figure 3.4] proclaimed that the abode had become one of imperial pomp (*makam-ı şevket oldu*) thanks to Abdülmecid.

The effect of these symbols was furthered by the presence of the *tuğra*, the Ottomans' dynastic monogram. When he visited Dolmabahçe, Louis Bunel, who wrote an account of his pilgrimage to the Holy Land, remarked: 'In the middle of the columns, the bas-reliefs, rosettes, and badges, appears surrounded by all the wealth and prestige of this art the cipher of the sultan, on its gold on green background.'[54] The *tuğra* was repeated around the palace: on mirrors, on frames, and in the painted ceiling in the *hamam* room [Figure 3.5]. On the exterior, the *tuğra* crowned every triumphal arch [Figure 3.6] and each façade [Figure 3.7]. The Parisian vocabulary (of symbols of plenty and power) proclaimed the message of Ottoman supremacy.

The Audience Hall of the Dolmabahçe Palace [Figure 3.8] was the site for ceremonial and balls described by *L'Illustration* and *Le Monde Illustré*. Its huge interior space was crowned by a dome whose exterior was hidden by a pitched roof so as not to break the rules of Ottoman architectural decorum (*adab*) to compete with mosques. Its painted decoration mirrored that of the Treasury Gate.

This echoing of ornament around the palace created a playful and sensory effect, and was another aspect of the *linguistic culture* of the Romantics. Motifs were repeated in different

The Balyan Family and the *Linguistic Culture* of a Parisian Education

Figure 3.5: *Dolmabahçe Palace (1856), ceiling of* hamam *room.* Alyson Wharton.

Figure 3.6: *Dolmabahçe Palace (1856), triumphal arch with* tuğra. Alyson Wharton.

Figure 3.7: *Dolmabahçe Palace (1856), entrance facade with* tuğra. Alyson Wharton.

Figure 3.8: *Dolmabahçe Palace (1856), Audience Hall.* Alyson Wharton.

techniques (stone carving, painted and gilded stucco), thus drawing attention to their artifice. Dolmabahçe is reminiscent of the Opéra of Garnier, his 'intuitive creative mode' and 'architectural empathy', most notably the changing functions of the rooms as spectators moved around.[55] There is a similar play between the motifs and techniques in ceremonial rooms and the use of decorative showpieces such as the crystal staircase by which visitors entered the palace [Figure 3.9]. Dolmabahçe, like the Opéra, provoked a reaction between the human senses and their environment.[56] However, at Dolmabahçe, this communicated Ottoman messages.

Elements of the decorative vocabulary had distinct symbolic meanings and reflected the aniconic tendency of Ottoman public and official art. Thus the *tuğra* took the place of portraits of the ruler, scrolls represented reforms, trumpets reflected Westernizing culture, and Constantinople's vistas showed territorial sovereignty. Although floral bouquets were

Figure 3.9: *Dolmabahçe Palace (1856), crystal staircase.* Alyson Wharton.

seen in the eighteenth century, at Dolmabahçe they were depicted in a theatrical composition, with frames and curtains. The bouquet of roses was incorporated into the Ottoman coat of arms because it was believed to signal to the magnanimity of the state.[57] Reflecting this heraldic role is the positioning of a bouquet at the apex of the crystal staircase, where it is depicted alongside militaristic symbols [Figure 3.10].

The *trompe l'oeil* dome of the Audience Hall similarly relied on symbols to communicate its message. In the pendentives, floral bouquets in urns, placed within golden frames and dramatic curtains, held an emblematic role [Figure 3.11]. In the cupola, triumphal arches formed a frieze as a reference to the *mihrab* (niche indicating the direction of prayer toward Mecca) of a mosque wherein arches pointed toward the *qibla* (the actual direction of Mecca). In the Ortaköy Mosque [Figure 3.12], also built by Nigoğos, rows of *mihrab*s were painted in the dome, echoing that in the prayer hall. In the Dolmabahçe Palace, these arches contained a cartouche that was a reminder of the *tuğra*, alluding to the sovereign power of the sultan.

The Dolmabahçe shows how Nigoğos had assimilated the methods of the Romantic rationalists. He used an ornamental overlay (in stone-carving and paintwork), including symbols and inscriptions, to express the function and meaning of the palace. However, although the vocabulary came chiefly from Europe (Renaissance, baroque, neoclassical), it was adapted to communicate an Ottoman message.

The Balyan Family and the *Linguistic Culture* of a Parisian Education

Figure 3.10: *Dolmabahçe Palace (1856), bouquet above stairs.* Alyson Wharton.

Figure 3.11: *Dolmabahçe Palace (1856), bouquets in pendentives of Audience Hall.* Alyson Wharton.

Figure 3.12: *Ortaköy Mosque (1854), dome.* Alyson Wharton.

The *linguistic culture* of the Romantics was tailored to a specifically Ottoman form at Dolmabahçe. The structure did not depart from plan types of Ottoman houses: its regularized façade housed a *sofa* (side spaces or *eyvan*s jutting out from a central hall).[58] The traditional house, including the *sofa*, became a focus of Turkish architectural historians in the early republic.[59] The *sofa* was even charted back to tents in early Turkic societies.[60] The *sofa* was consistently used in imperial palaces and pavilions, as Sedad Hakkı Eldem's studies have shown.[61] It is clear from his plan of Dolmabahçe that the palace consisted of consecutive *sofa*s, connected by corridors.[62] Masonry walls that gave the palace the exterior appearance of neoclassicism concealed this irregular plan.

The adherence to the *sofa* plan underlines that Nigoğos' practical approach was not fundamentally altered by his experience at the Sainte-Barbe: he continued to draw on local plan types. These traditional forms were given a new surface language in the form of neoclassical facades adorned with meaningful ornament. The tropes of romanticism were evoked through this expressive ornament. However, the imaginative power of Nigoğos' composition was manipulated to convey the flourishing state of the empire under Abdülmecid. This was *interactional expertise* utilized in the service of the sultan.

The Language of the Ecole Centrale: The Technical Education of Serkis Balyan

The Balyans' exposure to a Parisian technical education began at Sainte-Barbe. The school catered to students heading for the *grandes écoles* and the 1845 prospectus boasted of 'the force of the scientific education', led by Labrouste and Marie Parfait Alphonse Blanchet (1813–94).[63] Courses included geometry, descriptive geometry, arithmetic, algebra, and trigonometry.[64] Developed by Gaspard Monge (1746–1818) and promoted through the curriculum at the Polytechnique, descriptive geometry represented three-dimensional objects in two dimensions. It was used to solve spatial problems in the design process, breaking them down into parts, and allowing for the generation of complex forms. When he moved on to attend the Ecole Centrale in 1850, Serkis Balyan received a more thorough training in these technical skills.

The Ecole Centrale was established in 1829 to encourage industrialization.[65] Whereas the Polytechnique fed the military, the Centrale focused on the practical application of the sciences and the teaching of general subjects to explain the logic behind the theories. In the second year, students moved on from general subjects to a specialization in mechanics, construction, metallurgy, or chemistry. Armenian sources state that Serkis Balyan attended the Centrale.[66] Within the private archives of the school, student registers for 1850 and 1851 do list Serkis. However, unlike the other students, he had no specialty indicated. Instead, negative comments on his attendance and participation are noted, and a letter from his guardian states that Serkis 'made the decision to quit the school'. Serkis only attended two months in his second year, according to the register.

Despite this lack of commitment, Serkis learned scientific procedures at the Centrale during his first year that aided his subsequent works. In addition to mathematical skills like descriptive geometry, geometrical analysis, and mechanics, he attended courses in architectural and topographical drawing, metallurgy, machines of line, raising buildings, raising machines, industrial design, industrial physics, and transmission of movement. Moreover, a broader influence of Centrale pedagogy must have been the pragmatic approach of Louis-Charles Mary (1791–1870). Mary was professor of architecture and public works from 1833 until 1864. Student notebooks from Mary's architecture course show that its practical basis involved a logical progression from the analysis of 'elements of edifices' to 'examination of diverse edifices' (halls, markets, shops, etc.). Mary focused on problem solving and skills: his course on public works included instructions (tools, calculations, procedures) on how to construct roads, bridges, water flows, and artificial navigation.[67]

Serkis' proposal for an Ottoman school for arts and industry, written in 1881,[68] shows the impact of Centralien pedagogy. It espoused the same general education in the sciences followed by specialization. However, it also included lessons on classical and non-Western architecture and on antiquities that Serkis learnt from the Beaux-Arts, as well as skills from the building sites of his father. The language of Ottoman patriotism used in the proposal expressed how Serkis intended 'to benefit the peoples of varied regions by nurturing and equipping individuals with knowledge and training for the future'.[69] Serkis presented a collage of experiences, which he hoped would aid the empire's future.

Serkis' Ottoman Company for Public Works, established in 1873, also shows some impact of the Centrale's practical approach. This company engaged in activities resembling Mary's course. However, these engagements were, again, presented through the language of Ottomanism (promoting Ottoman power, resources, and self-sufficiency): for instance, it is stated that the company was founded to supply building projects with the justification that '[e]very country had its own factories, and because the Empire had to make continuous demands to Europe (for goods), it made losses'.[70]

Serkis' application of a pragmatic architectural language is shown in his 'building types'. At the Centrale, these were taught through the study of well-known examples. Student notebooks show that when teaching market halls, the plan, elevation, and dome of the Halle aux blés de Paris (grain exchange) was drawn in one class and Les Halles centrales was dealt with in the next. Among the models utilized were residential buildings, such as 5 rue de la Paix [Figure 3.13].[71] At the Beaux-Arts, types had an ornamental emphasis.[72]

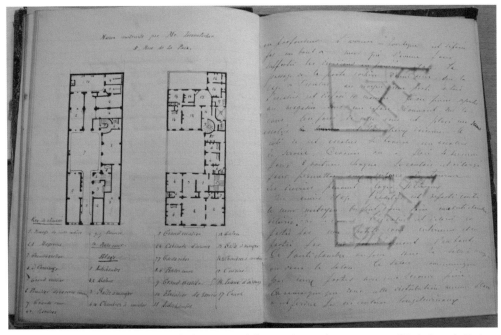

Figure 3.13: *Ecole Centrale student notebook, class on 5 rue de la Paix.* Alyson Wharton, courtesy of Ecole Centrale, Paris.

The Akaretler terrace or row houses [Figure 3.14], built in the early 1870s, shows Serkis' adjustment of a Parisian residential building to the Ottoman setting. Terrace houses were associated with simplicity and nobility in French architecture, as in the case of the Place Royale (now Vosges), built in 1612.[73] The Akaretler terraces recast this model as elegant residences for members of the sultan's court. Their uniform façade and rectangular plan stood in contrast to Constantinopolitan houses that continued to be wooden and used the *sofa* plan.[74]

Constructed on a steep slope as a route leading to the Aziziye Mosque of Abdülaziz, Akaretler required technical expertise that may have included instructions from Mary on how to level land [Figure 3.15].[75]

The design integrated Parisian approaches to urbanism: the terraces forming an entire quarter were reminiscent of the space around Garnier's Opéra, where 'axial streets and nodal squares converge in one continuously unfolding scenographic experience'.[76] However, Akaretler was on a much smaller scale than the complex arteries of Paris, and its function, to form the route of the sultan's procession (*selamlık*) from palace to mosque for Friday prayers, was a peculiarly Ottoman one.

Figure 3.14: *Akaretler (1872), Beşiktaş*. Alyson Wharton.

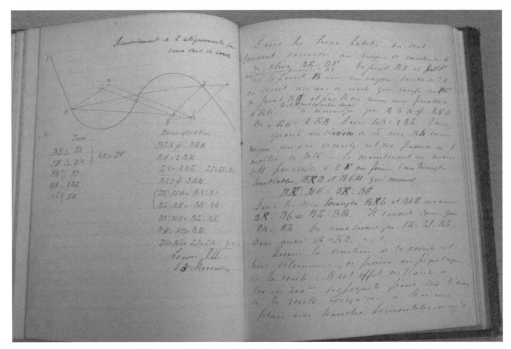

Figure 3.15: *Ecole Centrale student notebook, class on levelling land.* Alyson Wharton, courtesy of Ecole Centrale, Paris.

The ambiguity of Serkis' assimilation and adaptation of the language of the Centrale reflects his enrolment status as well as his continued attachment to his Ottoman identity. Serkis' works, such as his 1881 proposal and Akaretler, demonstrate how he combined elements from the Centralien, as well as the Beaux-Arts, approach. He, like Nigoğos, put these to use alongside local traditions of display and meaning. Serkis appropriated the methodology of the Centrale in order to build Akaretler; he implemented a Parisian notion of elite residences and choreographing the city. However, these aspects of Parisian *linguistic culture* were utilized in a way that communicated his Ottomanism.

The Language of the Beaux-Arts: Revivalist Ornament

Armenian sources assert that Serkis attended the Beaux-Arts.[77] On October 24, 1848, Serkis applied to the school as a foreign student,[78] but he did not attend until later. In an 1860 register for Architectes Aspirants, a 'Palean' is listed as a student of Juls Rebout.[79] There is a record of 'Palean' again on August 31, 1864, as a student of Louis-Jules André (1819–90), in Construction Générale.[80] These dates match Serkis' second stay in Paris between 1860 and 1864.

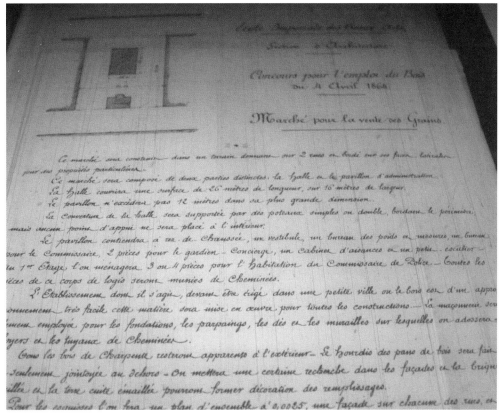

Figure 3.16: *Ecole des Beaux-Arts, project for market hall for the sale of grain*, Cours de Construction. *Archives Nationales, AJ/52/133*. Alyson Wharton, courtesy of Archives Nationales, Paris.

A focus of Beaux-Arts pedagogy was architectural composition. Courses would be assessed by *concours*, or competitions, for which the tutor would propose a type of building and each student would produce a project fulfilling the requirements (for 'construction in wood', a market hall for the sale of grain was proposed on April 4, 1864 [Figure 3.16]).[81] In the ateliers, students would improve their skills in drawing and composition.[82] As Blondel indicated, these competitions developed the passion and courage of the students so that they would produce winning designs that would gain the attention of judges.[83]

Style was of central importance to the *linguistic culture* of the Beaux-Arts. Although the projects set by course tutors did not always include specifications about style – this is the case for a 'colonial museum' in 1910, for instance[84] – many did offer a model to be followed, as was the case for a 'palace in the style of the Barberini Palace' [Figure 3.17], for which a plan and façade were provided.[85] As Van Zanten states: 'choice as the first act of the design process manifests the eclectic position taken by the École at the end of the century'. These

Figure 3.17: *Ecole des Beaux-Arts, project for a palace in the manner of Barberini Palace*, Cours de Construction. *Archives Nationales, AJ/52/133.* Alyson Wharton, courtesy of Archives Nationales, Paris.

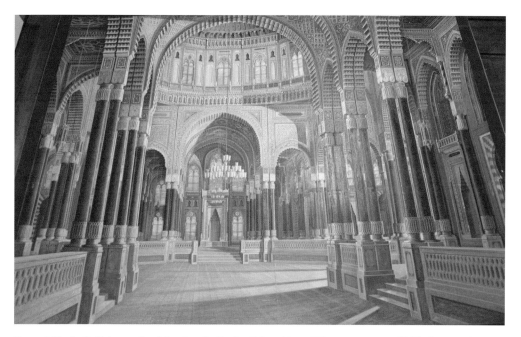

Figure 3.18: *Serkis Balyan undated drawings for Çırağan Palace.* Alyson Wharton, courtesy of Bibliothèque Nubar (AGBU), Paris.

choices or 'generative ideas', forming the 'battle of the styles', were then manipulated in order to achieve overall structural and decorative unity.[86]

By the late nineteenth century, the 'battle of styles' could encompass a wide range of models, as is shown in a text written by the professor of decorative arts Pierre-Henri Mayeux (1845–1929).[87] Within the three 'modes' of decoration were many possible choices including 'Louis XIII', 'Régence', and 'Byzantin'.[88] Ornament 'from nature' could be Egyptian, Persian, Japanese, or Gothic,[89] whereas 'geometric' art chiefly came from Arab and Moorish styles.[90]

Serkis Balyan's project drawings [Figure 3.18] showing the interior of the Çırağan Palace of Abdülaziz (completed 1871) expose his Beaux-Arts training. Serkis developed drawing technique in the ateliers, hoping to attract the attention of his patrons.[91] His sketches contrast with the two-dimensional traditions for architectural drawing in the Ottoman Empire. In his designs, Serkis delineated every aspect, from the bright colours and intricate design of the wall tiles [Figure 3.19], through the carved marble banisters, to the Gothic windows in the dome. He even signed the sketches, showing his vision of himself as an architect in the European sense.

Serkis' approach to planning also followed Beaux-Arts modes of communication. His plan for the Çırağan Palace, as drawn by Sedad Hakkı Eldem (1908–88), follows a version of the *sofa*.[92] However, in contrast to the plan of Dolmabahçe, the Çırağan is a single *sofa*

Figure 3.19: *Serkis Balyan undated drawings for Çırağan Palace.* Alyson Wharton, courtesy of Bibliothèque Nubar (AGBU), Paris.

Figure 3.20: *Serkis Balyan undated drawings for Çırağan Palace.* Alyson Wharton, courtesy of Bibliothèque Nubar (AGBU), Paris.

that is symmetrical and simplified. This axial and modular focus was a key element of the Beaux-Arts training;[93] Serkis had adapted it to an Ottoman plan type. Serkis' Çırağan Palace drawings show how he assimilated the Beaux-Arts 'battle of styles'. An exotic coating of Islamic ornament (arabesque patterns, multi-foil arches, *muqarnas*, interlocking stars, blind niches in primary colours, and gilding) was combined with attention-grabbing showpieces such as an internal fountain [Figure 3.20]. Ottoman features such as the cartouches of the wall decoration and turquoise hexagonal tiles making reference to the (early Ottoman) Green Mosque and Mausoleum of Bursa were combined with Gothic fenestration.

The Çırağan's incorporation of numerous historical styles reflected the teaching of the Beaux-Arts. In 1864, the same year that Serkis Balyan attended classes, Viollet-le-Duc taught aesthetics and the history of art (*esthétique et histoire de l'Art*).[94] Eugène Emmanuel Viollet-le-Duc (1814–79) emphasized that students should learn about theory, archaeological discoveries, and what different traditions had in common.[95] An outline of the class given by Lucien Magne (1849–1916), Viollet-le-Duc's successor, sheds light on Beaux-Arts pedagogy.⁹⁶ Magne dealt with the art of other cultures summarily: in a course concentrating on antiquity, Greece, and Rome, there was a section on 'modern architecture', which stretched from Latin, Byzantine, Gothic, Renaissance, monastic, and Arab architecture, to China, Mexico, and Peru. Arab architecture was defined simplistically as 'Byzantine [in] origin, modified by the oriental imagination, characterized by the use of the trefoil arch'.⁹⁷ There was a focus on exotic building types such as the 'palaces of Cairo', the Alhambra, the madrasas of Isfahan, and 'mosques surmounted with onion domes'. Encapsulating the generalizing conception of Islamic art is the comment that 'all of the countries of the Orient which have adopted the religion of Muhammad possess monuments of Arab architecture: Turkey, Persia, India etc.'⁹⁸

Despite his Orientalizing comments, Magne's approach had an analytical basis. Students produced plans, elevations, and drawings of historical monuments, such as the cloister of the hospital of Saint-Jean d'Angers [Figure 3.21].⁹⁹ That a related historicist methodology, involving some first-hand archaeological study of historical monuments, lay behind the design of the Çırağan Palace is suggested by a reference to Serkis' brother Agop sending artists to Spain and North Africa.¹⁰⁰

The meaning of the Islamic and Gothic elements seen in Çırağan Palace is indicated by a text by Viollet-le-Duc. In his introduction to *L'Architecture et Decorations Turques* (1874), written by his disciple Léon Parvillée, Viollet-le-Duc stressed how the Turks had adopted the art forms of those they had conquered as well as those of their religion and that it was difficult to identify anything 'local' within this mixture of Persian, Arab, and 'Hindu'.¹⁰¹ Viollet-le-Duc also identified relationships to European medieval and Crusader works.¹⁰²

The Pertevniyal Valide Sultan Mosque (1872), built by Serkis for the mother of Sultan Abdülaziz in Aksaray, shows a related vision of the confluence of architectural traditions. The exterior [Figure 3.22], covered with relief carving, displays various Islamic repertoires: Mughal onion domes, Seljukid pyramidal vaults, and Ottoman cartouches. The interior [Figure 3.23], decorated with bright paintwork, referenced Ottoman Bursa: blind niches, cartouches, and *muqarnas* (geometric) friezes, along with the Mughal onion dome of the *minbar* (pulpit in a mosque) and the classic Ottoman *mihrab*. As in the Çırağan Palace, Islamic inferences were combined with Gothic fenestration. As in the Dolmabahçe Palace and Ortaköy Mosque, a *trompe l'oeil* dome dominated the interior [Figure 3.24].

This dome in particular elucidates the nature of the Valide Mosque's revivalism. Within the illusionistic decoration, Islamic motifs such as *muqarnas* and multi-foil arches with *ablaq* (particoloured) decoration can be seen alongside more specific allusions, such as arabesques in the style of Ottoman Bursa and the central calligraphic medallion in classical Ottoman *thulth* (sloping 1/3) script. The bouquet of flowers in an urn, symbol of the magnanimity of the state, unifies these elements.

The categorization of the Valide Mosque and Çırağan Palace in the *Usul-u Mimari-i Osmani* (1873) as an 'Ottoman Renaissance' in fact explains the intention behind the syncretic nature of their decoration. Merging Ottoman and Islamic styles with Gothic fenestration, they displayed their (perceived) roots, according to theories such as those of Magne and

The Balyan Family and the *Linguistic Culture* of a Parisian Education

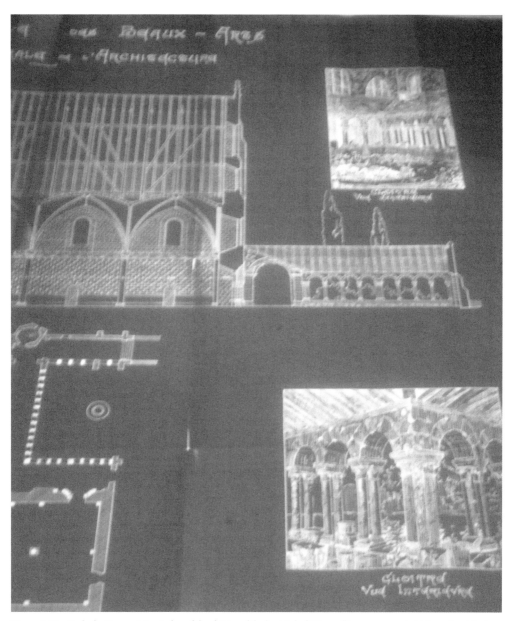

Figure 3.21: *Ecole des Beaux-Arts, studies of the cloister of the hospital of St Jean d'Angers, course in history of architecture by Magne. AJ/52/148.* Alyson Wharton, courtesy of Archives Nationales, Paris.

Figure 3.22: *Pertevniyal Valide Sultan Mosque (1872), Aksaray, Istanbul. Exterior.* Alyson Wharton.

Figure 3.23: *Pertevniyal Valide Sultan Mosque (1872), Aksaray, Istanbul. Interior, side wall.* Alyson Wharton.

Figure 3.24: *Pertevniyal Valide Sultan Mosque (1872), Aksaray, Istanbul. Interior, dome.* Alyson Wharton.

Viollet-le-Duc on the interrelation of historic styles. Bright colours and *trompe l'oeil* joined this vision of the genealogy of Ottoman architecture in order to evoke rebirth. The syncretic revivalism mixed seemingly contradictory styles (Gothic, Moorish, Ottoman, etc.) in one building in order to make a cohesive whole. It can be likened to the romantic eclecticism of the Marseilles Cathedral (1845–93) by Léon Vaudoyer, which blended Byzantine, Islamic, and European styles to communicate the role of the city as an intersection of cultures. Serkis Balyan's related invocation of historical styles was not a reflection of the interaction of European and Islamic influences, but was deliberately constructed to convey meaning.[103]

The choice of a syncretic approach can perhaps be attributed to the influence of André, who was one of Serkis' patrons in the ateliers.[104] André's works, such as the Museum of Natural History, followed Labrouste's lead in combining modern techniques with classical inspiration and epigraphic content communicating function and meaning. However, Ottoman architecture itself had, as Viollet-le-Duc pointed out, assumed a variety of traditions (being 'above all' a branch of Persian and Arab art).[105]

Although the 'Ottoman Renaissance' was an articulation of views that were circulating at the Beaux-Arts, crafted into a syncretic design whole, it was not Orientalist architecture. Instead, it was part of a spate of activities promoting Ottoman traditions in the 1860s and '70s. Ottomans joined the international expositions to increase international prestige and

Figure 3.25: *Sopon Bezirdjian, undated sketches.* Alyson Wharton, courtesy of the Bezirdjian/Clark family, London.

trade, by demonstrating the value of their handicrafts. These stressed Ottoman–Islamic heritage and identity: Salaheddin Bey, head of the delegation to the 1867 exposition, likened Abdülaziz's visit there to Harun al-Rashid's sending of presents to the 'greatest monarch of the Occident'.[106] Parvillée, who had worked on the Dolmabahçe Palace, conducted fieldwork in Bursa, aiming to distance Oriental style from '*une question de mode*' (a question of fashion/style). Instead of applying a certain number of motifs and borders to create '*un ensemble harmonieux*', he intended for his studies to identify 'the line, invisible but real, which comprises the taste, which can be called the art, of the civilization'.[107]

The decorator Sopon Bezirdjian (1841–1915) gives further evidence of this desire to use Beaux-Arts methodologies to rehabilitate the position of Oriental art. Bezirdjian published an album of designs in London in 1889, wherein he noted the passion of Abdülaziz for palaces 'in true oriental style' and his love for Turkish, Persian, and Arabian styles. Bezirdjian stressed the need for academic study to correct how 'Oriental peoples are improperly represented to Western nations'.[108] Bezirdjian's drawings show how he studied Oriental art forms, making sketches of recognizable Ottoman patterns [Figure 3.25], Far Eastern ones and historical Armenian architecture.[109] Bezirdjian's close working relationship with Serkis (he collaborated on nearly all of his works) suggests that his reference to palaces in 'true oriental style' can be seen as an accurate expression of Serkis' intent.

It is clear that Serkis Balyan took on aspects of the intellectual world and practical methods of the Beaux-Arts. These were circulated within his working milieu, including Parvillée and Bezirdjian, as well as the team responsible for the *Usul*, some of whom worked on his constructions.[110] Serkis expressed prevailing ideas on the genealogy of Ottoman architecture through syncretic revivalism in the Valide Mosque and Çırağan Palace, using an ornamental overlay to communicate a message of Ottoman resurgence.

Conclusion: Parisian Expertise Adapted to an Ottoman Core

At the Sainte-Barbe, the Centrale, and the Beaux-Arts, Nigoğos and Serkis were exposed to the *linguistic culture* of Parisian architecture and new methods of architectural communication. They assimilated these and adapted some of their elements to the Ottoman setting.

At the Sainte-Barbe, Nigoğos came into contact with romanticism, assimilated its tropes and formulated his own version of its architecture in the Dolmabahçe Palace. Nigoğos used external and internal ornament to express the function and meaning of the building, following practitioners such as Henri Labrouste. This ornament was employed in a highly original way, presaging the emotive architecture of Charles Garnier. However, Nigoğos used Parisian decoration and its vocabulary to express Ottoman sovereignty through inscriptions, symbolic motifs, and the display of the *tuğra*, as well as through the design of the palace, taking into account the competitive discourse of Ottoman architecture. Nigoğos made sure that Dolmabahçe remained rooted in the *sofa* plan of Ottoman residential architecture. Therefore, although its surface communication adapted the language of Parisian romanticism, its core did not depart from local traditions.

Serkis Balyan followed a similar approach. Although he attended the Sainte-Barbe, the Centrale, and the Beaux-Arts, Serkis used his new expertise alongside commitment to the traditions, practices, and identities of the empire. He built the earliest Ottoman terraced buildings, following models offered at the Centrale and the Beaux-Arts. However, Akaretler were not sold on the open market, but were reserved for the sultan's court and formed the sultan's route to Friday prayers. Parisian architectural modes were exploited to reinforce the structures of the empire. Serkis assimilated the Beaux-Arts approach to architectural communication and focused on the importance of composition and style. Following his exposure to the system of competitions, Serkis' drawings integrated formal and technical features engineered to catch attention. Notions about the history of Islamic architecture taught by Viollet-le-Duc and Magne were incorporated into the Valide Mosque and the Çırağan Palace, but, like Nigoğos, Serkis continued to use Ottoman floor plans.

On a pragmatic level, Nigoğos and Serkis learnt technical skills that helped their building works develop on a larger scale and that enabled Serkis to found his public works company. On a formal level, they gained an expertise that enabled them to use architecture to communicate in a different way. And yet, Nigoğos and Serkis continued to express Ottoman messages through their adaptation of Parisian *linguistic culture* and continued to build according to Ottoman structural types. This embodied the architectural form of *interactional expertise* used in the service of the sultan.

Notes

1 Rahip Yeprem Boğosyan, *Balyan Kertasdanı* (Vienna: Mekhitaryan Tparan, 1981), 133 on Nigoğos, 178 on Serkis, 245 on Agop.
2 Pars Tuğlacı, *The Role of the Balian Family in Ottoman Architecture* (Istanbul: Yeni Çığır, 1990), 303.
3 Kevork Pamukciyan, *Biografileriyle Ermeniler* (Istanbul: Aras, 2003), 97–100.
4 Aygül Ağır, 'Balyanlar'ın Eğitimleri Üzerine Notlar', in *Afife Batur'a Armağan. Mimarlık ve Sanat Tarihi Yazıları*, ed. Aygül Ağır, Deniz Mazlum, and Gül Cephanecigil (Istanbul: Literatür, 2005), 65–71.
5 My book (*Architects of Constantinople: The Balyan Family and the History of Ottoman Architecture* [London and NY: IB Tauris, 2015]) includes a chapter on the Balyans' education. The present chapter adds details on the educational experience and how this was adapted.
6 Celal Esad Arseven, *Türk San'atı* (Istanbul: Akşam Matbaası, 1928), 171.
7 Ibid., 172.

8   Sibel Bozdoğan, 'Reading Ottoman Architecture through Modernist Lenses: Nationalist Historiography and the "New Architecture" in the Early Republic', *Muqarnas* 24 (2007): 201.
9   Ibid., 202.
10 'Ottoman Renaissance' is given as *usul-i mimari-i 'Osmanının mebde-i ihyası* (reviving the source of Ottoman architecture). Ahmet Ersoy, 'On the Sources of the "Ottoman Renaissance": Architectural Revival and its Discourse During the Abdülaziz Era (1861–76)' (Ph.D. diss., Harvard, 2000), 269. Recently published as *Architecture and the Late Ottoman Historical Imaginary. Reconfiguring the Architectural Past in a Modernizing Empire* (Aldershot: Ashgate, 2015).
11 Ahmet Ersoy, 'Architecture and the Search for Ottoman Origins in the Tanzimat Period', *Muqarnas* 24 (2007): 133.
12 Ersoy, 'On the Sources of the "Ottoman Renaissance"', 311 n.6.
13 Ahmet Ersoy, 'Sarkis Bey's Dream: An Alternative House of Sciences and the Fall of the Traditional Builder', in *Armenian Architects of Istanbul in the Era of Westernization*, ed. Hasan Kuruyazıcı (Istanbul: International Hrant Dink Foundation Publications, 2010), 58–79.
14 Harold F. Schiffman, *Linguistic Culture and Language Policy* (London and New York: Routledge, 1996), 5.
15 Ibid., 7.
16 Jean-Claude Bringuier, Jean Piaget, *Conversations with Jean Piaget* (Chicago, IL: University of Chicago Press, 1980), 43. Piaget describes the process of 'accommodation' through which new techniques are implemented.
17 Ekmeleddin İhsanoğlu, *Science, Technology and Learning in the Ottoman Empire* (Aldershot: Ashgate, 2004), 62.
18 Harry Collins, 'Interactional Expertise as a Third Kind of Knowledge', *Phenomenology and the Cognitive Sciences* 3 (2004): 125–43 abstract, 125.
19 Ibid., 126.
20 Ibid., 127.
21 Harry Collins and Robert Evans, *Rethinking Expertise* (Chicago, IL: University of Chicago Press, 2007), 59. Contributory expertise is described as a kind of specialist expertise. It is 'the practical expertise that enables one to contribute to a domain of practice. To acquire contributory expertise one must work within the expert domain.' Full expertise is a complete practical training in a specialist area. Interactional expertise, in contrast, can be acquired from socialization alone. Harry Collins, 'Three Dimensions of Expertise', *Phenomenology and the Cognitive Sciences* 12.2 (June 2013): 3.
22 Collins, 'Interactional Expertise', 135.
23 Harry Collins, Robert Evans, and Michael E. Gorman, 'Trading Zones and Interactional Expertise', in *Trading Zones and Interactional Expertise: Creating New Kinds of Collaboration*, ed. Michael E. Gorman (Cambridge, MA: MIT Press, 2010), 15.
24 Teotik, *Teotik Amenun Daretsuytsi* (Bolis: Tpagr. V. yev H. Ter-Nersesian, 1907–29), vol. from 1921, 256–67; *Meğu*, March 10, 1858, 5; Boğosyan, *Balyan Kertasdanı*, 178; *Arşaluys Araradyan* 378 (1850); Boğosyan: *Balyan Kertasdanı*, 245; *Masis* 772 (1866).

25 Archives de Paris, D.50Z article no. 385, 1846–47 and 1851–52.
26 There is a 'Bellion' listed in D.50Z/385, 1846–47, which may be Nigoğos.
27 Marc Le Coeur, 'An Architect of Silence', in *Henri Labrouste: Structure Brought to Light*, ed. Barry Bergdoll et al. (New York: Museum of Modern Art, 2013), 44.
28 Archives de Paris, D.50Z/107, 24 Dec 1862.
29 Vartan Artinian, *The Armenian Constitutional System in the Ottoman Empire, 1839–1863: A Study of its Historical Development* (Istanbul: Isis Press, 1988), 62.
30 Archives de Paris, D.50Z/385, 1848–49 ; David Harvie, *Eiffel, the Genius Who Reinvented Himself* (Stroud, UK: Sutton, 2006), 7.
31 Robert Jarvis, 'Pierre Victor Galland', *The Art Amateur* 18.5 (April 1888): 108.
32 Charles Séchan, *Souvenirs d'un homme de théâtre 1831–55* (Paris: Calmann-Levy, n.d.), preface by Adolphe Badin.
33 Archives de Paris, D.11J/130, 1850, register of teaching personnel.
34 Ağır, 'Balyanlar'ın Eğitimleri Üzerine Notlar', 65–70.
35 Neil Levine, 'The Book and the Building: Hugo's Theory of Architecture and Labrouste's Bibliothèque Ste-Genevieve', in *The Beaux-Arts and Nineteenth-Century French Architecture*, ed. Robin Middleton (London: Thames and Hudson, 1982), 139.
36 David Van Zanten, 'Architectural Polychromy: Life in Architecture', in *The Beaux-Arts and Nineteenth-Century French Architecture*, ed. Robin Middleton (London: Thames and Hudson, 1982), 200.
37 *Meğu*, March 10, 1858.
38 Boğosyan, *Balyan Kertasdanı*, 178; *Masis* 319 (1858).
39 *Meğu*, March 10, 1858, 4.
40 Ibid.
41 Robert A. Nisbet, 'Genius & Milieu', *Proceedings of the American Philosophical Society* 126.6 (December 1982): 441.
42 Alice T. Friedman, 'Academic Theory and A.-L.-T. Vaudoyer's Dissertation sur l'architecture', *The Art Bulletin* 67.1 (March 1985): 118.
43 Ibid., 116.
44 *Meğu*, March 10, 1858, 6.
45 Théophile Gautier, *Constantinople of To-day*, trans. Robert Howe Gould (London: David Bogue, 1856), 300–01.
46 Ibid.
47 Roderic H. Davison, *Reform in the Ottoman Empire 1856–1876* (New York: Gordian Press, 1973), 28.
48 *Meğu*, March 10, 1858, 3.
49 Gülru Necipoğlu, *Architecture, Ceremonial and Power: The Topkapı Palace in the Fifteenth and Sixteenth Centuries* (Cambridge, MA: MIT Press, 1991), 8.
50 David Van Zanten, *Building Paris: Architectural Institutions and the Transformation of the French Capital 1830–1870* (Cambridge: Cambridge University Press, 1994), 105.
51 Gautier, *Constantinople of To-day*, 299–306.
52 David Graham Burnett, 'The Architecture of Meaning: Gautier and Romantic Architectural Visions', *French Forum* 7.2 (May 1982): 109.

53 Harriet Trowbridge Allen, *Travels in Europe and the East During the Years 1858–59 and 1863–64* (New Haven, CT: Tuttle, Morehouse A. Taylor, Printers, 1879), 106.
54 Louis Bunel, *Jérusalem, La Cote de Syrie et Constantinople en 1853* (Paris: Sangnier et Bray, 1854/Elibron Classics, 2005), 375.
55 Christopher Curtis Mead, *Charles Garnier's Paris Opéra: Architectural Empathy and the Renaissance of French Classicism* (New York and Cambridge, MA: MIT Press, 1991), 231.
56 Bruno Girveau, 'Une architecture qui parle aux yeaux, aux oreilles, au cœur et au passions', in *Charles Garnier Un Architecte Pour Un Empire*, ed. Bruno Girveau (Paris: Les Editions Beaux-arts de Paris, 2010), 14.
57 Selim Deringil, 'The Invention of Tradition as Public Image in the Late Ottoman Empire 1808–1908', *Comparative Studies in Society and History* 35.1 (1993): 7.
58 Sedat Hakkı Eldem, *Türk Evi Plan Tipleri*, 2 vols (İstanbul Teknik Üniversitesi, Mimarlık Fakültesi, 1954).
59 Bozdoğan, 'Reading Ottoman Architecture': 212–13.
60 Önder Küçükerman, *Türk Evi* (Istanbul: Apa Ofset Basımevi, 1985), 25–27.
61 Bozdoğan, 'Reading Ottoman Architecture': 213.
62 Eldem, *Türk Evi*, vol 2, 146.
63 Archives de Paris, D.50Z/107, booklet dated November 15, 1845.
64 Ibid.
65 Françoise Pothier, *Histoire De L'École Centrale Des Arts Et Manufactures* (Paris: Delamotte Fils et Cie, Libraires-Editeurs, 1887), 7–8.
66 *Luys* 52 (1880).
67 The (un-numbered) student notebooks or *cahiers spéciaux* are kept in the private archives of the Centrale.
68 BBK, Y.A. RES, D:9, G:27, 1298.S.02/1881.
69 BBK, YA.RES D:9, G:27, 1298.S.02/ 1881.
70 BBK, A)MKT.MHM, D:451, G:3, 1290.M.28/1873.
71 Ecole Centrale Private Archives, second-year student notebook, 1862–63.
72 Annie Jacques, 'Introduction', in *Les Dessins D'Architecture De L'Ecole Des Beaux-Arts*, ed. Annie Jacques and Riichi Miyaké (Paris: Arthaud, 1988), 8.
73 Pierre Lavedan, *L'urbanisme à l'époque moderne : XVIe–XVIIIe siècles* (Genève: Droz, 1982), 117.
74 Afife Batur, Atilla Yücel, and Nur Fersan, 'Reuse of Nineteenth Century Rowhouses in Istanbul' in *Conservation as Cultural Survival*, ed. Renata Holod (Geneva: The Aga Khan Award for Architecture, 1978), 60–65; Derin Öncel, 'Osmanlı Konutunun Gelişim Sürecinde Galata Apartmanları', Etkinlikler Voyvoda Caddesi Toplantılar 2005–06, accessed November 21, 2014, http://www.obarsiv.com/vct_0506_derinoncel.html.
75 Ecole Centrale Private Archives, second-year student notebook, 1862–63, Leçon II, 7 novembre: '*Nivellement*'.
76 Christopher Mead, 'Urban Contingency and the Problem of Representation in Second Empire Paris', *Journal of the Society of Architectural Historians* 54.2 (June 1995): 138.
77 Teotik, *Teotik Amenun Daretsuytsi* (1921), 263; *Dzarig* 56 (1899).

78 Tuğlacı, *The Role of the Balian Family*, 429; Teotik, *Teotik Amenun Daretsuytsi* (1921), 263; Boğosyan, *Balyan Kertasdanı*, 178.
79 Juls Rebout was a teacher in the ateliers of architecture from 1863–65. AJ/52/38.
80 Archives Nationales, AJ/52/161.
81 Archives Nationales, AJ/52/133.
82 Richard Chafee, 'The Teaching of Architecture at the École Des Beaux-Arts', in *The Architecture of the Ecole des Beaux-Arts*, ed. Arthur Drexler (New York: Museum of Modern Art, distributed by MIT Press: 1977), 82.
83 Jacques, 'Introduction', 6.
84 Archives Nationales, AJ/52/ 132, *Concours d'Emulation* from 1910.
85 Archives Nationales, AJ/52/133.
86 David Van Zanten, 'Architectural Composition at the Ecole Des Beaux-Arts from Charles Percier to Charles Garnier', in *The Architecture of the Ecole des Beaux-Arts*, ed. Arthur Drexler (New York: Museum of Modern Art, distributed by MIT Press, 1977), 115.
87 Henri Mayeux, *La Composition Décorative* (Paris: Société français d'editions d'art, 1885), 7–11.
88 Ibid., 42–48.
89 Ibid., 48–61.
90 Ibid., 64.
91 Jacques, 'Introduction', 6.
92 Eldem, *Türk Evi,* 2:152.
93 Van Zanten, 'Architectural Composition', 112, 124, 193.
94 Archives Nationales, AJ/52/39.
95 Eugène Viollet-le-Duc, *Lectures on Architecture*, trans. Benjamin Bucknall (London: Sampson Low, Marston, Searle, and Rivington Crown Buildings, 1877), 388.
96 Archives Nationales, AJ/52/41.
97 Ibid.
98 Ibid.
99 Archives Nationales, AJ 52/148.
100 Tuğlacı, *The Role of the Balyan Family*, 318.
101 Léon Parvillée, *L'Architecture et Decorations Turques* (Paris: Ve A. Morel, 1874), preface by Viollet-le-Duc, ii.
102 Ibid.
103 In contrast to this syncretic approach, the architectural works of Viollet-le-Duc were historicist in nature and geared toward the recreation of a particular historical monument to communicate national purity. Viollet-le-Duc disdained the pluralism that was encouraged by the Beaux-Arts, its superficial adopting of forms and 'grotesque medley of styles'. Viollet-le-Duc, *Lectures on Architecture*, 447–49.
104 Archives Nationales, AJ/52/460 and AJ/52/35.
105 Parvillée, *L'Architecture et Decorations Turques*, preface by Viollet-le-Duc, ii.
106 Salaheddin Bey, *La Turquie à l'Exposition universelle de 1867* (Paris: n.p., 1867), frontispiece.
107 Parvillée, *L'Architecture et Decorations Turques*, 2.
108 Sopon Bezirdjian, *Albert Fine Art Album* (London: John Heywood, 1889), 5.

109 Bezirdjian's drawings, formerly in a private collection, are now held by the Manchester Metropolitan University Library, Special Collections.
110 Eugène Maillard worked on Akaretler and Aziziye Mosque. BBK, HR.TO, 464/57, 1878.9.8. Pietro Montani worked on the Valide Mosque and Çırağan Palace. Ersoy, 'On the Sources of the "Ottoman Renaissance"', 98–99.

Chapter 4

Drawing Knowledge, (Re-)Constructing History: Pascal Coste in Egypt

Eva-Maria Troelenberg

The Expert as Agent

> […] order was given to all the leaders of the mosques to let me walk, measure and draw both inside and outside the buildings, and to provide me with protection against those who would hinder me. Equipped with this *firman*, I began to visit all the mosques of Cairo and of Old Cairo. I focused on the eight major ones, those most important by their typically Arab architectural character.[1]

This is how the Marseilles architect and engineer Pascal Coste (1787–1879) remembers the genesis of his publication *Architecture arabe ou monuments du Kaire* roughly six decades after the events described.[2] His first stay in Egypt between 1817 and 1822 is covered in a short but prominent passage of his two-volume memoir published in 1878. The Egyptian episode began when he was in his early thirties. As a young architect, he was commissioned by the Egyptian ruler Muhammad Ali Pasha (r.1805–48) to contribute to the planning and construction of a number of industrial and infrastructural projects; later on he was also asked to develop plans for representative buildings and mosques. This work prompted him to study the historical corpus of Cairo's medieval architecture in detail.

Seizing these opportunities abroad marked the beginning of Coste's career, which may be considered a paradigmatic one, shedding light on imperial and transnational trends of the nineteenth century shared between the western and eastern parts of the Mediterranean.

Scholars from various perspectives, not least including those interested in more recent approaches to artistic and architectural cultural exchange, have addressed the life and work of Coste. Based on the first systematic studies of the architect's estate in the Bibliothèque de l'Alcazar in Marseilles, a small volume of conference proceedings was published in 1990 with the explicit aim to present the career of this local personality as an instance of Mediterranean exchange.[3] In 1998, Marseilles participated in the *Année France-Egypte* with an exhibition titled *Pascal Coste: Toutes les Egypte*. This show was accompanied by a catalogue that provides fundamental information about Coste's ways of working and drawing as well as about the genesis and reception of *Architecture arabe*, while also hinting at its complex cross-cultural implications.[4]

Scholars of Orientalism in the arts, on the one hand, often place Coste's Egyptian work (as well as his later ventures in Persia)[5] in the larger context of Western, and particularly French, intellectual history of the period, shedding an interesting light on

Coste's professional career and profile, yet also creating a somewhat asymmetrical notion of Orientalism as a one-way trajectory, set against the canvas of a basically mute and receptive 'Orient'.[6] On the other hand, a rising tide of historiography on late modern Islamic or Islamicate art and architecture has led a number of scholars to touch upon Coste's presence in Egypt while also discussing urban developments in nineteenth-century Cairo, the Mamluk Revival, and local and foreign notions of Egypt's own heritage, thereby embedding the topic more strongly in a context of mutual, though often politically charged, cultural exchange. These approaches often refer only briefly to Coste, typically considering him among a number of other nineteenth-century Orientalists as a predecessor for later local as well as transcultural definitions of 'Old Cairo' in the age of historicism, and linking his work generally to a paradigmatic notion of Orientalist and Oriental medievalism.[7]

Taking up this path, this chapter seeks to revisit Pascal Coste's work as an engineer and an historian of architecture in and for Egypt,[8] yet placing this example against a wider horizon of transcultural intellectual history that even more obviously reaches beyond mere notions of revivalism or romantic Orientalist nostalgia. In this vein, the chapter also presents reasons to reflect on the role of the Middle East within the narrative of a larger modern Mediterranean world – something that must be understood in deliberately anti-nostalgic terms[9] and will contribute to the hitherto 'blocked narrative of Muslim modernity'.[10] The dependency paradigm of modern Area Studies has made a problematic imprint on the field of art history in this respect: while Mediterranean modernisms are primarily described for the region's European parts, the late and post-imperial areas of the Levant and North Africa have long been understood as a dependent periphery whose modernity is considered problematically at odds with claims for authenticity growing out of traditional or religious paradigms.[11] For the field of ethnology, Dieter Haller already identified a certain lack of '[…] actor centricity, the significance ascribed to the Mediterranean region on the level of identification and the degree to which it is relevant in terms of practical behaviour' a decade ago.[12] Meanwhile, agency-related theories have exerted their solid impact on the humanities, including art history. Particularly in the discussion of so-called 'cross-cultural' questions, these approaches add significantly to the methodological instruments of our discipline after the so-called 'Global Turn', allowing an identification and re-evaluation of agencies and their repercussions from a post-Orientalist point of view.[13] The work of Coste has so far often been described in terms of Orientalism on a rather positivistic level. My approach links the results of these approaches to an examination of the aesthetic eloquence of drawing, lines, and drafts to assess art's autonomous epistemological dimension. While the transnational character of Coste's career certainly could suggest a more system-related comparative approach, in this chapter I will thus deliberately consider the larger social, intellectual, and national systems only as an implicit background. The spotlight will be on the historian-expert as a mediating agent and on his impact on the image of nineteenth-century Cairo between historicization and modernization.

Drawing and the Establishment of Knowledge

The case of Coste offers a particularly apt example to demonstrate how this approach can be applied to visual material. The plates of his publication *Architecture arabe* had a significant impact on the image of Muslim-Egyptian architecture from about the mid-nineteenth century on [Figure 4.1].[14] An even more multifaceted and immediate testimony of his simultaneously active and passive visual agency is conveyed through the large corpus of drawings that he produced while in Egypt and later bequeathed to the municipal library of his hometown.[15]

The drawings, executed in different media ranging from pencil to watercolour, were mounted by Coste himself in 31 folios. Six of them relate to Egypt and hold a sum of

Figure 4.1: *Pascal Coste, Frontispiece*, Architecture arabe ou monuments du Kaire: mesurés et dessinés, de 1818 à 1825, par Pascal Coste *(Paris: 1839)*. The Miriam and Ira D. Wallach Division of Art, Prints and Photographs: Art & Architecture Collection, The New York Public Library.

1051 documents.[16] For conservation reasons the original folios were disassembled and re-mounted on neutral paper several years ago – yet their original sequence and organization was maintained.[17] Apart from a large number of studies for the plates of *Architecture arabe*, the albums also include a variety of other subjects and reveal the much wider scope of Coste's gaze towards Egypt. When organizing this material towards the end of his life, Coste apparently decided to follow an ordering principle that was only vaguely chronological. His main system of organization was rather one built around thematic categories that distinguish between studies of people and everyday items, ancient monuments, Arab Architecture, and plans for his own infrastructural or representative projects such as mosques and palaces. Almost all of the drawings are precisely dated and annotated in Coste's handwriting and in most cases it is clear that he did this in situ or during the immediate post-processing of what he had seen. Hence, the drawings reflect the speed and sequence of his work and his interest in the objects.[18] Seen together, the arrangement of the folios and the annotations form a most valuable paratext that provides important clues about his technique of establishing knowledge through his gaze and documenting it through the line. What follows is an examination of Coste's technique of understanding the 'Arab'[19] architecture of Egypt through a process-based description of some of his drawings.[20]

Six days after his arrival, on November 6, 1817, Coste executed a drawing that is paradigmatic for the typical preconditions and patterns of perception of a European draughtsman setting foot for the first time in the Levant: labeled 'antiquité d'alexandrie', it shows what is the so-called 'Pompey's Pillar', a monolithic symbol of Roman victory in the form of a monumental free-standing column [Figure 4.2].[21] Combining an ancient Egyptian base, an Ionian shaft, and a Corinthian capital, this eclectic combination of ancient Egyptian and classical elements had been the subject of modern travelogues and historiography and thus had gained some prominence.[22]

Obviously Coste, as an architect trained in the classical tradition, was familiar with the canonical and thus rational, comprehensible shape and proportions of this kind of monument: he aptly renders it in all of its detail, set against a low horizon, emphasizing its outstanding size and grandeur. The coastline of Alexandria with its ships, fortifications, and minarets is dwarfed in the background. A caravan in the middle ground and a number of Arabs with camels settle into the foreground, and their appearance as generic props for the timeless embodiment of the ancient heritage holds a recognizable aesthetic precedent. Contemporary Arab culture appears as scenography rather than being subject to the architect's analytical gaze yet.

Nevertheless, Coste also demonstrates an interest in contemporary Arab culture and society, an interest whose quality and method changes across his oeuvre over time. It seems to intensify only a few years into his sojourn, from 1820 onwards, when he begins drawing scenes of everyday life, connoting an ethnographic interest, with greater intensity.[23] Some of these documents even have a certain picturesque tint, thus betraying the classical Orientalist perspective with all its cultural asymmetries. At the same time, even his first studies of, say, *fellah*s working on watermills and wells clearly reflect the technical interest of the engineer who apparently deems such 'primitive' contraptions worthy of analytical study and

Drawing Knowledge, (Re-)Constructing History: Pascal Coste in Egypt

Figure 4.2: *Pascal Coste, drawing of 'Pompey's Pillar' in Alexandria, 6 November 1817.* Bibliothèque de l'Alcazar, Marseilles, Fonds Coste, MS 1308, fol. 68.

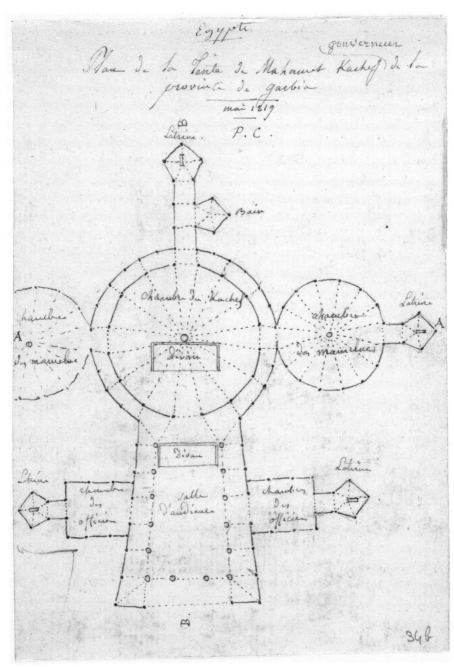

Figure 4.3: *Pascal Coste, systematic drawing of a tent, May 1819.* Bibliothèque de l'Alcazar, Marseilles. Fonds Coste, MS 1311, fol. 34.

description.[24] The same analytical gaze is directed towards animals and their proportions,[25] or towards the system of veils worn by women.[26]

Yet, the ultimate subject for the architect's taxonomic curiosity is initially the tent – both in its upscale and vernacular varieties. As early as 1819, Coste drew a systematic plan and section of a tent camp set up by the governor of the Province of al-Gharbiyah north of Cairo[27] [Figure 4.3]; studies of the tents of Muhammad Ali and of other dignities, as well as ordinary tribal tents would follow.[28] Remarkably, Coste seems to hardly distinguish between the different social strata involved – in each case he seems simply interested in how these structures work. The scrutiny he devotes to them also indicates that he has no reservations against considering common hierarchies in a teleological categorization of architecture. For him, even ephemeral textile structures deserve the same systematic taxonomic appraisal as monumental examples of ancient architecture.

Of course the overwhelming presence of these subjects between about 1818 and 1822 also indicates what would have been accessible to Coste at that time – and what was not, or not yet. During the same period, he also began to pay attention to the Arab architecture he encountered while traveling overland as well as in Cairo. Since, as was common for foreigners at that time, he did not have access to mosques and other religious buildings, it is not surprising to find only sporadic drawings of minarets, entry façades, or generic architectural silhouettes that reveal little in the way of detail. Crenellations, polygonal minarets, striped façades, and ribbed domes provide a rather vague summary of Mamluk architecture in these early folios – and yet, his fundamental interest in those details is discernible at this stage [Figure 4.4].[29]

Figure 4.4: *Pascal Coste, architectural sketches, 1819–20.* Bibliothèque de l'Alcazar, Marseilles, Fonds Coste, MS 1311, fol. 20.

His increasing interest in medieval and particularly Mamluk architecture from the early 1820s onwards coincided with the direction of his career, one determined largely by Muhammad Ali's commissions of representative buildings.[30] After working on infrastructural projects for several years, Coste was then commissioned to design two mosques in the urban centres of Cairo and Alexandria. As opposed to his secular building projects, which he envisaged as 'un petit Versailles',[31] Muhammad Ali's idea for these religious commissions was obviously more traditional and related to the aesthetic heritage of Muslim architecture in Egypt. In his memoir, Coste explains:

> I mentioned to him that, since I did not know the interior of these buildings and was not familiar with their religious ceremonies, I would end up designing a church for him, and not a mosque, and that therefore it was urgently necessary to give me permission to visit them.[32]

It is against this background that the privilege of the *firman* was issued to Coste in the spring of 1822. Subsequently, Coste spent several months studying what he identified as the eight main mosques of Cairo, determined by what he describes as '[…] their distinctly Arab type of architecture'.[33] This includes the mosque of Amr ibn al-As (641), the mosque of Ibn Tulun (876-79), the Fatimid structure of Al-Azhar (970-72), and the Mamluk mosques and complexes of Barquq (1384-86), Qala'un (1284-85), Sultan Hasan (1356-62), Al-Muayyad (1415-21), and Qa'itbay (1472-74), a list that defined the 'highlights' of medieval Cairene architecture.[34] To date, most of them have never been properly analyzed and described in the context of medieval Muslim architecture. In general, systematic knowledge about Muslim architecture was still scarce during that period.[35]

In some cases, Coste's drawings reveal a lack of familiarity with the lines, forms, and proportions, for instance with regard to the characteristic crenellations running along the rooftop of Ibn Tulun mosque,[36] which he only seems to have grasped after several attempts [Figure 4.5].[37] The lines in this study are a far cry from the elegant certainty of his renderings of antique columns, lintels, and capitals. Yet, at the same time, he instantly understands the significance of the unique stucco ornaments on the same building. His detailed studies show an appreciation for the reliefs, as well as for the position and character of this decoration within the larger architectural structure [Figure 4.6].[38] Coste grapples with the large stylistic variety found in the ornamentation he encounters, and yet the fact that this ornamentation is defined by its hybridity, merging, as it did in the first centuries of Islam, classical types and a new visual language, does play to his advantage. Coste chooses to detail a number of ornamental systems that seem to be more in line with the classical tradition, choosing, for example, bands of tendrils, rendered in a stylized way and closer to the acanthus leaf than to the arabesque, emphasizing symmetry and regularity over variety. His perception was filtered and directed by canonical categories and as a result his drawings appear less as true-to-fact copies and more as a visual contact zone between the familiar and the hitherto uncharted.

Similar observations can be made not only at the scale of ornament but also with regard to Coste's take on entire monumental structures. A case in point is his study of the funerary,

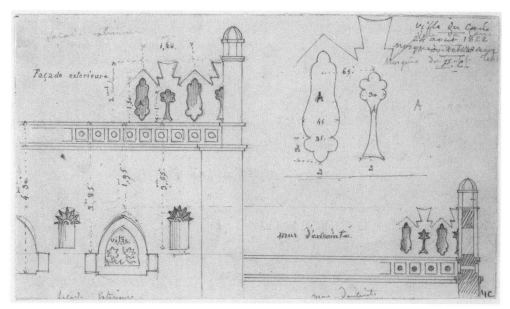

Figure 4.5: *Pascal Coste, sketches of façade and crenulation details, Ibn Tulun mosque, 24 August 1822.* Bibliothèque de l'Alcazar Marseilles, Fonds Coste, MS 1309, fol. 4c.

Figure 4.6: *Pascal Coste, sketches of stucco ornament details, Ibn Tulun mosque, July/August 1822.* Bibliothèque de l'Alcazar Marseilles, Fonds Coste, MS 1309, fol. 7d, 7c.

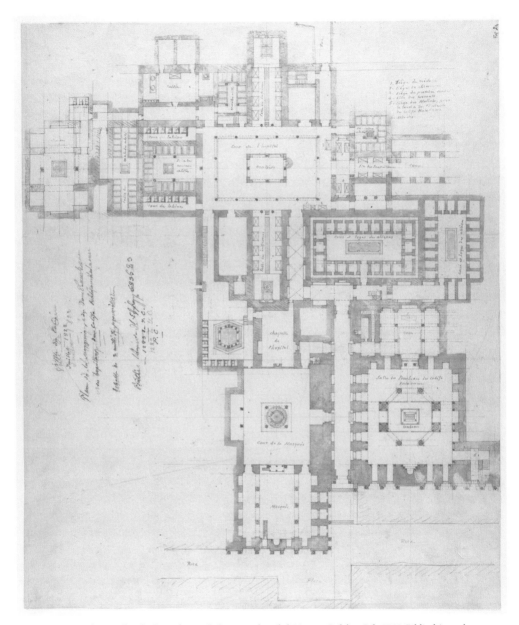

Figure 4.7: *Pascal Coste, fair drafting of ground plan, complex of al-Mansur Qala'un, July 1822.* Bibliothèque de l'Alcazar, Marseilles, Fonds Coste, MS 1309, fol. 24.

mosque, and *muristan* (hospital) complex of Sultan al-Mansur Qala'un, a densely organized cluster of rooms, combining representative, religious, and social functions behind a street façade with a length of over 35 metres.[39] When Coste worked at the complex in July 1822, he divided the building based on its functions and drew, for instance, the hospital section separately in his first sketches of the ground plan.[40] He later combined those parts for the detailed final drawing of the entire building's plan, which eventually also served as a template for the publication in *Architecture arabe* [Figure 4.7].[41] Compared to more modern ground plans of the same building, it is remarkable how carefully Coste captures its dimensions down to the smallest details [Figure 4.8].

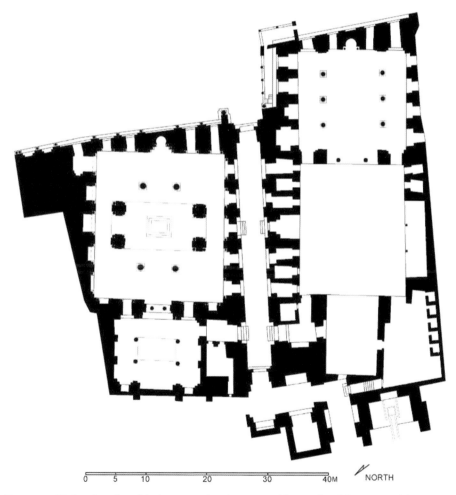

Figure 4.8: *Modern floor plan of the funerary and madrasa wing of the complex of al-Mansur Qala'un.* Nasser Rabbat / Aga Khan Program for Islamic Architecture, MIT. Drawing: Saeed Arida, 2003 (after M. Meinecke).

Figure 4.9: *Pascal Coste, fair drafting of street façade, complex of al-Mansur Qala'un, 1822 (left part, original drawing cropped).* Bibliothèque de l'Alcazar, Marseilles, Fonds Coste, MS 1309, fol. 25a.

Yet, it is equally striking how he forcibly adjusts several angles, particularly in the layout of the funerary wing, to fit the entire structure into an orthogonal system of right angles, seeking to define square and rectangular shapes as a kind of basic module that helps him to understand and represent it by purporting a rational matrix to a non-orthogonal system. His rendition of the street façade reflects the same approach, as he shows it in a very regular manner, using the street's direction as an axis for the drawing's central perspective, thereby also creating the impression of a boulevard rather than a narrow, irregular street [Figure 4.9].[42] It is also noteworthy that he chose a point of view that omits the entire

Drawing Knowledge, (Re-)Constructing History: Pascal Coste in Egypt

Figure 4.10: *Complex of al-Mansur Qala'un, street façade.* Ashmolean Museum of Art and Archaeology, K.A.C. Creswell Archive, Negative No.: EA.CA.4581.

madrasa complex, the part that protrudes significantly onto the street level to the left side of the entrance gate. Doris Behrens-Abouseif has pointed out that this building is '[…] the earliest Mamluk example to demonstrate an articulated urban aesthetic'.[43] The staggered character of the façade is an important and deliberate feature of this aesthetic, even more so as the building project was intended as an explicit response to the pre-existing structures on the opposite side of the street, the mausoleum of al-Salih Najm al-Din Ayyub (1250) and the early Mamluk madrasa of Sultan al-Zahir Baybars (1263).[44] Against this background, Coste's choice of perspective and standpoint is even more interesting, particularly when compared to modern photographs of the same site. These are usually taken from the roof of the opposite building, as it is almost impossible to take in the entire façade from street level due to lack of space [Figure 4.10].

Coste solved this problem by literally re-interpreting the entire ensemble as a vision of modernized urban space.[45] Here it becomes obvious how the draughtsman's method of understanding, measuring, and representing his subject automatically involves interpretation, or at least a symptomatic revelation of his own, very modern epistemic preconditions. It is not surprising that Coste's work was regarded highly by representatives of the rationalist French theory of architecture such as Eugène-Emmanuel Viollet-le-Duc (1814–79) and Jules Bourgoin (1838–1908) during later decades of the century.[46]

Drawing 'Aimed at Construction'

Joachim Rees has analyzed the fundamental function of drawing as a cross-cultural epistemological technique during the post-enlightenment age. He describes the paradigm of reportage through lines, as it were: the technique of drawing defines and expresses a set of rules governing knowledge. Accordingly, it submits 'foreign' objects and aesthetics to the gaze of an established, culturally and socially codified apparatus of visual categories. Through these categories, the object is primarily translated, i.e., reported, into the visual language of the modern, educated Western recipient. Rees develops his argument mainly with regard to travelogues, while taking into account the different levels of sophistication between dilettante and professional drawings.[47] In Coste's case this goes even further, confirming the autonomous professional function of drawing as a means of grasping, understanding, analyzing, and ultimately also shaping the world. This aim to establish knowledge for a wider audience is confirmed by the publication of the *Architecture arabe* as a condensed product of Coste's extensive drawing campaign, which he obviously considered to be a fundamental contribution to a universal history of architecture.

Yet we should not forget the practical purpose that was behind his entire approach to the Muslim architecture of Egypt. Coste's primary tasks in Egypt were of a more technical and infrastructural kind and his detailed examination of historical Arab architecture was initially prompted by the commission to design two new mosques for Cairo and Alexandria.

Hence, the drawings discussed here can certainly be considered as 'drawings aimed at construction',[48] that is, preparatory studies for new designs and not just documentation. What we witness in Coste's work is an early example of active reinterpretation of heritage, pointing towards an actual reshaping of a new architectural style, of urban spaces, and thus of the modern image of Egypt, be it in more nationalist or culturalist terms.

Looking mainly at the religious commissions of Coste, Nasser Rabbat has also hinted at this connection between historiographic and applied aspects in the architect's work: 'The two designs for the mosques in fact reveal how Coste, with a concern for symmetry and clarity characteristic of his architectural background, manages to synthesize and order a basic vocabulary for a neo-Mamluk style.'[49] Indeed, if we consider, for example, the mosque plans for Alexandria (which ultimately remained unrealized) [Figures 4.11 and 4.12],[50] these show a clear rectangular concept of space, derived from a basic square module, which results in a symmetrical composition of ground plan and main façade – a representative building that draws upon traditional elements such as the hypostyle prayer hall or the ribbed dome, while at the same time shaping and demanding the surroundings of an urban space organized according to modern principles.

Eventually, however, all this must be seen not only in light of a general rationalist aesthetic zeitgeist, but also in the context of Coste's more practical projects and their technical implications. He came to Egypt as an engineer, equipped with the contemporary toolbox of the topographic surveyor. His use of instruments, such as the plumb line, goniometer, and spirit level, points even more clearly to his way of grasping and understanding architecture in terms of regularity in space and measurement.[51]

A most interesting case in point, particularly against the background of his 1822 rendition of the *muristan* complex of Qala'un, is the design for a military hospital in Alexandria, ordered by Muhammad Ali in August 1826 [Figure 4.13].[52] It was part of a larger campaign for the improvement of public health, a reform project supervised by another French expert in Egypt, Antoine Clot-Bey (1793–1868).[53] The façades of the hospital again combine typical elements of the neo-Mamluk style, combined into a silhouette of arches, domes, and towers or minarets. Behind these façades, Coste envisaged the layout of a *castrum*-like structure on an almost square ground plan, its strict symmetry allowing for a clearly marked division between a '*Quartier des Mahometans*' and a '*Quartier des Européens*'. Again, the square and the right angle appear as principles of order, almost evoking the image of an ideal city behind the historicizing walls. The design thus combines the traditional image with a firm modernist and rationalizing resolution. Considering the function of this building as a hospital, which implies notions of social order and even control, it may even suggest a Foucauldian interpretation, thus turning it into a paradigmatically modern category of architectural space.[54]

This example renders the notion of the drawing as a contact zone particularly tangible: not just as a contact zone between the aesthetic heritage of the country and the modern draughtsman's gaze, but, in a more practical sense, a contact zone between 'eastern' and 'western' social orders and their mutually developing relations to tradition and modernism.

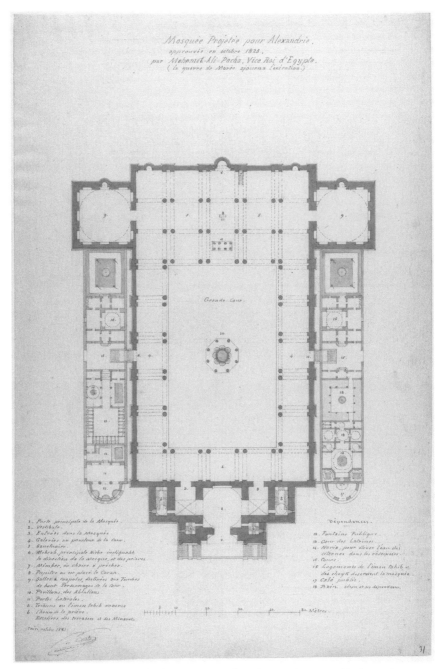

Figure 4.11: *Pascal Coste, floor plan for a mosque in Alexandria, October 1825.* Bibliothèque de l'Alcazar, Marseilles, Fonds Coste, MS 1306, fol. 31.

Figure 4.12: *Pascal Coste, main façade for a mosque in Alexandria, October 1825.* Bibliothèque de l'Alcazar, Marseilles, Fonds Coste, MS 1306, fol. 33.

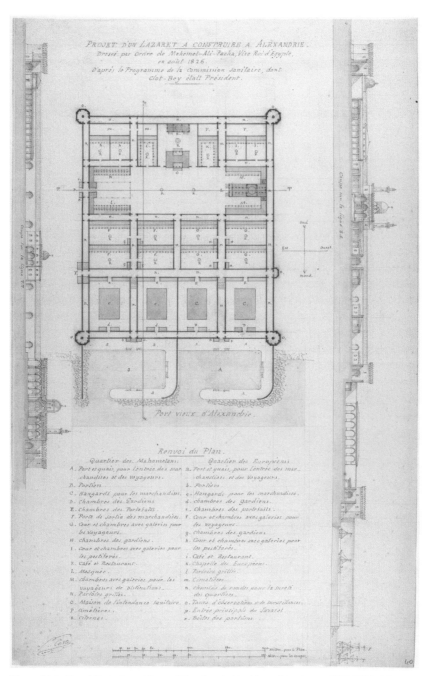

Figure 4.13: *Pascal Coste, layout for a military hospital in Alexandria, August 1826.* Bibliothèque de l'Alcazar, Marseilles, Fonds Coste, MS 1306, fol. 40.

It thus epitomizes in a paradigmatic manner the possibilities, as well as the limits, of cultural exchange at this stage of the imperial age.

Conclusion: Beyond Medievalism, Outside Orientalism?

In short, the final question remains: is Coste's work informed by a formally anti-romantic and anti-picturesque Orientalism, albeit a strictly Eurocentric one in its methods and definitions, that submits Egypt and its Arab culture to 'rational' Western criteria of perception? While these epistemic aspects are evident, this chapter suggests that Coste's agency at the same time transcends mere notions of asymmetric Orientalism. In fact, this case may hold exemplary potential for shedding light on often-neglected aspects of modernity within a history of the larger Mediterranean world.[55]

However, this dimension can only be understood by at least sketching a larger historical horizon as a backdrop to Coste's expertise: the presence of Western, particularly French, experts in Egypt during the reign of Muhammad Ali was part of an ambivalent, if strongly progressive project. Muhammad Ali was keen on developing economic and military strength. This was a means of consolidating and legitimating his domestic power, and at the same time underlined his claim to cultural and actual leadership and emancipation, in relation to the Ottoman Empire, but also as a message to the world at large.[56]

In this context, it is more than just trivial that Coste was also responsible for setting up the first telegraph line between Alexandria and Cairo, thus linking the rising Arab metropolis with the larger Mediterranean world through a modern means of communication.[57] Evidently, even as early as the first decades of the nineteenth century, Egypt should not be considered passively on the 'receiving end' of civilization, or of history, but rather actively communicating with modernity at large. The appropriation of knowledge and technique through the agency of Western experts was part of this communication process; the agency is thus a reciprocal one.[58]

In its active and applied aspects, Coste's agency as an expert links the historical perspective most tangibly to a genuine local, appropriative approach to progress and modernization.[59] In a way it thus also belongs to the immediate pre-history of a larger modern discussion, defining notions of cultural heritage within the Muslim world: during the nineteenth century, writers and thinkers of the Arab world developed reformist movements which still resonate even in late twentieth-century intellectual debates. In these discussions, the terms cultural heritage (*turath*) and authenticity (*asala*) are closely related to progress and contemporaneity (*muasara*).[60] Whatever the precise connection or dialectic between these concepts may be in detail, a process-based understanding of history is a basic precondition, just as the essentially material reassessment of historical architecture went hand-in-hand with the construction of modern mosques and representative buildings as well as factories and infrastructure. In this sense, the Arab revivalism introduced in Egypt by Muhammad Ali and through the agency of Pascal Coste is literally kindred to contemporary European historicism – though not in a derivative sense. It is not to be considered in terms of nostalgia, but rather as a symptom of the present in a universally historicizing age characterized by an active and at times even utopian re-interpretation of the past.

This illustrates that modernism, evolving dialectically from the variations of romanticism, is not an exclusively European phenomenon. This kind of historicism is not a retarding counter-movement to progress. It is, rather, a practical form of what Jörn Rüsen has described as 'functional teleology of historical thinking', defining a historical master narrative as a means of orientation for the present and future.[61]

Notes

1. Pascal-Xavier Coste, *Mémoires d'un Artiste. Notes et Souvenirs de Voyages (1817–1877). Egypte, Le Rhin, Hollande, Belgique, Sicile, Grèce, Turquie, Perse, Babylone (Mésopotamie), Syrie, Angleterre, Algérie, Maroc, Suisse, Italie, Allemagne, Espagne, Danemark, Norwège, Suède, Finlande, Russie et la France* (Marseilles: 1878), vol. 1, 30. The original reads: '[…] ordre était prescrit à tous les chefs des mosquées, de me laisser circular, mesurer et dessiner dans l'interieur comme à l'exterieur de ces monuments, et me donner protection à l'encontre de ceux qui s'y opposeraient. Muni de ce firman, je commencai à visiter toutes les mosquées du Caire et du Vieux-Caire. Je me fixai sur les huit principales, les plus importantes par leur caractère architectural du type arabe.' The relevant passage for Egypt is reprinted in Dominique Jacobi, ed., *Pascal Coste, Toutes les Égypte* (Marseilles: Parenthèses, 1998), 30-48.
2. Pascal-Xavier Coste, *Architecture arabe ou monuments du Kaire: mesurés et dessinés, de 1818 à 1825* (Paris: Hachette, 1937).
3. Daniel Armogathe and Sylviane Leprun, eds, *Pascal Coste ou l'architecture cosmopolite* (Paris: L'Harmattan, 1990).
4. Jacobi, ed., *Pascal Coste*; a number of the images referred to in this essay were published for the first time in this catalogue.
5. See Eugène-Napoleon Flandin, *Voyage en Perse de MM. Eugène Flandin, peintre et Pascal Coste, architecte … pendant les années 1840 et 1841: Relation du voyage*, 2 vols (Paris: Hachette, 1937).
6. See, e.g. Mercedes Volait, 'History or Theory? French Antiquarianism, Cairene Architecture and Enlightenment Thinking', *Ars Orientalis* 39 (2010): 231-54, esp. 244-48.
7. See Doris Behrens-Abouseif and Stephen S. Vernoit, eds., *Islamic Art in the 19th Century: Tradition, Innovation and Eclecticism* (Leiden: Brill, 2006). Here Mercedes Volait introduces Pascal Coste's mosque projects as forerunners to some of the later neo-Mamluk currents in nineteenth-century Cairo: Mercedes Volait, 'Appropriating Orientalism? Saber Sabri's Mamluk Revivals in Late-Nineteenth-Century Cairo', in Behrens-Abouseif and Vernoit, eds, *Islamic Art*, 131-55, esp. 131. One of the earliest discussions of this issue based on the evidence of visual material is Nasser Rabbat, 'The Formation of the Neo-Mamluk Style in Modern Egypt', in Martha Pollack, ed., *The Education of the Architect. Historiography, Urbanism, and the Growth of Architectural Knowledge* (Cambridge, MA: MIT Press, 1997), 363-86, on Coste esp. 368-373; Rabbat refers to primary archive material published in a

dissertation by Kara Marietta Hill, 'Pascal-Xavier Coste (1787-1879): A French Architect in Egypt', Ph.D. diss. (Massachusetts Institute of Technology, 1998), accessed March 15, 2015, http://dspace.mit.edu/handle/1721.1/13091. See also Nezar AlSayyad, Irene A. Bierman, and Nasser O. Rabbat, eds, *Making Cairo Medieval* (Oxford: Lexington Books, 2005), and particularly the chapter: Caroline Williams, 'Nineteenth-Century Images of Cairo: From the Real to the Interpretative', 95-124, on Coste's drawing methods, 97-99. Paula Sanders briefly refers to Coste with regard to a medievalist paradigm of Egyptian historicism: Paula Sanders, *Creating Medieval Cairo. Empire, Religion, and Architectural Preservation in Nineteenth-Century Egypt* (New York: American University in Cairo Press, 2008), esp. 56. Donald Reid includes Coste in his short chapter on 'Neo-Islamic Architecture', describing the applied aspects of the architect's design more as part of an Arab revival distinct from the dominating focus on the Pharaonic heritage of the country: Donald Malcolm Reid, *Whose Pharaohs? Archaeology, Museums, and Egyptian National Identity from Napoleon to World War I* (Berkeley, Los Angeles, London: University of California Press, 2002), esp. 239-42.

8 See e.g. Margaret S. Graves, 'Feeling Uncomfortable in the Nineteenth Century', in *Journal of Art Historiography* 6 (2012), accessed March 15, 2015, http://arthistoriography.wordpress.com/number-6-june-2012-2/.

9 Dieter Haller, 'The Cosmopolitan Mediterranean: Myth and Reality', *Zeitschrift für Ethnologie* 129.1 (2004): 29-47, on the anti-nostalgic notion as a necessary reaction to 'banal Mediterraneanism' esp. 32.

10 Edmund Burke III, 'Toward a Comparative History of the Modern Mediterranean, 1750–1919', *Journal of World History* 23.4 (2012): 907-39, esp. 911.

11 For a critical summary of the historiography of the modern Mediterranean, see Leila Tarazi Fawaz and C. A. Bayly, 'Introduction: The Connected World of Empires', in Leila Tarazi Fawaz and C. A. Bayly, eds, *Modernity & Culture. From the Mediterranean to the Indian Ocean* (New York: Columbia University Press, 2002), on the role of area studies and the dependista paradigm, 5–6. Especially for the field of Islamic art history, 'Mediterraneanism' is often still considered a pre-modern phenomenon; see e.g. the discussion by Mariam Rosser-Owen, 'Mediterraneanism. How to Incorporate Islamic Art into an Emerging Field', *Journal of Art Historiography* 6 (2012), accessed March 15, 2015, http://arthistoriography.wordpress.com/number-6-june-2012-2/.

12 See Haller, 'Cosmopolitan Mediterranean', 29.

13 Hamid Dabashi, *Post-Orientalism: Knowledge and Power in Time of Terror* (New Brunswick and London: Transaction Publishers, 2009); for a perspective on mutual agencies within the history of what has commonly been labelled 'Orientalism', particularly considering French-Arab relations, see also Francois Pouillon and Jean-Claude Vatin, eds, *Après l'Orientalisme. L'Orient crée par l'Orient* (Paris: IISMM-Karthala, 2011).

14 See esp. Mercedes Volait, 'Les monuments de l'architecture arabe', in *Pascal Coste*, ed. Jacobi, 97-130.

15 I thank Corinne Prévost and Thierry Conti at the Bibliothèque del Alcazar in Marseilles for making the material accessible to me. On the condition and preservation of the entire stock see Dominique Jacobi, 'La Collection "Pascal Coste" à la Bibliothèque Municipale de Marseille', in *Pascal Coste*, ed. Jacobi, 17-18.

16 Signatures MSS 1306 to MSS 1311.
17 Jacobi, *La Collection Pascal Coste*, 17.
18 Although in some cases I found the margins of the drawings cropped, cutting off small parts of the annotations or dates but typically leaving the month and year, though not the day of a drawing's execution. It is not clear whether these interventions were the work of Coste himself or occurred at a later stage.
19 It is important to note that Coste's own emphasis was on the use of the term 'Arabe', which especially during the nineteenth century could have racist undertones, but can also imply an affirmative culturalist notion that includes yet at the same time transcends the religious connotation. As it is the scope of my chapter to inscribe the agency of Coste into the modern image of an Islamic or Islamicate Middle East, I deliberately use the term 'Muslim' with a civilizational connotation – of course bearing in mind the necessary critical terminological and conceptual distinctions as described by Avinoam Shalem, 'What Do We Mean When We Say "Islamic Art"?' An Urgent Plea for a Critical Re-Writing of the Arts of Islam', *Journal of Art Historiography* 6 (2012), special issue, 'Islamic Art Historiography', eds Moya Carey and Margaret S. Graves, accessed 15 March 2015, http://arthistoriography.wordpress.com/number-6-june-2012-2/.
20 On the chronology of his working process see Volait, 'Les monuments de l'architecture arabe'.
21 MS 1308, fol 68; similar observations can be made with regard to a drawing of the so-called 'Obelisk of Cleopatra' which he executed two days earlier, extensively studying its proportions and entasis: MS 1308, fol 70. See also Jacobi, ed., *Pascal Coste*, 43; Coste's studies of classical capitals dated between November 1817 and January 1818, MS 1308 fol 63.
22 This certainly has to be considered in the context of the Egyptomania incited by the French campaign of 1798-1801, and the related project of the *Déscription de l'Egypte*, which mostly focused on the country's ancient heritage. On the pillar and the early nineteenth-century discussion regarding its date and meaning, see also Anon., 'Pompey's Pillar', *The North-American Review and Miscellaneous Journal* 3.8 (1816): 192-94.
23 See Anne Jouve, "Un Témoin de la Vie Quotidienne," in Jacobi, ed., *Pascal Coste*, 189-218.
24 See e.g. MS 1307, fol 38, which brings together three drawings executed between 1819-1821.
25 MS 1307, fol 50.
26 MS 1307, fol 58.
27 MS 1311, fol 34.
28 MS 1311, fol 32.
29 See e.g. MS 1311, fol 20. Though it should be noted that a small number of rather detailed plans of mosques are also dated as early as 1818, see e.g. a plan of Barquq mosque, MS 1309, fol 13.
30 The classical historiographic account of Muhammad Ali's reign from a contemporary Egyptian perspective can be found in the *History of Egypt* written by Abd al-Rahman al-Jabarti; the English translation: Jane Hathaway, ed., *Al-Jabarti's History of Egypt* (Princeton, NJ: Markus Wiener Publishers, 2009), esp. 245-345. An important critical reassessment of the common 'nationalist' reading of Muhammad Ali's reign is to be found in Khaled Fahmy,

All the Pasha's Men: Mehmed Ali, His Army and the Making of Modern Egypt (Cambridge: Cambridge University Press, 1997).

31 Coste, *Mémoires d'un Artiste,* 29.
32 Ibid., 30: 'Je lui fis remarquer que ne connaissant pas l'interieur de ces monuments et n'étant pas initié aux cérémonies religieuses, je lui ferais plutôt une église qu'une mosquée, et qu'il était urgent qu'il me permît de les visiter.'
33 Ibid., 30–31: 'Je me fixai sur les huit principales, les plus importantes par leur caractère architectural du type arabe.' He also specifies the names and – in some case tentative – dates for those buildings: '"Ces mosquées étaient celles d'Amrou", 613 de J.-C.; Touloum, 876; El-Azhar, 981; Barkauk, 1149; Kalaoun, 1296; Hassan, 1370; El-Mouaied, 1415; et Kaitbai, 1463'.
34 For surveys of medieval architecture in Cairo see: Doris Behrens-Abouseif, *Islamic Architecture in Cairo: An Introduction* (Leiden: Brill, 1989); Doris Behrens-Abouseif, *Cairo of the Mamluks: A History of the Architecture and its Culture* (London and New York: I.B.Tauris, 2007); Jonathan Bloom, *Arts of the City Victorious: Islamic Art and Architecture in Fatimid North Africa and Egypt* (New Haven, CT and London: Yale University Press, 2007).
35 The *Déscription de l'Egypte* includes several mosques and medieval buildings under the category '*Etat Moderne*' as opposed to the project's focus on ancient Egypt – yet, the descriptions and pictorial representations of these buildings are very general and emphasize the dilapidated state of Egypt, which was considered a consequence of the decay associated with Muslim societies during the imperial age. On the intellectual context of the *Déscription* and its genesis, see e.g., Jed Z. Buchwald and Diane Greco Josefowicz, *The Zodiac of Paris: How and Improbable Controversy over an Ancient Egyptian Artifact Provoked a Modern Debate between Religion and Science* (Princeton, NJ and Oxford: Princeton University Press, 2010). A professional interest in Islamic art and architecture only began to arise towards the turn of the twentieth century. See e.g., Stephen S. Vernoit, ed., *Discovering Islamic Art: Scholars, Collectors and Collections 1850–1950* (London: I.B.Tauris, 2000); *Journal of Art Historiography* 6 (2012), Carey and Graves eds.
36 For the mosque of Ibn Tulun, see e.g., Doris Behrens-Abouseif, *Islamic Architecture in Cairo: An Introduction* (Leiden: Brill, Supplements to Muqarnas III, 1989), 51–57.
37 MS 1309, fol. 4c.
38 MS 1309, fol. 7d, 7c.
39 See Behrens-Abouseif, *Cairo of the Mamluks*, 132-42.
40 MS 1309, fol. 26a, see also Volait, 'Les monuments de l'architecture arabe', 125.
41 MS 1309, fol 24. Compare Coste, *Architecture arabe*, pl. XV.
42 MS 1309, fol. 25b.
43 Behrens-Abouseif, *Cairo of the Mamluks*, 134.
44 Ibid., 134.
45 See also Volait, 'Les monuments de l'architecture arabe', 123, who describes his drawings of buildings as 'schémas spatiaux donnant une image idéale'. It is also worth noting how this virtually corresponds to or, indeed, partakes of the trend of 'metropolization' that was to reshape Middle Eastern cities during the nineteenth century as part of an international process of urban renewal. For the West, David van Zanten has hinted at the larger context

of these modern urbanistic trends even towards the mid-nineteenth century, that is, before the often-quoted wave of 'Haussmanisation' in Paris; see David van Zanten, 'Mais Quand Haussmann est-il Devenu Moderne?' in *La Modernité avant Haussmann. Formes de l'espace urbain à Paris 1801–1853*, ed. Karen Bowie (Paris: Èditions Recherche 2001), 153-64.

46 Volait, 'Les monuments de l'architecture arabe', 128.
47 See e.g. Joachim Rees, 'Die verzeichnete Fremde (Auf-)Zeichnen, 1800-1900', *Melton Prior Institute*, online feature 04/06/2006, accessed September 28, 2014, http://www.meltonpriorinstitut.org/pages/textarchive.php5.
48 Cf. Jutta Voorhoeve, 'Technische Zeichenmanöver. Zeichnen und Schreiben als Verfahren der Konstruktion', in *Welten Schaffen*, ed. Jutta Voorhoeve (Zurich: diaphanes, 2011), 7-16, esp. 7-8.
49 Rabbat, 'Formation of the Neo-Mamluk Style', 369; on the mosque project for Alexandria esp. 371.
50 MS 1306, fol 31, 33.
51 Claude Jasmin, 'Le Premier Ingenieur de l'Egypte Contemporaine', in *Pascal Coste*, ed. Jacobi, 71-96; on the technical devices, esp. 'Les Instruments de Coste', 76-77. On the variety of infrastructural projects by Coste, see also: Denise Jasmin, 'Les Dessins d'Architecture Civile', in *Pascal Coste*, ed. Jacobi, 131-62.
52 MS 1306, fol 40.
53 Rémy Kertenian, 'L'Oeuvre de Clot-Bey Médecin Marseillais', in *Pascal Coste*, ed. Jacobi, 235-44.
54 Michel Foucault, *Naissance de la clinique: une archéologie du regard medical* (Paris: Presses Universitaires de France, 1963); see also Peter Burke, *A Social History of Knowledge: From the Encyclopédie to Wikipedia*, vol. II (Cambridge: Polity Press, 2012), 188. This is also interesting in relation to the paradigm of (spatial) order, which Timothy Mitchell sees at work throughout Egypt's modernization process in the nineteenth century: Timothy Mitchell, *Colonising Egypt* (Berkeley, CA: University of California Press 1988).
55 Burke III, 'Toward a Comparative History', 911.
56 A recent essay by Marwa el Ashmouni and Katharine Bartsch only came to my attention during the final stage of editing: Marwa el Ashmouni and Katherine Bartsch: 'Egypt's Age of Transition: Unintentional Cosmopolitanism and during the reign of Muhammad Ali (1805–1848)', *Arab Studies Quarterly* 36.1 (2014): 43–74. As opposed to my argument, el Ashmouni and Bartsch largely discard the significance of Mamluk architecture for Muhammad Ali – but they provide an interesting interpretation of the cosmopolitan character of his rule, of historicist architecture and the role of non-Egyptian architects and craftsmen for the prefiguration of what later was to become the most important Middle Eastern metropolis.
57 Emile Temime, 'Rêves Méditerranéens et Présence Francaise en Orient au Milieu du XIXe Siècle', in *L'Orientalisme des Saint-Simoniens*, ed. Michel Levallois and Sarga Moussa (Paris: Maisonneuve et Larose, 2006), 19-31, on Coste, esp. 23.
58 For a larger perspective on this see Ghislaine Alleaume, 'Les Techniciens Européens dans l'Égypte de Muhammad Ali (1805-1848)', *Cahiers de la Méditerranée* 84 (2012): 185-95.
59 Temime, 'Rêves méditerranéens', esp. 22. See also Rabbat, 'Formation of the Neo-Mamluk Style', 373.

60 I am mainly referring to Stefan Winkler, 'Cultural Heritage – Authenticity – Tradition: On the Origin of the Exhibition's Title 'Mustaqbal al-asala – Asala(t) al-mustaqbal' (The Future of Authenticity – The Authenticity of the Future) in Contemporary Arab Discourse', in *The Future of Tradition – The Tradition of Future: 100 Years after the Exhibition Masterpieces of Muhammadan Art in Munich*, Chris Dercon, León Krempel, and Avinoam Shalem, eds. (Munich: Prestel 2010), 52-59.
61 Jörn Rüsen, 'Kann gestern besser werden? Über die Verwandlung der Vergangenheit in Geschichte', *Geschichte und Gesellschaft* 28.2 (2002): 305-12, esp. 314.

Chapter 5

A Bourguibist Mural in the New Monastir? Zoubeïr Turki's Play on Knowledge, Power, and Audience Perception

Jessica Gerschultz

The Murals

In 1962, Zoubeïr Turki (1924–2009) painted the mural he called *La Procession des Mourabtines* (The Procession of the Murabitun) in a second-storey lobby of the new Hôtel Ribat in the coastal city of Monastir. It was one of two murals commissioned for the hotel's stylishly decorated communal spaces. Measuring 60 square metres, the work portrayed the historic annual procession of the *murabitun* (volunteer warriors) and guardians of the faith in Tunisia's early Islamic history, in their dramatic march from Monastir's landmark Islamic monument, the eighth century *ribat* (a coastal fortification with military and religious functions) [Figure 5.1]. In the foreground, a group of sixteen stylized male figures of various ages appear with drums, horns, weapons, banners, and horses. Additional silhouettes in the background attest to the event's magnitude and exuberance. Executed in bold, flat colours, the figurative painting enlivened the hall's crisp whitewashed walls and sleek modern furnishings.

Turki executed a second mural, the *Ballet de l'Olive* (Olive Ballet), in an adjacent salon overlooking a seafront terrace. In this composition, four young women harvest olives as if in a dance, employing their sieves as drums [Figure 5.2]. Trees emulate the figures' gestures, and, in Turki's words, take on the forms of admiring cavaliers.[1] Not only do olives constitute a staple of Tunisian cuisine, but the fruit and its oil also commanded a significant place in the nation's agricultural production at the pinnacle of state-enforced collectivization. Partially visible in an early tourist brochure, the olive grove's bright colours complemented the verdant green and orange décor [Figure 5.3]. The scene's pairing with Danish teak furniture and patterned rugs woven in the newly reorganized National Office of Handicraft created an ambience of sophistication while retaining an essential *tunisianité*.

Like many murals designed by artists of the Ecole de Tunis, a prestigious group of Tunisian, French, and Italian painters committed to the articulation of a specifically Tunisian modernism, these two scenes are no longer extant. Ten years after its construction and three years after the official denouncement of Tunisian socialism, the Hôtel Ribat was demolished in 1972 to accommodate a shopping centre [Figure 5.4]. A handful of archival photographs testify to the murals' relationship to Monastir's architectural and political landscape under the bold reforms of the Parti Socialiste Dusturien (PSD). While some attention will be paid to the *Ballet de l'Olive*, this chapter focuses on hierarchies of expertise embedded in the creation of *La Procession des Mourabtines*. The work's iconography, position, and patronage are particularly salient evocations of the contentious relationships of power that underwrote the emergent artisanal and tourism industries during the decade of Tunisian socialism

Figure 5.1: *Hall of the Hôtel Ribat in Monastir with mural* La Procession des Mourabtines *by artist Zoubeïr Turki, 1962.* Gilbert Van Raepenbusch; Fonds Beit el-Bennani.

Figure 5.2: *Beachfront lounge of the Hôtel Ribat in Monastir with the mural* Ballet de l'Olive *by artist Zoubeïr Turki and textiles by the Office National de l'Artisanat, 1962.* Gilbert Van Raepenbusch; Fonds Beit el-Bennani.

A Bourguibist Mural in the New Monastir?

Figure 5.3: *Beachfront lounge of the Hôtel Ribat in Monastir with the mural* Ballet de l'Olive *by artist Zoubeïr Turki and textiles by the Office National de l'Artisanat, 1962. Undated brochure of the Société des Hôtels Tunisiens Touristiques for the Hôtel Ribat, Monastir.* Semerano-Scarinci/Société des Hôtels Tunisiens Touristiques, Office National du Tourisme Tunisien.

Figure 5.4: *The Hôtel Ribat.* Gilbert Van Raepenbusch, 'Monastir and its Hotel Ribat', *Tourism in Tunisia* 10 (December 1961): 5.

(1961–69). Moreover, the construction of the Hôtel Ribat was part of the grander reconfiguration of Monastir, the birthplace of former president Habib Bourguiba. Remarkably, Turki portrayed Bourguiba leading a chain of *murabitun* from the *ribat*. The artist's dual reference to Islamic sacred geography and the president's burgeoning cult of personality speak to his intellectual engagement with the reframing of religious and cultural identities in a contested political economy.

With its various subtexts and ambiguities, the mural invites an interrogation of power and expertise in three concentric areas. Firstly, in its broader historical context, Turki's imagery provides a lens into the fraught environment of demarcating the terms of Islam and engendering modernity in postcolonial Tunisia. In the late 1950s and early 1960s, competing claims to religious and political expertise underpinned contested strategies of decolonization and nation building. Bourguiba, a French-trained lawyer, invoked his claim to *ijtihad*, a specialized practice of interpretation in Islamic law, in drafting his reforms, while members of the PSD drew up algorithms and charted mechanisms for driving economic growth. The assassination of the main opposition leader, the restructuring of religious institutions such as the *habus* (endowment system) and the Zaituna-Mosque University, and questionable agricultural reforms fuelled dissent.[2]

Secondly, Turki's mural was commissioned in a system of patronage that supported hierarchical scales of artistry and authorship. The polemics of modernization directly affected the discursive frameworks of art, while the artistic field shaped by leading artists, architects, and consultants in turn reinforced the power of the administrative elite. Thus, senior architects paired the decorative programmes of the Ecole de Tunis with reinvented 'traditional' designs produced in the pilot ateliers of the National Office of Handicraft, a feminized industry that employed 80 per cent women from low status backgrounds. This approach to design generated a system of patronage embedded in class and gender distinctions whereby lower-status, anonymous artisans executed the designs of elite artists, as well as smaller objects considered 'craft'. Moreover, the institutional framework for articulations of 'modern' art and architecture relied on the expertise of architects such as Olivier-Clément Cacoub (1920–2008), who was charged with transforming Monastir into a premier city and seat of the nascent tourism industry. Entwined in these efforts were artisanal consultants, directors, and artists, whose shaping of art taxonomies operated in tandem with Bourguibist strategies for socio-economic development.

Thirdly, *La Procession des Mourabtines* invites a discussion of audience reception, as its multi-valence played on both local and foreign tourists' conceptions of a folkloric past and Tunisians' awareness of Bourguiba as the '*combattant suprême*' (Supreme Combatant). In terms of its varied Tunisian audiences, however, the mural's ambiguities defied a straightforward nationalist or class-based reading. Those familiar with media propaganda, whether members of the administrative elite or low-class seasonal staff, would have recognized the president's profile at the head of the *murabitun*. Turki thus suspended, if just for a moment, the seamless analogy positing Bourguiba as the spiritual and moral authority at the 'frontiers' of modernity.

The President

Turki, like other artists of the Ecole de Tunis who enjoyed governmental patronage, negotiated competing claims to spiritual and political ascendancy arising with the shifting constructs of Bourguibism. As the comprehensive personal ideology and development model enforced by Tunisia's first president Habib Bourguiba (in office from 1956 until 1987), Bourguibism underpinned the single-party state's social, cultural, and economic programming in the early post-Independence period. Its attendant restructuring of religious institutions, which dismantled or absorbed existing judiciary, inheritance, and educational systems, effectively consolidated presidential power beneath the veneer of modernization.[3] Furthermore, such reforms were predicated on Bourguiba's personal convictions that he, above all others, possessed the authority to steer the country on the 'correct' path of development.

Shortly after Independence in 1956, Bourguiba eradicated the existing ownership and administration of public, private, and mixed *habus* properties in land reforms that granted more than 1,500,000 hectares of *habus* land to the state.[4] *Habus* lands were formerly incontrovertible properties set aside as pious trust to support religious and charitable institutions or designated heirs. Bourguiba next abolished the existing Islamic and Jewish courts to create a homogenous, national judicial system. He legislated the Personal Status Code on August 13, 1956, which annulled Islamic family law by overturning the supremacy of the extended paternal lineage in inheritance, marriage, and divorce.[5] Bourguiba's Ministry of Education implemented extensive reforms in 1958, financed by up to one-third of the national budget, to convert the mentalities of ordinary Tunisians lodged in 'decadent' religious traditions. Free public schooling was intended to transform the youth into a unified, modern citizenry.[6] The Zaituna Mosque-University, Tunis's renowned centre of higher Islamic learning, lost its structure and autonomy after its forced integration into the national education system.

In order to avoid the binary conception of Bourguiba, a French-trained lawyer, as being purely secularist, it is important to note that he cast himself as a great Muslim reformer.[7] According to his perspective, he did not eschew Islam in drafting his all-encompassing reforms. Rather, Bourguiba claimed to use *ijtihad*, an Islamic legal concept that refers to the exercise of independent judgment by someone possessing sufficient expertise in theology, revealed texts, and legal theory, as well as a sophisticated capacity for reasoning. In his speech on February 9, 1961, Bourguiba asserted that he correctly interpreted the Qur'an according to principles decreed by the Prophet in order to simplify and facilitate Tunisian religious practices.[8] He framed the reforms in terms of what his conscience and intellect compelled him to do in order to 'liberate' Tunisians from stagnation, avowing:

> For the man before you, in whom the people have placed their trust, is firmly convinced that it is not because of Islam that we have these shackles that impede our progress and paralyse our intelligence. I affirm this emphatically. As I know, as I have studied and learned, as the Prophet himself, his companions, his contemporaries and successors have lived and practised, Islam is not a doctrine of intellectual asphyxiation.[9]

In conjunction with his institutional changes, Bourguiba negotiated with those in religious office. As he did with ministers, however, Bourguiba shuffled Islamic scholars from the court system and the Zaituna into religious leadership positions, only later to dismiss them for protesting his legitimacy.

In 1960 and 1961, Bourguiba's speeches pleaded for a *jihad* against underdevelopment, particularly against the Ramadan fast. He argued that observance of the fast drastically hurt an already weak economy, stating that: 'It is the reason I do not cease to repeat that our fight to rescue this Islamic nation from the under-development inherited from epochs of decadence is no less valuable than the *jihad*'.[10] While the president's actions generated a range of responses, in the sacred city of Kairouan, the abhorrence of the *ulama* was manifested through violent public protests against a perceived usurpation of religious scholarship and law.

The terms delineating the Bourguibist vision of Islam and modernity were thus created, understood, enacted, and contested through complex and locally specific discourses, as notions of the 'modern' and 'Islamic' took on charged and variant meanings. The predominant scholarly narrative emphasizes the struggle over the authority to define these terms for Tunisians, which erupted between Bourguiba and Salah Ben Yusuf (1910–61), rival leaders in the Neo-Dustur party, in the 1950s. Ben Yusuf's popularity and pan-Arab, pan-Islamic approach to decolonization ultimately resulted in his assassination in 1961 and the subsequent repression of his supporters. Thereafter, dissent surrounding Bourguibist strategies for socio-economic development – their methods of implementation, inefficiencies, contradictions, and shortcomings – created avenues for further political contestation and estrangement nationwide. The repercussions of top-down 'secularist' and socialist reforms were particularly acute in rural areas, the city of Kairouan, and the depressed mining region of the southern interior as the Bourguibist exploitation of Tunisia's religious, agricultural, and mineral resources alienated vast swathes of society that did not accept the imposition of expertise by the administrative elite.[11] Turki's processional image of triumphant *murabitun*, as well as the imposing structure of Monastir's *ribat* in the city centre, functioned as mutable ideological spaces within this struggle for authority.

The Infrastructure of Art and Architecture

In conjunction with Bourguibist religious reform, the murals of the Hôtel Ribat must be read against the rubric of development and tourism in Monastir. As part of the sweeping campaign against underdevelopment, the administrative elite initiated a vast expansion of the tourism industry centered in the coastal Sahel.[12] In Tunisia, the term 'sahel' refers to the narrow strip of coastal plain between Tunis and Sfax. It boasted fine beaches, urban centres, and the highest concentration of olive production and commercial activity in the country. The government harnessed tourism in the Sahel for the purposes of modernization and the strengthening of economic relations with Europe. Aiming at the European yearning for sun-kissed beaches, policy makers crafted a sea-sun-and-sand Mediterranean orientation, de-emphasizing an Arab or Islamic identity that could be viewed as a deterrent to the Europeans who comprised roughly 80 per cent of visitors.[13] Tunisia's Islamic heritage was presented as slightly exotic, folkloric, and subordinate to state-sponsored activities.[14] For instance, the *mawlid* (celebrations dedicated to the birth of the Prophet Muhammad) festival in Kairouan was marketed as 'an established tradition […] with numerous events of religious and artistic interest, not to mention folklore, under the patronage of President Bourguiba'.[15] By the 1970s, the package tourism industry, reliant on stereotypes of tropical paradise, had become the largest source of national revenue (approximately one-fifth of the annual total). The economic dependency on transnational flows of tourists and investment capital, ironically built as part of a 'regime of regulation' during the period of Tunisian socialism, propelled subsidiary economic growth in the agricultural, service, and artisanal industries.[16] However, this growth accentuated the existing power bases of the coastal elite and taxed local resources, as the positioning of Tunisia in an expanding capitalist market for global tourism and 'international division of leisure' served to legitimize Bourguiba's authority at home and in Euro-America.

The tourism industry thus represented a vital component in the state's Ten-Year Plan. Engineered by Minister of Planning Ahmed Ben Salah (1926–), the plan galvanized the so-called development decade. It centred on the recovery, stabilization, and expansion of Tunisian industries in concert with the expansion of public education and improved standards of living. Built on socialist development projects endorsed by the Neo-Dustur party, the Ten-Year Plan was slated to be in effect until 1971.[17] During this time, the party altered its name to the Parti Socialiste Dusturien in 1964 to reflect its economic orientation. However, the socialist plan collapsed in 1969 over disputed agricultural cooperatives, and Ben Salah was imprisoned for treason. The Hôtel Ribat was constructed during the first phase of the Ten-Year Plan, the so-called Triennial Plan, which spanned the period from 1962 to 1964. The Triennial Plan served as a test-run for initiatives that encompassed state-managed tourism, artisanal production, agriculture, phosphates, and factory-made textiles.[18]

Concurrently, Monastir was the site of extensive construction. The president bestowed the task of reimagining the city on Cacoub, a Tunisian-born, French-trained Jewish architect, who remapped the urban centre to balance the old quarters with new infrastructure [Figure 5.5].[19] Drawing from the expertise of local master masons such as Amor Bouzguenda (1890–1983), Cacoub designed more than thirty spaces, including several hotels, two schools, the convention centre, artisanal showrooms, the stadium, the party office, the park, a branch office of the Banque Centrale, Bourguiba's marble palace, and his mosque-tomb complex.[20] The *ribat*, situated between the medina and shoreline, was renovated and integrated into the modernized touristic beachfront. The fortress served not only as a tourist attraction, but also as a theatrical stage for plays that conjured its historical legacy, such as the performance of *Son et lumière à Monastir* (Sound and Light in Monastir) in 1965, sponsored by the Secretariat of State for Cultural Affairs.[21] The presidential architect sought to reconcile Monastir's glorious past with its present significance as Bourguiba's birthplace, the 'cradle' of the Neo-Dustur party (established in the nearby village of Ksar Hellal), and the nascent

Figure 5.5: *Map of Monastir by presidential architect Olivier-Clément Cacoub.* Olivier-Clément Cacoub, 'Monastir: la neuve', *Carthage: Revue Trimestrielle Tunisienne* 3 (October–December 1965): 49.

tourism industry. In conjunction with shared initiatives between the Ecole des Beaux-Arts in Tunis and the National Office of Handicraft, Cacoub strove to reinvigorate Monastir with an architectural style that harmonized modern comfort with *tunisianité*. Such a balance was achieved through the decorative programmes of the Ecole de Tunis and the reinvented 'traditional' forms of the modernizing craft industry, known in Tunisia as the *artisanat*.

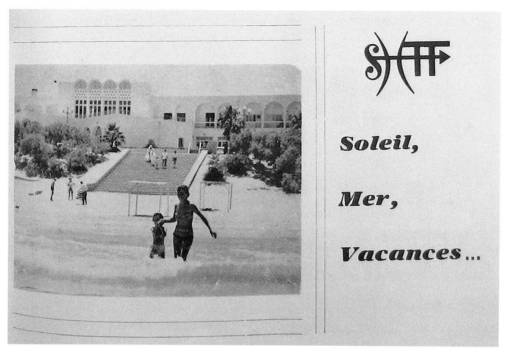

Figure 5.6: *Advertisement of the Société des Hôtels Tunisiens Touristiques showing the Hôtel Ribat, printed in* Femme, *the journal of the Union Nationale des Femmes Tunisiennes.* Femme 5 (1966): 69.

Concurrently with Cacoub's plan for the development of Monastir, the state-owned Société des Hôtels Tunisiens Touristiques (Tunisian Hotel and Tourism Society, or SHTT) constructed a series of hotels along the pristine Sahelian coastline of Monastir-Skanès in the early 1960s [Figure 5.6]. The SHTT was a public corporation established in 1959 to create a tourist infrastructure by building upscale hotels. SHTT hotels, which operated 90 per cent of all hotel capacity at this time, were strategically integrated into the evolving cultural and political landscape.[22] The Hôtel Ribat (built in 1960), located in the city centre, was one of four early enterprises decorated by the Ecole de Tunis, along with the Hôtel Esplanade (1961), the Hôtel les Palmiers (1961), and the Hôtel Skanès Palace (1964). In an undated SHTT brochure, a map of Tunisian tourist destinations signals the central prominence of Monastir-Skanès. Golden beams of light radiate outward from Monastir, connecting the city to the urban centres of Kairouan, Sousse, El Djem, and Mahdia [Figure 5.7]. As might be expected, the SHTT headquarters were in Monastir. Some officials in the National Tourist Office went so far as to delegate the city the second Capri.[23]

While boasting the newest luxury amenities, such as Danish furniture, Tunisian artisanal décor, modern heating, and a spacious dining room, the Hôtel Ribat claimed a historic

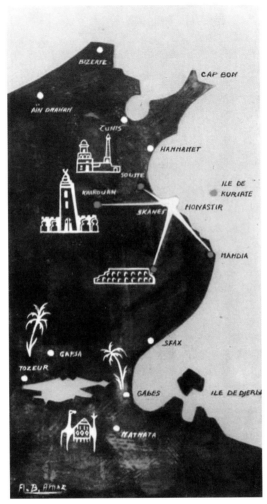

Figure 5.7: *Map of Tunisia featured in an undated brochure of the Société des Hôtels Tunisiens Touristiques for the Hôtel Ribat, Monastir.* Société des Hôtels Tunisiens Touristiques, Office National du Tourisme Tunisien.

link with Monastir's eighth-century *ribat*. *Tourism in Tunisia*, a publication of the National Tourist Office, lauded the hotel's connection to Monastir's Islamic history:

> The hotel is doubly privileged in the magnificent view it commands seaward and in the fact that it overlooks, or is overlooked by the Ribat fortress after which it has been named. The Ribat, dominating the entire town with its Mediaeval battlements, used once to be a combination of stronghold and convent for soldier-monks.[24]

Originally built in 795 CE by the Abbasid governor Harthama ibn Ayun, the *ribat* served both to defend against Byzantine incursions and to propagate Sunni Islam [Figure 5.8]. Continuously modified and expanded over the centuries, the fortress was part of a coastal warning system that safeguarded the North African interior (specifically Kairouan) and facilitated coastal commerce.[25] It was financed by Kairouani religious endowments until 1057 CE. Local hadiths attributed particular virtues to service rendered within the *ribat*. Slimane-Mostafa Zbiss, the Inspector of Historic Monuments in the early 1960s, cited one local hadith: 'three days garrison in Monastir begets access to Paradise'.[26] The bodies of members of the Zirid royal family and various Sufi saints were brought to Monastir for burial in the *ribat*'s vicinity, attracting pilgrims during Ramadan and 'Ashura. Trade, fishing, and agriculture sustained the pious population, whose purest olive oil reputedly lit the mosques of Mecca and Medina.[27] Until the nineteenth century, the *ribat* retained various military, economic, and religious functions. In Cacoub's rebuilding of Monastir, it served as a beacon of Islamic history and folklore for hotel clients and sunbathers a few hundred metres away [Figure 5.9].

Figure 5.8: *Photograph of the Monastir* ribat. Unknown photographer, 'The Sousse and Monastir Ribats', *Tourism in Tunisia* 8 (July 1961): 11.

Figure 5.9: *The beach of the Hôtel Ribat with the historic* ribat *in the background.* Unknown photographer, 'La Tunisie: Pays à facettes', *La Revue Française* 244 (July–August 1971): 12.

Turki's commission to paint a scene of the *ribat* in its namesake hotel came as artists of the Ecole de Tunis capitalized on orders to decorate the new tourism infrastructure. In 1962, the same year that Ben Salah implemented the Ten-Year Plan, the government reinstated the so-called '1% law'. This law mandated that 1 per cent of the budget for a new public building, including SHTT hotels, must be designated for its decoration by artist-designers whose approaches initially followed those found in the Ecoles des Arts in France.[28] Inherited from the French Protectorate, the law first took effect in 1950 after two members of the Ecole de Tunis, Pierre Boucherle (1895–1988) and Yahia Turki (c.1901–69), pushed for increased government patronage for Tunisia's 'professional artists'.[29] A committee of Ecole de Tunis artists, colonial architects, engineers, and bureaucrats determined commissions for decorative programmes that included murals, tapestries, ceramic tile panels, and stone fountains, with the senior architect appointed as chief director.[30] Between 1962 and 1969, most new construction fell under the purview of approximately 160 state-run enterprises, which led to the commission of Ecole de Tunis artworks in numerous facilities: SHTT hotels, banks, post offices, schools, conference centres, refineries, and other civic edifices. To manage this demand, Ecole de Tunis artists Safia Farhat (1924–2004) and Abdelaziz Gorgi (1928–2008) established the Société Zin in 1963. They, along with Turki, Jellal Ben Abdallah (1921–2017), and Ali Bellagha (1924–2006), designed an array of monumental works through this enterprise, frequently using artisanal materials: tapestries, ceramic tile panels, bas-reliefs, mosaic murals, and obelisks.[31] Often executed with the assistance of artisans whose expertise and contributions have been marginalized or undocumented, these works were seen to synthesize modern design and an authentic *tunisianité*, imbuing new venues with tasteful artistry.[32]

In tandem with the growth of tourism, the National Office of Handicraft was itself undergoing vast reorganization. The hotel industry served as client, ordering artisanal products for the dining halls, lounges, lobbies, and rooms of new hotels. Rugs, blankets, ceramic ware, ashtrays, and birdcages were among the various items purchased by hotels, while some hotels also sold artisanal wares in their gift shops.[33] To assist with the establishment of a new system of pilot ateliers that fulfilled the demand for artisanal work, the French tapestry artist Jean Lurçat (1892–1966) visited Tunisia as a senior consultant for the state *artisanat*.[34] Habib Bourguiba, Jr solicited Lurçat, a global figure in the modernist movement to revive tapestry, for his conceptual expertise and technical support.[35] Appearing in various Tunisian publications, including *Tourism in Tunisia*, Lurçat avowed that his overall impression of the *artisanat* was favourable.[36] However, in order to advance the industry, he advocated for 'traditional' artisans to move beyond what he perceived to be the cycle of repetitive forms prescribed by Islam. While acknowledging the role of Islamic artistry in the general history of art, he described it as stunted, admonishing that an art that did not move with the times would cease to be an art.[37] Recapitulations of this view circulated among Bourguibist officials, who asserted that the *artisanat* was in dire need of specialists drawn from the upper class: 'modern' artist-designers trained in the Beaux-Arts were thus sought to guide a 'stagnant' industry.[38] As one article published by the National Tourist Office stated, 'Traditional models, often decadent ones, continued to be slavishly reproduced [which] brought artisanship to a standstill'.[39] Lurçat's grim perception of what he called 'Saracen' art dovetailed with Bourguibist attitudes toward certain 'decadent' Islamic religious and cultural traditions deemed stifling to economic advancement and public health.

In addition to Turki's murals depicting Monastir's historic procession from the *ribat* to the idyllic olive groves in its vicinity, the Hôtel Ribat commissioned a monumental tapestry from the Gafsa ateliers of the National Office of Handicraft. A brief description of its production highlights the messy and hierarchical employment of art terminology among Tunisian administrators, who assigned taxonomies such as 'modern', 'traditional', and 'Islamic' to class and gender-based tiers of expertise or perceived lack thereof. As a renowned centre for women's weaving, Gafsa and its rural environs were targeted by the National Office of Handicraft, which employed mostly women, for the modernization of women's 'traditional' high-warp textiles. Sent by their fathers to weave in newly inaugurated state-run cooperatives, thousands of young, unmarried women from the lower classes entered the low-wage economy on terms that did not fundamentally alter the Tunisian 'personality', as historically most women wove in the home.[40] In a 1963 interview with the Tunisian newspaper *La Presse*, artisanal director Hamida Ben Naceur discussed his renewal of a 'dying' industry, using as his culminating example a tapestry in the Hôtel Ribat.[41] Woven by a 12-year-old Muslim girl by the name of Meriam, the tapestry was fifteen metres long, had a white background, and required six months to produce. Unfortunately, no photographs of this tapestry are known. Tellingly, Ben Nacuer asserted that Gafsien women's compositions pre-dated the *hijrah*.[42] In disassociating Islam from a series of women's motifs in the midst of economic revival, he reified the official emphasis that conjoined modern art forms with Tunisia's ancient heritage. This linkage corresponded with reports that contemporary Muslim artisans were repetitive, lodged in tradition, and lacking the creativity necessary for resuscitating Tunisian textile traditions.[43] The idea that the 'traditional' female Muslim artisan required liberation from spiritual and intellectual constraints, not merely stylistic and technical ones, resonated with the administrative elite charged with implementing social programmes and economic initiatives for women.[44]

Zoubeïr Turki and *Tunisianité*

The pairing of Ecole de Tunis decorative commissions with artisanal objects in tourist hotels resulted in an aesthetic programme associated with elite notions of *tunisianité*. While artists of the Ecole de Tunis did not issue mandates, they shared a deep-seated interest in exploring thematic concerns and artistic motifs and practices seen to characterize the Tunisian personality.[45] Their paintings portrayed local landscapes and figures, interior scenes, quotidian life, and artisanal production. This orientation did not preclude representations of female nudes, sunbathers, and still lifes, but rather stressed historic transcultural linkages, cross-influences, and Tunisian 'openness'. To a large extent, the Ecole de Tunis located *tunisianité* at the crossroads of past and present Mediterranean civilizations in alignment with the official narrative of the postcolonial period, which was cultivated for tourism, diplomacy, and economic relations to convey a positive image of Tunisia abroad.

The transformations in the political, economic, and arts infrastructure thus far described engendered shifts in the processes and modes used by the Ecole de Tunis to create an iconography of *tunisianité*. While trained as painters, Farhat, Gorgi, Ben Abdallah, and Bellagha reoriented their scope of production from drawing and painting to the design of monumental artworks executed in materials derived from the artisanal industry: wool, ceramics, wood, ironwork, and stone. With the establishment of the Société Zin, Farhat and Gorgi fielded decorative commissions through their close connections to the administrative elite. Turki, a graduate of Zaituna Mosque-University, the Ecole des Beaux-Arts in Tunis, and the Academy of Art in Stockholm, participated in this postcolonial entrepreneurial and aesthetic shift by turning to mural design and illustration. During the period in which Turki produced the murals for the Hôtel Ribat, he also served on the editorial board of the Bourguibist-leaning, feminist journal *Faïza*, directed by fellow artist Safia Farhat. Turki illustrated numerous issues of *Faïza*, as well as contributed articles pertaining to art and

A Bourguibist Mural in the New Monastir?

Figure 5.10: *Advertisement for the Office National des Pêches illustrated by Zoubeïr Turki. Faïza 50 (1965): 3.*

culture. In addition, he designed advertisements for state-owned companies that appeared in nationalist periodicals. His commissions and contributions to these publications indicate Turki's accord with the Bourguibist agenda, although he was known to be slightly satirical in his portraiture of Tunisian citizens. The artist published the occasional caricature of the president in *Faïza*.[46]

Turki's drawing for the National Office of Fisheries exemplifies the artist's portraiture style [Figure 5.10]. Rendered in thick, fluid lines, the archetypal Tunisian fisherman opens his net to display three arching fish. The sweeping contours of the figure's head-wrap and face are echoed in his neckline, shoulders, forearm, and thumbs, as well as in the bodies of the fish in the draping net. Turki's energetic line is similarly present in his paintings, into which the artist inserted raw planes of colour. As acknowledged by Czech critic Miloslav Krajný in 1963, the artist 'creates an individual paraphrase of Fauvist aesthetics which combines the rhythmical interaction of colour planes and of line to form the main means of expression'.[47] Articles authored by Turki in *Faïza* attest to the artist's critical engagement with international art styles and the legacies of avant-garde artists who appropriated form and colour from Maghribi art, notably Henri Matisse and Paul Klee.[48] Throughout the 1960s Turki maintained his position that in order for Tunisian modernists to contribute to international art movements, their work must be rooted in *tunisianité*. The portraits featured in Turki's illustrations, paintings, and murals were therefore based on quintessential figures such as musicians, artisans, chess players, brides, muezzins, merchants, and olive producers.[49] In

Figure 5.11: *Maquette by Zoubeïr Turki for his mural in the Radiodiffusion Télévision Tunisienne, 1962, detail, ink and paper.* Jessica Gerschultz/ Collection of Dorra Bouzid.

some works, these characters were based on real individuals: a famous singer, poet, server in a café, or jasmine vendor.

Turki's largest mural of 52 square metres comprises such historic cultural figures. Painted in 1962 in the headquarters of the Radiodiffusion Télévision Tunisienne in Tunis, this mural depicts the singer Saliha (1914–58) seated on a carpet amidst a crowd of musicians, dancers, and intellectuals, including violinist Mohamed Battikh (1871–1910), writer Arbi al-Kabbadi (1880–1961), poet Chédli Khaznadar (1881–1954), and lower-status members of the service industry who worked in and around the cafés that popularized the style of Arab-Andalusian music known as *maluf* in the early to mid-twentieth century.[50] In the far right-hand side of the composition, Turki incorporated a well-known jasmine merchant known as Baga, who sold flower buds to patrons of the Café des Nattes in Sidi Bou Saïd [Figure 5.11].[51] The artist was delighted to learn that his monumental representation of musicians elicited surprise amongst viewers employed at the broadcasting headquarters.[52] Like Turki's lively choreography of characters in the Radiodiffusion Télévision Tunisienne, the vibrant *murabitun* of the Hôtel Ribat were intended to provoke audience response.

The Audience

In 1962, the editorial team of *Faïza* interviewed Turki about his shift to painting murals.[53] The artist had recently returned from a six-year period of study and art production in Sweden, where he had made more than 350 easel paintings. Despite his financial success abroad, Turki sought to participate in the 'awakening' of his country. He discussed his desire for art to arouse curiosity in wider Tunisian audiences and his intent to initiate a population without a pictorial tradition. He remarked that while painting on canvas remained an elite privilege, murals had the capacity to reach the general public. In addition to outlining his aesthetic approach, Turki clarified the conception of his project for the Hôtel Ribat. He explained that he intended *La Procession des Mourabtines* to be a historical scene of the *murabitun*. In conducting the research for the mural, he had consulted the national library and the *ribat*'s conservator. He was particularly interested in rendering both the details of medieval costume and the overall effect of the twelfth-century procession. While a representation of the *ribat* itself was seemingly absent from his composition, its massive exterior walls and distinctive conical tower would have been visible from the hotel's beachfront terraces.

According to historian Néji Djelloul, the author of official publications on the *ribat*s of Monastir and Sousse, the twelfth-century imam and patron saint of Monastir Abou Abdullah El Mezri described the processional scene illustrated by Turki:

> The ascetics gathered after the night prayer and went onto the ramparts by torchlight imitating soldiers and chanting: Glory to Allah the almighty. The procession then crossed

the town and walked down the streets, passing by the butchers and rubbish dumps to the ramparts.[54]

Amor Bouzguenda (1956–), former director of the *ribat* museum, contends that during the twelfth century, the activities of the *murabitun* occurred as tensions between religious and political factions mounted.[55] He writes that El Mezri sought to transcend the brewing strife and guard the spirit of independent thinking with the study of Maliki thought, and was considered an expert in science, religion, medicine, astronomy, agronomics, law, and architecture. El Mezri attracted followers and students from throughout the Maghrib and al-Andalus during his lifetime. However, Djelloul reports that the Fatimid *qadi* (judge) of the nearby city of Mahdia deplored the parades in Monastir as crude and likened the 'tasteless' costumes of the *murabitun* to those of Christian monks.[56] In the lifetime of Monastir's patron saint, the *ribat* was embroiled in the politics of religious interpretation. Under the Bourguibist regime, the *ribat* took on renewed significance as the country's Islamic monuments, symbolism, and institutional structures were made subordinate to their rebranding of Tunisia. In the closing lines of the performance *Son et lumière à Monastir* in 1965, the *ribat* under Bourguiba became a personification of the Father of the Nation himself:

> I am the remembrance and prayer facing the powers of the night. See my walls as outstretched arms. See my stones as degrees of will. See my towers as the flags of progress. I am the eternal Ribat of Tunisia, and her hope.[57]

In rendering *La Procession des Mourabtines*, Turki chose to deviate from historical accuracy by inserting a portrait of Bourguiba on horseback at the head of the sequence [Figure 5.12]. The president's strongly defined facial features, particularly his thick eyebrows, are recognizable, and he is the only adult figure depicted without facial hair. The artist claimed this rendition to be a spontaneous decision:

> In my maquette, I already had wanted to make this procession a sort of apotheosis. I found myself there in the hometown of the president, and then, imposed on me in perhaps somewhat of a mystical impulse abstracted from time, was the idea that the head of these combatants and these joyful, proud people, the rider of the black horse, was to be president. This took me a few days longer, for I had not planned on this in my maquette. It was necessary to preserve a likeness in a style in which it is difficult to accommodate resemblances…[58]

Turki's 'sudden' vision to create an apotheosis of the president thus launched the mural into dialogical relation with innumerable images in mass circulation during a formative period in which Bourguiba's cult of personality was enacted. This cult relied heavily on visuals of a triumphant Bourguiba, the self-identified *combattant suprême*, processing through city and country.

A Bourguibist Mural in the New Monastir?

Figure 5.12: *Detail of* La Procession des Mourabtines *by artist Zoubeïr Turki, 1962.* Gilbert Van Raepenbusch; Fonds Beit el-Bennani.

The most famous photographs of an exultant Bourguiba were taken on June 1, 1955 and continuously circulated during his rule [Figure 5.13]. These images captured the leader's homecoming from France, where he had been negotiating the terms of Tunisian independence, as his ship pulled into the historic port of La Goulette. Gazing down from the deck, the returning hero received a passionate welcome from scores of waving supporters on the ground. Thereafter, countless reproductions of photographs of Bourguiba appeared in

Figure 5.13: *Press photograph of Habib Bourguiba's Homecoming in La Goulette, Tunisia, June 1, 1955.* Unknown photographer/Fonds Beit el-Bennani.

print media, posters adorned public spaces, and the Poste Tunisienne issued commemorative postage stamps [Figure 5.14]. These images served to cultivate what Laryssa Chomiak refers to as an adulatory, 'regime compliant citizenry'.[59] Moreover, the self-selected title *combattant suprême*, or *mujahid al-akbar*, implied a 'special Islamic virtue' congruent with the popular Tunisian belief in Bourguiba's moral authority at the height of independence.[60]

In manipulating the content of his mural in relation to its architectural position, Turki juxtaposed Bourguibist ideologies of modernity with an evocation of the city's Islamic history. The multiple tonalities evinced by the composition are debatable. Turki seemingly directed this segment of the mural toward the hotel's Tunisian guests and staff as part of his intent to arouse their curiosity [Figure 5.15]. It is unlikely that the majority of European tourists, unfamiliar with the visual tropes of Bourguibism, would have had the capacity to identify the president's stylized profile within the horde of figures. To a foreign visitor, the mural may well have embodied local folklore pertaining to a distant Islamic past. But how might astute Tunisian spectators – low-wage labourers in the service industry as well as members of the political elite – have interpreted Turki's gesture? The painting of *La Procession des Mourabtines* codified an epistemic, iconological form of expertise accessible to Tunisians but not the majority of foreign beachgoers.

Waleed Hazbun posits that many SHTT construction projects were 'meant to illustrate the new prestige of the regime and serve as symbols of modernity by catering to party and

A Bourguibist Mural in the New Monastir?

Figure 5.14: *Stamp designed by the Ecole de Tunis artist Abdelaziz Gorgi for the tenth anniversary of Tunisian independence.* Unknown photographer, *Carthage: Revue Trimestrielle Tunisienne*, 6 (Summer 1966): 21.

Figure 5.15: *Zoubeïr Turki and an unidentified spectator before his mural* La Procession des Mourabtines. Unknown photographer, 'Notre ami Zubeïr Turki en Tchécoslovaquie', *Faiza* 24 (April 1962): 13.

trade union officials and their conferences'.⁶¹ While the majority of tourists were indeed European, Tunisian bureaucrats and businessmen comprised an important clientele, and the entire hotel enterprise relied on seasonal wait staff, cooks, maids, bellhops, drivers, artisans, and entertainers. On one level, Turki's mural may well have functioned in a nationalistic sense to conjure a historical continuity between past and present, in which the *combattant suprême* was the spiritual, moral, and political head of Monastir's *ribat* and new modern city. Yet, on another level, Turki's depiction may have been viewed as playful, witty, bordering on satirical, as the anachronistic insertion of Bourguiba into a scene of twelfth-century *murabitun* was absurd. From this standpoint, Turki invited a subtle challenge to the president's reinscription of Islam into the nation's infrastructure to disrupt the seamless analogy permeating the mass media. Viewers cognizant of Bourguiba's visual cult, whether university-educated members of the administrative elite or illiterate low-class seasonal staff, would have recognized the president's profile at the head of the *murabitun*. In addressing multiple contingents, Turki activated the politically charged questions of just what might be construed as 'modern' and 'Islamic', and by whom. To his Tunisian audiences, Turki's ambiguity certainly drew attention to, if not satirized, the president's spiritual and political authority on the frontiers of modernity.

Given the political tones infused in his depiction of Bourguiba, Turki's imagery in the *Ballet de l'Olive*, though less provocative in the anonymity of its idyllic female labourers, nonetheless merits a revisiting. In this mural, vibrant young women collect olives in a scenic grove. While picturesque in the rendering of *tunisianité*, the image portends the crises to come as the state attempted to force growers to form state-run cooperatives. Alleging the indispensability of rescuing olive cultivators from centuries of decadence, misery, and colonialism, the PSD sought to graft privately owned land into state-managed, collectivized farmland.⁶² Strong protestations against the failed restructuring of agriculture, and olive production in particular, contributed to the premature unravelling of the decennial plan. In 1969 Bourguiba denounced Tunisian socialism and the Ten-Year Plan, accusing Ben Salah of trickery and treason. With Ben Salah imprisoned, the PSD, which nonetheless retained its socialist-inspired name until 1988, soon adopted a course of economic liberalization.⁶³

This brief analysis suggests that the iconography and architectural placement of Turki's mural *La Procession des Mourabtines* may illuminate the power differentials underpinning not only its production, but also the attempted re-articulation of Monastir as an urban space and in its entire social fabric. Moreover, the disputed delineations of the 'modern' and 'Islamic' were embedded in highly variant, often contradictory perceptions of expertise, leading to the mutability and manipulation of these terms by those in positions of power. The wider polemics of modernization thus cut across the genealogies and entanglements of local art nomenclatures, particularly as the art/artisanal infrastructure of the 1960s converged with Bourguibist programming. Moreover, stark class distinctions divided the population, as wealth and access to services remained uneven as the Ten-Year Plan unfolded. In a provocation that invited Tunisian spectators to reconsider the terms of presidential power, Turki momentarily transcended class and religious divisions with an expertly mediated, sweeping gesture.

Notes

1 'Zoubeïr Turki et les fresques', *Faïza* 30 (1962): 30–35. *Faïza* was founded in 1959 by Safia Farhat, the only woman artist of the Ecole de Tunis. Turki was a main illustrator for many issues in the early to mid–1960s.
2 See Christopher Alexander, *Tunisia: Stability and Reform in the Modern Maghreb* (London and New York: Routledge, 2010); Lisa Anderson, *The State and Social Transformation in Tunisia and Libya, 1830–1980* (Princeton, NJ: Princeton University Press, 1986); Kenneth J. Perkins, *A History of Modern Tunisia*, 2nd ed. (Cambridge: Cambridge University Press, 2014).
3 For further reading on Bourguiba's restructuring of religious institutions, see Clement Henry Moore, *Tunisia Since Independence: The Dynamics of One-Party Government* (Berkeley and Los Angeles: University of California Press, 1965), 48–61; Perkins, *A History of Modern Tunisia*; Norma Salem, *Habib Bourguiba, Islam, and the Creation of Tunisia* (London: Croom Helm, 1984).
4 Moore, *Tunisia Since Independence*, 50–53.
5 Mounira M. Charrad, *States and Women's Rights: The Making of Postcolonial Tunisia, Algeria, and Morocco* (Berkeley and Los Angeles: University of California Press, 2001).
6 Russell A. Stone and John Simmons, eds, *Change in Tunisia: Studies in the Social Sciences* (Albany, NY: State University of New York Press, 1976).
7 Moore, *Tunisia Since Independence*.
8 Habib Bourguiba, 'La texte du discours présidentiel', *La Presse de Tunisie*, February 9, 1961, 1–6.
9 'Car l'homme qui est devant vous, en qui le peuple tunisien a placé sa confiance est fermement convaincu que ce n'est pas à la religion musulmane que nous devons ces entraves qui ont arrêté notre marche et paralysé nos intelligences. Je l'affirme catégoriquement. Telle que je la connais, telle que je l'ai étudiée et apprise, telle qu'elle a été vécue et pratiquée par le Prophète lui–même, ses compagnons, ses contemporains et ses successeurs, la religion musulmane n'est pas une doctrine d'asphyxie intellectuelle.' Ibid.
10 'C'est pourquoi je ne cesse de répéter que notre lutte pour arracher cette nation musulmane au sous–developpement hérité des epoques de la décadence n'est pas moins valable que la jihad.' Ibid.
11 Henri de Montety described the emergence and intellectual background of Tunisia's 'new elites' in his essay 'Old Families and New Elites in Tunisia', in *Man, State, and Society in the Contemporary Maghrib*, ed. I. William Zartman (New York: Praeger, 1973), 171–80.
12 For analyses of Tunisia's tourism industry, see Mohamed Bergaoui, *Tourisme et Voyages en Tunisie: Le Temps des Pionniers 1956-1973* (Tunis: Simpact, 2003); Waleed Hazbun, *Beaches, Ruins, Resorts: The Politics of Tourism in the Arab World* (Minneapolis, MN: University of

Minnesota Press, 2008); Robert A. Poirier and Stephen Wright, 'The Political Economy of Tourism in Tunisia', *Journal of Modern African Studies* 31.1 (March 1993): 149–62.

13. Hazbun, *Beaches, Ruins, Resorts*; Poirier and Wright, 'The Political Economy of Tourism in Tunisia'.
14. 'Summer Festivities', *Tourism in Tunisia* 5 (September 1960): 5.
15. Ibid.
16. Hazbun, *Beaches, Ruins, Resorts*.
17. See Ahmed Ben Salah, 'Le plan de développement', *La Revue Française* 166 (July 1964): 66–67; Sadok Bahroun, *La Planification Tunisienne* (Tunis: Maison Tunisienne de l'Edition, 1968); Pierre Rossi, *La Tunisie de Bourguiba* (Tunis: Editions Kahia, 1967).
18. Ben Salah, 'Le plan de développement'.
19. Olivier Clement Cacoub, 'Monastir la neuve', *Carthage: Revue Trimestrielle Tunisienne* 3 (October–December 1965): 46–55.
20. Amor Bouzguenda (son of mason Amor Bouzguenda, Sr. and former director of Monastir's *ribat* museum), interview with the author, June 14, 2014; Michael Ragon, *Olivier Clément Cacoub: Architecture de Soleil* (Tunis: Cérès Productions, 1974).
21. Manuelle Peyrol, 'Son et lumière à Monastir', *Carthage: Revue Trimestrielle Tunisienne* 1 (January–March 1965): 38–43.
22. Hazbun, *Beaches, Ruins, Resorts*, 10.
23. 'Monastir and its Hotel Ribat', *Tourism in Tunisia* 10 (December 1961): 4–5.
24. Ibid., 5.
25. See Hassan S. Khalilieh, 'The Ribat System and Its Role in Coastal Navigation', *Journal of the Economic and Social History of the Orient* 42 (1999): 212–25; Slimane–Mostafa Zbiss, *Inscriptions de Monastir* (Tunis: Secrétariat d'Etat à l'Education Nationale and Institut National d'Archeologie et Arts, 1960).
26. Slimane–Mostafa Zbiss, *Monastir ses Monuments* (Tunis: Secrétariat d'Etat aux Affaires Culturelles et à l'Information, 1964).
27. '*Tenir pendant trois jours garnison à Monastir ouvre l'accès du Paradis*'. Mohamed Bergaoui, *Monastir: Fragments d'histoire* (Tunis: Simpact, 1997).
28. While there is no treatise defining *décoration* in Tunisia, the conceptualization of this term follows French definitions from the late nineteenth century concerning the integration of art and ornament into architectural design. In mid-twentieth century Tunisia, 'decoration' encompassed the design of modernist works such as murals and tapestries, as well as art created by artisans to fulfil the plans of artist-designers and architects in both secular and religious buildings.
29. Letter from Pierre Boucherle and Yahia Turki to the Résident Général de la République Française, 1948, National Archives of Tunisia, SG 12 251–14.
30. Minutes from the *Commission chargée des Commandes aux Artistes de Tunisie pour la décoration des Bâtiments Civils*, 1950, National Archives of Tunisia, SG 12 251–14.
31. For an overview of artworks created by Safia Farhat during this period, see Aïcha Filali, *Safia Farhat: une biographie* (Tunis: MIM Editions, 2005). The categorization of decorative programmes produced by artists of the Ecole de Tunis during both iterations of the 1 per cent law is the subject of my current book manuscript.

32 Due to the institutional framework established by the 1 per cent law in 1950, artists classified as 'artisans' frequently assisted 'fine artists' with the execution of their designs. Moreover, the administrative elite held the view that the *artisanat* was a 'civilizing discipline' that could elevate a 'backwards' population. With few exceptions, only the artists claimed authorship and signed their work.
33 I consulted official receipts and memos from 1962–64 in the archives of the Office National de l'Artisanat, Den Den, Tunis in June of 2014.
34 I am grateful to Xavier Hermel of the Académie des Beaux–Arts in Paris, who located private papers recording Jean Lurçat's consultation in Tunisia during his visit to Lurçat's home in Paris on July 11, 2013.
35 Jean Lurçat was known internationally for his initiatives, consulting work, publications, and exhibitions. In addition to Tunisia, Lurçat worked in other countries on the African continent, including Morocco, Egypt, and Senegal. At the time of his visit to Tunisia in 1960, Lurçat was involved with co–founding the Centre International de la Tapisserie Ancienne et Moderne (CITAM) in Lausanne, Switzerland, as well as the Lausanne International Tapestry Biennales.
36 'Tunisian Artisans Link up with 3000 Years of Artistic Tradition', *Tourism in Tunisia* 5 (September 1960): 10–11.
37 'Les Tapis Tunisiens et leur rénovation: entretien avec Jean Lurçat', *Faïza* 7 (June 1960): 22–23.
38 Jessica Gerschultz, 'The Interwoven Ideologies of Art and Artisanal Education in Postcolonial Tunis', *Critical Interventions: Journal of African Art History and Visual Culture* 8:1 (2014): 31–51.
39 'Tunisian Artisans Link up with 3000 Years of Artistic Tradition', 10.
40 Sophie Ferchiou, '"Invisible" Work, Work at Home: The Condition of Tunisian Women', in *Middle Eastern Women and the Invisible Economy*, ed. Richard A. Lobban (Gainesville, FL: University Press of Florida, 1998), 187–97.
41 'Resurrection de la tapisserie à Gafsa, par S.S.' *La Presse de Tunisie*, November 13, 1963. A newspaper clip of this article was saved with the private papers of Jean Lurçat in Paris.
42 Ibid.
43 Abdelaziz Gorgi's statements concerning the stagnant nature of artisanship were published in Tunisian periodicals; see, for example, M.L.T., 'L'art dans la vie et des formes nouvelles en s'inspirant du passé', *La Presse*, May 28, 1965.
44 See Gerschultz, 'The Interwoven Ideologies'.
45 For further reading on the Ecole de Tunis see Dorra Bouzid, *Ecole de Tunis* (Tunis: Alif, 1995); Mustapha Chelbi, *La quête de la tunisianité* (Tunis: Finzi, 2002); Ali Louati, *L'aventure de l'art moderne en Tunisie* (Tunis: Simpact, 2002).
46 Turki's caricature of Habib Bourguiba in the journal *Faïza* is published in his article 'La Russie, en Artiste', *Faïza* 10 (1960): 18–21.
47 Miloslav Krajný, *Zoubeïr Turki* (Prague: Editions de Belles Lettres et d'Art, Prague, en collaboration avec le Secrétariat d'Etat aux Affaires Culturelles et à l'Information, Tunis, 1963), 20.
48 See, for example, Zoubeïr Turki, 'Zoubeïr Turki défend la peinture Tunisienne', *Faïza* 57 (1967): 12–15.

49 Turki published a compendium of 28 such drawings in *Tunis naguère et aujourd'hui: dessins et textes de Zoubeïr Turki; adaption française de Claude Roy* (Tunis: Sud Editions, 2005). See also Dorra Ben Ayed, 'Tunis naguère et aujourd'hui un livre de Zoubeïr Turki', *Faïza* 15 (1961): 15–19.
50 'Zoubeïr Turki et les fresques'.
51 Dorra Bouzid, interview with the author, June 23, 2014. Dorra Bouzid is a former journalist at *Faïza*, friend of Zoubeïr Turki, and owner of the *maquette* for the mural in the Radiodiffusion Télévision Tunisienne.
52 'Zoubeïr Turki et les fresques', 35.
53 Ibid.
54 Néji Djelloul, *The Monastir Ribat* (Tunis: Ministère de la Culture et de la Sauvegarde du Patrimoine and Agence de mise en valeur du Patrimoine et de Promotion Culturelle, 2007).
55 Amor Bouzguenda, 'L'imam Abou Abdullah El Mezri (453 H- 536 H/ 1061-1141)' *Sites et Monuments* 28 (Novembre 2010): 35–38.
56 Néji Djelloul, *The Monastir Ribat*, 15.
57 'Je suis le souvenir et la prière, face aux puissances de la nuit. Voyez mes murs comme des bras étendus. Voyez mes pierres comme des degrés de volonté. Voyez mes tours comme les étendards du progrès. Je suis le Ribat éternel de la Tunisie et de son espérance.' Manuelle Peyrol, 'Son et lumière à Monastir', 42.
58 'Sur ma maquette, j'avais déjà voulu faire de cette procession une sorte d'apothéose. Je me trouvais là–bas dans la propre ville du Président, et s'est alors imposé à moi dans un élan un peu mystique peut–être et abstraction faite du temps, l'idée qu'à la tête de ces combattants et de ce peuple joyeux et fier, la cavalier du cheval noir devait être le Président. Cela m'a pris quelques jours de plus car je n'avais pas prévu sur ma maquette. Toute une étude devait être faite sur le profil du Président. Il fallait conserver une ressemblance dans un style qui s'accomode mal des ressemblances…' 'Zoubeïr Turki et les fresques', 34.
59 See Laryssa Chomiak, '"Spectacles of Power" Locating Resistance in Ben Ali's Tunisia', *Portal* 9.2 (Spring 2013): 70–83. Chomiak, in turn, builds on the scholarship of Lisa Wedeen.
60 Moore, *Tunisia Since Independence*, 48.
61 Hazbun, *Beaches, Ruins, Resorts*, 6.
62 Mongi Goaied, 'Trente-Cinq Millions d'Oliviers', *Carthage: Revue Trimestrielle Tunisienne* 4 (February 1966): 64–66.
63 In 1988 the party changed its name to the Rassemblement Constitutionnel Démocratique (Democratic Constitutional Rally), or RCD.

Chapter 6

Expertise in the Name of Diplomacy: The Israeli Plan for Rebuilding the Qazvin Region, Iran

Neta Feniger and Rachel Kallus

Introduction

On September 1, 1962, an earthquake measuring 6.9 on the Richter scale struck the Iranian province of Qazvin,[1] killing more than 12,000 people [Figure 6.1].[2] The earthquake occurred shortly before Israeli Minister of Agriculture, Moshe Dayan, was scheduled to visit Iran in mid-September for meetings with the Shah and with his Iranian counterpart, to discuss Israel's possible role in the 'White Revolution', a plan for land reform and the modernization of rural Iran.[3] Israel's expertise in development was valued around the world at the time, particularly in housing and regional planning.[4] The meeting was postponed due to the earthquake, but Dayan realized that the disaster presented an opportunity for Israel to offer even more technical assistance to Iran, thus creating the opportunity for deeper involvement with the Shah's national modernization plans.

Shortly after the earthquake, two planning experts were sent from Israel to assist with Iranian relief activities. After touring the region and meeting with the Iranian minister in charge of relief efforts, they were assigned to rebuild the village of Khuznin, located in the centre of the Qazvin region [Figure 6.2]. Other teams, both Iranian and foreign, had also arrived in the region to offer assistance and expertise in the reconstruction activities. Each team was assigned one village or more for planning and rebuilding. Over the course of three months, the Israeli team built hundreds of houses in the village that they had been assigned. Afterwards, Israel received a bid for a larger project administered by the United Nations Technical Assistance (UNTA) programme.[5] For the UNTA project, a larger team of Israeli experts prepared a comprehensive regional plan for the area most devastated by the earthquake, an area of 170,000 square kilometres, as well as reconstruction plans for several other villages.

Focusing on the UNTA project, this chapter examines transnational planning by the Israeli team working in Qazvin. The sources of evidence include the personal documents of and in-depth interviews with team members; the Israeli report prepared for UNTA;[6] material in the Israel State Archive (ISA); and contemporary newspaper articles. As Israelis, we cannot visit Iran and therefore do not have access to the site or Iranian sources, but this research has enabled us to discuss the export of Israeli expertise in the context of the period's political atmosphere. It also presents an opportunity to explore the prevalent professional discourse within which the planning and strategies for implementation were envisioned and outlined as well as employed for diplomatic purposes. The success of the implementation of the plan in Qazvin is outside the scope of our investigation as it requires research in Iran.

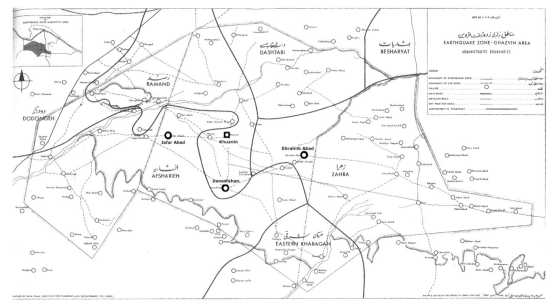

Figure 6.1: *Location of villages highlighted on regional boundaries map.* Village Planning & Reconstruction of the Earthquake Zone in the Ghazvin Area – Iran (Tel Aviv: United Nations Technical Assistance [UNTA] Team and Institute for Planning and Development [IPD], 1968).

Figure 6.2: *Map of the Qazvin project location.* Neta Feniger.

The roles of different actors in post-WWII transnational planning have been the focus of many studies.[7] Yet, the diversity of these projects and the actors involved, their different goals, and their varied perspectives are sometimes disregarded. The Qazvin project was shaped not only by the architectural experts, but also by the goals of diverse teams of experts and administrators. For example, the objectives of the Israeli professionals differed from those of their national government, even though these objectives were interrelated. On the Iranian side, the 'locals' – the Shah, the government, experts involved in the project, local villagers – had diverse, and at times conflicting, perspectives. In an effort to better understand the ways in which diversity was negotiated in the Qazvin project, the following questions are addressed: how did the Israeli experts respond to the Iranians' conflicting objectives? How did the experts deal with the political objectives? How did these affect their planning?

Bilateral Relations in a Cold-War Arena

Israel and Iran maintained friendly diplomatic relationships between 1950 and the Iranian Revolution in 1979. These relations were never formalized or publicized, but were nonetheless close and mutually beneficial.[8] Ideologically, the relationship was based upon the shared outlook of the two countries as non-Arab nations in the Middle East promoting modernization;[9] however, in the fraught political atmosphere of the region, the relationship was far more crucial for Israel.[10] Because the entente was fragile, the Israeli government actively sought ways to reinforce its diplomatic status in Iran.

Diplomatic relations between Israel and the Shah's regime were rooted in the power balance of the Cold-War era and based on both countries' geopolitical policies. The alliance was also beneficial to both states in their relationships with the United States. The support of Israel and Iran was important to the Western presence in the region, and for this reason diplomatic relations between the two countries were strongly encouraged.[11]

In the 1950s, the Shah asked the United States to support Israel in order to protect Western interests in the Middle East. Iran and Russia had long been at odds, and the Shah was also threatened by pro-Soviet groups such as the Iranian Tudeh (People's) Party. He was also concerned about Egyptian president Gamal Abdel Nasser's pan-Arabism, which was supported by the Soviet Union.[12] Although the United States' decision to support Israel financially, militarily, and politically was not a direct outcome of the Shah's efforts, it derived from similar interests. In the 1960s, when the United States was more involved in Iran, and more important for Israel's foreign policy, it was clear that contributions by Israel to the Shah's regime would be viewed favourably by America. Thus, the relationships between the United States, Iran, and Israel were beneficial for all three countries.

The relationship between Iran and Israel started soon after the establishment of the State of Israel in 1948. The Shah's eagerness for Westernization and modernization, and his antagonism towards Russia and the Arabs, made the relationship with Israel logical. For Israel, it was part of its 'periphery doctrine' in which attempts were made to establish relationships with non-Arab states on the periphery of the Middle East (e.g., Turkey, Iran, and Ethiopia). In the words of Shimon Peres, who served as the Deputy Minister of Defence, the doctrine was intended to 'surround the circle of hatred with newly-established friendships'.[13] From the beginning, Israel's foreign policy was to create sustainable connections in the region even if they were not necessary for its survival.[14] Furthermore, Iran was a potential trading partner, which was important for the politically and economically isolated country and, finally, Israel wished to maintain close contact with the large Jewish community still living in Iran.[15] Unlike Jews who trace their roots to Arab countries, relatively few Iranian Jews immigrated to Israel after the establishment of the state. Although most of them supported the State of Israel, they did not wish to leave their homeland.[16]

Until the Six-Day War in 1967, the Iranian intellectual elite were largely favourable towards Israel, even though the country's government had a close relationship with the Shah, who was an unpopular figure in these circles. Jalal al-e Ahmad, a renowned Iranian left-wing writer known for his criticism of Iran's adoption of Western mores and the loss of Iranian culture and identity, travelled to Israel in 1962. Upon his return, al-e Ahmad described his general enthusiasm for what he saw there, including a visit to a kibbutz, in his book *The Israeli Republic*.[17] Like other Iranian leftists, he saw Israel as a Middle-Eastern entity that was capable of creating its own culture independent of Western influence and therefore a model from which Iranians could learn.[18] For many Iranians, Israelis were associated with development projects rather than with helping the Shah to consolidate his autocracy by providing him with tools for the oppression of the Iranian people (such as the SAVAK, the notoriously brutal Iranian secret police, which the Israeli Mossad intelligence agency helped to establish and train).[19]

Both governments saw the use of Israeli expertise as a way to further strengthen the relationship between them. Parsi claims that the Shah ordered that Israeli experts be hired in many fields – even when they were not needed – as a way to cement the relationship.[20] The work of Israeli experts in Iran was no small endeavour. Civil servants were hired for numerous development projects, particularly in the area of agriculture in which they trained about 10,000 Iranians. Iranians also participated in international development conferences held in Israel during the 1960s.[21]

Disaster and Diplomatic Opportunity

In the early 1960s, Moshe Dayan, the Israeli Minister of Agriculture, was invited by the Shah to visit Iran in order to discuss Israel's consultation on the country's modernization efforts in agriculture, the water supply, and cooperative organizations.[22] Dayan was scheduled to tour the Qazvin region, an area under consideration for the implementation of the Israeli consulting project. This rural region, situated between western Tehran and the city of

Qazvin, was mostly underdeveloped, although the trans-Iranian railway passed through it. Dayan's visit was intended to initiate the bilateral planning project, which originally did not include architecture, but the devastation of the region by the earthquake gave rise to a larger plan, which provided Israel with an opportunity to more fully demonstrate its expertise and express its goodwill.

The export of its knowledge of planning and development as well as technical assistance was a crucial plank in Israel's diplomatic strategy as it combined the country's aspiration for political legitimacy in the global arena with a genuine concern for the economic improvement of their fellow emerging societies.[23] Israeli architects had participated in post-WWII reconstruction projects, lending technical assistance to projects ranging from infrastructure development and rural and regional planning, to public buildings, housing, hotels, and commercial facilities. By the 1960s, Israeli architects, planners, and engineers were employed across Latin America and Africa,[24] as well as in Southeast Asia, Turkey, and Greece.[25] For the most part, the projects were commissioned by construction firms or contractors, or by state agencies such as MASHAV (Hebrew acronym for the Department of International Cooperation in the Ministry of Foreign Affairs), which was established to provide advice and technical assistance to developing countries.[26] The nature of the projects was determined by the host country, local planning policies, and by the funding entity, which was usually an international organization such as the United Nations or the Organization for Economic Cooperation and Development (OECD), but sometimes by the host country (or, rarely, Israel itself).

After the earthquake, like many other countries, Israel contributed medical and material aid to the relief operation.[27] However, Dayan recognized that technical assistance could consolidate the two countries' bilateral relations. Six days after the quake, he sent a letter of condolence to his Iranian counterpart, Dr Sayyid Hassan Arsanjani, in which he also offered Israeli architectural expertise to Iran:

> Wouldn't it be better if, instead of building houses in the old-fashioned way, you adopt new building ideas […] to use the funds efficiently in a rational manner? If you will accept our help, we offer it gladly.[28]

An official in Israel's Ministry of Foreign Affairs reported to the Israeli Embassy in Washington that Arsanjani welcomed the offer, and asked whether Israel could also ensure funding from the United States government. Dayan could not guarantee this, but implied that the Americans would probably agree to fund the project, if it were based on modern planning methods.[29]

In mid-September, Israeli agricultural expert Micha Talmon and architect Yehuda Drexler, both civil servants, arrived in Qazvin. After touring the devastated region, Drexler sent a report to the Israeli Ministry for Foreign Affairs describing the ongoing relief efforts by foreign and local organizations. He noted that locals already 'began to collect local building materials and plan to rebuild their mud houses'.[30] A great believer in modernization, he undoubtedly saw it as a missed opportunity, commenting in the letter that because the ongoing construction had not embraced modern architectural methods, 'these houses will again be destroyed in the next quake'.[31] Soon after, the Israelis met with Arsanjani, who approved their plans and asked that they be implemented in the village of Khuznin, which had been completely destroyed by the earthquake:

> The Agriculture Minister caught on to our suggestion, and approved it on the spot, ordering his staff to implement it in one village immediately with the Israelis. He also brought it to the king stating that with the help of the Israelis it will be built in two weeks...[32]

The plans included a new village layout and small family-housing units, described in an Israeli newspaper as 'rows of white houses like cubes' [Figure 6.3].[33] Public amenities included a school, a clinic, a clubhouse, and an agricultural centre at which Israeli experts would teach modern agricultural methods.

For the Iranian government, reconstruction presented an opportunity for modernization, as part of the 'White Revolution'. The Iranian press commented on 'the good that came out of the disaster' in Qazvin.[34] However, the project was not funded by the Iranian government, but by international organizations such as United Nations International Children's Emergency Fund (UNICEF), United Nations Educational, Scientific and Cultural Organization (UNESCO), World Health Organization (WHO), Food and Agriculture Organization (FAO), as well as Iranian organizations, including the Red Lion and Sun, and the National Iranian Oil Company (NIOC). While the Israeli team planned one village, the combined relief efforts and reconstruction of infrastructure featured contributions from many teams

Figure 6.3: *Houses in Khuznin.* Plan for the Development of Qazvin Region: Survey Report (Tel Aviv: TAHAL, 1963).

from different countries and organizations. For example, the World Council of Churches planned the village of Esmatabad; the NIOC, one of the project's major contributors, sent a team to build in Boeen; and a team from the University of Tehran built the village of Rudak [Figure 6.4].[35]

In due course, the Israeli emissaries learned that the Iranians had detached the relief efforts – their priority – from the comprehensive regional plan.[36] It was obvious that external funding was needed to implement the plan, and this Israel could not offer. The UNTA's decision to fund a regional plan for Qazvin paved the way for the contribution of Israeli expertise. In October 1962, Ernest Weissmann, the director of UNTA and an influential figure in promoting projects for the developing world, approached the Israeli delegation to the United Nations.[37] An architect of Jewish descent from Croatia, and a member of the Congrès Internationaux d'Architecture Moderne (CIAM), he immigrated to the United States before World War II and became head of the UN Centre for Housing, Building and Planning and UNTA.[38] In the aftermath of World War II and the colonial era, international organizations, especially the UN, became an important force in transnational planning.[39] As head of UNTA, Weissmann acted as liaison between foreign professionals and the nation-states seeking planners for development projects.[40]

In the three months after the earthquake, but before signing the UNTA contract in December 1962, Israeli efforts were concentrated in the diplomatic arena in Iran and the UN.[41] A key part of the diplomatic and relief effort was to send the first team to Iran two weeks after the earthquake as Israel recognized that speed and effectiveness on the ground were crucial to receiving a larger project.[42]

Although Israel's interest in the diplomatic gains presented by the disaster might be considered 'disaster capitalism',[43] most of the personnel involved viewed their role as benevolent and altruistic, as evidenced by letters from the Tehran embassy to the Foreign Ministry:[44]

> The diplomats praised Israel's planning and execution of the project and the dedication of the engineer Badni, whose tent was set up on-site.[45]

> Our people are the best in the world [...] are full of pioneering and professional enthusiasm, and capture the hearts of the Iranians.[46]

> [...] appreciation for Israel's experts, who are trusted more than those from more developed countries [...][47]

These letters reflect genuine Israeli pride in the country's expertise in the areas of development and reconstruction. They also show an instinctive identification with emerging nations and national liberation movements.[48]

The administration of the Qazvin project, including the recruitment of experts, was undertaken by the Institute for Planning and Development (IPD), a non-profit public firm established by the Israeli government in the late 1950s when there was an increase in

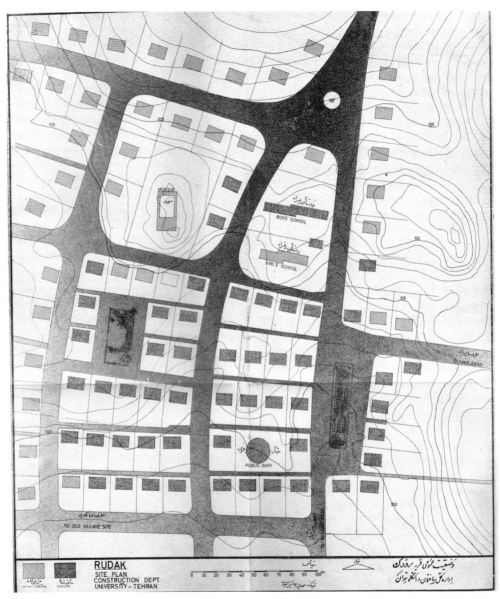

Figure 6.4: *Plan for the village of Rudak.* Jacob Dash and Elisha Efrat, 'Lakhish Regional Plan', in *The Israel Physical Master Plan*, Ministry of Interiors – Planning Department (1964), 54. Michael Boneh Collection, Israel Architecture Archive.

international demand for Israeli development expertise. A pamphlet published by the IPD states that:

> Feeling the experience in planned development in Israel, can contribute much elsewhere, in particular in developing countries, the Government of Israel established the Institute for Planning and Development Ltd., for the purpose of consolidating in one institution the entire experience of Israel in this field, and of co-ordinating its activities in this sphere vis-à-vis developing countries.[49]

The IPD was an agency for recruiting ad-hoc teams of experts according to the needs and requests of each individual mission. The project in Qazvin was one of its first, and as it represented the State of Israel, the Foreign Ministry supervised the recruiting process in order to ensure quality expertise.

According to one of its founders, Raanan Weitz, Israeli expertise in regional planning was unique in its institutional approach, which assigned an administrative team to see a plan to its completion.[50] Moreover, Weitz advocated remaining 'behind the scenes' while working abroad so as not to be perceived as a colonizing force.[51] A successful plan, he believed, required skilled administrators as much as planners. For the Qazvin project, the administrator with political skills was Arie Lova Eliav.[52]

Transnational Planning: From Lakhish to Qazvin

The UNTA project (January 1963–February 1964) was part of a larger mission made up of three Israeli teams, each engaged under a separate contract. The largest contract was between the Iranian Planning Organization (PO)[53] and Israel's water-planning company TAHAL (Hebrew acronym for Water Planning for Israel) to redesign Qazvin's water system in order to increase agricultural productivity.[54] The second contract was between the Iranian government and MASHAV for the purpose of creating and operating farms to teach modern techniques of agriculture. The third contract, which is the focus of this chapter, was between UNTA and IPD. Although the Israeli experts were divided into different teams, they collaborated and cooperated under the leadership of Eliav, who managed and coordinated the entire mission.[55] He also acted as an intermediary between the teams and the Israeli government, and between the Iranian government and the United Nations. Eliav was enlisted for the Qazvin mission by Prime Minister David Ben-Gurion after successfully managing the regional development in Lakhish, Israel.[56] He was not a professional planner by training, but had become involved at an early stage with Israel's nation building, both as an administrator and as a politician who later became a parliamentary representative of Israel's Labour Party.

The Lakhish Plan was initiated by the Israeli government as part of its nation-building effort [Figure 6.5]. This rural development plan was based on Israel's regional approach to

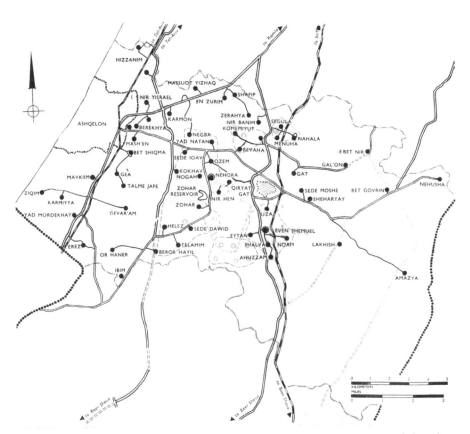

Figure 6.5: *Plan of Lakhish region.* Jacob Dash and Elisha Efrat, 'Lakhish Regional Plan', *Israel Physical Master Plan* (Tel Aviv: Ministry of the Interior-Planning Departmnt, 1964), 54.

its peripheral regions. According to Smadar Sharon, the intellectual roots of the Lakhish Plan were to be found in the ideas of the German geographer, Walter Christaller, and even more notably in the Italian colonization paradigm used in Libya.[57] Weitz adopted these ideas during his doctoral studies in Agronomy at the University of Florence (1932–37). Sharon also notes that the regionalist approach (attributed to Lewis Mumford) influenced important planners, like Artur Glikson,[58] who worked in the Israeli planning institutions involved in the Lakhish Plan. Its objectives were to retain territorial continuity in geopolitically unstable areas; to de-urbanize and de-centralize; and to create new settlements and jobs for new immigrants.[59] An extensive survey was conducted by teams of experts in sociology, anthropology, economy, agriculture, water and soil engineering, and planning and architecture. The three main components of the plan were: comprehensive regional planning, cooperation at different political levels (national and regional), and the cooperation of experts from different disciplines. The regional plan consisted of the organization of clusters of settlements around rural centres, and a rural scheme of mixed agriculture.[60]

In the 1950s 'Lakhish became a planning model, a paradigm, almost an article of faith, for its participants'.[61] Their confidence made it a 'universal settlement model'.[62] It became a destination for others who wished to learn from the Israeli regional development experience, and was used as a 'master class' in international conferences and symposia on housing, regional planning, and rural planning in Israel in the 1960s.[63] Israel began to export the model in the early 1960s; plans based on the Lakhish model were deployed in Argentina,[64] Burma,[65] Crete,[66] Sierra Leone,[67] and eventually in Qazvin. Most of the experts sent to Qazvin had been members of the Lakhish planning team.

The UNTA Project

For Eliav, architecture was the key to the Qazvin mission's success. Soon after his arrival in Qazvin, he wrote to the Israeli Minister for Foreign Affairs to explain that:

> I feel (after long talks with Arsanjani) […] that, as well as long- and short-term planning, they will want speedy results 'on the ground'. Here, architects can achieve more than water and agriculture experts, for whom planning and execution naturally take longer. It was a real godsend that Weissmann approached us about the architectural planning […] Please cut the 'red tape' and send the architects as fast as possible.[68]

This insight suggests that the plan administrator understood that the Israeli objectives lay in the diplomatic realm. Expertise, especially architectural expertise, was the key to diplomatic success. Eliav's letter also highlights the perception that the ability to plan and build quickly – as evidenced by the reconstruction of Khuznin – was very attractive to the Iranian government.

Project visibility was important for Iran and Israel, but also for the United States. Moshe Shoked, a team member, claimed that the United States was more preoccupied with building new facilities, such as modern dairy farms, than with bringing real change to the villagers' lives, and that the United States was more likely to give financial aid to projects that 'looked good', in terms of size and modernity.[69] Israel's contribution was important in terms of providing visible improvement. As Qazvin was close to the border with the USSR, it was important for the United States to demonstrate its presence and influence in Iran. An Israeli Embassy official claimed that 'the United States ambassador told me, with great satisfaction [...] [that] the official completion and delivery of the three villages in Qazvin [built with American funds] to the Shah was on the eve of the Soviet president's arrival.'[70]

The Survey

The Israeli team for the UNTA project included: two architects, Arieh Fatran (team leader) and Michael Boneh; sociologist Moshe Shoked (Minkovitz); construction expert David Brenner; and the building expert who also worked in Khuznin, Eliyahu Badni [Figure 6.6]. The two objectives of the plan, as established by the Iranian Government and the UN, were to find solutions to the housing problems in the area affected by the earthquake and to define the principles of regional socio-economic planning based on the agrarian reforms.[71] The goal was to 'avoid errors made in the past in some communities where those in charge of planning and implementation insisted solely on rapid economic changes, without regards to resulting dislocations in the demographic and social structure of these communities'.[72] The team prepared a comprehensive survey of the physical conditions as well as other features including demography, administrative structure, transport, public and commercial institutions, and health and educational services [Figure 6.7]. They interviewed many villagers and the village leaders. Afterwards, they prepared a master plan for the region that included new roads, infrastructure and social institutions, and detailed plans for three villages [Figure 6.8].

The survey, prepared in collaboration with the other Israeli teams working in the region, focused on water and agriculture. The regional plan was designed according to the national agrarian land reform, which provided farmers with private land that was held in cooperatives.[73] As the Qazvin region is semi-arid, it required the construction of new water systems capable of supporting modern agriculture. This was planned by TAHAL, Israel's water planning firm. The firm had experience in projects of this nature as it had previously planned a water delivery system for Lakhish. While the plan for Qazvin was based on the Lakhish model, the historical circumstances of its construction were different. Lakhish had been largely uninhabited after the 1948 War during which the Palestinian inhabitants had been driven out. The locations of the new towns in Lakhish, which were designated for new

Expertise in the Name of Diplomacy

Figure 6.6: *Arieh Fatran explaining the plan to the UNTA representative.* Arieh Fatran personal archive.

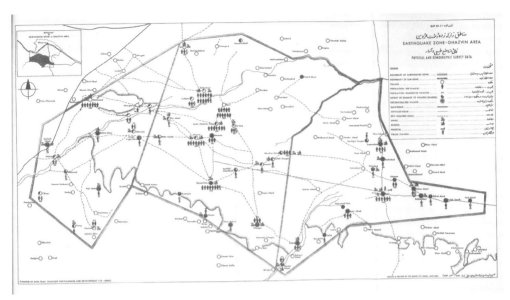

Figure 6.7: *Map of physical and demographic survey data.* Village Planning & Reconstruction of the Earthquake Zone in the Ghazvin Area - Iran (Tel Aviv: United Nations Technical Assistance [UNTA] Team and Institute for Planning and Development [IPD], 1968).

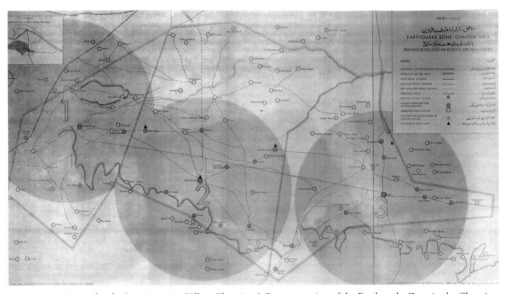

Figure 6.8: *Master plan for Qazvin region.* Village Planning & Reconstruction of the Earthquake Zone in the Ghazvin Area - Iran (Tel Aviv: United Nations Technical Assistance [UNTA] Team and Institute for Planning and Development [IPD], 1968).

Jewish immigrants, were determined by the planners.[74] In the case of Qazvin, the villages that had been destroyed by the earthquake were to be rebuilt in their original locations, maintain their pre-earthquake sizes, and accommodate the local population. Planning for a region that was currently inhabited presented a new challenge for the Israeli team. In Lakhish, the team created an evenly distributed hierarchy of settlements; however, in Qazvin they had to work with the existing settlement structure.

To achieve a pattern of distribution similar to Lakhish, the region was divided into three sub-areas, each defined by a set of villages. At least one village in each group, distinguished by its size and regional importance, was made into a commercial and social centre. The team designed detailed plans for one sub-area that contained three ruined villages: Danesfahan, a large village with 800 dwelling units, became the commercial and social centre of the region and the two other villages, Ebrahim-Abad and Jafar-Abadhad, had 250 and 80 dwelling units, respectively [Figure 6.9].[75] The plans called for a new parcelling of land and included the designs for dwelling units, farmhouses, and public buildings such as schools, *hamam*s (baths), and mosques.

The plan's boundaries were originally delineated according to the extent of the damage inflicted by the earthquake. However, the team suggested that the planned region be extended beyond these boundaries to cover a larger, more geographically contiguous area.[76] Since detailed maps of that area were not available, the survey map became the basis for drafting the final plan.

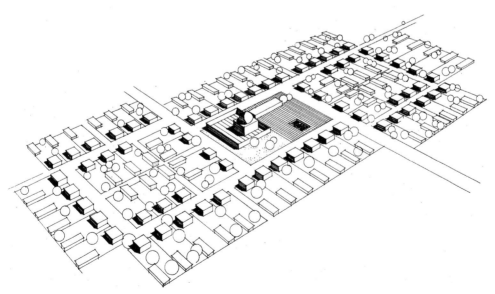

Figure 6.9: *Perspective view of a small village.* Village Planning & Reconstruction of the Earthquake Zone in the Ghazvin Area - Iran (Tel Aviv: United Nations Technical Assistance [UNTA] Team and Institute for Planning and Development [IPD], 1968).

While the Lakhish region was designed as part of a national project for land colonization, Qazvin was planned without any preconceptions concerning its effect on the rest of Iran. The team proposed the creation of an administrative authority to manage the plan's implementation, which mirrored the administration of Lakhish. However, Qazvin's inhabitants were given a voice in a way that the inhabitants of Lakhish were never offered. The village leaders were given an opportunity to contribute ideas to the planning team, and it was suggested that they become agents of the proposed administration. This and other administrative suggestions were included in the report to the Iranian government and to UNTA, though the plan could ultimately have been implemented without these changes.[77]

The Site Plan

The schematic plan for Danesfahan, the central and largest village in the middle sub-region included the zoning and road systems [Figure 6.10]. The detailed plan demarcated two types of dwelling plots: a larger one for farmers and a smaller one for others [Figure 6.11].[78] Some of the latter were clustered in a separate neighbourhood at the entrance to the village in accordance with traditional village organization.

The orthogonal village layout contained three neighbourhoods arranged around the axis connecting the village to the main road plus the smaller workmen's neighbourhood at the entrance. The large neighbourhoods were planned so that extended families could live together, a concept originally employed in the Israeli *moshav* (semi-cooperative agricultural settlement) in Lakhish.[79] In the neighbourhoods, public plots were designated for a *hamam*, kindergarten, shops, mosque, and a small park. Each was planned with a small open public space next to which the neighbourhood shop was located. Other public amenities were interspersed among the blocks of dwelling units. In the centre of the village was a boulevard lined with public buildings: clinics, administrative offices, schools and clubs, sport facilities, a commercial centre, a central mosque with gardens, and a large *hamam*. The dwelling units were set perpendicular to the boulevard. The village that became the rural hub contained warehouses for agricultural produce and agricultural industrial enterprises, a bazaar, a police station, a post office, a bus station, and workshops. The plan also took into account the potential for the village's future expansion by creating an adjoining road network.

Design

The plan indicates that the designs of the dwelling units considered the local climate by making use of natural ventilation. Each house was designed by the construction expert, Brenner, to withstand earthquakes and included a walled garden, according to local custom, for growing household produce and to ensure family privacy. The plan took into account the

Expertise in the Name of Diplomacy

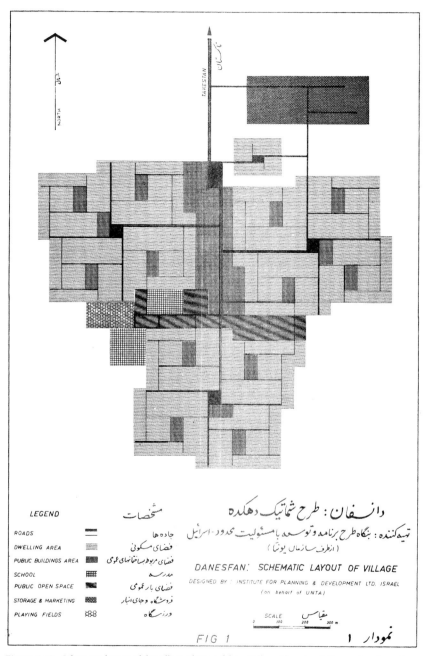

Figure 6.10: *Schematic layout of the village of Danesfahan.* Village Planning & Reconstruction of the Earthquake Zone in the Ghazvin Area - Iran (Tel Aviv: United Nations Technical Assistance [UNTA] Team and Institute for Planning and Development [IPD], 1968).

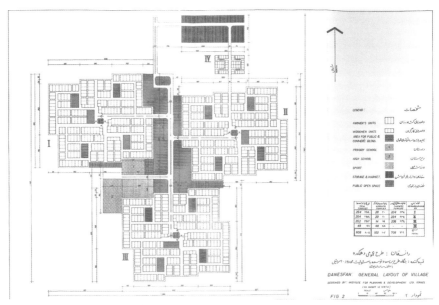

Figure 6.11: *Plan of the village of Danesfahan.* Village Planning & Reconstruction of the Earthquake Zone in the Ghazvin Area - Iran (Tel Aviv: United Nations Technical Assistance [UNTA] Team and Institute for Planning and Development [IPD], 1968).

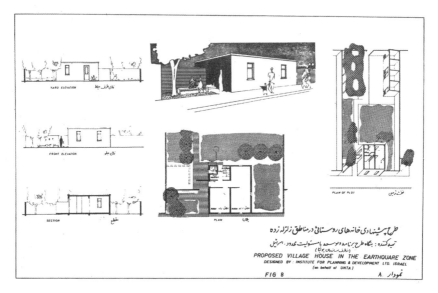

Figure 6.12: *Plan for a housing unit.* Village Planning & Reconstruction of the Earthquake Zone in the Ghazvin Area - Iran (Tel Aviv: United Nations Technical Assistance [UNTA] Team and Institute for Planning and Development [IPD], 1968).

possible future expansion of each house as well as its connection to a sewage system (at the time, unplanned) without detriment to the natural ventilation or the street facade.

The plan states that the houses were designed according to aesthetic considerations without elaborating on these considerations.[80] The illustration in the plan depicts a rather simple and functional building design with no indication of a particular architectural style or adornment [Figure 6.13]. The comprehensive and elaborate survey neither addressed the issue of local building traditions and style nor sought to adopt any particular style, which makes the assertion concerning aesthetic consideration seem rather perfunctory.

The region had strong building traditions, and it is surprising that the team refrained from using, or even studying them, given the state of current discourse on international modernism in architecture. The importance of locale and local traditions in architecture had been discussed in CIAM meetings, particularly at the ninth meeting in Aix-en-Provence (1953).[81] While most European architects working outside Europe still used a modernist façade, they experimented with incorporating local traditions (the work of Ecochard and ATBAT Afrique in Morocco is one example[82]), both in terms of the specific needs of the

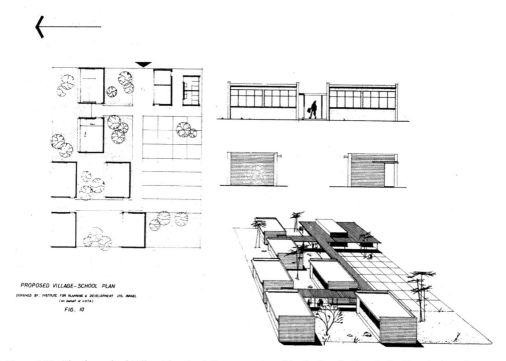

Figure 6.13: *Plan for a school.* Village Planning & Reconstruction of the Earthquake Zone in the Ghazvin Area - Iran (Tel Aviv: United Nations Technical Assistance [UNTA] Team and Institute for Planning and Development [IPD], 1968).

habitat as well as aesthetic considerations. Gwendolyn Wright observes that architects, both foreign and local, who worked in the Middle East in the mid-twentieth century tended to incorporate arches, domes, and patios into their designs, even if the overall effect was naive.[83] Iranian architects, however, were encouraged by the Shah to create a national architecture derived from European modernism and mixed with local traditional styles. While this occurred with public buildings, Iranians tended to adopt the modernist style in the design of private houses.[84] In early 1960s Israel, high modernism was still the prevailing trend and therefore Israeli architects disregarded the local vernacular.[85] It is in this context that the Israeli architects' inattention to local architectural tradition in Iran as well as their references to the aesthetic satisfaction of functional design should be understood. Other reconstruction teams working in the region during the early relief project were more influenced by local building methods like mud brick building and incorporated the dominant local features such as arched doorways and flat roofs, which could be used for sleeping during the summer, into their designs.[86]

Although concrete blocks or burned mud bricks, the most common building material in Iran, were recommended by the plan, concrete was mainly used. As Fatran explained:

> We planned according to what we knew, which wasn't what the Persians knew… What was the Persian building? It was mud work […] but the damage (from the earthquake) was due to the mud. So we told them […] we would build from concrete and showed them examples […]. We succeeded, and in the end, they were very pleased […][87]

Concrete was chosen because the Israeli planners believed it would withstand earthquakes better than the traditional mud construction. As the most commonly used building material at the time in Israel, it was also familiar. Fatran did not make clear whether he was referring to the locals or the politicians as being pleased with the work.

As mentioned previously, one project objective was to train local professionals. However, working with local professionals posed challenges for the Israeli team due to differences in working methods. Fatran made a request for student assistance at Qazvin to the School of Architecture at the University of Tehran, as he thought that they would want to participate in 'real planning'. Nobody volunteered. When he consulted with the dean, Fatran was told that the students were more interested in planning opera houses and office buildings than in Iran's rural architecture. Later, two technicians from Tehran were sent to work with him, but they would not meet with the villagers. The urban technicians and the local villagers came from different social classes and had little in common; beyond this, the Iranian technicians found it difficult to come to terms with the hands-on approach of the Israelis:

> We went into destroyed and semi-destroyed houses and huts to talk to people. They (the technicians) didn't come with us. When we came out after interviewing a village leader who had miraculously survived, they told us we were crazy. When we asked why, they

said: 'Why plan for these animals?' I realized that these were two absolutely different worlds.[88]

Moshe Shoked, the team's sociologist, stated that his job was to suggest ways of implementing the changes that modernization was expected to bring to the region: 'The Sociological survey of Gahzvin area was undertaken for the purpose of ascertaining the likely interplay between existing demographics and social structure of the farming population and the proposed plans for economic and agricultural development of the area.'[89] Shoked had trained as a sociologist in Israel in the early 1950s, a time when theories of modernization were dominant in the discipline. While working in Lakhish, he began to embrace new anthropological methods based on his fieldwork and interviews with locals. By the time he reached Qazvin, Shoked had already begun to question the dogma of modernization in social planning. His experience in Qazvin led him to pursue studies in anthropology after the completion of the mission.[90]

Like Fatran, he recalled the differences in methodology and attitudes between himself and the Iranian sociologists from the University of Tehran that had been assigned to learn from his experience. Although Shoked and his Iranians colleagues shared similar professional and socio-economic statuses in their respective countries, their work style and professional practices were different. While the Israelis wore blue-collar style work clothes, the Iranians wore professional Western style suits and ties. The Israelis wanted to work directly in the field; the Iranians placed an emphasis on the collation and statistical analysis of data from an office set in the city of Qazvin.[91]

Shoked made suggestions as to how the architecture could be more sensitive to local traditions, such as planning neighbourhood units according to the inhabitants' occupations. Traditionally, families involved in maintaining the water system (*qanat*) tended to live in the same neighbourhood. Based on this model, Shoked suggested that a separate neighbourhood be created for non-farming workmen's families. The school was designed for a small teaching staff; as one teacher often taught several age-groups, he proposed that the architects design the classroom to permit a teacher to move easily between two or more classes of different age groups. Thus, the architects designed the school to be organized in clusters of classrooms, connected by a shaded, open-air corridor [Figure 6.13]. On the other hand, the plan for the *hamam* corresponded with the simple bathing facilities of the kibbutz,[92] rather than the local architectural and social traditions [Figure 6.14].[93] Another team working on the reconstruction of the Rudak village designed a more elaborate *hamam* that was based on local architectural traditions including concentric spaces with shared bathing areas for the hot and cold water pools [Figure 6.15].[94]

We have no evidence regarding whether the Qazvin plan was ultimately successful in the eyes of its inhabitants. However, Shoked claims that when he visited the region at the end of the 1960s, it had been developed according to the plan and that the local residents were pleased. However, he also recalled that the villagers had enlarged their houses with

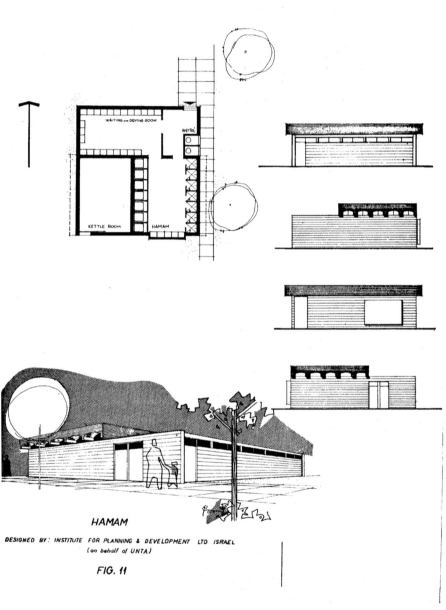

Figure 6.14: *Plan for a* hamam. Village Planning & Reconstruction of the Earthquake Zone in the Ghazvin Area - Iran (Tel Aviv: United Nations Technical Assistance [UNTA] Team and Institute for Planning and Development [IPD], 1968).

Expertise in the Name of Diplomacy

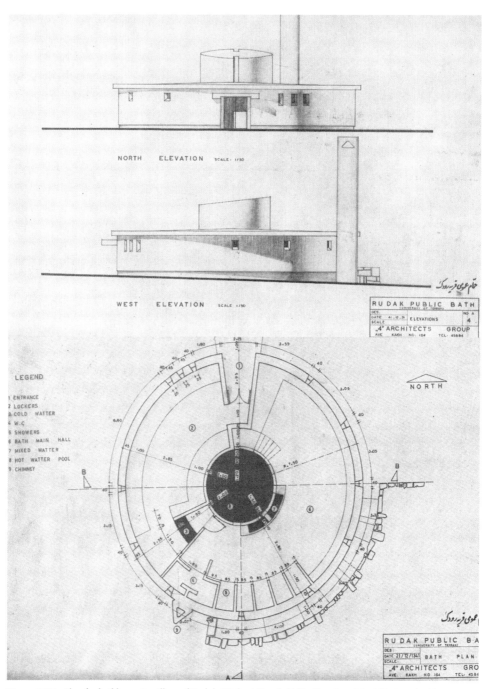

Figure 6.15: *Plan for bathhouse in village of Rudak.* Michael Boneh Collection, Israel Architecture Archive.

traditional mud work around the concrete core, in order to make them as large as they were before the earthquake.[95]

The Qazvin project was not the first attempt to develop and 'modernize' rural Iran.[96] The Ford Foundation had been working towards the same goals since 1953; however, they admitted that they had not been able to achieve their objectives with the project in 1963 and ceased activity in the region.[97] Nemchenok explains that what he described as a failure resulted from the differing goals of the Ford Foundation, the United States, and the Shah and his officials. The goals of The Ford Foundation, as set forth in its mission statement, were to undertake projects that promoted democracy and maintain high professional standards in the engagement of experts to implement these projects. The United States' foreign policy towards Iran was intended to stabilize the Shah's regime; therefore, the government felt that funds should be invested in strengthening the middle class, a source of political unrest, rather than rural populations. The Ford Foundation experts shared the views of some of the Israeli experts[98] that the Shah was only interested in US dollars,[99] and did not view development as a route to democracy, but rather as a means of strengthening his regime. It is important to note that, although the Qazvin team was aware of corruption among the Shah's clerks and his autocratic oversight,[100] like most Israelis,[101] it regarded the Shah as a benevolent dictator, considered his endeavours to be for the general public good, and were proud to be a part of his modernization project.

Conclusion

The Ford Foundation's mission was similar to the UNTA plan in that both were inextricably linked with a diplomatic agenda. In both cases, the nation states (the United States and Israel) sent missions with the goal of creating a new reality of cooperation and modernization in Iran, albeit for different reasons. For the United States, it was a part of their Cold War agenda. For Israel, it was to establish an alliance with another Middle Eastern country with the hope that by helping to advance Iran's modernization project, the two nations would grow closer thereby establishing a 'new Middle East', one in which Israel could be a participant. Of course, Iran also had its own goals. In this complicated context, the Israeli team met its goals while the Ford Foundation did not, at least not by its own standards. The evidence suggests that the Israeli team, led by a politician, was able to negotiate and manage the project in a way that contributed more meaningfully to its overall agenda. The project was not only developed and implemented according to plan, which was regarded as a success by the team,[102] but was also the beginning of a fifteen-year period of increased Israeli consultation and collaboration in Iran,[103] thus achieving the diplomatic goals. Whether the project was a long-term success and how it was perceived by the inhabitants remains to be researched.

The regional planning approach used by the team in Qazvin was based on the model implemented in Lakhish. However, it was adapted to the Iranian context based on the survey results, with particular attention paid to the sociological concerns. The adaptations are attributable to the different circumstances encountered by the Israeli experts in Qazvin, which influenced the nature of their engagement with the local population. In Qazvin, Shoked, the sociologist, was able to work with the region's indigenous people, while in Lakhish he worked with newly arrived immigrants, some of whom had not been given a choice about where to live or whether they wished to become farmers.[104] While both cases are examples of state-imposed modernization, the encounter with the villagers in Qazvin led to a different understanding of the needs of the inhabitants, and ultimately affected the plan.[105]

One of the goals of the Qazvin mission was to assist the State of Israel in building a framework for international relations and breaking its political isolation. The Qazvin project not only advanced the country's political agenda in the Middle East, but also established Israel as a prominent player in the area of international development, where there was an appreciation for the expertise developed during the project of nation building following the establishment of the state. This goal was achieved in the short term, but failed greatly in the long run. Israel had been an ally of the Shah, and the Israeli experts, though acting with the best of intentions, served an oppressive regime. Ram suggests that the alliance with the Shah's regime is one of the reasons for Iran's continued animosity towards Israel.[106] After becoming an occupying nation in 1967, and especially after the October War in 1973, Israel's role as an expert in development was rejected by many countries, notably in Africa.[107] Nonetheless, architecture outlives diplomatic relations and continues to affect the lives of its inhabitants. Relations between Israel and Iran may remain hostile to the present day, but remnants of the former relationship still exist on the ground in the rural region of Qazvin, as well as in other parts of Iran.

Our study of the Qazvin project and its historical context has been shaped by information obtained mainly from Israeli sources. The absence of Iranian archival records and the Iranian point of view is an indisputable shortcoming of this research. Despite these limitations, the present chapter aims to make a contribution to scholarship on the history of modern planning and development in Iran by focusing on the perceptions and experiences of the Israeli planning team in their encounters with the local villagers and professionals in Iran, with different ways of life, and with different needs and expectations. It highlights the positive intentions of the planners, as well as the impossibility of understanding all aspects of local environments in a High Modernist top-down plan. Our research demonstrates the extent to which the local context in Qazvin affected Israeli planning principles over the course of this transnational exchange. Finally, we hope that this chapter will open up opportunities for further research on rural Qazvin to Iranian scholars, who, until now, have not had access to the original plans.

Notes

1 In 1960s documents, Qazvin was spelled Ghazvin.
2 Known as the Buyin-Zahra earthquake in which 12,225 people died, 2776 were injured, and 21,130 houses were destroyed in 249 villages. These figures were taken from M. Berberian,

'The 1962 Earthquake and Earlier Deformations among the Ipak Earthquake Fault', *Geological Survey of Iran* 39 (1976): 419–27. A cover story with photos from the devastated region was published in *Life Magazine* on September 21, 1962.

3 The 'White Revolution' was the Shah's project for agrarian and land reform and the modernization of rural areas; it started in 1962. See Ervand Abrahamian, *Iran between Two Revolutions* (New Jersey: Princeton University Press, 1982), 424–25.

4 Shimon Amir, *Israel's Development Cooperation with Africa, Asia, and Latin America* (New York: Praeger, 1974).

5 In other publications this UN department, headed by Ernest Weissmann, is called Technical Assistance Administration (TAA), see: Tom Avermaete and Maristella Casciato, *Casablanca Chandigarh: A Report on Modernization* (Zurich: Canadian Centre for Architecture and Park Books, 2014): 58–59; and David Webster, 'Development Advisors in a Time of Cold War and Decolonization: The United Nations Technical Assistance Administration, 1950–1959', *Journal of Global History* 6.6 (2011): 249–72. According to Webster, it operated in the years 1950–59 and thereafter was absorbed into another UN section. As the project's report refers to it as UNTA, this acronym is used in the present chapter.

6 *Village Planning & Reconstruction of the Earthquake Zone in the Ghazvin Area – Iran* (Tel Aviv: United Nations Technical Assistance [UNTA] Team and Institute for Planning and Development [IPD], 1968).

7 Joe Nasr and Mercedes Volait, eds., *Urbanism: Imported or Exported?* (Chichester: Wiley-Academy, 2003); Anthony D. King, *Spaces of Global Cultures: Architecture, Urbanism, Identity* (London: Routledge, 2004); Patsy Healey and Dell Upton, eds., *Crossing Borders: International Exchange and Planning Practices* (London and New York: Routledge, 2010); Duanfang Lu, ed., *Third World Modernism: Architecture, Development and Identity* (London and New York: Routledge, 2010); Lukas Stanek, ed., 'Cold War Transfer: Architecture and Planning from Socialist Countries in the "Third World"', Special Issue, *The Journal of Architecture* 17.3 (2012): 299–307.

8 Baruch Gilaad, 'Israel–Iran Relations (1949–1979): Diplomacy Undercover', in *Ministry for Foreign Affairs: The First Fifty Years,* ed. Moshe Yeger, Yosef Govrin, and Arieh Oded (Jerusalem: Ministry for Foreign Affairs, 2002), 251–256 [Hebrew].

9 Haggai Ram, *Iranophobia: The Logic of an Israeli Obsession* (Stanford, CA: Stanford University Press, 2009).

10 Trita Parsi, *Treacherous Alliance: the Secret Dealings of Israel, Iran and the U.S.* (New Haven: Yale University Press, 2007).

11 Ibid., 19–28.

12 Ibid., 22.

13 Shimon Peres (1963) as quoted in Benyamin Neuberger, *Israel's Relations with the Third World (1948–2008)* (Tel Aviv: The S. Daniel Abraham Center for International and Religious Studies, Tel Aviv University, 2009), 14.

14 Uri Bialer, 'Top Hats, Tuxedos and Cannons: Israeli Foreign Policy 1948 to 1956 as a Field of Study', *Israel Studies* 7.1 (2002): 1–23.

15 Gilaad, 'Israel-Iran Relations', 253.

16 See Lior Sternfeld, 'Reclaiming Their Past: Writing Jewish History in Iran during the Mohammad Reza Pahlavi and Early Revolutionary Periods' (1941–1989)' (Ph.D. diss., University of Texas at Austin, 2014).
17 Jalal Al-e Ahmad, *The Israeli Republic,* trans., Samuel Thrope (New York: Restless Books, 2014). For more on Al-e Ahmad's travelogue, see the book review by Lior Sternfeld: https://notevenpast.org/the-israeli-republic-by-jalal-al-e-ahmad-2014/, posted March 5, 2014.
18 Eldad Pardo, 'Israel as a Model for the Iranian Left in the 1960s', *Iyunim Bitkumat Israel (Studies in Israeli and Modern Jewish Society)* 14 (2004): 337–65 [Hebrew].
19 Ram, *Iranophobia,* 58–59.
20 Parsi, *Treacherous Alliance,* 24.
21 Ruth Gruber, *Science and the New Nations: The Proceedings of the International Rehovot Conference 1960* (New York: Basic Books Publishing, 1961).
22 ISA-mfa-InterCooperation-0007wme. This reference and those in the following notes are to document numbers in the system of classification used by the Israel State Archive.
23 Neuberger, *Israel's Relations,* 13.
24 On Israeli development missions in the new African nations, see: Zach Levey, *Israel in Africa 1956–1976* (Amsterdam: Martinus Nijhoff, 2012) and Neuberger, *Israel's Relations*. On Israeli architecture in Africa, see: Inbal Ben-Asher Gitler, 'Campus Architecture as Nation Building: Israeli Architect Arieh Sharon's Obafemi Awolowo University Campus, Ile-Ife, Nigeria', in *Third World Modernism: Architecture, Development and Identity,* ed., Duanfang Lu (London and New York: Routledge, 2010), 113–40; Ayala Levin, 'Exporting Architectural National Expertise: Arieh Sharon's Ife University Campus in West Nigeria', in *Nationalism and Architecture,* eds, Raymond Quek, Darren Deane, and Sarah Butler (London: Ashgate, 2012), 53–66; Haim Yacobi, 'The Architecture of Foreign Policy: Israeli Architects in Africa', *OASE Architectural Journal* 82 (2010): 35–54. On the work of Israeli architects in Latin America, see Uriel Kon, '"A Menorah Etched in the Pampas": The Export of Planning Knowledge from Israel to Argentina 1963–1970: The Test Case of Las Pirquitas' (Master Thesis, Technion – Israel Institute of Technology, 2013) [Hebrew].
25 On Israeli projects in Crete see Rachel Kallus, 'The Crete Development Plan: A Post-WWII Israeli Experience of Transnational Professional Exchange', *Planning Perspectives* 30.3 (2015): 339–65.
26 On MASHAV, see http://www.mashav.mfa.gov.il/MFA/mashav/Pages/default-old.aspx
27 Articles on Israel's relief package were published on September 6, 1962 in major Farsi-language Iranian newspapers, including *Setareh Tehran, Mehr Iran, Payghman Emrouz,* and *Kayhan.*
28 Letter from Moshe Dayan, September 6, 1962: ISA-mfa-Political-000wudo.
29 Letter from Haim Divon of the Israeli Foreign Ministry to the US embassy September 21, 1962: ISA/RG130/MFA/3435/10.
30 Report dates to September 28, 1962: ISA-mfa-Political-000wudo.
31 ISA-mfa-Political-000wudo.
32 Ibid.
33 'Israel Pays an Old Debt to King Cyrus' Successors', *Yediot Aharonot,* December 30, 1962 [Hebrew].

34 Articles on Israel's relief package were published in Iranian newspapers in December, 1962. An article in English was published in *Kayhan International*, December 10, 1962.
35 The Iranian government published several pamphlets describing the rebuilding efforts. Two were found in Boneh's archive: Michael Boneh Collection in the Israel Architecture Archive (IAA). See Ed Holting, 'Earthquake Village: Rubble to Reconstruction', *The Tehran Journal*, November 22, 1962, for an article in English about the other villages being rebuilt in the first phase of reconstruction (there is no mention of the Israeli project in Khuznin).
36 Report dates to September 28, 1962: ISA-mfa-Political-000wudo.
37 Letters from the Israeli UN delegation to the Foreign Ministry: ISA-mfa-Political-000wudo.
38 Ijlal M. Muzaffer, 'The Periphery Within: Modern Architecture and the Making of the Third World' (Ph.D. diss., Massachusetts Institute of Technology, 2007).
39 Lukasz Stanek, 'Introduction: The "Second World's" Architecture and Planning in the "Third World"', *The Journal of Architecture* 17.3 (2012): 299–307.
40 Stephen V. Ward, 'Transnational Planners in the Postcolonial World', in *Crossing Borders: International Exchange and Planning Practices*, eds Patsy Healey and Robert Upton (London and New York: Routledge, 2010), 47–72.
41 ISA-mfa-Political-000wudo.
42 Correspondence between the foreign ministry and the Israeli 'embassy' in Iran: ISA-mfa-InterCooperation-0007z75.
43 This phrase is taken from the title of Naomi Klein's book, *The Shock Doctrine: The Rise of Disaster Capitalism* (New York: Picador, 2007).
44 Israel had only unofficial representation in Iran, though Israelis and Iranians referred to it as an embassy and to its head as the ambassador.
45 Letter from Ambassador Ezry describing a tour given to foreign diplomats by Arsanjani on January 4, 1963: ISA-mfa-Political-000wudo.
46 Letter from Zvi Doriel, March 4, 1963: ISA-mfa-InterCooperation-0007z70.
47 Letter from Moshe Gilboa, March 17, 1963: ISA-mfa-InterCooperation-0007z75.
48 Amir, *Israel's Development Cooperation*, 9.
49 ISA/RG130/MFA/496/8.
50 Raanan Weitz explained his views in a meeting at the Foreign Ministry on May 8, 1954: ISA-mfa-InterCooperation-0006sd8. The institutional approach was a top-down command hierarchy.
51 See Raanan Weitz, *New Roads to Development* (Westport, CT: Greenwood Press, 1986).
52 Arie Lova Eliav, *Autobiography: Rings of Dawn* (Tel Aviv: Am Oved, 1984).
53 The Planning Organization (known as the PO) was a pseudo-ministry for housing and development. See Ali Madanipour, 'Urban Planning and Development in Tehran', *Cities* 23.6 (2006): 433–38.
54 The *qanat* water system was mostly destroyed in the earthquake, but even earlier, the Iranians had wished to improve the water supply in order to increase agricultural productivity.
55 *Village Planning & Reconstruction*, 2. The three teams worked together under one leader at the special request of the Iranian Ministry of Agriculture.
56 Israeli Prime Minister David Ben-Gurion wrote to Eliav, on behalf of himself, the Foreign Minister Golda Meir, and the Agricultural Minister Moshe Dayan, asking him to take the

57 Smadar Sharon, '"Not Settlers but Settled": Immigration, Planning, and Settlement Patterns in the Lakhish Region in the 1950s' (Ph.D. Diss., Tel Aviv University, 2013), 66–68 [Hebrew].
58 Rachel Kallus, 'Humanization of the Environment: Glikson's Architecture and the Poetic of the Everyday', *Journal of Architectural and Planning Research* 21.2 (2004): 152–70.
59 Kallus, 'The Crete Development Plan'.
60 Moshe Schwartz and Paul A. Hare, *Foreign Experts and Unsustainable Development: Transferring Israeli Technology to Zambia, Nigeria and Nepal* (Aldershot: Ashgate, 2000), 13.
61 Schwartz and Hare, *Foreign Experts*.
62 Ibid.
63 On the centrality of the Lakhish Plan in the curriculum of planning conferences and symposia, see: ISA-mfa-IsraeliMissionsAbroad-000oip8, ISA-mfa-InterCooperation-0007khu, ISA-mfa-InterCooperation-0007vad, ISA-mfa-InterCooperation-0007vae, ISA-mfa-InterCooperation-0007as3.
64 Kon, 'A Menorah Etched'.
65 ISA-mfa-InterCooperation-0007kid.
66 Kallus, 'The Crete Development Plan'.
67 Ayala Levin, 'From Survey to Plan: The 1965 Israeli National Urbanization Plan for Sierra Leone' (paper presented at the European Architectural History Network, Second International Meeting, Brussels, Belgium, May 31–June 3, 2012).
68 Letter from Eliav to the Ministry of Foreign Affairs, December 27, 1962: ISA-mfa-InterCooperation-0007z75.
69 Moshe Shoked, interview, June 8, 2010. Shoked believed that too much money was incorrectly invested.
70 ISA-mfa-InterCooperation-0007wm.
71 *Village Planning & Reconstruction*, 12. A more detailed description of the job can be found in Supplement A of the report.
72 Ibid., 37. The full sociological survey conducted by Shoked appears in Appendix I of the report.
73 *Ibid.*, 4.
74 Some locations were specifically chosen to avoid the return of the previous Palestinian residents.
75 A dwelling unit is defined as housing for one family.
76 *Village Planning & Reconstruction*, 13–14.
77 Ibid., 7.
78 Ibid., 49–55. The report refers to 'Workmen': villagers who work in the services sector, especially as part of the *Boneh* group tasked with building the qanat water system. The survey suggests keeping the families of this group together.
79 Sharon, 'Not Settlers but Settled', 127. On the role of extended families in the planning of the *Moshav*, see Dana Shevah and Rachel Kallus, 'Past Forward: Planning in the Light of Historical Knowledge', *Journal of Planning History* (2014) DOI: 10.1177/1538513214553909.

80 *Village Planning & Reconstruction*, 27–29.
81 See: Tom Avermaete, *Another Modern: The Post-War Architecture and Urbanism of Candilis – Josic – Woods* (Rotterdam: NAi Publishers, 2005); and Eric Mumford, *The CIAM Discourse on Urbanism, 1928–1960* (Cambridge, Mass.: MIT Press, 2002).
82 Monique Eleb, 'An Alternative to Functionalist Universalism: Ecochard, Candilis, and ATBAT-Afrique,' in *Anxious Modernisms, Experimentation in Postwar Architectural Culture*, eds Sarah Goldhagen Williams and Réjean Legault (Cambridge, MA: MIT Press, 2001), 55–73.
83 Gwendolyn Wright, 'Global Ambition and Local Knowledge', in *Modernism and the Middle East: Architecture and Politics in the Twentieth Century,* eds., Sandy Isenstadt and Kishwar Rizvi (Seattle, WA: University of Washington Press, 2008), 55–73.
84 Talin Grigor, *Building Iran: Modernism, Architecture, and National Heritage under the Pahlavi Monarchs* (New York: Prestel, 2010).
85 Alona Nitzan-Shiftan, 'Seizing Locality in Jerusalem', in *The End of Tradition?*, ed., Nezzar AlSayyad (London: Routledge, 2004), 231–55. Nitzan-Shiftan claims that the adoption of the (Arab) vernacular in Israeli architecture occurred after the 1967 war.
86 Ed Holting, 'Earthquake Village'. Pamphlets in Farsi on the planning of villages in the first relief mission appear in the Michael Boneh Collection in the IAA (Israel Architecture Archive).
87 Fatran, interview, 2011.
88 Ibid.
89 *Village Planning & Reconstruction*, 37.
90 Shoked earned a Ph.D. in Anthropology at the University of Manchester.
91 Interviews with Fatran (2011) and Shoked (2010).
92 Fatran, interview, 2011.
93 'Bathhouses', Encyclopedia Iranica, last updated December 15, 1988, http://www.iranicaonline.org/articles/bathhouses.
94 A plan for the circular public bath for the village of Rudak, designed by "4" Architects Group, appears in a pamphlet in the Michael Boneh Collection in the IAA (Israel Architecture Archive).
95 Shoked, interview, 2010.
96 On other architectural exports from the United States to Iran, see Jeffery W. Cody, *Exporting American Architecture 1870–2000* (London: Routledge, 2003), 140–51.
97 Victor V. Nemchenok, '"That So Fair a Thing Should Be So Frail": The Ford Foundation and the Failure of Rural Development in Iran, 1953–1964,' *Middle East Journal* 6.2 (2009): 261–84.
98 Shoked, interview, 2010.
99 Nemchenok, 'That So Fair', 265.
100 Interviews with Fatran (2011) and Shoked (2010).
101 Ram, *Iranophobia*, 47.
102 *Village Planning & Reconstruction*, 1.
103 On other projects of Israeli architects in Iran, see: Neta Feniger and Rachel Kallus, 'Building a "New Middle East": Israeli Architects in Iran in the 1970s', *The Journal of Architecture* 18.3

(2013): 381–401; Neta Feniger and Rachel Kallus, 'Israeli Planning in the Shah's Iran: A Forgotten Episode', *Planning Perspectives* 30.2 (2015): 231–251.
104 Sharon, 'Not Settlers but Settled', 109–51.
105 On this subject, see James C. Scott, ed., *Seeing Like a State: How Certain Schemes to Improve the Human Condition Have Failed* (New Haven: Yale University Press, 1998).
106 Ram, *Iranophobia*, 62.
107 Levey, *Israel in Africa*, 157–76.

Chapter 7

Industrial Complexes, Foreign Expertise, and the Imagining of a New Levant

Dan Handel and Alona Nitzan-Shiftan

> For me, the term 'Middle East' has no real meaning. Rather, I see two areas separated by their ownership of oil resources, whereby those of us without oil are the Eastern Mediterranean countries that formed the old 'Levant'.
>
> (Stef Wertheimer in The Tefen Model)[1]

Introduction

In the 1970s, the industrialist Stef Wertheimer (1926–) pioneered a new industrial model in the Galilee – a rural region in northern Israel. Fifteen years later, he suggested using this model to develop a new transnational industrial frontier in the Eastern Mediterranean. Surprisingly, and in sharp contradiction to the prevalent Zionist depiction of Israel as an island of progress in a decadent Arab Orient, Wertheimer advanced his project under the heading 'The New Levant'. In doing so, he echoed the dramatic shift in Israeli politics after the 1977 elections, in which the Labour Party lost power for the first time since Israeli independence. The new right-wing coalition, to which he was elected as a parliament member, led a transition from a socialist to a liberal economy, and launched the historic peace process with Egypt. Once the horizon of a peaceful region started looming, the developmental logic of the post-World War II Marshall Plan – infrastructure sponsored by a transnational funding scheme – seemed to Wertheimer relevant and applicable. In this New Levant, Wertheimer envisioned a scheme of 100 industrial gardens – each an extraterritorial enclave of knowledge and expertise that would transcend the national conflicts haunting the region and yield a new era of economic prosperity.

Wertheimer's vision relied on two profound shifts he foresaw in positioning Israel in the Middle East. The first distinguished between oil- and non-oil-producing countries, and identified in this distinction an opportunity for new economic blocs. This geopolitical, economically based reading allowed Wertheimer to advance yet another shift. Instead of the old Zionist reading of the Levant, imbued with Orientalism and associated in Israel with the perennial risk of its Arabization and decline, Wertheimer now advanced a New Levant – a Mediterranean network of development. Such reading de-Arabized the context of economic collaborations and perfectly matched the optimism surrounding the historic visit of an Egyptian president to Jerusalem. Eventually, Wertheimer's vision of a transnational Levantine network approximated the scholarly depiction of the historic Old Levant – a territory in which extraterritorial capitulations, encounters with foreign experts, and inherent pragmatism facilitated transnational economic exchange.

Wertheimer entrusted to experts the transformation of this new concept into an economic engine. His road to a New Levant, therefore, uncovers a trajectory of expertise that connects post-war American industrial parks, organizational experts in Ivy League universities, and complex economic arrangements that lead back to American markets. By pioneering the import of such expertise, Wertheimer eventually transformed Israel's industrial landscape, and aspired to expand it to regional dimensions.

In order to understand the power of his undertaking, this chapter first associates Wertheimer's use of the Levant framework with the liberal political ideology he advanced as a member of the Israeli parliament. It then considers the development of his industrial complexes, highlighting what one may understand to be radical spatial propositions in which architecture rejects its immediate context to become a register of proto-global economic processes. In conclusion, the chapter posits that the transnational scheme of the New Levant, anchored as it is in specific geographic and economic conditions, can shed critical light on notions of globalization and regional identity.

Oil Boundaries

The 1970s were a particularly transformative decade in the history of the Middle East. After the withdrawal of the British from the Persian Gulf and the post-1973 spike in oil prices, the region saw the emergence of oil regimes that nationalized their resources and began constructing extraction and distribution infrastructure on a massive scale.[2] However, the prosperity brought by the black gold was not evenly distributed among OAPEC (Organization of Arab Petroleum Exporting Countries) members. Although the gross domestic product of Saudi Arabia increased by more than 1000% between 1970 and 1977, and that of the United Arab Emirates, Kuwait, and Libya grew by more than 400%, Egypt and Syria contributed only 11.5% to OAPEC's gross national product, even though their combined populations were more than 50% of the total population of all OAPEC member countries.

The growing disparities between oil- and non-oil-producing countries soon became evident on two levels. First, it became evident in domestic investment that financed development projects, defence mechanisms, and welfare services, and expanded the growth of financial institutions. Second, it became clear in the growing liberalization of economies in non-oil-producing countries, an outgrowth of their desire to attract foreign investment. This shift, known as *infitah* (opening up), was most developed in Egypt, where President Anwar Sadat in 1974 introduced a thorough restructuring of the economy, 'based on the encouragement of foreign investment, the reorganization of the public sector, […] and the liberalization of foreign trade'.[3] Sadat's policy enabled the internationalization of the Egyptian economy, reduced the level of state planning in the economy, and allowed a substantial growth in imports.

This policy can be understood as part of a larger process in which Middle Eastern economies became part of the international economy both as oil suppliers and as markets for primary and manufactured goods. In turn, this process led Middle Eastern countries to rapidly expand their participation in total world trade.[4] Another effect was the growing involvement of foreign experts in newly liberalized economies, whose impact was felt mostly in the financial and industrial sectors. In Egypt in 1980, many multinationals already established their hold on the country, looking to build plants for products targeted at Egyptian and foreign markets.[5] These industrial facilities were built either by the local subsidiaries of international companies or by joint ventures created to benefit from government grants and tax breaks. The knowledge required to build these facilities often came from abroad. Most of them were constructed by foreign companies with little local labour, and usually were handed over to their users as turnkey projects.[6]

As economic liberalization pushed foreign expertise deeper into non-oil-producing countries, it paved the way for regional and economic definitions that were not necessarily anchored in Arab nationality. This is evident when looking at non-OAPEC economies in the region, such as Turkey and Israel. In both, we see highly planned economies suffering from a surge in energy prices, going through a crisis, receiving international support, and then adopting an export-oriented, market-driven set of policies in the 1980s.[7]

For the Israeli economy, the 1970s was an especially volatile and dramatic decade. Being on the other side of the oil embargo, Israel suffered a series of crises that lowered growth rates, worsened the balance of payments, and ultimately caused spiralling inflation. As economist Paul Rivlin notes: 'Increasing oil prices and other import costs as well as the international recession had deleterious effects on the economy […] the oil import bill rose from $98 million in 1972 to $1.8 billion in 1980.'[8] During these years, the government attempted to liberalize the economy and develop a more independent industrial sector several times. The most dramatic experiment was the economic liberalization plan inspired by Milton Friedman (1912–2006), passed in 1977, which introduced monetary-oriented reforms that led eventually to hyperinflation that would be contained only by the stabilization plan of 1984. However, as Rivlin observes, the most significant features of a long-term liberalization of the economy were the trade agreements signed with the European Community and with the United States in 1975 and 1985, respectively. These marked, as for other countries in the region, 'a move from import substitution toward reliance on exports as the motor of growth'.[9] This was the immediate economic context in which Wertheimer first introduced his Tefen Model and developed his regionalist concepts, based on export and special trade agreements.

The Model

The Tefen Model began as a complex developed in the Galilee region in the north of Israel – a triad composed of a communal settlement, a production base, and an educational–industrial compound, which Wertheimer promoted under the title 'industrial garden' as a new model for Israeli industry with an idiosyncratic architecture. The garden was conceived as a pioneering attempt to create enabling environments for entrepreneurs, insulated from governmental structures. Its ambition was to allow companies to develop in (what in later years would be known as) 'incubators' until they reached a predetermined capacity. At that point, the companies were expected to relocate and stand on their own feet. Rather than focusing on specific industries, Tefen accepted companies based on the sole criterion of their products' export capacity.

The industrial garden idea had its origins in the United States, stemming from Wertheimer's encounters with new developments along the East Coast, which followed his work on a knowledge agreement signed with the New Jersey Adamas Carbide Corporation in 1956. Visiting industrial areas in New Jersey and the Route 128 industrial parks in Massachusetts, Wertheimer saw in them the models for his own vision: 'The first industrial gardens were built there. I looked at them, and dreamed that one day we would build things in the same way.'[10] The planning and architecture of these environments were fundamental to their success: 'Everything had to be rational, in its place, without redundancies or masquerades [...] these principles guided me throughout.'[11] However, this was not the vision of a single mind. Rather, the industrial gardens were designed through a frequent correspondence with an array of American management, planning, and architecture experts.

Wertheimer first encountered the case method at a 1962 conference in Israel, which included Massachusetts Institute of Technology (MIT) and Harvard Business School (HBS) experts. His interest formalized through long-lasting relationships with these institutions. During the 1970s, Wertheimer sent his managers to programmes at HBS. He also led an intensive communication with Professor Dick Rosenbloom (1933–2011) from HBS, who focused on corporate strategy, and Professor Ed Roberts (1935–) of the MIT Sloan School of Management, who theorized high-tech business development. This correspondence would gradually shape the programmatic requirements of the industrial garden.

At the same time, Wertheimer became interested in the work of American developer and planner James Rouse (1914–96). Purportedly the person who introduced the term 'urban renewal' in the 1950s, Rouse spent the following decades promoting the idea of planned communities. His most ambitious experiment, the new town of Columbia, Maryland, was composed of twelve villages, sharing central amenities and responding to the challenges of 'our cities of today'. Wertheimer visited Columbia in 1978; in 1979, Rouse travelled to Israel, where he toured the site on which Wertheimer's 'new town' was to be built; and in 1979, Werthheimer and his planner Harry Brand (1936–) made several subsequent visits to Columbia. 'There has never been a private new town developed in Israel', wrote Rouse.

> There are lofty and rational goals, but little knowledge of how to fulfil them. Our kind of assistance and direction is needed. It remains to be seen whether or not it is wanted on a basis acceptable to us.[12]

A business relationship was not established. However, Wertheimer fused Rouse's observations with those of others in a first generic plan for the industrial garden, produced as an appendix to Wertheimer's report to the Israeli government *c.*1979 [Figure 7.1].[13] Rosenbloom's and Roberts's

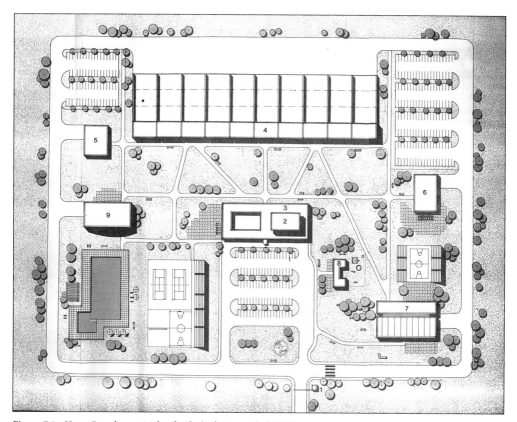

Figure 7.1: *Harry Brand, generic plan for the 'industry garden', 1979.*

ideas found their expression in the modulation of production facilities, which suggest internal flexibility. The economic rationale for the industrial garden was anchored in space modules of 250 square metres that would house the enterprises, from the smallest (one unit) to the largest (four units). Wertheimer, using a terminology that echoes Rouse's in describing his industrial incubator, recalled: 'I used to tell Brand "Make it small, like a village. Don't give me big buildings. Make small units, so people will have to get out of here once their companies grow."'[14] Rouse's ideas also resonate in the distribution of shared services in the plan and in the addition of educational and recreational facilities that would become the Tefen Model trademark. Wertheimer compressed them all in an organic plan that surrounds a well-manicured, open space.

Beyond the work of foreign experts, Tefen was also a manifestation of a political ideology Wertheimer developed during his time in national politics. In addition to economic shockwaves, Israel also experienced a thorough reconfiguration of its political map in the 1970s. Labour Zionism – the workers' party, which was synonymous with the country's socialist ethos – was challenged and defeated by the right flank of Zionism and by the liberal parties. These parties, influenced by a conservative brand of American liberalism, brought to the government

Figure 7.2: *Dan Reisinger's 'Industree' graphic, commissioned by Stef Wertheimer to visualize his liberal Zionism idea. At the bottom, the small houses of early pioneers stand for 'the roots' of land settlement. The straight trunk-figured middle part embodies the collective task of building a functioning society based on military power, and the upper branches represent industry, signified by the cogwheels breaking free from the state tree and into the world.*

an emphasis on individual rights and private initiative.[15] In this context, Wertheimer, who was a parliament member for the Liberal Party, formulated his own liberal redefinition of Zionism. According to Wertheimer, during the Mandate period, Zionism had its roots in agriculture; then, during the first decades of statehood, it focused on military force; and in the late 1970s, it should evolve and develop industries that, through export, would 'bring economic independence and promote peace' [Figure 7.2].[16] In other words, Wertheimer reconstructed the collective, socialist roots of early Zionism into an accumulation of individual pursuits.[17]

These pursuits could be materialized only if their promoters – that is, entrepreneurs – could be insulated from the bureaucracies of central government. Once Wertheimer's party entered the parliament in 1977, he sought to define an environment that could do just that. The opportunity to develop this idea soon appeared. At this point, the problems of Israeli new towns, resulting many times from poor economic planning, were becoming a political issue. Established under the auspices of a developmental agenda, and tellingly called 'development towns', these settlements were provided with industrial areas that housed mostly state-owned factories. The architecture of these plants, already alluded to in the renderings of the first national (Sharon) plan produced for Israel in 1951, mostly followed a standard, low-cost prefabricated structure and saw-tooth roof design. As the logic went, these industrial areas would turn their hosting towns into product and service centres for their rural environment. However, their planners failed to recognize several factors that prevented this goal from materializing. First was the underestimation of the agricultural lobbies that established their own cartels instead of relying on new towns for services. Second, there was the general lack of capital investment and finance mechanisms for industry until the late 1950s. These difficulties were layered with the profile of the population in new towns, mostly new immigrants from North African or Arab-speaking countries, who were, for lack of political organization (as well as prejudice among the ruling parties), more likely to be sent to inhabit new settlements in remote locations.

The result was settlements that quickly evolved into hotbeds of social and economic problems, which prompted the government to take action.[18] Although it was recognized that industry can play a key role both in diversifying the economies of new towns and in supplying a stable source of employment for their inhabitants, the government again demonstrated its preference for geopolitical considerations over economic ones by creating a subsidy system that was designed to support enterprises in designated 'priority areas'. The degree of priority was 'higher the farther a region was from the metropolitan areas of the coastal plain', and the economic criteria for getting subsidized were 'somewhat loosely' defined.[19] This policy meant that support for new industrial developments was not conditional on feasibility studies and that the development of industry remained confined and inefficient.[20]

As the inhabitants of development towns constituted an important part of right-wing voters who brought the Likud to power in 1977, the government attempted to respond to their problems. It commissioned Wertheimer, versed in industrial development, to propose solutions. Instead of amendments, he concluded that new towns should be left behind and substituted by an entirely different model. In the report written on the subject, consulted by Brand, he writes: 'With the onset of the post-industrial era, and after recognizing the need and importance of ecological balance […] it is necessary to consider a new industry–

settlement model [...] which will be a crucial step towards economic independence.'[21] This model also intimated a withdrawal of central planning from industry, much like the one put into effect in Egypt several years earlier. In the minds of Wertheimer and his committee, the model offered the spatial equivalent of their updated Zionism idea: a new scheme in which national goals could be materialised through individual initiatives. However, in practice, the site allocated for Tefen, which presented a specific set of regional problems, complicated this ambition. The Galilee had been a contested region for decades and was a focus of state planning agencies, which sought to populate it with Jewish settlers as a way of countering a perceived demographic problem. The first national plan of 1951 exposed this obsession by allocating urban centres in these areas against all professional considerations.[22]

These efforts continued in the 1960s with the establishment of seventeen agricultural settlements and the new town of Carmiel, and in the 1970s with concentrated efforts by a new generation of planners in the ministry of housing who emphasized regional urban development. This flurry of planning was complemented by frequent land appropriations by the government, which in 1976 resulted in the first organized anti-government protests of the Arab population, known as the 'Land Day'. This moment, some argued, marked the Arab population's point of entry into Israeli public politics.[23] The government promoted further Judaization of the region with its 1979 'observatories plan',[24] in which 30 new Jewish settlements were designated.[25]

The governmental response to Wertheimer's plan cannot be separated from this context. Although he promoted a system completely isolated from governmental influence, the land allocated for the project, the development of its infrastructure, and the creation of its municipal entities were all facilitated by public agencies. In a curious Israeli dynamic, Wertheimer succeeded to establish an environment for private entrepreneurship by juxtaposing extraterritorial arguments with an alignment between private and national interests. As such, Tefen is arguably a mediator between nationalist ideology and proto-global capitalism. Wertheimer, on his side, never openly admitted this implicit agenda. Instead, he used the impressive array of experts he gathered in order to argue for his project in the most rational terms on both economic and social levels. The Tefen master plan, produced by Brand around 1982, reiterated almost entirely his earlier generic scheme from the 1979 report, but with minor alterations. The garden was now slightly more compact, and the production facilities were distributed around the central garden in a more explicit way. The first phase was built as it appears in that plan [Figure 7.3].

The architecture of the Tefen Model registers these divergent, sometimes opposing, ambitions. It can be described as a radical break from the earlier generation of industrial buildings, mostly through its capacity to capture and enable the fluctuating flows of economic processes in its organization and its envelope system. Brand and Moshe Zarhy (1923–2015) – Wertheimer's long-time friend and one of Israel's prominent architects – designed the buildings on the grounds. Their architecture clearly express the demand for internal flexibility and the strict underlying economic rationale with one important distinction: whereas Brand gave a direct interpretation to this idea by creating serially compartmentalized, prefabricated

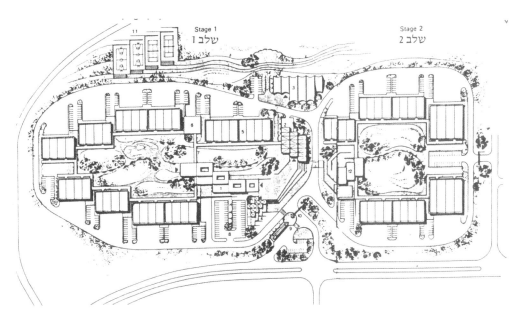

Figure 7.3: *Harry Brand, Tefen Masterplan, 1982.*

buildings, sometimes with a hint of symbolism, Zarhy pursued a more radical strategy in which flexibility was allowed through a sophisticated treatment of the envelope.

The use of the term 'envelope' here seeks to contextualize it within architectural discourse, in which it indicates a divergence from the architectural façade. Whereas façades were used at times polemically to expose the rationale of buildings, arguing for material and ideological neutrality,[26] the architectural envelope serves mostly to demarcate inside from outside. As such, it is understood as carrying technological, social, and political content. Peter Reyner Banham (1922–88) was early to touch upon this concept in 1965, calling to substitute the building's exterior with a 'membrane' that would enable a controlled environment.[27] Literary critic Frederic Jameson, in analysing the Bonaventure Hotel in Los Angeles, California, as a spatial symptom of the postmodern condition, further explored this idea.[28] For him, the architectural skin not only allows for a controlled interior but also dissociates the Bonaventure from its surroundings. It thus enables the game of mirrors that became synonymous with Jameson's theorization of postmodernism. Partly building on that work, Reinhold Martin analysed the screen wall as an architectural register of the nexus of post-war organizational culture,[29] and Alejandro Zaera-Polo argued that the envelope should be understood as a composite of technology, organization, environmental effects, and representation. 'The envelope has become', he writes 'the last realm of architectural power'.[30]

Under these terms, Zarhy's buildings for Tefen can be seen in a new light. While still prefabricated, the envelope of these buildings acts as enabling shells for the relentless reorganization of economic processes. This focus on the technological, structural, and aesthetic

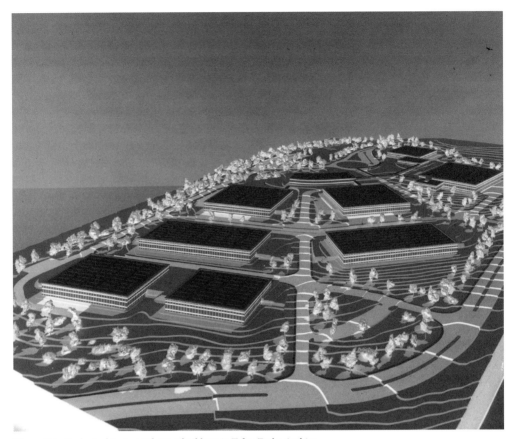

Figure 7.4: *Zarhy Architects, production buildings in Tefen.* Zarhy Archive.

qualities of the envelope is the essence of the radicality of these buildings; although they may superficially resemble earlier industrial structures, their immaculate articulation, down to the level of the prefabricated detailing, highlights a completely different architectural trajectory.

Around 1982, Zarhy explicitly used the term when writing about 'envelope buildings', which are based on a two-phase process: 'The first includes the expedited construction of the building's envelope and the main supply and clearing systems. In the second phase, the subdivision, interior design and secondary systems are structured.' This separation of inside and outside allows the envelope building to have 'universal qualities, allowing flexibility in its internal subdivision'.[31] The envelope in the Tefen projects is developed to allow for this quality. Consequently, Zarhy introduced into Israeli architecture projects that were blatantly devoid of symbolic content – buildings that serve as the unmediated expression of economic processes. In the regional scheme Wertheimer developed later, this architecture of economy became an efficient vehicle for the negotiation of cultural boundaries [Figure 7.4].

Regional Argument

This negotiation became apparent as the project scaled up. By 1988, the Tefen Industrial Garden already housed more than 20 new companies with total sales of almost $30 million.[32] It was soon followed by a second phase, planned by Zarhy, as well as by the establishment of additional industrial gardens in Lavon (1988), Tel Hai (1992), and Omer (1995). The success of the Tefen Model brought Wertheimer national and worldwide recognition and led him to develop the transnational argument for the New Levant. In this argument, both national and regional designations became obsolete, as he writes in the quote that opens this chapter. If the boundaries could be redrawn in accordance with economic potentials, coexistence could be again a viable option:

> among the 'nonoil' countries are those that would choose to compete on world markets and seek economic independence, such as Jordan, Turkey, Israel, and, potentially, Lebanon and the Palestinian Authority. Successful advancement along this path can lead the countries of our region towards the creation of a thriving economy, towards a work ethic based on reason and responsibility and towards the achievement of peaceful coexistence between like-minded neighbours.[33]

The development of this export capacity was dependent on the funding of 100 industrial parks, based on the Tefen Model. As in the Marshall Plan, which served as a point of reference, Wertheimer's initiative proposed that funding from donor countries would be channelled through non-governmental organizations and used for infrastructure, industrial development, and technical training.[34]

It is notable that Wertheimer identifies many similarities between post-war Europe and the Eastern Mediterranean. Both regions are understood as entrenched in complex and problematic political circumstances, and both are struck by conflict and lag in industrial development. Therefore, the Marshall Plan is used here not only for the sake of historic analogy but as an actual structural inspiration for a system that would construct the New Levant through the agency of international financial institutions and experts, and with minimal interaction from state bureaucracies.

That said, the potential of the Levant to act as an economic, cultural, and regional framework for proto-global transactions still demands scrutiny. To that end, it is worthwhile here to recount briefly the nature and characteristics of the 'Old Levant' to which Wertheimer refers. Much like the 'Orient', the 'Levant' served archaeologists and writers as a vague designation of a geographical region based on a generalizing gaze toward the (Near) East. The term, originating from medieval French, became more specific to the lands controlled by the Ottoman Empire around the sixteenth century with the development of commercial activities. The French were the first to institutionalize a relationship with the Ottoman Empire through capitulations that were agreed upon in the 1560s.[35] These agreements were to last in one form or another for more than three centuries and, as Philip Mansel points out, had a decisive influence on the region:

> The modern Levant was born from one of the most successful alliances in history […] the history of the region and its cities would be dominated by the changing balances of influence – political, cultural and economic – between Constantinople and Paris.[36]

From the start, this alliance was as political as it was commercial, a result of *Realpolitik* more than shared ideology. Toward the mid-eighteenth century, trade with the French accounted for up to 65 per cent of all Ottoman trade.[37] The French influence in the region was due not only to the volume of commercial activity, but also to a different organizational agenda. While the English tended to concentrate on a small number of cities as their trading hubs, the French took a different approach, 'penetrating' deeper into the hinterland of the Ottoman Empire and operating in places such as Bursa, Ankara, and Aleppo. This involvement at all of the *échelles* (scales) of the Ottoman Empire was always connected with French diplomatic efforts in the region, which kept France as the empire's most favourable trading partner until the end of the eighteenth century.

By that time, decades of interaction furnished the emergence of a very specific brand of interchange, in which Enlightenment ideas intersected with everyday cosmopolitan practices on the boundary between Europe and the Muslim world, and affected the idea of cosmopolitanism in both.[38] In this process, the notion of free trade was gradually loaded with nationalistic, Eurocentric, and then imperial undertones.[39] While such notions anticipated the colonialist approach of the following century, the Ottoman Empire's economy nevertheless benefited during this time, as the dense networks established by European traders allowed the empire's constant growth and integration into the world economy.[40]

It is also necessary to note the meaning the Levant carried in Israel. Since the Levant, as a concrete geography and a mentality, was affiliated with the Ottoman Empire and with cosmopolitan cities, it became something of an antithesis to European modernity, intimately connected with national identity and ideological zeal. As a result, the term acquired an anachronistic and derogatory aura throughout the nineteenth and twentieth centuries. In the context of the newly founded nation state of Israel, the transnational infrastructural and cultural networks that connected cities in mandatory Palestine to places like Alexandria or Beirut had to be severed.

Ironically, once the flow of Jewish immigrants from Arab countries increased, the war against the Levant had to be fought on two levels. On the first level, it entailed a denial of 'externalities', such as Islamic buildings or Arab cities, while on the second, it entailed a centralized attempt to suppress the Arab identity of Jewish immigrants and align their identity with the hegemonic Eurocentric Zionist narrative.[41] This effort was and still is a contested subject and the source of some of the more bitter struggles dividing Israeli society, but in the mid-twentieth century, the Levantinization of Israeli society was conceived as a concrete danger, well captured in the statement by David Ben-Gurion (1886–1973): 'We do not want the Israelis to be Arabs. It is our duty to fight against the spirit of the Levant that ruins individuals and societies.'[42]

Nevertheless, the Levant, beyond a geographical designation, can be understood as a dynamic boundary between Islam and the outside world, and as a framework for the constant negotiation of identity. It is a regional concept shaped by the presence and expertise of foreign agents, extraterritorial concessions and a tendency to prefer pragmatism over ideology. Wertheimer's scheme was built upon these nuances and contradictions, projecting a trajectory of development in which the region will experience an effortless, almost spontaneous, resolution of ideological conflicts, cultural disparities, social inequalities, and even unfavourable forms of government. Once absorbed into the language of the economy through the sole criterion of exports, these frictions would become disposable elements in the circulation of capital, channelled, worked, and released back into the world economy through the cogwheels of 100 Tefens.

Instances

Although the complex realities of the region usually hindered such post-national ambitions, Wertheimer's idea was considered positively on both local and international levels. In the 1990s, he received support from the Israeli and Palestinian governments for a twin industrial park scheme – one Palestinian and the other Israeli – on both sides of the Israeli border with the Gaza Strip, near the Sufa border crossing. In 1999, a working team headed by Dr Sa'adi el-Krunz, minister of industry for the Palestinian Authority, and Wertheimer met to discuss the principles of the joint project. The memorandum that followed stated the ambition in the following way: 'The endeavour is intended as an economic project; however, it will play an important role in developing good neighbourly relations and increased "cooperation on the benefit of both peoples."'[43] In this memorandum, too, economic pragmatism preceded ideological differences.

The project's guidelines included the possibility of declaring the park a free-trade area and stressed the importance of relationships with 'donating states'. The memorandum also specified the structures of planning with great detail, including steering committees, working teams, and a joint planning team. Wertheimer invited a small group of Harvard University experts, headed by Professors Alex Krieger and Carl Steinitz of the Harvard Graduate School of Design, for a five-day workshop to identify potential sites for the project, which they did from a helicopter and then through short site visits.[44] The team subsequently met in Jerusalem for two days and 'sketched schematic designs for how [the twin industrial park scheme] would work'.[45] These designs were presented to high-level Israeli and Palestinian officials, including three ministers from each side. Krieger and Steinitz discussed the planning and landscape elements of the projects, recommending three sites out of the initial ten for serious consideration. The team worked in isolation, with Zarhy Architects later developing the planning schemes [Figure 7.5].[46] In principle, the project was to 'be modelled on the industrial parks previously

Figure 7.5: *Tour to the Israeli-Palestinian industrial gardens project site, 1999. The Harvard team includes Carl Steinitz, Alex Krieger, and students.* Zarhy Archive.

built by Mr. Stef Wertheimer in Tefen, Omer, Lavon, and Tel-Hai'.[47] Steinitz reflected that the ground rules were clear: 'There was a *parti* [the basic scheme or concept of an architectural design] that had minor variations because of site conditions. There's a pattern, which can vary in certain ways and not others.'[48] Accordingly, the plans proposed by Zarhy Architects placed identical 'Tefen elements' on both sides of the 'no-build zone', projecting economic incentive systems, development stages, and connection to ground and air infrastructures [Figure 7.6]. The industrial incubators on both sides of the border were to look the same. In fact, the rejection of architectural contextualism was so radical that buildings from previous industrial gardens were used in the artist impression of the project [Figure 7.7].

This moment of regional and global optimism ended abruptly as the second *intifada* broke out in 2000.[49] The project was frozen and Wertheimer moved to promote the Aqaba International Industrial Estate project in Jordan, using an initial concept design produced by the planning firm Uzi Gordon Ltd. The US government positively appraised the feasibility of this project, as American consulting firms had already conducted previous studies on

Industrial Complexes, Foreign Expertise, and the Imagining of a New Levant

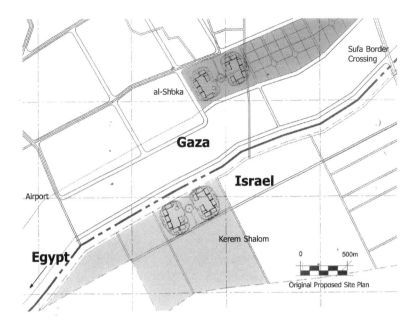

Figure 7.6: *Zarhy Architects, initial scheme of the joint Israeli-Palestinian industrial gardens project, 1999.* Zarhy Archive.

Figure 7.7: *Zarhy Architects, joint Israeli-Palestinian industrial gardens project perspective, 1999.* Zarhy Archive.

Figure 7.8: *Buildings at the Gebze industrial garden.* The Tefen industrial parks website.

Jordan's industrial capacity. In a diplomatic communication cable from 2002, the Aqaba project was recognised as '[benefiting] from the services of a development management team from Parsons Brinckerhoff, and is supplemented by support in the Aqaba Special Economic Zone from master developer Bechtel'.[50] This interest was not coincidental, and resulted from intense efforts on Wertheimer's side. Another cable refers to the fact that Wertheimer had hired former US Senator George Mitchell (1933–) and former US Congressman Robert Livingston (1943–) 'as consultants and Washington lobbyists for his plans'.[51] The Aqaba project also came to a halt, and Wertheimer turned his attention to Turkey, where he managed to develop an industrial garden in Gebze, outside of Istanbul. In this case, too, American approval was instrumental, as the concept was based on the suitability of Gebze as a Qualifying Industrial Zone – a special designation that allowed (through the involvement of Israeli companies) areas in countries around Israel to benefit from Israel's free-trade agreements with the United States. In order to achieve that, the Tefen Company entered the project under the scheme of a joint venture, as a 49-per-cent-share partner. Five years after its completion, the Gebze industrial garden contained 80 companies and employed 680 research and development (R&D) personnel.[52]

The programme and layout of the project were strikingly similar to those of other Tefen projects, with six rentable buildings of around 2000 square metres each, intertwined with open areas and public buildings on a 120,000-square-metre site. The application process for interested companies was also similar, focusing on software and R&D companies with export potential.[53] Istanbul-based Tekeli-Sisa Architecture Partnership designed the buildings, completed in 2008. Although the layout dictated a dense building composition, the architects attempted to pay attention to the forming of outer spaces that 'enrich social life'. Following the Tefen scheme, the project also allocated areas for 'social responsibility projects': technology workshops and art studios. The architecture remained confined to the expression usually chosen for the project's predecessors in Israel. The six buildings intentionally avoid any local or national characteristics, and although they were described at a certain point as having 'sculpture like qualities', they do in fact present a slick architectural expression with functionalist undertones [Figure 7.8].[54]

Networks

The series of attempts to materialize the industrial garden in its regional phase, in the Gaza, Aqaba, and Gebze projects, came close, through their minute economic, infrastructural, and architectural organization, to the materialization of a functionalist, transnational economic hub. That was partly due to the fact that they were located outside Israel, and, at least in the case of Gebze, managed to navigate through complex diplomatic, ideological, and social waters.[55] From an economic standpoint, we see a curious trajectory in which American expertise is being exported in order to enable the organization of the industrial gardens in one location (Israel) to be then replicated in another (Turkey) in order to export knowledge and products back into the American market, and so a cycle of transactions and interactions is circumscribed.

Under these terms, the Gebze project can be better evaluated vis-à-vis the New Levant concept. First, we can argue that the clear demarcation of the project's boundaries and the way it presents itself organizationally and architecturally reinforces its enclave extraterritoriality and brings to mind the capitulations in Turkish territories that were fundamental to the definition of the historic Levant. Other features of the project support these links as the industrial gardens promote a pragmatism that has the potential, once developed to its logical conclusion, to transcend the national conflicts haunting the region. Additionally, the project is calibrated according to the commercial interests of world powers and while these powers are now different, it can easily be argued that the French and British empires were simply substituted by a new global empire.

The association of globalization and the Levant has been made before. Mansel writes:

> The true heirs of the Levant are some of the richest cities of today: London, Paris and New York – Dubai, Bombay and Singapore. Their mixed populations [...] make them increasingly different from their hinterlands, but they are protected by national armies and police forces.

This observation leads him to conclude that 'Ben-Gurion was blind to denounce "the spirit of the Levant" [...] Levantine cities are the future, as well as the past. Globalization means we are all Levantines now.'[56]

However, what the industrial gardens demonstrate slightly differs from this celebratory statement; the model according to which they are structured avoids the identification of the Levant with urban settings, and, as such, follows a more nuanced territorial understanding, closer to the French demarcation of *échelles* (scales). In other words, the industrial gardens attempt to structure networks between hubs of different scales that go deep into the hinterlands – enclaves of knowledge economy, which are enabled through a combination of central planning and private capital. This composite character is challenging received ideas about the weakening of the role of the state under global capitalism. As such, the New Levant, as imagined and as partly materialized, is making the case for a regional concept with well-defined planning and architectural articulation that is anchored in its geography, economy, and history. These features, registered in its architecture, allow the New Levant the potential of not succumbing to the all-encompassing thrust of globalization.

Notes

1 Stef Wertheimer, quoted in Tefen Enterprises, *The Tefen Model* (Israel: Tefen, 2005), 65–66.
2 For a more nuanced account of the oil embargo from the perspective of exporting countries, see Yusif A. Sayigh, 'Arab Oil Policies: Self-Interest Versus International Responsibility', *Journal of Palestine Studies* 4.3 (1975): 59–73.
3 Roger Owen, 'The Arab Economies in the 1970s', *MERIP Reports* 100/101 (1981): 5.
4 Saudi Arabia, for instance, became the seventh-largest American world market by 1979.
5 For a detailed list of these companies and their operations, see Fran Rivier, 'Le Politique Industrielle en Egypte: De Nasser à Sadat', *Mahgreb/Machrek* April/May/June (1981): 57.
6 Ibid., 10.
7 In the Turkish context, the five-year plans of the 1960s were substituted by planning that was geared toward trade agreements with Europe. As the debt crisis worsened, the country adopted a set of stabilization policies c.1980. See Merih Celâsun and Dani Rodrik, 'Turkish Economic Development: An Overview', in *Developing Country Debt and Economic Performance*, vol. 3, *Country Studies: Indonesia, Korea, Philippines, Turkey*, ed. Jeffery Sachs (Chicago, IL: University of Chicago Press, 1989), 617–29. See also Merih Celâsun, *Sources of Industrial Growth and Structural Change: The Case of Turkey*, World Bank staff working papers 614 (Washington, DC: World Bank, 1983).
8 Paul Rivlin, *The Israeli Economy* (Boulder, CO: Westview Press, 1992), 11.
9 Ibid., 59.
10 Interview with Stef Wertheimer, Tefen Industrial Garden, Galilee, Israel, March 2012.
11 Ibid.
12 James W. Rouse. 'Letter to Matthias J. DeVito', July 19, 1979. The James Rouse Archives, Columbia, MD, RGI-S1-5-38-F10.
13 Wertheimer Committee for the Allocation of Failed Enterprises and Mivnei Ta'asiya Ltd., *Industrial Gardens: A Conceptual Plan (1979)*.
14 Interview with Stef Wertheimer.

15 See, for instance, Amnon Rubinstein, *The Zionist Dream Revisited: From Herzl to Gush Emunim and Back* (New York: Schocken Books, 1984).
16 Stef Wertheimer and Yeshayahu Ben Porat, *Conversations with Stef Wertheimer* (Tel-Aviv: Sifriyat Poalim, 1998).
17 In that, he also followed the ideas of his peers in the Liberal Party, such as Amnon Rubinstein, mentioned in note 15.
18 Arie S. Shachar, 'Israel's Development Towns', *Journal of the American Institute of Planners* 37.6 (1971): 367.
19 Ibid., 362–72.
20 'Very seldom did the decision to establish an industrial enterprise take into account alternative regional or local locations; thus, local specialization of industry based on relative location advantages was hindered.' Ibid., 368.
21 Wertheimer Committee, *Industrial Gardens*, 5.
22 An internal memo of the planning department exposed this when arguing that: 'Founding new towns in a mountainous area such as the Galilee presents a tough problem […] economically speaking, there is almost no justification for establishing these centres […] security and political considerations led to the decision that despite these difficulties additional urban centres need to be established in these parts of the region that are currently mostly populated by Arabs.' Israel State Archives, Ministry of Interior, File 56, 15.8, 1950.
23 Oren Yiftachel, 'Ethnocracy: The Politics of Judaizing Israel/Palestine', *Constellations* 6.3 (1999): 372.
24 It is noteworthy that the term 'Judaization' was frequently used in the public discourse surrounding the plan, and did not necessarily carry the critical undertones we associate with it today.
25 For an overview of the region as an arena of territorial struggle, see Oren Yiftachel, *Planning a Mixed Region in Israel: The Political Geography of Arab–Jewish Relations in the Galilee* (Aldershot: Avebury, 1992), 385.
26 Alan Colquhoun, 'The Facade in Its Modern Variants', *Werk, Bauen + Wohnen* 12 (2005): 13–20.
27 Peter Reyner Banham, 'A Home Is Not a House', *Art in America* 2 (1965): 109–18.
28 Frederic Jameson, *Postmodernism, or the Cultural Logic of Late Capitalism* (Durham, NC: Duke University Press, 1991), 82.
29 Reinhold Martin, *The Organizational Complex: Architecture, Media, and Corporate Space* (Cambridge, MA: MIT Press, 2003).
30 Alejandro Zaera-Polo, 'The Politics of Envelope: A Political Critique of Materialism', *Volume* 17 (2008): 79.
31 Moshe Zarhy, *High Technology Industry Campuses* (Tel Aviv: self-published, 1985).
32 Tefen Enterprises, *Tefen Model*, 65–66.
33 Ibid., 6.
34 Ibid., 98.
35 These capitulations established freedom of commerce between the two states and an extraterritoriality for French subjects that included the freedom of dress and worship, freedom from forced labour, and freedom from Ottoman taxation.

36 Philip Mansel, *Levant: Splendour and Catastrophe on the Mediterranean* (New Haven, CT: Yale University Press, 2011), 5.
37 Edhem Edlem, 'French Trade and Commercial Policy in the Levant in the Eighteenth-Century', *Oriente Moderno* 18 (1999): 28.
38 For a thorough development of this argument, including an overview of the complexity of society under Ottoman rule, see Ian Coller, 'East of Enlightenment: Regulating Cosmopolitanism between Istanbul and Paris in the Eighteenth Century', *Journal of World History* 21.3 (2010): 447–70.
39 Ibid., 469.
40 Elana Frangakis-Syrett, 'Market Networks and Ottoman–European Commerce, *c.*1700–1825', *Oriente Moderno* 25.(86)1 (2006): 109–28.
41 This process was termed 'de-Arabization' by some writers, arguing that it followed closely the de-Arabization of the land. See Amnon Raz-Krakotzkin, 'The Zionist Return to the West and the Mizrahi Jewish Perspective', in *Orientalism and the Jews*, ed. Ivan Davidson Kalmar and Derek Jonathan Penslar (Waltham, MA: Brandeis University Press, 2005), 162–81.
42 Ella Shohat has argued that this was not an isolated remark, but part of an attitude toward Arab Jews in which one can identify parallels with colonialist conceptions. See Ella Shohat, 'Sephardim in Israel: Zionism from the Standpoint of Its Jewish Victims', *Social Text* 19/20 (1988): 1–35.
43 Stef Wertheimer and Saadi El-Krunz, *Memorandum of Understanding*, March 11, 1999, Zarhy Archives.
44 Interview with Carl Steinitz, London, September 2014.
45 Ibid.
46 See Harvard University Graduate School of Design, 'Towards a Joint Palestinian–Israeli Industrial Development', in *Al-Shoka and Kerem Shalom: An Assessment of Location and Future Planning Flexibility* (Cambridge, MA: Harvard University Graduate School of Design, 2009). Steinitz had collaborated with Wertheimer before on a number of Harvard University Graduate School of Design-sponsored design studios that focused on alternatives for the Galilee region. See Carl Steinitz, ed., *Alternative Futures in the Western Galilee, Israel* (Cambridge, MA: Harvard University Graduate School of Design, 1998).
47 Wertheimer and El-Krunz, *Memorandum*.
48 Interview with Steinitz.
49 'Everybody went home, and that was it. Right after that, things blew up and nothing happened'. Ibid.
50 'Jordan's Unused Industrial Capacity', Internal Cable, Ref: 02AMMAN6288, Tuesday, October 29, 2002, 7:41a.m., accessed October 3, 2014, https://github.com/alx/cablegate/blob/master/cables/02AMMAN6288.txt.
51 'Wertheimer Apparently Giving Up on "Marshall Plan" for the Middle East', Internal Cable, Ref: 04TELAVIV1362_a, Thursday, March 4, 2004, 14:43, accessed October 3, 2014, https://www.wikileaks.org/plusd/cables/04TELAVIV1362_a.html. Mitchell had first-hand knowledge about the Middle East as an author of the Mitchell Report, which was initiated by the Clinton Administration to inquire into the events of the second *intifada* and to propose possible solutions.

52 GOSB (Gezbe Organized Industry Zone) Teknopark, A.S., 'About Us', accessed October 7, 2014, http://rgp.sabanciuniv.edu/technopark.
53 Ibid.
54 In that regard, much as in the Israeli context, these decontextualized projects actually echoed earlier experiments in the modern forms of *Yeni Mimari* ('new architecture') in Kemalist Turkey, pushing for a modernist national architectural expression. See Sibel Bozdoğan, *Modernism and Nation Building: Turkish Architectural Culture in the Early Republic* (Seattle and London: University of Washington Press, 2001), 59.
55 The first decade of the 2000s saw the rise of right-wing conservatism and nationalism in both Israel and Turkey, followed by a gradual deterioration of diplomatic relations and economic cooperation.
56 Philip Mansel, *Levant: Splendour and Catastrophe on the Mediterranean* (New Haven, CT: Yale University Press, 2011), 356.

Chapter 8

Mobilities of Architecture in the Global Cold War: From Socialist Poland to Kuwait and Back

Łukasz Stanek

A visitor to Kuwait City in 1983 described it as a 'showplace for the world's architectural prima donnas'.[1] The landscape of the city was indeed shaped by architects of international renown, with Arne Jacobsen's National Bank of Kuwait (1976), the airport by Kenzo Tange (1979), the National Assembly Building by Jørn Utzon (1984), followed by structures designed by Rifat Chadirji, Arthur Erickson, Hassan Fathy, Mohamed Makiya, Reima and Raili Pietilä, The Architects Collaborative (TAC), and Skidmore, Owings and Merrill (SOM).[2] Yet behind what appears to be an exemplification of familiar modalities of architectural globalization, including the emerging star system, boutique architects, and large corporate design offices, complemented by a small group of esteemed specialists in 'Arab' architecture, the production of space in Kuwait in the late 1970s and 1980s was defined by yet another actor: architects from socialist countries including Bulgaria, Czechoslovakia, Hungary, Poland, and Yugoslavia.[3] This chapter will discuss their work with a particular focus on a group of Polish architects, mostly from Wrocław, who left for Kuwait by the late 1970s after a decade of successful professional work in socialist Poland. They were employed by Kuwaiti design offices and, together with other expatriate and local professionals, they contributed to a change in the townscape of the city state by designing and supervising construction of the first generation of high rises, and of housing neighbourhoods, commercial buildings, and public-use buildings. Architects from socialist countries working in Kuwait and elsewhere hardly fit the familiar image of architectural globalization that juxtaposes an architectural elite shaping urban icons to the cultural practices of migrant workers associated with 'globalization from below'; and yet they were crucial, if rarely accounted for, agents of globalization of architectural practice.[4]

The Gulf has become a favourite example of such processes and, in *The Global Architect*, Donald McNeill describes the 'rapid intensification' of architects' travel, when 'territorial boundaries that had kept most architects tied to a small set of national markets no longer make much sense for design firms capable of operating in the dynamic economies of the Gulf and China'.[5] McNeill sees these processes as a facet of the globalization of capitalism, which accelerated after 1989 when 'the geopolitical fixities of the Cold War softened up to create new markets in East and Central Europe'.[6]

By contrast, this chapter shows that, far from being a 'new market' opened to the globalization of architectural practice after the fall of the Soviet Bloc, socialist countries played an important role in the global mobility of architectural services in the 1970s and 1980s. Consequently, this mobility is not to be understood as 'Americanization' or 'Westernization'; neither can it be explained with the unilateral scheme of 'diffusion' of architectural and planning knowledge from metropolitan centres.[7] It appears, rather, as multidirectional, both in the sense of competition and collaboration among professionals coming to Kuwait from around the world, and in the sense that the Wrocław architects, while in Kuwait, learned at least as much as they brought with them. This knowledge proved an asset for those who returned to Wrocław after 1989 and the end of socialism in Poland.

The work of architects from socialist countries in the Gulf, more generally, was conditioned upon and contributed to the emergence of a global market of architectural resources which, besides labour, included building materials and technologies, discourses, and images, most often combined on the ground with resources from local and regional networks. But the insistence on the global, rather than 'transnational', character of the exchanges discussed in this chapter stems also from its larger context. The present chapter is part of a research project focused on what I have identified elsewhere as architecture's 'mondialization',[8] that is to say the emergence of architecture as a worldwide techno-scientific phenomenon after World War II from within competing visions of global cooperation and solidarity. Socialist internationalism and the Non-Aligned Movement were among such visions that programmatically took the world as a dimension of practice and imagination in the context of the Global Cold War.[9] They became frameworks for the recruitment of architects and planners from Eastern Europe since the late 1950s, hired for contracts abroad.[10]

Within this larger research project, the focus in what follows on a spectrum of actors and practices in Kuwait in the late 1970s and 1980s allows historicizing of the mobilities of architectural resources in the economic, cultural, and techno-political conditions of the final two decades of the Cold War. The work of the Wrocław architects will be shown as dependent on the institutional framework created by socialist Poland at a time when the authorities in Warsaw were putting increased stress on the economic benefits of labour export and on securing employment for large groups of intellectual workers of big state companies, and as waning ideas of 'socialist internationalism' were being paid lip service at best. This shift was paralleled by a change in architectural terms. The previous generation of Polish architects can be seen as agents of the mondialization of modernism, orientating their work abroad in large part according to the principles of CIAM (Congrès internationaux d'architecture moderne), however adapted and modified. The Wrocław architects in Kuwait, though, responded to a pervasive disenchantment with these principles that was felt as much in the Gulf as in socialist Eastern Europe.

The response to such disenchantment had been articulated in the work of the Wrocław architects before they travelled abroad, and this will be accounted for in the first part of this chapter, together with a review of the institutional conditions of their employment in Kuwait. The second part will show how their work in Poland reverberated with the critique of post-oil urbanization in the Gulf and with the shift in international architectural culture associated with postmodernism. Their designs in Kuwait responded to this new climate of opinion, characterized by a turn to what were perceived as 'local', 'traditional', or 'familiar' forms and ways of use, and often at odds with the social reality of the rapidly urbanizing Gulf. These tensions will be discussed in the third part of this chapter by focusing on the ways the Wrocław architects reimagined the relationship between the pedestrian and the car in Kuwait. Rather than following authors who discuss architecture as a 'mediation' between (global) technology and (local) culture,[11] however, this part will show that techno-scientific expert systems (technologies of prefabrication, managerial and logistical schemes, Computer-Aided Design software, or CAD) facilitated an engagement with the specific 'context' of the Gulf. The chapter's final section will show how these expert systems, characterized by Science and Technology Studies (STS) scholars in terms of their capacity for de-territorialization and re-territorialization,[12] found a pendant in the intersubjective 'profile' of architects from socialist countries working abroad.

From Socialist Poland to Kuwait

In simpler terms, this is a story about a group of friends. Andrzej Bohdanowicz, Ryszard Daczkowski, Wojciech Jarząbek, Edward Lach, Krzysztof Wiśnowski, and most other protagonists of this study graduated from the architectural school of Wrocław Polytechnic in the late 1960s. Some of them were invited to join the Chair of History of Urbanism at the Institute of History of Architecture, Art, and Technology,[13] where their research addressed questions of regional architecture. Composing various teams, they worked together on numerous competition projects, some of which they won. One of these was the competition for a section of the City Centre Housing Estate in Łódź (1969), which became a flagship project of the regime of Edward Gierek, first secretary of the Polish Communist Party from 1970 to 1980. Among other projects reflecting Gierek's modernization effort were competitions for city centres and new housing districts, in particular the Kozanów neighbourhood in Wrocław, a project that received first prize in 1974.[14]

In spite of this success, these architects became disillusioned with the conditions of work in Poland, which was characterized by the submission of architecture to the apparatus of the Party and the state-controlled building industry, the domination of planning over architecture, and the increasingly apparent economic and political crisis of the 1970s. Their competition entry for Kozanów is a case in point. Breaking with the 'real existing modernism'[15] of undifferentiated, homogenous apartment blocks being constructed in Poland since the early 1960s, Kozanów was designed as a 'small city within a big city' [Figure 8.1]. Their design was a topographically sensitive composition of diverse housing typologies, linked by a cluster of low pavilions with social facilities. In spite of the fact that the project won the first prize in a national competition, it was rejected by the Ministry of Construction, which did not accept the flexible prefabrication system proposed by the architects. As one of them recalled, 'I had to go back to designing the very same apartment blocks that, we were told during our studies, don't work'.[16]

In this context, the invitation to Kuwait, mediated by a Palestinian alumnus of Wrocław Polytechnic employed in a Kuwaiti architectural office, was a welcomed change. The first group to come to Kuwait included Lach and Daczkowski in 1976, who were employed in the

Figure 8.1: *Kozanów Estate, competition model, design 1974.* K. Wiśniowski archive, Kuwait City.

Gulf Engineering Office (GEO), and later co-opted Jan Matkowski and Mieszko Niedźwiecki. Wiśniowski and Bohdanowicz were employed in 1977 by the office Shiber Consultants, headed by Victor Shiber, brother of the renowned Palestinian architect and urban planner Saba George Shiber who worked in Kuwait from 1960 until his death in 1968.[17] In 1978, Jan Urbanowicz, Jacek Chryniewicz, and Jarząbek replaced Wiśniowski and Bohdanowicz in Shiber's office, where they cooperated with the Industrial & Engineering Consulting Office (INCO). INCO's director, Mohammad Al-Sanan, recalls the group's successful competition entries for Site C of the Sabah Al-Salem district (designed in 1977, constructed in 1982) and for the Kuwaiti National Theatre (designed in 1978, unrealized).[18]

The competitions that were won allowed them to legalize their employment in the Gulf. They signed contracts with Polservice, the foreign trade organization (FTO) in socialist Poland, which mediated contracts of labour export. Over the course of the 1970s, the Polish authorities increasingly foregrounded the mercantile interest in export of intellectual labour, which generated the foreign currency needed to finance the Gierek regime's modernization efforts and, later, to pay off its debts.[19] Such tripartite contracts between foreign commissioners, professionals, and mediating institutions were typical for architects from socialist countries employed abroad, including Czechoslovak and Yugoslav architects working in Kuwait.[20] Polish architects coming to Kuwait recommended others, including their wives and partners: Danuta Bohdanowicz, Zdzisława Daczkowska, Elżbieta Niedźwiecka, Rudolf and Ewa Staniek, Anna Wiśniowska, and Marian Żabiński. Architects from other Polish cities were arriving as well, including Janusz Krawecki, who was invited by his former student at the School of Architecture of Kraków University of Technology, and Włodzimierz Gleń of the Kraków state office Miastoprojekt, whose earlier extensive experience in Baghdad proved very useful in the Gulf.[21] Krawecki and Gleń contributed to the first high-rise buildings in Kuwait.[22] These architects found employment in various Kuwaiti offices: INCO, SSH, the SOOR Engineering Bureau, the Arabi Engineer Office, the Kuwait Engineering Office (later the Kuwait Engineering Group, or KEG), and GEO (later Gulf Consult).[23] The professional links with Poland were rarely severed and Jarząbek, for example, sent plans for the church of St Mary Queen of Peace in Wrocław-Popowice (1994) from Kuwait, the details of which resemble those of the Al-Othman Centre he co-designed in Hawally (with Lach for KEG, 1995). After the declaration of martial law in Poland (1981) most of them decided not to return, and the monthly fee imposed on them by Polservice (often paid in cash to the Polservice representative in Kuwait) was one more incentive to break with the state socialist system.[24]

Labour conditions for the Wrocław architects in Kuwait on Polservice contracts were different from those of Western consultants in the Gulf, such as Constantinos Doxiadis or Michel Ecochard, and from employees of large state-socialist companies working in the region, such as Energoprojekt of Yugoslavia or Bulgaria's Technoexportstroy. The daily routine of the Polish architects was characterized by their intense engagements with clients and contractors, and direct supervision of the building sites, where many details were drawn when needed.[25] They cooperated with Kuwaiti professionals, mainly educated in the United Kingdom and the United States, with professionals from the region (Egyptian, Iraqi, Lebanese, Palestinian), as well as with architects and engineers from India and Pakistan. Exchanges were intense with British professionals in Kuwait, commissioned to design schools, hospitals, and housing since the period of the protectorate, as were exchanges with offices from the United States.[26] The latter were based on financial links between the United States and Kuwait and often resulted from joint-venture agreements between Kuwaiti and foreign firms; such agreements were increasingly required for larger projects by the authorities and private clients alike.[27]

Architects from other socialist countries contributed to this cosmopolitan character of Kuwait. The designer of the Sava Centar in Belgrade (1977–79), Stojan Maksimović, was invited by the Kuwaiti government to participate in the competition for the Conference Center at Bayan Park, which he won in 1980 (the realized project, however, has little to do with the design which he prepared together with the Kuwaiti office Archicentre).[28] After winning the international competition for the Amiri Diwan, which included the offices of the ruler prominently located next to the Seif Palace, Archicentre delivered the final design in cooperation with a group of Czech and Slovak architects on contract with Polytechna, the Czechoslovak FTO.[29] But it was the Yugoslav construction firm Energoprojekt that had been the pioneer in establishing contacts with Kuwait; as early as the 1960s, Energoprojekt's architects Dragomir Bakić and Ljiljana Bakić had designed a number of housing layouts and public facilities.[30] The Hungarian office KÖZTI followed, with designs for housing neighbourhoods and mosques within the Coastal Strip Development Project, the urban design of which was delivered by Miastoprojekt-Kraków from Poland.[31] Bulgarproject of Sofia designed the slaughterhouse in Kuwait and bid for other projects, including the Arab Cities Organization Building; the latter was not constructed, in contrast to several buildings in the UAE designed by Bulgarproject.[32]

State companies from socialist countries operated in Kuwait within a highly competitive market, divided between South Korean, Indian, and Pakistani contractors (receiving commissions for which cheap labour provided competitive advantage); and Japanese, European, and American firms (competing for technically challenging projects), who were increasingly joined by Kuwaiti and Saudi contractors.[33] Companies from socialist countries were part of the latter segment, either individually or as subcontractors. Some of these were highly visible commissions: Yugoslavia's Union Inženjering constructed the Kuwait Towers (1977), the icon of modern Kuwait; Energoprojekt was responsible for the Ministries Complex (1981) and the military hospital (1987); and Strojexport and Armabeton of Czechoslovakia contributed to the construction of the Water Towers (1977).[34] The planetarium for Kuwait was supplied by an East German firm (1986), and the steel sections of the new telecommunication tower (1993) were provided by Poland's Mostostal-Zabrze, which in the 1980s counted Kuwait as one of its main clients.[35]

In a 1983 interview, the Kuwaiti ambassador to the United States, Sheik Saud Nasir Al-Sabah, complemented Yugoslav companies and explained to a US journalist: 'You have to understand [that] Kuwait is a completely open market, no political consideration is given as far as the tender is concerned'.[36] This attitude followed the attempts of Kuwaiti diplomats to secure the 'neutrality' of their country within Cold War geopolitics in the Middle East: Kuwait maintained close relations with the West while accepting Soviet military assistance and securing its economic interests as a founding member of OPEC.[37] On this 'open market', the relatively modest fees of architects from Eastern Europe were used as bargaining leverage by mediators such as Polservice and Polytechna. However, even after the Wrocław architects decided to break with Polservice and stay in Kuwait on their own, their salaries remained lower than those of Western experts. This showed the persistence of Cold War cultural hierarchies in the Gulf, reinforced by reports in the local press about the inferior quality of technology from socialist countries and their outdated managerial models.[38]

Beyond Post-Oil Urbanization

'Upon my first landing in Kuwait, I saw a forest of cranes and I decided to stay', recalled Lach.[39] This construction boom was taking place 'among parked cars [and] the ruins of what remains of Kuwait's stock of single-storey courtyard family houses', as another observer put it.[40] The Kuwait that confronted the architects from Wrocław was the result of three decades of rapid urbanization, financed by the state's oil revenues, and defined by state policy of land acquisition and resettlement.[41] The first master plan of Kuwait by the British planners Minoprio, Spencely, and MacFarlane, in 1951, had envisaged a transformation of what was then a settlement of courtyard houses into a commercial and business 'city centre', surrounded by new residential suburbs linked by a system of radial and ring roads. While much of the urban fabric of Kuwait was erased, only a few urban projects were realized, and the next master plan, commissioned in 1968 from the British consultants Buchanan and Partners, took this condition as its starting point. Revised in 1977 and endorsed by the Municipal Council, this plan suggested a linear development following the coast, consisting of housing neighbourhoods with new centres, and the construction of two new towns in the south and the north.[42] A specialist on car traffic in cities, Buchanan suggested a renewal of the city centre by assigning specific areas to commercial uses and civic and government programmes, filling the gap in the urban fabric and laying out pedestrian zones.[43] This plan defined the development of Kuwait from the late 1970s until the Iraqi invasion in 1990, and formed the framework for architectural practices of this period.

The architects from Wrocław, during their work in the Gulf, were exposed to and contributed to a critical rethinking of the boom-era urban development in Kuwait. Falling oil prices, the disruptive effect of the Iran–Iraq War and the crash in 1982 of the Suq Al-Manakh, the unofficial stock exchange, contributed to a more reflexive climate of opinion. Prefigured by some forewarnings by Saba George Shiber from the mid-1960s,[44] calls abounded over the course of the next decade to preserve the little that was left of the old Kuwait.[45] The 1981 revision of the master plan declared the Behbehani compound, the American Mission, the traditional suq, and part of the Sharkh frontage as conservation areas. The Al-Ghanim Dasman, the Naif Palace, and all historical mosques were to be preserved.[46] The architect Ahmad Al-Ansari suggested that plazas in the Green Belt be used for the display of Kuwaiti traditions and folklore,[47] in line with the broad definition of heritage promoted by the National Museum, itself designed by Ecochard and opened in 1983. The Kuwaiti architect Ghazi Sultan supervised the first renovation of a historical building that was pursued by the municipality: the Old Kuwait Courts (1987).[48] Fathy, the Egyptian architect of international renown, designed the Beit Al-Reihan house praised in the Saudi architectural journal *Albenaa* (Construction) as following 'the pattern of Arabian palaces which observe the Arabian Kuwaiti environment characteristics'.[49] Similarly, the project for senior housing in Sharkh by Jarząbek and Lach referenced the scale, disposition, sequence of spaces, materials, and details of the disappearing courtyard houses in this area, photographs of which were included in all presentation drawings [Figure 8.2].[50]

The unbuilt Jarząbek and Lach design fed into the general critique of post-oil urbanization in the Gulf press, both popular and professional, which debunked 'modern architecture' and lamented that the city-state was becoming 'a dumping ground for alien architectural landmarks'.[51] Hence, commentators writing in *Albenaa* targeted forms that they considered to be alien to the Gulf: apartment blocks with oversized spaces between them ('similar to

Figure 8.2: *W. Jarząbek, E. Lach, Senior Citizens Housing, design, 1970s.* E. Lach archive, Wrocław.

the theory of Le Corbusier'), private villas with large spaces around them, the car-oriented city, and the gridiron plan.[52] The critique included the analysis of the courtyard house as a flexible and multi-purpose space, opposed to the reductive understanding of the division and separation of functions imputed to the CIAM tradition.[53] This shift in opinion sometimes happened very quickly: if in 1978 the Al-Sawaber project by Erickson in Kuwait City was praised by the daily press as 'modernistic, breaking with the stereotyped, impersonal, rectangular blocks of bricks', already in 1980 the idea of high-rise blocks was criticized as not allowing for privacy, and hence against Islamic tradition.[54]

Debates about 'Islamic', 'Arab', and 'Muslim' architecture and urban design took place in a number of conferences in the Gulf countries over the course of the 1980s. During these events, the widespread demand for operative guidelines for design practices was confronted by scholars through a discussion of the constructivist character of such concepts, often based on the extrapolation of specific urban forms, which only slowly shed Orientalist fantasies and Western-centred theories of culture and urbanization.[55] Published in journals in Arabic and in English, and hence accessible to expatriate architects, most of these voices differed little from the discourse of a modernism 'adapted' to local conditions, which had proliferated since World War II in colonial 'tropical' modernism and its postcolonial mutations.[56] But new themes were emerging as well. Besides the widely argued (if rarely realized) postulates of accounting for specific local conditions in terms of climate, social structures, customs, and local materials and technologies, the debates introduced architectural form as a self-sustained condition and not a 'result' of other factors. The Iraqi architect Kahtan Al-Madfai, for example, argued for a continuation of traditional forms, which he catalogued as either monumental or domestic.[57] Another example is the discussion of the *mashrabiyya* which stressed its synthetic character in the way it serves multiple functions: anchoring the building in a visual tradition, regulating climatic conditions, negotiating the relationship between public and private, and linking the building to local economies, craftsmanship, and materials. Some authors engaged in a speculative enterprise of translating the laws and values of the sharia into architectural and urban-planning principles, while others explicitly opposed the association between architecture, which is constantly evolving, and religion, immutable and eternal.[58]

Some of these debates resonated with international discussions on postmodernism, to which architects from socialist countries who were working in Kuwait gained easy access by means of journals, exhibitions, and newly constructed buildings. For example, in 1985 the journal *Middle East Construction* published Basil Al-Bayati's designs of a mosque in the form of an oversized open book and of a telecommunication tower shaped as a gigantic palm tree.[59] These designs could have been included in any of the postmodernism manifestos that Charles Jencks had been publishing for a decade, and which were reflected by authors writing in Kuwait since that time.[60] Jarząbek, by reading *The Architectural Review* in Kuwait, discovered the work of James Stirling, his ferryman to postmodern architecture, which then reverberated not only in his Kuwaiti designs, but also in those he drew in Poland upon his return in the 1990s. Professionals in the region followed the development of Baghdad closely as it was led by Chadirji under Saddam Hussein with the participation of Denise Scott Brown, Robert Venturi, Ricardo Bofill, and Erickson: a 'laboratory of postmodernism' where new urban typologies were tested.[61]

Beyond academic and professional discussions, the dissatisfaction with post-oil urban development in Kuwait was shared by inhabitants of state-subsidized housing, interviewed for the first time in the mid-1970s by the National Housing Authority (NHA). With the aim of guaranteeing every Kuwaiti citizen an accommodation, the NHA divided housing into two categories: LIG (Low Income Group) and AIG (Average Income Group); their dimensions were often generous and, for example, in the Messila neighbourhood, LIG housing was built on lots of 300 sq. metres, and AIG housing on lots of 500 sq. metres.[62] These housing areas were realized by the NHA, together with mosques, shopping malls, and schools, for which Mieczysław Rychlicki and Daczkowska delivered type designs in the early 1980s (for Gulf Consult).[63] The NHA interviews conveyed the uneasiness with the typologies that had until then been applied by the housing authority, ultimately deemed foreign and unsuitable. Instead, the inhabitants expressed preference for one-storey courtyard houses that included the *diwaniyya* (semi-public/semi-private room for male visitors), accessible from both inside and outside the dwelling unit, usable roof space, and a paved courtyard with an area for plants.[64]

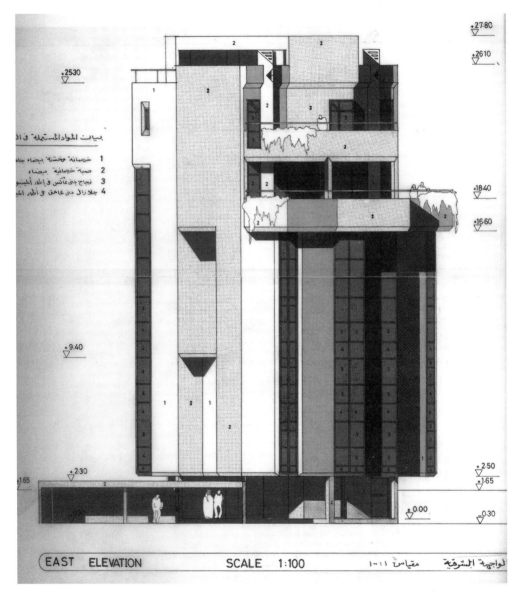

Figure 8.3: *A. Bohdanowicz, Al-Mazidi Building, Fintas, elevation drawing (1982).* A. Bohdanowicz archive, Kuwait City.

Reference to an often-unspecified 'Islamic tradition' was becoming a standard requirement by the 1970s in governmental commissions in the Gulf, and foreign designers needed to comply.[65] The London-based office Fitzroy Robinson Partnership designed banks in Dubai, Abu Dhabi, and Muscat in a generic modern idiom, for example, but its design for the Ministry of Foreign Affairs in Muscat was given a 'vernacular appearance'.[66] Similarly, the design of the Kuwait Law Courts by Basil Spence Partnership evolved in order to accommodate stylistic recommendations, and the sequence of its seven façade variants shows a transformation from the abstract grid of the competition project into a display of 'familiar elements of Islamic geometry and decoration'.[67]

Yet it was precisely such a 'cosmetic' application of ornamental motifs on the façade that was debunked by the most notable architects from the region.[68] Their differing design positions notwithstanding, Chadirji, Makiya, Sultan, and Abdel Wahed el Wakil agreed in their search for a tectonic facade and a more organic connection between the skin and the structure. Examples included Chadirji's housing project in Hawally (1968), Makiya's State Mosque in Kuwait City (1985)[69] and, less known, the integration between the plan and the façade in the Al-Mazidi building in Fintas, designed by Bohdanowicz (1982, demolished). The plan of the building was based on an eight-point star; in the words of the designer, 'an Arab geometry', the *gestalt* of which appeared only in the pronounced balcony of the penthouse, otherwise resulting in an abstract checkerboard of bright stone and tinted glass [Figure 8.3].[70]

Negotiating Urban Typologies

What this overview shows is a sentiment, shared by many among Kuwaiti elites, professionals, academics, journalists, and inhabitants that urbanization patterns of the previous two decades needed to be left behind. The Wrocław architects projected into this sentiment their own uneasiness with post-war urban designs in Poland, as it had been expressed in projects such as Kozanów. Yet this overview also shows that the concomitant demands for a more 'contextual' design differed widely in motivations and references, and that calls for a 'local', 'traditional', or 'familiar' environment in the Gulf, more often than not, were either going in incommensurable directions or left unspecified. The architects from Wrocław responded with a variety of proposals and, in what follows, these will be reviewed by focusing on urban typologies that negotiated the relationship between the pedestrian and the car in Kuwait. This focus will allow a bringing together of questions of technology, lifestyle, and rhythms of everyday life, and will also demonstrate that this 'contextual' turn at times foregrounded tensions within the processes of space production in the Gulf, rather than assuaging them.

Pedestrians and cars were at the centre of one of the first designs in Kuwait by the architects from Wrocław: the competition entry for Site C in the Sabah Al-Salem district, submitted in 1977. This community of 60,000 people, combining LIG and AIG housing, was designed as a part of the linear-urbanization scheme proposed by the Buchanan plan. Sabah Al-Salem was one of the biggest districts planned in Kuwait in the 1970s, organized in neighbourhoods of *c.*3000 housing units with social facilities, further divided into 'sites' of 300–500 housing units.[71]

After the competition was won by Bohdanowicz and Wiśniowski for Shiber Consultants, it was developed together with Jarząbek and INCO, and realized in 1982. The design comprised sand bricks and cement blocks for walls, with ceilings and staircases in reinforced concrete poured on site, and after several years it was retrofitted with elevators [Figure 8.4]. The competition brief by the NHA included requests for an 'Arab design' and floor plans that sustained traditional customs, and the designers responded with an interpretation of Kuwaiti courtyard typology. This typology, they argued, allowed to secure privacy, enhanced by a split-level disposition, with the day area below and the night area above.[72] The day area included two larger rooms, one of which could be separated from the rest of the apartment and used as a *diwaniyya*, while the night area could be used as a living room for the entire family. This differentiation of privacy in the apartment followed the recommendations of the NHA, as did the possibility of transforming the terrace into an additional bedroom.[73] The ground floor apartments were extended by a small garden or patio, separated from the public space by a wall [Figure 8.5].

Another key attempt to respond to the 'local tradition' was, in the words of the architects, the careful design of external spaces, topography, and greenery. In contrast to other neighbourhoods in Sabah Al-Salem and the AIG Al-Qurain district (Bohdanowicz, R. Singh and Wiśniowski for INCO, 1988), Site C was furnished with a network of pedestrian-only pathways. Inspired by the urban fabric of Sharkh, these pathways linked the houses to the local community centre with its mosque, kindergarten, and shops, situated diagonally across the neighbourhood. Perpendicular to the pedestrian paths, a grid of roads was introduced for vehicle traffic, with parking spaces shaded by the overhangs resulting from the split-level section of the apartments [Figure 8.6].[74]

The relationship between the pedestrian and the car had been recognized in Kuwait since the 1960s not only as a problem of urban planning and technology, but also as an architectural challenge. This recognition was, for instance, the starting point for a 1968 brief of the studies of urban development of Kuwait City, commissioned by Leslie Martin from BBPR, Candillis-Josic-Woods, Reima Pietilä, and Alison and Peter Smithson.[75] A typology that took hold was a reinterpretation of the suq, combining garages, shops, offices, and cafes; and equipped with up-to-date air-conditioning systems, elevators, and telecommunications facilities. Developing the typology of the suqs constructed since the 1960s along Fahad Al-Salam Street, the Suq Al-Kuwait (SOM with SSH, 1975) was divided by a double atrium, and the Suq Al-Wataniya (TAC with PACE, 1979) included a 'village' of duplex courtyard houses on the roof.[76] Architects of the Wrocław group designed the Suq Dawliyah, combining a multi-storey parking garage with an atrium and an office block (Daczkowski and Lach for GEO, 1978), and imagined as a nodal point within the new pedestrian zones of the master plan for Kuwait City [Figure 8.7].[77]

The tense relationship between the pedestrian and the car was captured in the design of the Al-Othman Center, a commercial and residential complex in Hawally. The centre consists of three floors of shopping and office areas, twin ten-floor residential towers, and a multi-storey car park for 350 vehicles [Figure 8.8]. The foundations were ready before

Figure 8.4: *A. Bohdanowicz, W. Jarząbek, and K. Wiśniowski for Shiber Consult/ INCO, site C, Sabah Al Salem, 1982.* Photograph by Ł. Stanek taken in 2014.

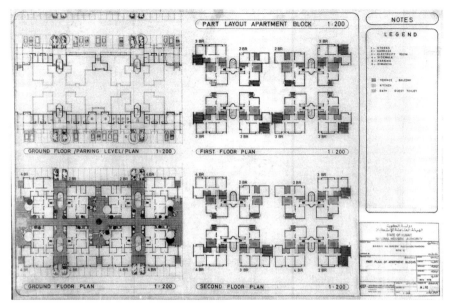

Figure 8.5: *A. Bohdanowicz, W. Jarząbek, K. Wiśniowski for Shiber Consult/ INCO, site C, Sabah Al Salem, 1982, first floor, drawing.* K. Wiśniowski archive, Kuwait City.

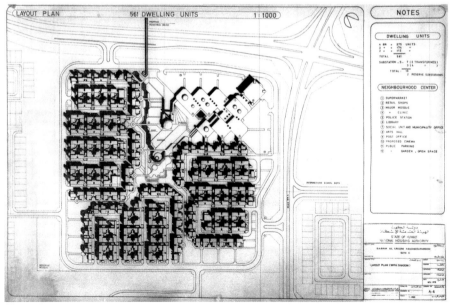

Figure 8.6: *A. Bohdanowicz, W. Jarząbek, K. Wiśniowski for Shiber Consult/ INCO, site C, Sabah Al Salem, 1982, general plan.* Wiśniowski archive, Kuwait City.

Figure 8.7: *Z. Daczkowski, E. Lach for GEO, Suq Dawliyah during construction, Kuwait City (1978).* Photograph, E. Lach archive, Wrocław.

the Iraqi invasion, but the building was not finished until 1995, four years after liberation. The department store comprised a number of small shops located around a narrow central atrium with escalators. The building is located at a major intersection of Al-Othman and Ibn-Khaldoun Streets, and its arcaded entrances are located on the corners of the allotment. Yet in spite of the arcades, the building is introverted: the shops on the ground floor were designed not as opening directly to the streets, but rather to a passage shielded from the streets by a set of kiosks with stairs between them so as to accommodate the slope of Ibn-Khaldoun Street.[78] While these kiosks were eliminated in the realized building, the stairs were built according to the first design – narrow, sparsely distributed – and at odds with the image of the arcade. The long stretches from the street entrances to the atrium contrast with the short connection between the atrium and the car park at the point where the two buildings, designed on skewed construction grids, touch each other [Figure 8.9].

A similar hiatus between an image of urban space and its ways of use can be seen in three apartment buildings constructed in Salmiya in 1978, according to the design by Bohdanowicz

Figure 8.8: *E. Lach, W. Jarząbek for KEG, Al Othman Center, Hawally, 1995.* Photograph by Ł. Stanek taken in 2014.

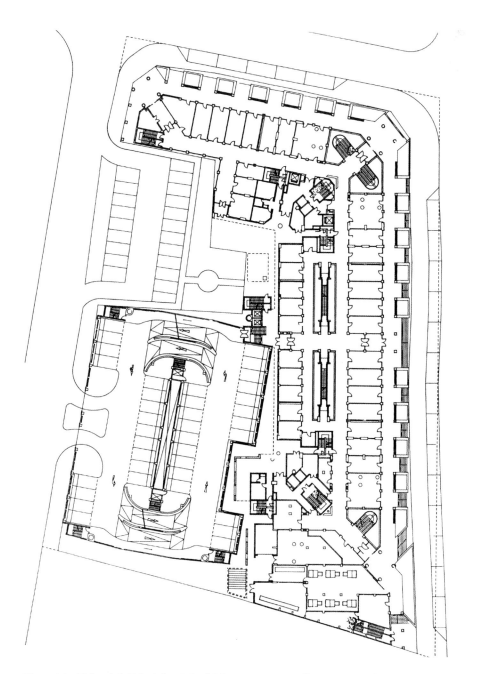

Figure 8.9: *W. Jarząbek, E. Lach for KEG, Al Othman Center, Hawally, 1995, ground floor plan.* E. Lach archive, Wrocław.

for Shiber Consultants. They are distinguished among the neighbouring structures by a careful sequence of transitional spaces sandwiched between the apartment buildings and the streets [Figure 8.10]. However, these shared spaces are hardly maintained, nor are the streets nearby, which often have no sidewalks. This poor level of maintenance reflects the fact that immigrants to whom these buildings are rented out have few instruments for putting pressure on the authorities and landlords. According to the 1980 census, more than 59 per cent of the population in Kuwait and three-quarters of the labour force consisted of immigrants, which included the skilled, the semi- and unskilled occupations. At the same time, only citizens were entitled to housing provisions. As a result, housing districts in Kuwait have been divided into low-density villas, inhabited by citizens and set along landscaped avenues, and areas inhabited by *Bidoon*s (stateless people) and immigrants, with the latter ranging from upper-grade apartments for better paid professionals, to workers' apartment blocks, overpopulated and surrounded by poorly maintained streets.[79] While Kuwaitis expected the government to provide welfare services, non-citizens could, at best, associate in district neighbourhood councils in order to coordinate self-help and to petition the government.[80]

The design of spaces with an appearance at odds with their uses cannot be explained by the allegedly formalist approach of the Wrocław architects, since the commissioners sometimes demanded such spaces. A case in point is the Baloush bus station, resulting from a competition won by INCO (Leopold Chyczewski, Wiśniowska, and Wiśniowski, 1986) [Figure 8.11]. After the competition, the Kuwait Public Transport Company changed the programme and replaced the commercial spaces the architects had proposed with publicly accessible spaces with no commercial use.[81] Yet the programme of a bus station implied that the building was to be frequented mainly by low-income, non-Kuwaiti residents, the primary users of public transportation in Kuwait.[82] In spite of the station's multiple gestures towards public space – pronounced eaves, two open-entrance pavilions, and the basilica section of the main hall – it could not have become a space where people of different backgrounds meet, as it was unable to fill the gap of such spaces left in a city centre that had been severely depleted during the process of post-oil urbanization.[83]

These examples show that the Wrocław architects responded to the climate of opinion in Kuwait in the 1980s by reimagining the pre-oil urban fabric (Salah Al-Salem), by alluding to images acculturated in the Middle East by colonial urbanism (Al-Othman Center, the Baloush bus station), or by reinterpreting the 1970s suq (Suq Dawliyah). These buildings engaged the voices in Kuwait that demanded putting an end to the architectural and planning patterns of the two post-oil decades, patterns widely considered to be alien and alienating. However, it was against the background of these more familiar images that the 'other within' appeared: the migrant, the non-citizen, the *Bidoon*. This is particularly visible in the Port Complex in Shuwaikh, another competition project that was won by Bohdanowicz and Wiśniowski for INCO (1984), one in which the designers wanted to see their scheme as being inspired by the courtyard-house typology in the region. When visiting today, in spite of the sophisticated landscape of stairs and ramps, the only pedestrians one meets around

Figure 8.10: *A. Bohdanowicz for Shiber Consult, residential building in Salmiya, 1978.* Photograph by Ł. Stanek taken in 2014.

Figure 8.11: L. Chyczewski, A. Wiśniowska, K. Wiśniowski for INCO, Baloush Bus Terminal, 1988. Photograph by Ł. Stanek taken in 2014.

Figure 8.12: A. Bohdanowicz, K. Wiśniowski, Port Authority Shuwaikh, 1984. Photograph by Ł. Stanek taken in 2014.

the Port Complex building are immigrant blue-collar workers trying to catch a minibus. They must wait for it on the artificially watered lawn next to the expressway, as there is no other place a bus can stop without disturbing the traffic of the private cars of white-collar employees [Figure 8.12].

Technologies in Context

The projects of the Wrocław group that are discussed above might appear to be a confirmation of the familiar narrative of architecture's role as a cultural 'mediator' of modern technology, as postulated by a variety of post-war architectural idioms, from 'tropical architecture' to 'critical regionalism'.[84] The technologies of the car, the escalator, the elevator, the highway, and prefabricated construction systems appear to be integrated into floor plans inspired by courtyard houses, arranged according to morphologies derived from familiar urbanization patterns, and covered by details abstracted from pre-oil monuments in Kuwait. In the final part of this chapter, however, it will be argued that several of these imported expert systems themselves facilitated the re-contextualization of Kuwaiti architecture – and that these technologies found their subjective pendant in the portable, shared 'profile' of the Wrocław architects.

Much of the disappointment with 1950s and 1960s buildings in Kuwait stemmed from the rapid pace of their deterioration, and this concerned, in particular, the one material most strongly associated with the modern movement: reinforced concrete. While most buildings in Kuwait were less than 20–30 years old, concrete structures quickly deteriorated in the hot, humid, dust-laden climate of the Gulf [Figure 8.13]. Expatriate architects were accused of specifying building materials that often proved unsuitable, especially in light of the fact that maintenance protocols were usually not adhered to.[85] A 1987 study estimated the life expectancy of a concrete building in the Gulf to be 10–15 years (in comparison with 60–80 years in less trying environments). This was soon challenged, and another study extended this span to 27 years, which was hardly an optimistic estimation either, and meant that buildings constructed during the boom years would need to be demolished by the end of the century.[86] The oil boom brought about rising costs of land, construction, and rents, followed by the shift among main investors in real estate from individuals to developers and governmental agencies. This shift contributed to the professionalization of the building industry and to tighter supervision. Yet the fast pace of construction during the boom period had an adverse impact on the quality of construction.[87]

Private investors and government agencies introduced a number of control measures and encouraged the use of prevention techniques (coated rebar, dense concrete, and pulverized fuel ash as an alternative to cement, anti-chloride surface coating, and prefabricated cladding with protective finishing for façades).[88] This was supported by the emerging Kuwaiti and Saudi building industries, which were increasingly able to supply materials produced with foreign licences that had been adapted to the requirements of the local market.[89] These

Figure 8.13: *Anwar Al-Sabah Complex at the Fahad Al-Salam street, early 1960s.* Photograph by Ł. Stanek taken in 2014.

adaptations included protective measures against the climate and also accounted for aesthetic proclivities by means of ornamental rubber moulding for prefabricated concrete elements, and with cladding elements with openings in the shape of ogee arches.

More generally, the shift beyond the townscape of post-oil urbanization in Kuwait was facilitated by innovations in the building industry. These included the organization of building sites, and over the course of the 1970s the NHA argued against large housing projects, which proved to be too difficult to manage. The construction site of the Sabah Al-Salem neighbourhood was a case in point in October 1980, when 3500 workers went on strike because their employer, the National Construction Company, owned by the Pakistani government, had not paid their wages for two and a half months. This was a consequence of the company's inability to accommodate rising prices of building materials, which had been underestimated in the tender documentation submitted two years earlier.[90] The NHA proposed that no single contractor was to be given more than 500 units to build and opted for increasing the share of contracts going to locally registered joint ventures. While the main aim was to support local contractors[91] (in order to divert profits back to the country, to provide more efficient procedures of capacity control and risk management, and to enhance the knowledge and expertise of local firms)[92] this regulation brought to an end the large, uniform housing projects of the 1960s and early 1970s.

During the same period, the NHA introduced the requirement of computerization of the design and construction process. The aim was the acceleration of information flow between all actors involved, facilitation of communication between them, and ensuring their accountability.[93] For many Western firms, in particular from the United States and the United Kingdom, the Middle East became one of the first places to develop CAD on a commercial scale. CAD was particularly useful for managing commissions within the 'design and build' procedure that was increasingly favoured in the Middle East, when contractors were expected to submit design proposals together with building cost estimates.[94] For example, CAD was used in Kuwait by John S. Bonnington, the designer of the Stock Exchange (1984) and by Arup, the designer of the Salhia Complex (1979). Representatives of the latter stressed the necessity of CAD for an exceptionally fast-moving contract programmes, and the use of dynamic databases allowed for a quick response time to contract programme updates and forecasts.[95]

Salah Salama, the head engineer of KEG, recalled that the General Drafting System (GDS) was bought by the office in the early 1980s for the working drawings of the Fintas Center project in the Fintas area, because of its size, complexity, and the particularly short timing of the commission.[96] For this project, the conceptual design was delivered by Erickson and the execution drawings were worked on by a number of architects from Wrocław employed by KEG. In the wake of the unrealized Fintas Center, CAD technology was used in other KEG projects,[97] including the Audit Bureau, designed by Jarząbek and Lach before the invasion, and then completed in 1996. The building is located at Ahmed Al-Jaber Street in the heart of Kuwait City and includes office spaces, a conference hall, a library, an emergency shelter, and parking for 650 cars [Figure 8.14]. Within the narrative sensitivity developed in their Kuwaiti projects, Jarząbek and Lach took the punched computing card as a direct inspiration for the façade, combining this with complex, ornamental *mashrabiyyas*, themselves drawn in CAD [Figure 8.15]. The technology was also used in the design of the Al-Othman Center, which, as with the Audit Bureau, was only finished after the Iraqi invasion. The designer argued that the building's careful details, including the decorative geometry of the tiles, would not have been possible without CAD, and they appear exceptional within the decline of building expertise in Kuwait during the 1990s.[98]

In this way, the implementation of CAD and other technologies in Kuwait through the 1980s displays the processes of de-territorialization and re-territorialization of expert systems across diverse social and cultural environments, which have been described by STS scholars in studies on global knowledge transfer. Accordingly, the Kuwaiti offices which implemented CAD in order to cooperate with Western architects and construction firms could be seen as 'technological zones', discussed by Andrew Barry as sites where differences between technical practices, procedures, and forms are reduced and common standards are established.[99] Similarly, the implementation of computerized management systems at construction sites in Kuwait could be analysed as unstable 'global assemblages', as studied by Stephen J. Collier and Aihwa Ong, in which impersonal forms of techno-science are assimilated and contested within specific, situated arrangements.[100] Barry, Collier, and Ong

Figure 8.14: *W. Jarząbek, E. Lach for KEG, Audit Bureau Headquarters Building, 1996.* Photograph by Ł. Stanek taken in 2014.

Figure 8.15: *W. Jarząbek, E. Lach for KEG, Audit Bureau Headquarters Building, 1996, CAD rendering, photograph.* W. Jarząbek archive, Wrocław.

stress that such 'technological zones' and 'global assemblages' forge a separation between 'global/Western' and 'local' regimes (political, economic, social, and ethical). By contrast, I argue that several of the expert systems discussed above bridged this separation and facilitated a 'contextual' response, in line with the new architectural climate of opinion in Kuwait in the 1980s. In particular, the prefabricated systems and CAD software accommodated the demand for a visual environment into which collective identities could be projected. This shift, from the self-assigned mediation between 'technology' and 'context' (as postulated by various regionalisms, 'critical' and otherwise) toward their conflation testified to a reshuffling of architectural culture in the Gulf, to which architects from Wrocław contributed.

At the same time, their professional approach displayed a similar dynamic of de-territorialization and re-territorialization. Their generational experience of disenchantment with post-war modern architecture in Poland, as well as the specific interest in architectural history shared by many of them, was an important resource for their practice in Kuwait. At least equally significant for their employers, however, was a set of more generic attitudes: flexibility, professional ambition, the willingness and ability to learn and to implement innovations, whether in architectural culture, building technology, or construction management.[101] These attitudes were delineated in a collective 'profile' of 'specialists abroad' as specified by Polservice in a 1972 manual. Polservice stipulated the advantages of Polish specialists by their professional qualifications, efficiency, and dedication; an ability to adapt to the environment; the 'selfless' transfer of know-how to local staff; and good knowledge of languages, while it explicitly prohibited their employees from 'getting involved in political or religious debates' in the host countries.[102] In Polservice's recruitment procedures during the final decades of the Cold War, a general profile such as this took precedence over specific experience with post-war reconstruction, such as the state-led rebuilding of Warsaw or the construction of new towns, which had legitimized earlier Polish master plans for cities in Algeria, Libya, Syria, and Iraq.[103] Aspects of this profile had been provided by the typically Central European training of the Wrocław architects, straddling engineering, architecture, and urban planning, which was valued in Kuwaiti offices, often headed by civil engineers – all the more so as it came with a modest price tag.[104] Such training furnished them with a broad set of portable rather than localized skills, which were advantageous within the expanding global market of architectural services: a market that Polservice and state companies from other socialist countries, as this chapter demonstrates, not only took advantage of, but also helped to define.[105]

Afterword: From Kuwait to Poland

The 1990 Iraqi invasion resulted in the destruction of many buildings in Kuwait, and also in the closure of several Kuwaiti architectural offices including Archicentre, and in foreign professionals leaving, some of whom moved to Dubai and Abu Dhabi in the years that followed.[106] The invasion coincided with the end of socialism in Eastern Europe, and most architects of the Wrocław group who were leaving Kuwait decided to return to Poland. Upon their arrivals there, they became known by the nickname 'Kuwaitis', and they helped shape the urban landscape of post-socialist Wrocław. Jarząbek used CAD technology, for example, which he had previously utilized in the Audit Bureau and Al-Othman Center projects, to design the Solpol department store (1993), the first in the Wrocław city centre after 1989. Lach was responsible for the Dominikańska department store alongside the medieval town (1999), among other projects.[107] In 1994, when the construction of the church in Popowice was completed, the cardinal who consecrated the building associated its interior with Islamic architecture – and went on to jokingly thank Jarząbek for designing 'such a beautiful mosque'.[108]

Beyond anecdotal references, the experience of working in the Gulf, the Middle East, and North Africa in the 1980s was a decisive career step that prepared architects from Poland and other then-socialist countries for practising architecture after the political transformations. They distinguished themselves by their professional knowledge and familiarity with programmes with which architects that had remained practising in state socialism had little experience, such as underground car parks, middle-class housing, office parks, shopping malls, and modern department stores.[109] They benefited from the experience with current building processes, from CAD through construction technologies and advanced materials, the organization of the office and the construction site, to contacts with international developers and construction firms. No less important was the acquaintance with postmodernism, embraced by investors and the public alike. While postmodern tendencies were present in Polish architecture since the 1970s, it was only after the end of socialism that they were turned into a new mainstream, facilitated by imported programmes, materials, building technologies, and capital. Yet while boosting individual careers, the work on 'export' contracts often came with a sympathetic association with developers and construction firms, reinforced by the experience of a 'public' deemed too fragmented and contingent to become an obligation for an architectural project, and an architectural culture valorizing the detachment of architectural images from broader processes of space production. These experiences dovetailed with the new professional habitus in 1990s Eastern Europe, which linked the conditions of labour of Polish architects back in the Middle East with those in post-socialist Poland.

Notes

1 Neil Parkyn, 'Kuwait Revisited', *Middle East Construction* (hereafter *MEC*) 9 (1983): 39.
2 Stephen Gardiner, *Kuwait: The Making of a City* (London: Longman, 1983); Lawrence Vale, *Architecture, Power, and National Identity* (New Haven: Yale University Press, 1992), 248–78; Udo Kultermann, *Contemporary Architecture in the Arab States: Renaissance of a Region* (New York: McGraw-Hill, 1999), 167–78. Here and in what follows, unless otherwise specified, the dates indicate the construction year of the building in question.

3 For a rare notice, see Kultermann, *Contemporary Architecture*, 173–75; see also: Łukasz Stanek, 'Second World's Architecture and Planning in the Third World', *The Journal of Architecture* 17.3 (2012): 299–307; Łukasz Stanek, 'Miastoprojekt Goes Abroad: The Transfer of Architectural Labour from Socialist Poland to Iraq (1958–1989)', *The Journal of Architecture* 17.3 (2012): 361–86; Łukasz Stanek, *Postmodernism Is Almost All Right: Polish Architecture after Socialist Globalization* (Warsaw: Fundacja Bęc Zmiana, 2012).

4 Donald McNeill, *The Global Architect: Firms, Fame and Urban Form* (London and New York: Routledge, 2009); see also: Murray Fraser and Nasser Golzari, eds, *Architecture and Globalisation in the Persian Gulf Region* (Aldershot: Ashgate, 2013); Yasser Elsheshtawy, ed., *The Evolving Arab City: Tradition, Modernity and Urban Development* (London and New York: Routledge, 2008); Yasser Elsheshtawy, *Dubai: Behind an Urban Spectacle* (New York: Routledge, 2010).

5 McNeill, *Global Architect*, 1.

6 Ibid.

7 Steven Ward, 'Re-Examining the International Diffusion of Planning', in *Critical Readings in Planning Theory*, eds S. Fainstein and A. Scott (Chichester: Wiley-Blackwell, 2012), 479–98; see also: Fraser and Golzari, *Architecture and Globalisation*; Łukasz Stanek, 'Architects from Socialist Countries in Ghana (1957–1967): Modern Architecture and Mondialisation', *Journal of the Society of Architectural Historians* 74.4 (December 2015): 416–42.

8 The concept of mondialization was developed by Henri Lefebvre and Jean-Luc Nancy, see Stanek, 'Architects from Socialist Countries'.

9 Ibid.; for the concept of the Global Cold War, see Odd Arne Westad, *The Global Cold War: Third World Interventions and the Making of Our Times* (Cambridge: Cambridge University Press, 2005).

10 Stanek, 'Architects from Socialist Countries'.

11 Yasser Mahgoub, 'Globalization and the Built Environment in Kuwait', *Habitat International* 28 (2004): 505–19.

12 Stephen J. Collier and Aihwa Ong, 'Global Assemblages, Anthropological Problems', in *Global Assemblages: Technology, Politics, and Ethics as Anthropological Problems*, eds Collier and Ong (Malden, MA: Blackwell, 2005), 3–21; Andrew Barry, 'Technological Zones', *European Journal of Social Theory* 9.2 (2006): 239–53.

13 They included Krzysztof Wiśnowski, Andrzej Bohdanowicz, and Ryszard Daczkowski.

14 The team composition differs in various sources, and among its members are listed Bohdanowicz, Daczkowski, Lach, and Wiśniowski, as well as Mieszko Niedźwiecki and Marianne Ludwin; see: *Krzysztof Wiśniowski, Anna Wiśniowska, Magdalena Wiśniowska, Jan Wiśniowski: 1969–2006* (Wrocław: Muzeum Architektury, 2006); e-mail exchange with Mieszko Niedźwiecki, October 2015.

15 Łukasz Stanek, ed., *Team 10 East: Revisionist Architecture in Real Existing Modernism* (Warsaw: Museum of Modern Art/Chicago: University of Chicago Press, 2014).

16 Interview with Edward Lach, Wrocław, April 2011.

17 Joe Nasr, 'Saba Shiber, "Mr. Arab Planner". Parcours professionnel d'un urbaniste au Moyen-Orient', *Géocarrefour* 80.3 (2005): 197–206; Saba George Shiber, *Kuwait Urbanization: Documentation, Analysis, Critique* (Kuwait: Kuwait Government Printing Press, 1964).

18 Interview with Krzysztof Wiśniowski, Kuwait City, January 12, 2014; interview with Mohammad Al-Sanan, Kuwait City, January 13, 2014. The design for the National Theatre by Bohdanowicz and Wiśniowski was a finalist, together with that by Denis Lasdun.
19 See also Stanek, 'Miastoprojekt'.
20 Interview with Stojan and Mirjana Maksimović, September 14, 2014, Nahant, MA.
21 See the following personal dossiers in SARP Archive, Warsaw: 279, 351, 353, 363, 480, 533, 983, 1091, 1138, 1218.
22 They included the Al-Fintas towers (Gleń, J. Damija, N. Fatteh for Arabi Engineer Office, 1984) and the Al-Qibla tower (Krawecki for Gulf Consult, 1988), SARP dossier 1091; Janusz Krawecki archive, Kraków.
23 See also Jacek Wozniak, *Contemporary Architecture in Kuwait* (n.d.), 282–93.
24 Interview with Andrzej Bohdanowicz, Kuwait City, January 15, 2014.
25 Interview with Krzysztof Wiśniowski.
26 Tanis Hinchcliffe, 'British Architects in the Gulf, 1950–1980', in *Architecture and Globalisation*, eds Fraser and Golzari, 23–36.
27 Telephone interview with Janusz Krawecki, March 2014.
28 The team working for Archicentre in Kuwait included Mirjana Maksimović, Sonja Živković, Branislav Jovin, Jovan Katarnic, and Radomir Mihajlović; see Zoran Manević, *Stojan Maksimović: Stvaralaštvo* (Belgrade: Centar VAM, 2006), 76–78.
29 Archicentre's Principal Manager was Kuwaiti engineer Jasem Qabazard, its Project Design Director was Iraqi architect Akram Augaily, and its Project Architect and Planner was Vaclav Bašta, a Czech architect who had been Professor at Baghdad University in the 1960s and 1970s. Bašta was also the consultant of the Amiri Diwan competition project and he invited a group of architects from Prague to work on the execution design. For the full list of contributors, see Archicentre, 'Ministry of Public Works, Amiri Diwan and Council of Ministers, Predevelopment Study. Conceptual Design Stage 4. Technical Report' II-a (n.d.): 0–10, private archive, Prague.
30 'Naselje 23 dvojne kuče za rentu šeika Duaj Ibrahim Al-Sabaha u Kuvajtu', 'Šest vila za Mr. Youset al Shaye u Kuvajtu', 'Kuće za izdavanje Mr. Abdulatif Al Touenija u Kuvajtu', *Architektura Urbanizam* 58 (1969): 46–47; Ljiljana Bakić, *Anatomija B&B arhitekture* (Belgrade: Ljiljana Bakić, 2012).
31 The designers were Tibor Hübner, Attila Eműdy, and László Szabados; 'KÖZTI Középülettervező Vállalat' (n.d.), KÖZTI Archive, Budapest; Attila Eműdy archive, Budapest; 'Coastal Strip Development Project,' private archive of Kazimierz Bajer, Kraków.
32 Stanka Dundakova archive, Sofia; Dimitar Andreychin archive, Sofia.
33 'Building and Construction Industry. Kuwait Times Special Supplement', *Kuwait Times*, August 31, 1980, 5–10.
34 'Building and Construction Industry'; Peter Kilner and Jonathan Wallace, *The Gulf Handbook*, vol. 3 (London: Trade & Travel Publications, 1979), 360; Renata Holod and Darl Rastorfer, eds, *Architecture and Community: Building in the Islamic World Today* (Aga Khan Award for Architecture, 1983), 252.
35 M. Kwiecień, 'Trudny eksport usług budowlanych', *Rynki Zagraniczne* 31 (1986): 6.
36 'Kuwait Is an Open Market', *MEC* 4 (1983): 15.

37 Michael S. Casey, *The History of Kuwait* (Westport: Greenwood Press, 2007).
38 'East Bloc Managers Fail to Keep Up with Trends', *Kuwait Times*, April 4, 1982, 12; interview with Wiśniowski. On Cold War division of intellectual labour in architecture, see Stanek, 'Architects from Socialist Countries'.
39 Interview with Lach.
40 'Kuwait Revisited', 42.
41 Asseel Al-Ragam, 'The Destruction of Modernist Heritage: The Myth of Al-Sawaber', *Journal of Architectural Education* 67.2 (2013): 243–52; Farah Al-Nakib, 'Kuwait's Modern Spectacle: Oil Wealth and the Making of a New Capital City, 1950–90', *Comparative Studies of South Asia, Africa and the Middle East* 33.1 (2013): 7–25.
42 Gardiner, *Kuwait*.
43 Ministry of Transport (UK), *Traffic in Towns* (London: Penguin, 1964); Shankland/Cox Partnership, 'Master Plan of Kuwait: City Centre', Library of Congress, Geography and Map Reading Room, Washington, DC, G7604.K9G45 1977.S5.
44 Shiber, *Kuwait Urbanization*.
45 'The Changing Suq', *MEC* 11 (1982): 14.
46 'A Master Plan to Reshape the City Centre', *Kuwait Times*, November 8, 1981, 19.
47 'Purposive Architecture for the Urban Development of Kuwait', *Kuwait Times*, May 10, 1978, 5.
48 'An Architect from Kuwait', *Albenaa* 7.38 (1987/1988): 10–11.
49 'Kuwait, Beit Al-Reihan', *Albenaa* 8.43 (1988): 10–11, 24–29.
50 Edward Lach archive, Wrocław.
51 Jim Antoniou, 'The Challenge of Islamic Architecture', *MEC* 10 (1979): 16–17.
52 Ahmed Farid Moustapha, 'Islamic Values in Contemporary Urbanism (1)', *Albenaa* 7.41 (1988): 18–24, 26–33.
53 'Islamic Architecture and Modernism', *Albenaa* 5.26 (1985/1986): 69–73.
54 'Kuwait's Huge Housing Plans', *Kuwait Times*, March 23, 1978, 7; 'Building and Construction Industry'.
55 Nezar AlSayyad, *Cities and Caliphs: On the Genesis of Arab Muslim Urbanism* (New York: Greenwood Press, 1991).
56 For bibliography, see Stanek, 'Second World's Architecture'.
57 Kahtan Al-Madfai, 'Elements of Heritage', *MEC* 5 (1980): 58–59.
58 Moustapha, 'Islamic Values'; Ahmed Farid Moustapha, 'Islamic Values in Contemporary Urbanism (2)', *Albenaa* 7.42 (1988): 14–19, 16–23; Christa Udschi, 'International Symposium on Islamic Architecture and Urbanism', *Albenaa* 2.10 (1981): 2–6.
59 'A Future for the Past', *MEC* 10 (1985): 31–33.
60 Charles Jencks, *The Language of Post-Modern Architecture* (New York: Rizzoli, 1977); Huda Al-Bahar, 'Contemporary Kuwaiti Houses', *Mimar* 15 (1985): 63–72.
61 'Urban Renaissance in Baghdad', *Albenaa* 4.21–22 (1985): 76–88; Stanek, 'Miastoprojekt'.
62 'A Road Network Sized for the Products of Detroit', *Construction Today – Middle East* 3 (1979): 30; National Housing Authority (NHA, Kuwait), *National Housing Programme*, 5 vols (London: Buchanan, 1976).
63 SARP Archive, dossier 1138.

64 'Household Interviews', *National Housing Programme*, vol. 4.
65 'Sunshine and the Rule of Law: Kuwaiti Law Courts Scheme', *Building Design* 501 (June 20, 1980): 24; see also Nezar AlSayyad, 'From Modernism to Globalization: The Middle East in Context', in *Modernism and the Middle East: Architecture and Politics in the Twentieth Century*, eds Sandy Isenstadt and Kishwar Rizvi (Seattle: University of Washington Press, 2008), 255–63.
66 'Calling the Tune', *MEC* 8 (1985): 20–21.
67 'Sunshine and the Rule of Law', 25.
68 Al-Bahar, 'Contemporary Kuwaiti Houses'.
69 'Islamic Architecture and Modernism'.
70 Andrzej Bohdanowicz archive, Kuwait City.
71 'Housing the Arab Population', *MEC* 1 (1983): 27–34; 'A Road Network,' 30–31.
72 Interview with Wiśniowski.
73 'Household Interviews'.
74 Krzysztof Wiśniowski archive, Kuwait City.
75 'Proposals for Restructuring Kuwait', *Architectural Review* 156.931 (1974): 179–90.
76 Sara Saragoça Soares, 'Modernization or Change?', *YourAOK Pages* 1 (Summer 2013): 53–59.
77 SARP dossier 480.
78 Lach archive, Wrocław.
79 Abdulrasool A. Al-Moosa, 'Kuwait: Changing Environment in a Geographical Perspective', *British Society for Middle Eastern Studies*: *Bulletin* 11.1 (1984): 45–57; Farah Al-Nakib, 'The Bidoon and the City: A Historical Account of the Politics of Exclusion in Kuwait', *Al Manakh 2*, eds Rem Koolhaas et al. (Amsterdam: Stichting Archis, 2010), 384–87.
80 For an overview of the history and typologies of Kuwaiti housing, see Al-Ragam, 'The Destruction of Modernist Heritage'.
81 Interview with Wiśniowski.
82 Bruce G. Hutchinson and Galal M. Said, 'Spatial Differentiation, Transport Demands and Transport Model Design in Kuwait', *Transport Reviews: A Transnational Transdisciplinary Journal* 10.2 (1990): 91–110.
83 Farah Al-Nakib, 'Public Space and Public Protest in Kuwait, 1938–2012', *City: Analysis of Urban Trends, Culture, Theory, Policy, Action* 18.6 (2014): 723–34.
84 Jane Drew and Maxwell Fry, *Tropical Architecture in the Humid Zone* (New York: Reinhold, 1956); Kenneth Frampton, 'Towards a Critical Regionalism: Six Points for an Architecture of Resistance', in *The Anti-Aesthetic: Essays on Postmodern Culture*, ed. Hal Foster (Port Townsend: Bay Press, 1983), 16–30.
85 'Facing Facts', *MEC* 3/4 (1987): 19–20.
86 'As Solid as Concrete?', *MEC* 4/5 (1987): 20–21.
87 'Building Maintenance in Kuwait', *MEC* 1 (1980): 51–53.
88 'As Solid as Concrete?'.
89 'Innovation: Computer Screen Printing', *MEC* 2 (1986): 17.
90 Simon Dunkley, 'Housing Project Runs into Difficulties', *MEC* 12 (1980): 11.

91 'Fi Mutab'eh tahliliyeh men ra'ys al'etihad alKuwaiti litijarah wa sina'eh al'ensha' litusrihat wazeer al'eskan', *Al-Siyasah*, April 19, 1982, 7.
92 'Ambitious Housing Projects Keep the Market Buoyant', *Kuwait Times*, November 8, 1981.
93 Ibid.
94 'Design and Build', *MEC* 5 (1984): 29; 'Number One for Jubail', *MEC* 5 (1985): 21–23; 'Dynamic Management', *MEC* 4 (1986): 32–33.
95 John A. Davison, 'Computer Aids in Modern Architectural Practice', *Albenaa* 2.9 (1981): 52–54; 'Salhia Complex Kuwait', *Arup Journal* 14.2 (July 1979): 2–5.
96 Interview with Salah Salama, Kuwait City, January 16, 2014.
97 KEG Archive, Kuwait City.
98 Interview with Wojciech Jarząbek.
99 Barry, 'Technological Zones'.
100 Collier, Ong, 'Global Assemblages'.
101 *Krzysztof Wiśniowski*; Bohdanowicz archive; Andrzej Wyżykowski, 'Zagraniczna twórczość architektoniczna Janusza Kraweckiego', *Kwartalnik architektury i urbanistyki* XLI.3–4 (1996): 339–42.
102 Stanisław Grzywnowicz and Jerzy Kiedrzyński, *Prawa i obowiązki specjalisty* (Warszawa: Wydawnictwa UW, 1972), 26, 49–50.
103 Stanek, 'Miastoprojekt'; Łukasz Stanek, 'PRL™ Export Architecture and Urbanism from Socialist Poland', *Piktogram. Talking Pictures Magazine* 15 (2011): 1–54.
104 Interview with Al-Sanan.
105 See also Donna C. Mehos and Suzanne M. Moon, 'The Uses of Portability: Circulating Experts in the Technopolitics of Cold War and Decolonization', in *Entangled Geographies: Empire and Technopolitics in the Global Cold War*, ed. Gabrielle Hecht (Cambridge: MIT Press, 2011), 43–74.
106 Muhannad A. Albaqshi, 'The Social Production of Space: Kuwait's Spatial History' (Ph.D. diss., IIT, 2010); Yasser Mahgoub, 'Kuwait: Learning from a Globalized City', in *The Evolving Arab City*, ed. Elsheshtawy, 170.
107 Stanek, *Postmodernism*.
108 Ibid., 73.
109 See also Stanek, *Postmodernism*.

Chapter 9

Form Follows Faith: Swedish Architects, Expertise, and New Religious Spaces in the Stockholm Suburbs

Jennifer Mack

In 2007, the city of Stockholm initiated the Järva Lift, an urban renovation project around Järva Field, a former military training ground that is the nucleus of several Stockholm suburbs. These neighbourhoods have received consistently negative media attention and public criticism almost since their beginnings in a state-sponsored housing initiative known as the 'Million Programme' (*miljonprogrammet*). This Social Democratic project created more than one million dwelling units across Sweden between 1965 and 1974 and employed late modernist notions of 'utopian living'.[1] Government research stipulated that not only housing interiors but also urban amenities needed to be standardized, typically placing shops, community centres, postal services, spaces for volunteer associations, and health clinics around a town square.[2]

While the 'Million Programme' town centres sometimes offered discreet churches, secular structures eclipsed sacred ones in importance and visibility. The Järva Lift's current incarnation pays explicit attention, however, to new spaces for religious practice, especially mosques, reflecting the area's 'multicultural' population of over 60,000 people with backgrounds from Somalia to Iran.[3] One 2009 municipal report explained this as follows:

> There is a great demand for a mosque in the area, which [...] brings together many worshippers under the same roof and is tailored for this function. Many town-centre spaces and cellar spaces have turned out to be unsuitable for different reasons, and the question of the suitable placement of a new building should be prioritized.[4]

While this official line encourages mosque construction, planners have often sought to restrain the considerable architectural aspirations of 'New Swedish'[5] faith groups during negotiations over the (legally binding) local development plan (*detaljplan*). Several groups currently hold prayer services in so-called 'cellar mosques' (*källarmoskéer*, retrofitted spaces in basements, storefronts, or apartments) but have long hoped for a purpose-built mosque. As Johan,[6] a development engineer, described to me, such ambitions received political ambivalence until recently:

> It was a little divided before: should we encourage this or not? But now the politicians have put their foot down and said that we want more mosques to be located in Järva. They probably think that this is good from the perspective of integration because there are so many Muslims there. So, they thought that they should let them have their own space in the name of being reasonable: a church to go to.[7] Like the Christians built churches in Sweden before.

As a result, three mosques are now working their way through the planning process for this single suburban zone [Figure 9.1].

In each case, the faith group has hired a Swedish architectural firm, despite sometimes procuring initial designs from architects in Kuwait or Saudi Arabia. These local architects have been tasked with making mosques appropriate for a cold and dark Scandinavian setting. More critically, however, they must also make them conform, both to planning regulations and to expectations from a larger Swedish public that often expects immigrant groups to have little visible impact on the urban environment. Intriguingly, all three of the Swedish offices – ranging from boutique to corporate – have never before designed a mosque.

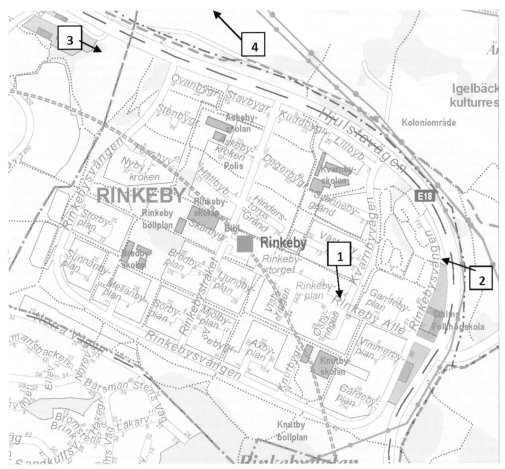

Figure 9.1: *Locations of the three mosque projects in Rinkeby-Tensta, as shown in a slide show given by the Urban Development Authority of the City of Stockholm. The offices associated with each plot are as follows: Celsing (1), Spridd (2), and Tengbom/Rashid (3). The proposed mosque at position 4 has been delayed. City of Stockholm.*

Drawing on ethnographic research among planners and designers involved in Järva mosque projects (including interviews and fieldwork at offices and meetings) and a survey of recent media coverage of them, this chapter examines how mosque projects travel from suburb to city centre and across domains of expertise, both via the design ideas brought by clients from abroad and through the planning regimes of the Swedish capital. I investigate why Swedish architects' experience and connections have particular value for their clients as they elucidate an opaque planning bureaucracy, use forms that cater to the tastes of the Swedish public, and even incorporate Sweden-specific architectural typologies as prototypes. Does this 'local knowledge' trump the design experience that a more seasoned mosque architect might bring?

The Language of Bureaucracy

With different faith groups behind them, the three mosques under consideration for Järva are Johan Celsing's Rinkeby Mosque for the Islamic Federation Järva, Spridd's Islamic Cultural Centre, and a project for the Stockholm Large Mosque Organization with collaboration from the Tengbom Group. The Rinkeby Mosque is intended to occupy a central site on a corner crossing between the Rinkeby Allé and Kvarnbyvägen [Figure 9.2]. The Islamic

Figure 9.2: *The Rinkeby Mosque, rendering by Johan Celsing Arkitektkontor, 2013.* Johan Celsing Arkitektkontor AB.

Figure 9.3: *The Islamic Cultural Centre, rendering by Spridd, 2014.* Spridd AB.

Cultural Centre is planned for a site on the outer edge of Rinkeby, defined by the curvilinear highway on one side and the neighbourhood grid on the other [Figure 9.3]. The Stockholm Large Mosque Organisation building will appear in the zone between the neighbourhoods of Rinkeby and Tensta, close to the highway, with funding from private sources in Saudi Arabia.

The esteem for these architectural offices within the ranks of Swedish design (albeit at different levels and for disparate reasons) lends these suburban projects profiles as high design commissions in culturally central settings. Johan Celsing Arkitektkontor is led by its namesake and has completed prestigious projects in Stockholm, including the Bonnier Art Gallery and the ABBA Museum. Spridd is a boutique firm with two principals, Ola Broms Wessel and Klas Ruin, whose oeuvre bridges the divide between research and practice and focuses on rethinking the spaces of the 'Million Programme'. Finally, established in 1906, Tengbom, which serves as the project architect for the mosque originally designed by Rashid Engineering in Saudi Arabia, is today a large, corporate-style firm employing more than 500 people across Sweden and Finland.

All three are known quantities within Sweden and have experience with planning, thus possessing skills for developing complicated and potentially controversial projects. In fact, in May 2013, critic Elisabeth Andersson penned a major article about Celsing's mosque, which appeared along with a slideshow of his drawings in the Swedish national newspaper *Svenska Dagbladet*.[8] Describing the complexities of the commission and his design process, Andersson noted the architect's particularly respected professional position, writing: 'Johan

Celsing is possibly the country's most exclusive architect, and he is as humble and unaffected as one with that indisputable status can be'.[9] Indeed, the weight of Celsing's public persona lends the plans a prominent critical reception that they would likely not otherwise receive.

Even so, positive media attention has appeared alongside a variety of harsh and xenophobic portrayals depicting mosques as the standard-bearers of a Sweden under threat from foreign invaders. Bloggers, social media groups such as 'Mosque in Sweden: No, thank you!', anonymous commentators on Internet venues like Flashback Forum, and supporters of the anti-immigration Sweden Democrats claim that mosques will exacerbate segregation, increase traffic, ruin the natural landscape, and cause the 'Islamization' of Sweden.[10]

A 2013 Swedish public radio programme about mosques stated that protests were registered against mosques in eleven different places in Sweden that year, and, in late 2014 and early 2015, unknown individuals committed arson attacks against several mosques.[11] When the Uppsala Mosque was planned in 1994, the Sweden Democrat party included blocking its construction as a campaign issue in the elections (and failed).[12] In 2017, the Christian Democrat party argued publicly that international financing for mosque construction had encouraged terrorism. Indeed, the source of funding for the Tengbom-Rashid mosque precipitated the following objection from a neighbour to the site: 'To allow a totalitarian dictator system like Saudi Arabia to carry out a project like this in Sweden would be like if Swedish authorities had allowed a Stalinist propaganda centre in Sweden during the Cold War.'[13] When anti-mosque groups place such hurdles onto the course of the planning process, the choice of an architect like Celsing or Spridd appears all the more potent.

In the context of such heated polemics, even finding a plot on which to build a mosque may become a major component of the architect's initial role in the process. The faith group behind the proposed Islamic Cultural Centre currently rents over 1000 square metres of space in Rinkeby Centrum from a private owner. Non-coterminous prayer spaces for men and women mean that the men's mosque fronts the plaza while the women's lies in another building on the back of the town-centre complex. According to members of the mosque's steering group, this unfavourable situation and the high cost of the rents encouraged them to seek out a more permanent and affordable spatial solution.

The Stockholm Urban Development Authority could find no additional land for a mosque, however, and encouraged them to accept their current spatial conditions. Faced with this negative response, the group hired Spridd as consultants. As development engineer Johan told me:

> It was very wise of this organization to hire a consultant who is familiar with the Swedish codes: who can speak them, who knows how civil servants think, and who knows how politicians think. Spridd found a small plot. They talked to the Planning Office and found out that it was parkland. Normally, you're not allowed to build on parkland. But it was also peripherally located and rather uninteresting, so the Planning Office said, 'It's okay if you build a multicultural centre here because it won't be a problem'. And they got a land allocation for it.

Thus, architects well versed in the subtleties of how the Swedish planning process works and the relative 'official' value of different sites were able to overcome the obstacles. As Valdemar, an architect involved in the project, acknowledged, 'We actually found this plot for them. They were very frustrated because they've had a lot of different projects. It kind of never worked out.'

With Swedish design professionals on board, groups hoping to build mosques in the existing suburban landscape are unhindered by seemingly hidden regulations that foreign architects might not be able to foresee or to challenge, or that might entail a protracted process of site selection with representatives sent from a Kuwaiti or Saudi architecture firm. With specific knowledge of the neighbourhood of Rinkeby-Tensta and a local presence, Stockholm firms are able to scout a potential site quickly, reducing the time between seeing and doing. Politically charged and often considered formally suspect, these projects thus have a greater chance of being completed in the hands of an embedded Swedish architect.

Form and the Future

As they navigate the design and planning processes, 'New Swedish' mosques must function programmatically and symbolically while also appealing to the constraints of a larger Swedish public that often approves of mosques in theory but expresses a 'NIMBYist' attitude in practice. Concerns touch not only upon both exterior appearance and formal integration into a larger urban environment, but also on how these buildings will be used in connection to Swedish cultural standards, especially around gender equality. Spridd, Rashid with Tengbom, and Celsing are all designing buildings with divided internal prayer spaces for men and women. Furthermore, the mosques with which their clients are familiar – either as illustrious sources of inspiration abroad or from their own countries of origin – make the inclusion of intricate details on façades and expensive building materials like gold or marble highly desirable but often not affordable.

Several planners and architects described gender-separated spaces and intricate ornamentation as 'un-Swedish' for social or formal reasons, respectively. For instance, when Spridd's client provided sketches of a mosque designed by a Kuwaiti firm [Figure 9.4], Valdemar realized that translating the project to the Swedish context would require more than just climatic adaptations:

> When they want to build a mosque, they can go to Kuwait in this case and get someone to draw a generic mosque that they give to us. This is the 'Islamic Cultural Centre in Sweden'. You will see that this has nothing to do with the site, or with anything else. It's kind of really crazy, very generic, but also the very specific way that you do a mosque, I would say, in a much warmer country than Sweden. The façades and the plans don't even match. But this is something that they gave to us and said that we should really look into. We considered it more as input into the brief.

Form Follows Faith

Figure 9.4: *Renderings provided to Spridd by the client, as drawn by a Kuwaiti firm.* Spridd AB.

Likewise, Celsing's mosque is one of many designs to have been proposed for this central plot on the Rinkeby Allé, formerly the site of the Neighbourhood Administration. Initially, the young Swedish architect Johanna Wickström received the commission, which was then passed onto others.[14] Stefan, a planner at the city of Stockholm, described one sketch by a French firm as 'a gigantic mosque in a Spanish style, like the Alhambra'. This plan included, he continued,

> […] mosaics, very classical. A little old-fashioned, important-looking and big and beautiful. But then Göran [another planner] had a lot of opinions. It couldn't be too high. It had to fit into the landscape. And there were windows here, there, and everywhere. They had to change the mosque quite a bit then. I don't know how much contact they had with the architect. Instead, it was the ones in Sweden who did the changes so that it would fit in.

Swedish planning has, at least since the rise of Functionalism in the 1930s, emphasized standardization in the built environment as a tenet of modern living, yet religious buildings

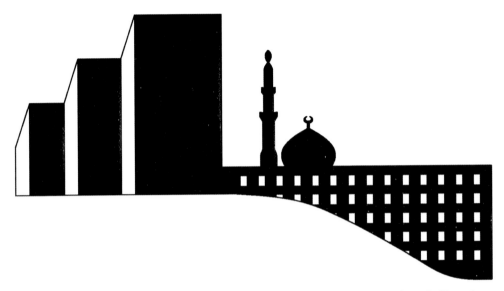

Figure 9.5: *Iconic representation of the Islamic Cultural Centre in the context of the existing modernist buildings of Rinkeby, originally created for the 2012–2013 exhibition, 'Stockholm on the Move', held at Färgfabriken in Stockholm.* Spridd AB.

have the potential to be iconic structures that separate themselves visually from these supposedly 'monolithic' late modernist suburbs [Figure 9.5]. Andersson noted that this increases their appeal as commissions, since architects rarely have such opportunities in central Swedish cities, and few churches are built today. Even so, the description of the local development plan for the Islamic Cultural Centre presents it as striking a perfect balance:

> The mosque's design has been based on the encounter between a Muslim formal world and a Scandinavian modernist building tradition with the goal of being adjusted to Nordic architecture, even while retaining a basic design influenced by classic mosque architecture with the dome and minaret and sparingly playful decorations. The façade material will mainly be carried out in concrete in a bright colour. In some parts of the building, such as on the minaret and around windows, cast concrete or stucco in geometric patterns is used.[15]

In this sense, Swedish architects facilitate expedient problem solving. This places hybrid mosque buildings within the pantheon of Swedish architecture at large, rather than marking them as 'foreign', as one earlier Swedish mosque, the Fittja Mosque, has sometimes been. Designed by the Turkish architect Eray Ercan Aygün for another Stockholm suburb, it was begun in the late 1990s, was inaugurated in 2007, and is considered to display a distinctly

Turkish style of mosque architecture.[16] Andersson writes that the group behind the Rinkeby Mosque explicitly sought another path:

> For Bashir Aman Ali and Ibrahim Bouraleh, with origins in Somalia, an architect who is active in Sweden was an obvious choice. 'We want this to be a Swedish architecture', says Ibrahim Bouraleh, adding that they also need the support of a person who is grounded in Sweden and well acquainted with everything from the climate to the legal framework. Along the journey, they have increasingly realized how important it is to be able to navigate their way through the Swedish bureaucracy. 'We've actually been working on it since the early 1990s. But the problem was that we didn't understand the Swedish bureaucracy, we didn't know how we should do it', says Bashir Aman Ali and recounts years of fruitless labour.[17]

The strong culture of consensus in Swedish planning and architecture lends political undertones to the programming of mosque spaces. In this context, architects seem also to expect their designs to play a culturally transformative role. For instance, Valdemar suggested a future-oriented approach made possible by the flexible panelling system of the office's mosque design. When complete, the panels will allow for the gender-separated prayer that the Somali-Swedish worshippers practise in their current spaces [Figure 9.6]. As

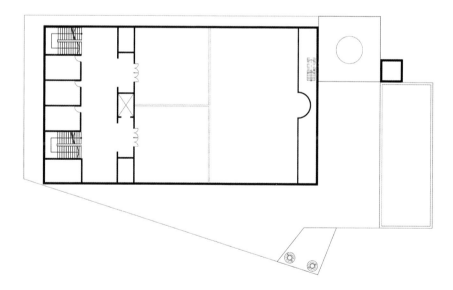

Figure 9.6: *Floor plan for prayer spaces within the Islamic Cultural Centre, showing the removable panels rendered as grey lines, 2015.* Spridd AB.

these panels are movable, however, Valdemar argued that the system (and the gender divisions) 'may disappear in the future'. With this, he avoided perhaps more provocative language while also expressing an assumption that attitudes within the group would shift, more closely adhering to current Swedish social norms and requiring the building to change along with them. Moreover, such design moves acknowledge the possibility that gender-separated prayer spaces may trigger negative reactions from the local community during the approval process for changes to the neighbourhood plan. With both training in forms that are palatable to the Swedish public and in-depth knowledge of the multifaceted and often extensive planning process, Swedish architects serve as a strategic bridge to success for communities that have seen earlier projects stall.

A Mosque for the People

In 2012, an article in the Järva newspaper *Norra Sidan* reflected on the intriguing mixture of functions included in all three mosques, arguing that each includes programmatic space well beyond a mere room for religious services and will thus be 'more than a place for prayer'.[18] In their original 1964 plans for Rinkeby and Tensta, Igor Dergalin and Josef M. Stäck followed the then-current trends in planning, including strict traffic separation and the use of rectilinear blocks.[19] 'Service' was a self-evident component of these projects, and the mosques, in a sense, replicate the blended functions offered in these nearby neighbourhood centres.[20] At the same time, this mixture allows them to take on the other traditional role of the mosque: a community centre.[21]

While the majority of users may appear on the site for Friday prayer services, varying subsets of the groups (as well as non-members) may use a mosque's other programmatic features. These include restaurants and cafés, retail stores, offices, community and educational facilities, and gym and other health-focused spaces. Spridd's mosque is 1900 square metres and includes retail space, a café, a youth centre, a library, classrooms, and a women's area with sauna and exercise equipment. The Stockholm Large Mosque Organization's new complex will be 7875 square metres and over five storeys in height, with offices, shops, a library, classrooms, and a restaurant. Finally, the Rinkeby Mosque includes a restaurant, gym, and youth centre. In connection with this, some Järva mosque architects referenced the Swedish *kulturhus* (House of Culture) as a precursor to their design approach.

This twentieth-century European architectural type combined spaces for community gathering, political debate, education, and entertainment, and it was particularly popular in Sweden. Most notable among the Swedish examples is the *kulturhus* located in central Stockholm, designed by Johan Celsing's father, Peter, and completed in 1974. In conversation, Valdemar explicitly described the firm's longstanding interest in Islamic architecture and how they had discovered a potentially exciting synergy with the *kulturhus*:

> We have been interested in not so much studying this as being a religious building, but more like this being a complex. If you look at old mosques, they have all these functions.

So, what we have realized now is that this really is not a building that is surrounded by a lot of rules, or things that you should do or should not do, but it's really an open programme.

Echoing this in an essay on Swedish mosques, architectural historian Johan Mårtelius writes:

[T]he mosque's program is simple, to contain prayer and to mark the direction toward Mecca. No specific symbolism or iconography is expected, so the architecture has, in principle, been able to be formed completely for the place and the local conditions.[22]

In Järva, then, designers not only have the opportunity to design major new iconic buildings, but are also afforded the chance to work with a flexible megastructure with limited rules around programming.

Furthermore, combining functions may also be potentially strategic, since the planned structures may then be labelled 'cultural centres' instead of mosques. Indeed, the original name for Spridd's project was the Multicultural Centre (Mångkulturellt Centrum), only recently having been changed to its current designation. As the planner Stefan told me:

We notice a tendency among these religious organizations. In the past, they wanted to build a church or a mosque. That's not how it is anymore. Instead, they now want to build a 'multicultural centre', and there is then also a mosque included. But there is also education, commercial activity with some shops, a meeting point for girls, babysitting; anything is possible. There is a larger concept. And it also becomes a little less charged. When you go to the media, it's better to say that we have allocated land for a multicultural centre than that we have allocated it for a mosque. Many people react to the word *mosque*.

Drawing on local architects' expertise, these projects thus remake elements of the original plans for the 'Million Programme' neighbourhoods (especially the town centre) while challenging the status and categorization of Swedish faith spaces. At the same time, like their formal mixture of Islamic and Nordic building traditions, these mixed-use, suburban structures incorporate the multifaceted programming found both in mosques abroad and in the mythologized, typically-urban *kulturhus* of Sweden. Such megastructures allow the groups commissioning them to capitalize on an interstitial programmatic identity, becoming a centre, and thus, as the article described it, 'more than a mosque'.

Following Faith

Aiming a periscope through the deep seas of bureaucratic constraints, formal and programmatic concerns, and the question of typology, both clients and architects follow their 'faith' in the production of new Swedish mosques. On the one hand, the religion of Islam and its material expression in mosque buildings meet new challenges from the logics of a 'Scandinavian modernist building tradition' and the regulatory mechanisms of the municipal planning process. As clients and professional designers travel a path opened, as development engineer Johan described, by the political will to build new structures of this type, it is a path nonetheless laden with roadblocks. Here, in the suburbs of Järva, the centres of power retain ostensible control. Mosque clients explicitly recognize that their best hope of altering contemporary urban space lies in the commissioning of Swedish expertise via Swedish architects.

While none of these architects have designed a mosque before, knowing 'how officials think' and what colours on a façade will successfully make it through a planning process predicated on public consensus are just as – or even more – important. This also reflects negotiations around mosque form and function occurring in other European contexts, such as the 2009 compromise around the call to prayer for the Grand Mosque of Marseille: a (silent) ray of light projected in a colour without significance for the ships travelling through that city's harbour.[23] Grounded in their experience with the Swedish planning regime and public expectations for local architecture, Celsing, Tengbom, and Spridd have the ability to make 'foreign' typologies and forms adhere to Nordic traditions. Years of frustration and nonstarters among their clients have made the choice of a Swedish architect a shrewd one.

Beyond Järva Field, many other new mosques are currently appearing in the planning dockets of other Swedish cities. This occurs even as anti-immigrant political forces appear to be gaining ground nationally, with the Sweden Democrats receiving nearly 13 per cent of the vote in the 2014 national elections, and in the context of rising defacements and the mosque arsons of December 2014 and January 2015. While not the first of such structures to be built in Sweden, the planned mosques of Järva Field lead the way in demonstrating that one token mosque for areas with large and diverse Muslim populations will no longer do. Likewise, as the groups behind the commissions learn how to make plans for new purpose-built spaces appear in material form, they also become, like their architects, experts in exhausting and experimenting with the content of these processes. Here, both clients and architects transform peripheral sites into new centres for a New Sweden.

Acknowledgements

I would like to thank the editor, the two anonymous reviewers for the *International Journal of Islamic Architecture* who evaluated an earlier version of this piece, and Moa Tunström for their invaluable comments. I also thank the planners and architects who shared their experiences of the mosque commissions with me, and I thank colleagues at the Institute for Housing and Urban Research at Uppsala University and the School of Architecture at KTH Royal Institute of Technology for their thoughtful insights into the larger study. Finally, I am deeply grateful for the funding that made this research possible, which I received from the Formas-funded research environment Architecture in Effect, Forte (the Swedish Research Council for Health, Working Life, and Welfare), and Vetenskapsrådet (the Swedish Research Council).

Notes

1. See Thomas Hall and Sonja Vidén, 'The Million Homes Programme: A Review of the Great Swedish Planning Project', *Planning Perspectives* 20 (2005): 301–28.
2. The following Swedish government reports outline expectations for town centres: SOU 1968:38; SOU 1970:68; SOU 1971:26; SOU 1971:27; SOU 1971:28; and SOU 1973:24.
3. The official brochure is available online as 'Vision Järva 2030,' accessed September 10, 2014, http://bygg.stockholm.se/Alla-projekt/Jarvalyftet/.
4. Utlåtande 2009: RV (Dnr 319-2070/2008, 336-2252/2004), Vision Järva 2030. Projekt 830 årsrapport 2003 ytterstadssatsning, stadsdelsförnyelse. All translations from the Swedish are my own.
5. For more on the terms used over time, see Ingvar Svanberg and Mattias Tydén, *Tusen år av invandring: en svensk kulturhistoria* (Stockholm: Dialogos, 2005).
6. In the interest of protecting informants' identities, all of their personal names are pseudonyms, and the specific dates upon which personal communications with them took place are not provided.
7. Although he was explicitly discussing mosques, Johan used the word *kyrka* (church) rather than *moské* (mosque) at this juncture.
8. Elisabeth Andersson, 'En moské blir till', *Svenska Dagbladet*, May 5, 2013, accessed May 30, 2013, http://www.svd.se/kultur/titta-in-i-modellen-avstockholms-forsta-moskebyggnad_8143752.svd.
9. Elisabeth Andersson, 'Arkitektens skisser till nya moskén', *Svenska Dagbladet*, May 5, 2013, accessed September 13, 2014. http://www.svd.se/kultur/arkitektens-skisser-till-nya-mosken_8142218.svd.
10. Ibid.
11. 'Moské väcker motstånd', *Människor och tro*, Sveriges Radio, November 14, 2013.
12. Eva Wikström, *Rum för Islam – moskén som religiöst rum i Sverige* (Stockholm: Riksantikvarieämbetet, 2005), 37.
13. Överklagande av beslut tagit av Stadsbyggnadsnämnden10/5-2012 gällande Lackes 2, Dp 2010-04433-54. Beslut i ärende § 9, Stockholm, June 8, 2012.
14. 'Johanna har ritat en moské', *Nya Åland*, January 17, 2010, accessed January 16, 2015, http://www.nyan.ax/nyheter/index.pbs?news_id=49680.
15. Planbeskrivning, Detaljplan för del av fastigheten Akalla 4:1m.fl., moské vid Rinkebysvängen, i stadsdelarna Rinkeby och Kista, S-Dp 2013-02091. Nearly identical language is used in the description of the Rashid Engineering-Tengbom collaboration: Kvalitetsprogram för gestaltning gällande KV LACKES 2, TENSTA, Stockholm, May 2011.
16. The architectural historian Johan Mårtelius argues that the Fittja Mosque's design can be linked both to fifteenth-century Ottoman architecture and many modern Turkish mosques, particularly in the location of its major prayer space under a dome and in the design of its primary façade to include an arcade and three small domes. For more, see his chapter, 'Minareternas sång' in *Stockholm Global Stad*, ed. Ulf Sörenson, Series *Samfund S:t Eriks Årsbok* (Stockholm: Langenskiöld, 2012): 154–57.
17. Andersson, 'En moské blir till'.

18 Rouzbeh Djalaie, 'Ny moské ska bli mer än böneplats', *Norra Sidan*, April 10, 2012, accessed March 30, 2014, http://www.direktpress.se/norra_sidan/Nyheter/Ny-moske-ska-bli-mer-an-boneplats/.
19 See Igor Dergalin and Josef M. Stäck's articles, 'Generalplan för Rinkeby, Spånga kyrka och Tensta', *Arkitektur* 64.5 (1964): 119–24, and 'Rinkeby, Spånga kyrka och Tensta', *Plan* 3 (1964): 101–07.
20 See also Jennifer Mack, 'Eat, Pray, Shop! The Mosque as Centre of the Town', in *Future People's Palace: Remaking the Architecture of the Welfare State*, eds. Ola Broms Wessel, Jennifer Mack, and Tim Anstey (Stockholm: Arvinius, forthcoming).
21 Jocelyne Cesari highlights this expanded role, as well as the constraints of the typically limited spaces afforded to Muslim groups in European cities, in 'Mosque Conflicts in European Cities: Introduction', *Journal of Ethnic and Migration Studies* 31.6 (2005): 1015–24.
22 Mårtelius, 'Minareternas sång'.
23 Steven Erlanger, 'French Mosque's Symbolism Varies with Beholder', *The New York Times*, December 27, 2009, accessed February 15, 2015, http://www.nytimes.com/2009/12/28/world/europe/28marseille.html.

Notes on Contributors

Peter H. Christensen is Assistant Professor of Art History at the University of Rochester, where he teaches courses in global modern architecture and infrastructure. He is the author of *Germany and the Ottoman Railway Network* (2017) and co-editor of *Architecturalized Asia: Mapping a Continent Through History* (2014), *Instigations: Engaging Architecture, Landscape and the City* (2012), and *Home Delivery: Fabricating the Modern Dwelling* (2008).

Neta Feniger is a landscape architect and holds a Ph.D. from the Technion – Israel Institute of Technology. Her dissertation, entitled 'Building a "New Middle East": Israeli Architects in Iran', focused on the work of Israeli architects in Iran from the 1950s to the late 1970s. Her Master's thesis in architectural history is entitled 'Theory and Planning of the Public Open Space in Kauffmann's and Geddes' Plans for Tel Aviv' (Technion – Israel Institute of Technology, 2009).

Jessica Gerschultz is Assistant Professor in the Department of African and African American Studies at the University of Kansas. She is a 2018 Hans-Robert Roemer Fellow at the Orient-Institut Beirut. Her research and teaching centre on African and Arab articulations of modernism with a particular emphasis on tapestry. She has published articles in *ART Margins* (2016), *International Journal of Islamic Architecture* (2015), and *Critical Interventions: Journal of African Art History and Visual Culture* (2014). Gerschultz was an American Council of Learned Societies Fellow in 2016 for the writing of her first book on Tunisian modernism (Penn State Press, forthcoming). She has held fellowships and awards from the American Philosophical Society, the Max Weber Foundation, the American Association of University Women, the US Fulbright Council, the American Institute for Maghrib Studies, and the Andrew W. Mellon Curatorial Internship Program. She serves on the board of AMCA, the Association for Modern and Contemporary Art of the Arab World, Iran, and Turkey.

Dan Handel is an architect whose work focuses on economic models and industrial architecture. He holds degrees from the Harvard Graduate School of Design and the Bezalel Academy. His writing has appeared in *Thresholds, Journal of Landscape Architecture* (JOLA),

Frame, San Rocco, Pin-Up, Bracket, and *Cabinet* among others. He is the co-editor of *Aircraft Carrier: American Ideas and Israeli Architectures after 1973* (Hatje Cantz, 2012) and of *Manifest: A Journal of American Architecture and Urbanism.*

Rachel Kallus is a faculty member in the Architecture and Town Planning Department of the Technion, and Head of the Social Hub for Community and Housing. Her research focuses on the sociopolitical production of the built environment, particularly in ethno-nationally contested spaces. Her work has been published widely in academic journals and books. Her current project, funded by the Israel Science Foundation, is entitled 'Development from the periphery: The export of nation building knowledge from Israel, 1950–1970'.

Jennifer Mack is a researcher at the Institute for Housing and Urban Research at Uppsala University and at the School of Architecture at KTH Royal Institute of Technology. She combines history, ethnography, and formal analysis to study social change and the built environment. Mack has published work on the architecture of large-scale mosques, the design of mid-twentieth-century youth centres, the politics of landscape in allotment gardens, and the Swedish town centre (*centrum*). Her recent book *The Construction of Equality: Syriac Immigration and the Swedish City* (University of Minnesota Press, 2017) investigates how 'users' become makers, focusing on how immigrant-instigated architectural projects and spatial practices have altered the Swedish city's built environment 'from below' over a 50 year period. Her work has received support from the American-Scandinavian Foundation, Architecture in Effect, Formas, Forte, the Fulbright US Student Program, the Graham Foundation, the Society of Architectural Historians, Vetenskapsrådet, and more. Mack holds a Ph.D. in architecture, urbanism, and anthropology from Harvard University, an MArch and MCP from MIT, and a BA from Wesleyan University.

Alona Nitzan-Shiftan is an architectural historian and theorist. She currently teaches at the University of Chicago while on sabbatical from the Technion, where she is the designate Head of the Arenson Built Heritage Research Center, and Founding Editor of the centre's *Testimony* book series. She received her S.M.Arch.S and Ph.D. from MIT, and her work was sponsored by the Center for Advance Study in the Visual Arts (CASVA), the Getty/UCLA programme, and the Frankel Institute at the University of Michigan. Her research on the politics of architecture and heritage, on architectural modernism in Israel and the United States, and on critical historiography has been published in journals such as *Theory and Criticism, Journal of Architecture, Architectural History, Perspecta,* and *TDSR,* as well as in numerous anthologies. As the first Chair of the Architecture Department at the Technion, she implemented a new curriculum that integrates design and research, and after serving as the President of the European Architectural History Network (EAHN), she co-chaired its third thematic conference, *Histories in Conflict*. Her book *Seizing Jerusalem: The Architectures of Unilateral Unification* was recently published by University of Minnesota Press.

Mrinalini Rajagopalan is Assistant Professor in the Department of the History of Art and Architecture at the University of Pittsburgh. She is an architectural historian of South Asia whose research focuses on topics such as the history of preservation, urban memory, and the colonial and postcolonial framings of architecture. She is the author of *Building Histories: The Archival and Affective Lives of Five Monuments in Modern Delhi* (University of Chicago Press, 2017), and is the co-editor of *Colonial Frames, Nationalist Histories: Imperial Legacies, Architecture, and Modernity* (Ashgate, 2012).

Łukasz Stanek is Lecturer at the Manchester Architecture Research Centre, The University of Manchester. He authored *Henri Lefebvre on Space: Architecture, Urban Research, and the Production of Theory* (University of Minnesota Press, 2011) and edited Lefebvre's unpublished book about architecture, *Toward an Architecture of Enjoyment* (University of Minnesota Press, 2014). Stanek also studies the Cold War transfer of architecture from socialist countries to West Africa and the Middle East, and published the book *Postmodernism Is Almost All Right: Polish Architecture After Socialist Globalization* (Fundacja Bec Zmiana, 2012)

Eva-Maria Troelenberg is Chair for Modern and Contemporary Art History at Utrecht University. She has directed the Max-Planck-Research Group 'Objects in the contact zone – The cross-cultural lives of things' at Kunsthistorisches Institut in Florenz – MPI. She has taught Islamic art history and transcultural modern and contemporary art history in Munich, Vienna, Zürich, and Heidelberg. Her publications include the volume *Images of the Art Museum: Connecting Gaze and Discourse in the History of Museology* (2017) and the special issue of the *Mitteilungen des Kunsthistorischen Institutes in Florenz*, 'Visualizing otherness in modern Italy' (2017).

Deniz Türker is a postdoctoral fellow at University of Cambridge's Centre of Islamic Studies and an affiliated lecturer in the departments of the History of Art and Asian and Middle Eastern Studies. Prior to that she held the Fari Sayeed Fellowship in Islamic art at Pembroke College. She is a graduate of Harvard University's dual degree programme in the History of Art and Architecture and Middle Eastern Studies. She is a historian of Islamic art and architecture and has published on Ottoman collectors of Islamic art as well as Ottoman garden and landscape histories in the eighteenth and nineteenth centuries. She has recently co-curated an upcoming exhibition at ANAMED (Istanbul) titled *Ottoman Arcadia: The Hamidian Expedition to the Land of Tribal Roots (1886),* which is centred on a set of photograph albums gifted to Otto von Bismarck by Sultan Abdülhamid II. She is currently completing her book manuscript on the architectural history of Yıldız, the last Ottoman palace complex.

Alyson Wharton received her doctorate from SOAS, University of London, with a thesis entitled 'Building the Tanzimat: The Power of the Balyan Family in the Age of

Re-Organizations' (2011), recently published as the book *The Architects of Ottoman Constantinople: The Balyan Family and the History of Ottoman Architecture* (I.B.Tauris, 2015). As an Assistant Professor at Mardin Artuklu University in Turkey, she carried out research on Armenian architects working in the region in the nineteenth century. She is now a lecturer at the University of Lincoln (UK), School of History and Heritage.

Index

Note: Page numbers in *italics* refer to figures and/or captions.

A
Abdülaziz (sultan), 28, 40–41, 87
Abdülhamid (sultan), 24
Abdülmecid (sultan), 23, 28–29, *33*, 87, 94
acculturation, 88
agency theory, 126
agriculture, 189, 192
AIG Al-Qurain district, 250
Akaretler terrace, 103–04, *103*
Alai Darwaza gateway, 59
Alai Minar, 59
Al-Ansari, Ahmad, 245
Al-Azhar mosque, 132
Al-Bayati, Basil, 247
al-e Ahmad, Jalal, 184
Al-Ghanim Dasman, 245
Ali, Bashir Aman, 281
Allen, Harriet Trowbridge, 94
Al-Madfai, Kahtan, 247
Al-Mazidi building, *248*, 249
Al-Muayyad mosque, 132
Al-Othman Centre, 243, 250, 253, *254–55*, 256, 264
Al-Sabah, Saud Nasir, 244
al-Salih Najm al-Din Ayub, mausoleum of, 138
Al-Sanan, Mohammad, 242
Al-Sawaber project, 246
American Mission (Kuwait), 245
Amiri Diwan, 243
Amr ibn al-As mosque, 132
Ancient Delhi (Cole), 53, 69, 76–77
Andersson, Elisabeth, 276
André, 113
anthropology, 10, 13, 191, 201
Anwar Al-Sabah Complex, *260*
Aqaba International Industrial Estate, 228, 230
Aqaba Special Economic Zone, 230
Arab Cities Organization Building, 244
Arab revivalism, 143
Arabization, 215
Archaeological Society of Delhi (ASD), 54, 57, 66, 70–71, 79–80n21, 80nn22–23
Archaeological Survey of India (ASI), 54, 66, 70–71, 76
archaeology, 54, 57
Archicentre, 243
architects
  Polish, 239–45, 249–50, 256, 263–64
  from socialist countries, 239–43, 264
Architects Collaborative, The (TAC), 239
architecture
  Arab, 110, 125, 128, 132, 146n19, 239, 246
  Cairene, 132
  and the envelope concept, 223–24
  and expertise, 5–7
  Hindu, 57–58
  historic, 16
  Islamic, 116, 126, 246, 248–49, 264

in Kuwait City, 239
Mamluk, 131–32, 138, 148n56
mondialization of, 240
mud brick, 13–15
Muslim, 132, 138, 146n19, 246
Muslim-Egyptian, 127
neo-Mamluk, 139
Nubian, 11
Ottoman, 15–16, 87–88, 91, 94, 97, 115–16
Parisian, 115
pharaonic, 10
rural, 200
and technicalism, 4–5
tropical, 259
urban typologies, 249–50
Western texts on, 57
Architecture arabe ou monuments du Kaire (Pascal Coste), 125, 138
   frontispiece, *127*
archives, 66, 76–77, 78n5
Area Studies, 126
Armabeton, 244
Arsanjani, Sayyid Hassan, 185–86
Arseven, Celal Esad, 87–88
Arup, 261
Āṣār-us-Ṣanādīd (Traces of Noblemen), 53, 78n8
   as archive, 66
   chronology of Delhi's monuments, 55, 70–71, *72–74*, 76
   comparison with Cunningham's account, 55, 66–70
   differences between editions, 55–56, 67, 70–71, 77–78n3, 79n14, 82n52
   first page of urban geneology of Delhi, *74*
   historical and discursive context of, 55–59
   images of the Qutb Minar, 55, 59–62, *60–61*, *63*, 64–66, *65*
   list regarding building forts and cities of Delhi, 72–73, 83n56
   poetry in, 55
   translation of, 56, 79n13

Asiatic Society, 56
Audit Bureau (Kuwait), 261, *262*, 264
authenticity, 143
Aygün, Eray Ercan, 280

B

Badni, Elliyahu, 192
Bakić, Dragomir, 244
Bakić, Ljiljana, 244
Ballet de l'Olive (Olive Ballet) mural, 153, *154*, *155*, 174
Baloush Bus Terminal, 256, *258*
Balyan, Agop, 87, 89, 110
Balyan, Karapet, 87, 91
Balyan, Léon, 90
Balyan, Nigoğos, 16, 87
   architectural education of, 87–90, 115–16
   designs for Dolmabahçe Palace, 91–101, 115–16
   Odian's obituary for, 90–91
Balyan, Serkis, 16, 87
   architectural education of, 87–89, 101–02, 104–05, 107, 109–10, 115–16
   architectural projects, 103–04
   designs for Çırağan Palace, 107, 109–10, 116
   designs for Pertevniyal Valide Sultan Mosque, 110, 113, 116
   drawings for Çırağan Palace, 107, *107*, *108–09*
   proposal for Ottoman school for arts and industry, 101–2
Banham, Peter Reyner, 223
Barquq mosque, 132
Basil Spence Partnership, 249
Bechtel, 230
Beglier-Bey Summer Palace, *26*
Behbehani compound, 245
Behrens-Abouseif, Doris, 138
Beit Al-Reihan house, 245
Bellagha, Ali, 165
Ben Abdallah, Jellal, 165
Ben Naceur, Hamida, 166

Ben Salah, Ahmed, 159, 164, 174
Ben Yusuf, Salah, 158
Ben-Gurion, David, 189, 226–27, 231
Bernier, François, 56
Beşiktaş Palace, 26
Beylerbeyi Palace, 27
Bezirdjian, Sopon, 115
Blanchet, Marie Parfait Alphonse, 101
Blondel, Jacques-François, 93
Bode, Christian Ludwig, 28
Bofill, Ricardo, 247
Bohdanowicz, Andrzej, 241–42, *248*, 249–50, *251–52*, 253, 256, *257*
Bohdanowicz, Danuta, 243
Boneh, Michael, 192
Bonnington, John S., 261
Boox, Franz, 25
Bostandji-Bachi kiosk, *25*
Boucherle, Pierre, 164
Bouraleh, Ibrahim, 281
Bourgoin, Jules, 138
Bourguiba, Habib, 17, 156–59, *171*
    photographs of, 171–72, *172*
    in Turki's *Mourabtines* mural, 170, 174
Bourguiba, Habib Jr., 165
Bourguibism, 157, 172, 174
Bozdoğan, Sibel, 88
Brand, Harry, 218, *219*, 221–22
Brenner, David, 192, 196
Buchanan and Partners, 245
Bulgarproject, 244
Bunel, Louis, 94
Buyin-Zahra earthquake (Iran), 181, 205–06n2

C
Cacoub, Olivier-Clément, 156, 159–61
Candillis-Josic-Woods, 250
capitalism, global, 222
cellar mosques, 273. See also mosques
Celsing, Johan, 275–77, 279, 284
Celsing, Peter, 282
Cemaran Mektebi school, 87

Cezayirliyan, Mıgırdiç, 90
Chadirji, Rifat, 239, 247, 249
Choiseul-Gouffier, Marie-Gabriel-Florent-Auguste de, 24
Chomiak, Laryssa, 172
Christians/Christianity, 40–41
Chryniewicz, Jacek, 242
Chyczewski, Leopold, 256, *258*
CIAM (Congrès internationaux d'architecture moderne), 240, 246
Çırağan Palace, 15, 23, 87–88, 115
    gardens, 31–34, *32–33*
    Serkis Balyan's drawings for, *107–09*
    sofa plan, 107, *109*
Çırağan Palace
City Centre Housing Estate (Łódź), 241
Clot-Bey, Antoine, 139
Coastal Strip Development Project, 244
Cold War era, 183, 204, 239–40, 244, 263, 277
Cole, Henry Hardy, 53, 69, 76–77, 78n4
Collège Sainte-Barbe, 87, 89–91, 101, 115
Collier, Stephen J., 261
colonialism, 3, 16, 66–67, 77, 191, 234n42
Computer-Aided Design (CAD) software, 241, 261, *262*, 263–64
Conference Center (Bayan Park), 243
contemporaneity, 143
Corot, Jean-Baptiste-Camille, 90
Coste, Pascal
    architectural sketches (1819–20), *131*
    commissions for mosques, 132, 138–39
    design for Alexandria mosque, 139, *141*
    design for military hospital, 139, *142*
    drafting of ground plan for Sultan al-Mansur Qala'un complex, *134*, 135
    drawing of Obelisk of Cleopatra, 146n21
    drawing of 'Pompey's Pillar', 128, *129*
    drawings of mosques, 132, *133*, 139
    expertise and agency of, 143–44
    floor plan for Alexandria mosque, *140*
    folios of drawings, 127–28
    stay in Egypt, 16, 125, 127–28, 131–32, 138–39, 143–44

study of Cairo mosques, 132
  systematic drawing of a tent, *130*, 131
Coxiadis, Constantinos, 243
Critical Regionalism, 10, 259
cultural heritage, 143
cultural memory, 54
culture
  Arab, 128
  Iranian, 184
  linguistic, 87–88, 91, 93–94, 100, 105, 115
Cunningham, Alexander, 58, 64, 66, 76
  architectural expertise of, 69
  on the Qutb Minar, 67–70

D

Daczkowska, Zdzisława, 243, 247, 250, *253*
Daczkowski, Ryszard, 241
Dalberg, Karl Theodor von, 28, 31
Dargah Quli Khan, 56
Dayan, Moshe, 181, 184–85
de-Arabization, 234n41
decolonization, 158
decoration (*décoration*), 164, 176n28, 176n31
Delhi
  built environment of, 58
  historic architecture in, 16
  historical accounts of architecture of, 56–57
  map, *75*
  as series of imperial capitals, 70
  urban evolution of, 70–71
Dergalin, Igor, 282
Derrida, Jacques, 66
de-territorialization, 263
Dirks, Nicholas, 71
disaster capitalism, 187
Djelloul, Néji, 169
Djenné, construction in, 13–15
Dolmabahçe Palace, 31, 87, 115–16
  Audience Hall, 91, 94, *97*, 98–99
  bouquet above stairs, *99*

bouquets in pendentives of Audience Hall, *99*
ceiling of *hamam* room, 94, *95*
crystal staircase, 97, *98*
entrance façade, *96*
ornament on seaside façade, *93*
Ottoman traditions in, 91, 100
sofa plan, 100–01
Treasury Gate, 91, *92*, 93–94, *94*
triumphal arch, *95*
view from Bosphorus, *92*
Dominikańsak department store (Wrocław), 264
Drexler, Yehuda, 185

E

earthquake, in Iran, 181, 205–6n2
earthquake relief
  housing unit plans, *198*, 199
  in Qazvin, 201
  school plans, *199*
  using concrete blocks, 200
Ecochard, Michel, 243, 245
Ecole Centrale, 87, 101–03, 115
  student notebook, *102*, *104*
Ecole de Tunis, 153, 156, 161, 164, 166
  stamp designed by, *173*
Ecole des Beaux-Arts (Paris), 16, 87, 102–05, 109–10, 113, 115
  project for market hall, *105*
  project for palace, *106*
  studies of the cloister of the hospital of St. Jean d'Angers, 110, *111*
Ecole des Beaux-Arts (Tunis), 160
Egyptomania, 146n22
Eiffel, Gustave, 89
El Mezri, Abou Abdullah, 169
el Wakil, Abdel Wahed, 249
Eldem, Sedad Hakkı, 107
Elias, Jamal, 64
Eliav, Arie Lova, 189, 191
el-Krunz, Sa'adi, 227
Energoprojekt, 243–44

English landscape garden, 30
Ensle, Jacob, 25–26
entrepreneurship, 221–22
envelope concept, 223–24
Erickson, Arthur, 239, 246–47
Ersoy, Ahmet, 88
Essay on the Architecture of the Hindus (Ram Raz), 57
expertise
    American, 231
    architectural, 3–7, 69–70, 191
    contributory, 89, 117n21
    development, 189
    exporting, 181
    full, 89, 117n21
    German Fountain, 7–9
    of Hassan Fathy, 10–13
    horticultural, 15, 23
    industrial, 216
    interactional, 88–89, 101, 117n21
    Israeli, 184, 189
    knowledge management theory of, 14–15
    of Max Spitta, 7–9

F
Faiz Ali Khan, 55
Farhat, Safia, 164, 166, 176n31
Fathy, Hassan, 245
    New Gourna Village (Upper Egypt), 10–13
Fatran, Arieh, 192, *193*, 200
Fergusson, James, 58, 64, 68–70, 80n28, 82n48
Finch, William, 56, 70
Fintas Center, 261
Fittja Mosque, 280–81, 285n16
Fitzroy Robinson Partnership, 248
Food and Agricultural Organization (FAO), 186
Ford Foundation, 204
foreign investment, 216
Fossati, Giuseppe, 41
Frankl, Ludwig August von, 36–37, 39

Friedman, Milton, 217
Functionalism, 279

G
Galland, Pierre Victor, 90
garden art and design
    English, 30
    German, 23, 30–31
    in Istanbul, 15, 36–39, 43–44, 45n1
    Ottoman, 23
Garnier, Charles, 94, 97, 103, 115
Gautier, Théophile, 90–91, 93
Gebze industrial garden, 230–31, *230*
General Drafting System (GDS), 261
Gentil, Jean-Baptiste, 56
GEO. *See* Gulf Engineering Office
German Fountain, 7
    design, *8*
    symbols and inscriptions, 9
    vandalism of, 9–10
German Hospital, 41
Ghanim, Fathi, 11
Ghazvin Area (Iran), map of earthquake zone, *194*
Gierek, Edward, 241
Gleń, Włodzimierz, 243
global assemblages, 261, 263
globalization, 15, 231–32
    architectural, 239
Gorgi, Abdelaziz, 164–65
Great Trigonometrical Survey, 54
greenhouses, 44
gridiron plan, 246
Guha-Thakurta, Tapati, 58
Gulf Engineering Office (GEO), 242, *253*

H
Hahn-Hahn, Ida (Countess von), *33*
Haller, Dieter, 126
Hammer-Purgstall, Joseph von, 26
Harvard Business School (HBS), 218
Heber, Bishop, 56
Henry, Charles, 44, 49n78

Herder, Gottfried, 30, 31
heuristics, 7–15
high modernism, 205. See also modernism
Hirschfeld, Christian Cay Lorenz, 30
historiography, 3, 66, 126, 128
Hodgson, Marshall, 6
Hôtel Ribat, *155*, 159, 162–63, 169
    advertisement, *161*
    beach, *164*
    construction of, 153, 156
    demolition of, 153
    tapestry in, 166
    Turki's murals in, 153, *154–55*

I

Ibn Battuta, 70
Ibn Tulun mosque, 132, *133*
identity
    Iranian, 184
    negotiation of, 227
Ihlamur Kiosk, 87
ijtihad, 156, 157
Iltutmish (sultan), 62, 81n36
    tomb of, 59
immigrant labor, 221, 256
imperialism, 3
    economic, 66–67
INCO. See Industrial & Engineering Consulting Office (INCO)
India
    archaeology in, 54
    architectural history in, 54
    archival history of, 53–54
    as British colony, 66–67, 79n10
    surveys of, 54
'Industree' graphic, *220*
Industrial & Engineering Consulting Office (INCO), 242, 250, *251–52*, 256, *258*
industrial garden idea, 217–19, *219*, 232
    Aqaba International Industrial Estate, 228, 230
    Gebze industrial garden, 230–31

    Israeli-Palestinian industrial gardens project, 227–29, *228–29*
    Tefen Industrial Garden, 217–19, 221–24, *223–24*, 225–27
Institute for Planning and Development (IPD; Israel), 187, 189
Iran
    diplomatic relations with Israel, 183–84
    earthquake in, 181, 205–6n2
    earthquake relief from Israel, 17, 181, 183, 185–86, 205
    earthquake relief from other agencies, 187
    map of Qazvin project location, *182*
    reconstruction after earthquake, 181, 183
    reconstruction of Khuznin, 191
    Village Planning & Reconstruction of the Earthquake Zone in the Ghazvin Area, *182*
    Westernization in, 183, 184
    'White Revolution' in, 181, 186, 206n3
Iranian Revolution, 183
Islam. *See also* mosques
    in Sweden, 283–84
    in Tunisia, 17
Islamic Cultural Centre (Sweden), 275–76, *276*, 277, 280
    floor plan for prayer spaces, *281*
    iconic representation, *280*
    renderings by Kuwaiti firm, *279*
Islamic Federation Järva, 275
Islamic law, Bourguiba's interpretation of, 156–58
Israel
    African development missions, 207n24
    diplomatic relations with Iran, 183–84
    earthquake relief for Iran, 17, 181, 183, 185–86, 205
    earthquake relief in Qazvin, 201
    economic liberalization in, 217
    'periphery doctrine,' 184
Israeli-Palestinian industrial gardens project, 227–29, *228–29*
    initial scheme, *229*

296

project perspective, *229*
tour of site, *228*
Istanbul, 15
   imperial gardens after Sester, 43–44
   imperial gardens by Sester, 36–39
   See also Turkey

J
Jacobsen, Arne, 239
Jameson, Frederic, 223
Janissary corps, 23–24
Järva Lift, 273, 284
Jarząbek, Wojciech, 241–243, 245, 247, 250, 261, 264
   architectural projects, *246*, *251–52*, *254–55*, *262*
Jencks, Charles, 247
Johan Celsing Arkitektkontor, 276. *See also* Celsing, Johan

K
KEG, 261, *262*
knowledge economy, 232
Koch, J. D. H., 44
Konak Pier (Izmir), 89
Kozanów Estate (Wrocław), 241, *242*
KÖZTI, 244
Krajný, Milosalv, 168
Krawecki, Janusz, 243
Krieger, Alex, 227
Kritovoulos of Imbros, 91
kulturhus, 282–83
Kumar, Sunil, 59
Kuwait, 18
   architectural conservation in, 245
   architecture in, 239–41
   construction materials in, 259–60
   urbanization in, 244–49
Kuwait City
   architecture in, 239
   urban development of, 250
Kuwait Law Courts, 249
Kuwait Public Transport Company, 256
Kuwait Towers, 244
Kuwaiti National Theatre, 242

L
La Procession des Mourabtines (The Procession of the Murabitun) mural, 153, *154*, 156, 169–72, *173*, 174–75
labour export, 242
Labour Zionism, 219
Labrouste, Alexandre, 89–90, 101
Labrouste, Henri, 89–90, 115
Lach, Edward, 241, 244–45, 250, 261, *262*
   architectural projects, *246*, *253–55*
Lakhish Plan (Israel), 189, *190*, 191
Lehmann, Henri, 90
Lelyveld, David, 56, 70
Leopold, Prince (Duke of Brabant), 33–34
Levant, 17, 126, 128, 215, 225–27, 231–32
Libya, Italian colonization of, 191
lithography, 79n12
Livingston, Robert, 230
Lurçat, Jean, 165, 177n35

M
Mackenzie, Colin, 71
Magne, Lucien, 109–10, 116
Mahmud II (sultan), 23, 25–29, 31
Makiya, Mohamed, 239, 249
Maksimović, Stojan, 243
Mansel, Philip, 226, 231
Marchand, Trevor, 13–15
Marshall Plan, 17, 215, 225
Mårtelius, Johan, 283, 285n16
Martin, Leslie, 250
Martin, Reinhold, 223
Mary, Louis-Charles, 101
mashrabiyya, 247, 261
Massachusetts Institute of Technology (MIT), 218
Matkowski, Jan, 242
Maulvi Imam Baksh Sahba'i, 55
Mayeux, Pierre-Henri, 107
McNeill, Donald, 239

297

Mehmed II (sultan), 24, 91
Mélick, Jacob, 90
Melling, Antoine Ignace, 26
Metcalfe, Thomas, 57
Miastoptojekt, 243
Miastoprojekt-Kraków, 244
Middle East
   economic liberalization in, 216–17
   oil production in, 215–17
   participation in world trade, 216–17
   See also Iran; Israel; Kuwait; Libya; Tunisia; Turkey
military hospital (Kuwait), 244
Million Programme, 273, 276, 283
minarets, 67
   minaret at Ghazni, 67, *68*
   See also Qutb Minar
Ministries Complex (Kuwait), 244
Minoprio, Spencely, and MacFarlane, 245
Mirza Sangin Beg, 56
Mirza Shah Rukh Beg, 55
Mitchell, George, 230
Mitchell, Timothy, 71
Mitra, Rajendralal, 57–59
modernism, 4, 143–44, 241
   colonial 'tropical', 246
   combined with local traditions, 199–201
   high, 205
   in Scandinavia, 284
   in Tunisia, 153, 168
modernity
   in Egypt, 143
   Muslim, 126
   in Tunisia, 156, 158, 172
modernization
   in Iran, 17, 181, 183, 185–86, 201, 204
   in Tunisia, 156–57
Monastir (Tunisia), 169–70
   construction in, 159–60
   map of, *160*
   tourism industry in, 158–66
Monastir *ribat* (Tunisia), 162–64, *163–64*
Monge, Gaspard, 101

monumental writing, on the Qutb Minar, 62, 64–65
Moreau, J.M. (le jeune), *24*
mosques
   Al-Azhar, 132
   Al-Muayyad, 132
   Amr ibn al–As, 132
   Barquq, 132
   in Cairo, 132
   cellar mosques, 273
   design of, 18
   Fittja, 280–81, 285n16
   gender-separated prayer spaces in, 281–82
   Ibn Tulun, 132, *133*
   mix of functions in, 282–83
   'New Swedish,' 278
   Ortaköy, 87, 98, *100*
   Pascal's plan for, 139, *140–41*
   Pertevniyal Valide Sultan, 87–88, 110, *112*, *113*, 115
   popular opposition to, 277
   preservation of, 245
   Qa'itbay, 132
   Qala'un, 132, 139
   Quwwat-ul Islam, 59–61, *60–61*, 70, 81n31, 81n33
   Rinkeby, 275, *275*, 281–82
   Stockholm Large Mosque Organization, 275–76, 282
   Sultan Hasan, 132
   in Sweden, 18, 273, *274*, 275–84
   Uppsala, 277
Mostostal-Zabrze, 244
mud brick masonry, 13–15, *14*
Muhammad Ali, 139, 143, 148n56
Mysore Survey, 54

N

Nadar, Tournachon, 90
Naif Palace, 245
Naim, C.M., 56, 70
Nasser, Gamal Abdel, 183

National Assembly Building (Kuwait City), 239
National Bank of Kuwait, 239
National Construction Company (Kuwait), 260
National Housing Authority (NHA) (Kuwait), 247, 250, 260–61
National Iranian Oil Company (NIOC), 186–87
National Office of Handicraft (Tunisia), 156, 160, 165
nationalism, 222
Naval Ministry building, 87
Nemchenok, Victor V., 204
neo-imperialism, 17
New Gourna Village (Upper Egypt), 10–13
 representational scheme, *11*
New Levant, The, 17, 215–16, 225–27, 231–32
Niedźwiecka, Elżbieta, 243
Niedźwiedki, Mieszko, 242
Non-Aligned Movement, 240

O

OAPEC (Organization of Arab Petroleum Exporting Countries), 216
October War (1973), 205
Odian, Krikor, 90–91
oil production, 215–17
Old Kuwait Courts, 245
Ong, Aihwa, 261
OPEC (Organization of Petroleum Exporting Countries), 244
Orbán, Balázs, 41
Orientalism, 125–26, 128, 143, 215
Ortaköy Mosque, 87, 98
 dome, *100*
Osten, Anton Graf Prokesch von, 40–41
Ottoman architecture, 15–16, 87–88, 91, 94, 97, 115–16
Ottoman Company for Public Works, 102
Ottoman court, foreign head-gardeners in, 25–28

Ottoman Empire, and the Levant, 225–26
Ottoman Renaissance, 110, 113, 117n10

P

Palais Indiens, 56
pan-Arabism, 158, 183
Panis, Jules Ernest, 90
Pardoe, Julia, 27, *32*
Parsons Brinckerhoff, 230
Parvillée, Léon, 90
Pasha, Ahmed Fethi, 28
patronage system, 156–57
Peres, Shimon, 184
Perpignani, Nicholas, 41
Pertevniyal Valide Sultan Mosque (Aksaray), 87–88, 110, 115
 exterior, *112*
 interior, *112*
 interior dome, *113*
Pietilä, Raili, 239
Pietilä, Reima, 239, 250
planetarium (Kuwait), 244
Planning Organization (PO; Iran), 189
Polservice, 242–44, 263
Polytechna, 243
'Pompey's Pillar', 128, *129*
Port Authority Complex (Shuwaikh), 256, *258*, 259
postcolonialism, 246. See also colonialism
postmodernism, 223, 247, 264. See also modernism
post-nationalism, 227
post-Orientalism, 126. See also Orientalism
Pückler-Muskau, Hermann Ludwig von, 30

Q

Qa'itbay mosque, 132
Qala'un mosque, 132, 139
Qazvin region, Iran
 architecture and the rebuilding project, 191–92
 earthquake in, 181, 205–6n2
 funding for reconstruction project, 187

houses in Khuznin, *186*
Israeli earthquake relief in, 181, 183, 185–86, 189, 201, 205
layout of village of Danesfahan, *197*, *198*
map of, *182*
master plan for rebuilding, *194*, 195
perspective view of a small village, *195*
plan for a bathhouse, *203*
plan for a *hamam*, 201, *202*
plan for a housing unit, *198*, 199
plan for a school, *199*, 201
redesign of water system, 189, 208n54
site plan, 196
survey of, 192, 195–96
UNTA project, 191–92
village design, 196–97
Qutb Minar, 59–62, *61*, *63*, 64–66, *65*, 81–82n39, 82n44. *See also* Quwwat-ul Islam mosque
British colonial restoration work, 65–66
British pavilion, *63*, 66
minaret inscriptions, 62, 64–65
as palimpsest, 64–65
site plan, *60*
'Smith's folly' cupola, 65–66, *65*
Quwwat-ul Islam mosque, 59, 70, 81n31, 81n33
courtyard, *61*
defacing of Hindu idols, 60–61
figural columns, 60–62
site plan, *60*

R

Rabbat, Nasser, 4, 139
Ram Raz, 57–59
Rashid Engineering, 276
Rathy, Hassan, 239
Rationalism, 90
Red Lion and Sun, 186
Rees, Joachim, 138
Reisinger, Dan, *220*
relational theory, 15
re-territorialization, 263

Rinkeby Mosque, 275, *275*, 281–82
Rivlin, Paul, 217
road systems, 196
Roberts, Arthur Austin, 56, 71
Roberts, Ed, 218–19
romanticism, 90–91, 93, 98, 100, 115
Rosenbloom, Dick, 218
Rouse, James, 218
Royal Asiatic Society, 57
Rudak (Iran)
plan for a bathhouse, *203*
plan for (earthquake reconstruction), *188*
Ruin, Klas, 276
rural development, 189, *190*, 191
Rüsen, Jörn, 144
Russia, relationship with Iran, 183
Rychlicki, Mieczysław, 247

S

Sabah Al-Salem district, 242, 249–50, *251–52*, 260
Sadat, Anwar, 216
Sair-ul-Manazil, 56
Salah Al-Salem, 256
Salaheddin Bey, 115
Salama, Salah, 261
Salhia Complex, 261
Salmiya residential building, *257*
Sava Centar (Belgrade), 243
Schiffman, Harold F., 88
Schlerff, Adam, 44
Science and Technology Studies (STS), 241
Sckell, Carl Ludwig von, 28
Scott Brown, Denise, 247
Séchan, Charles, 90
Selim III (sultan), 25–26, 31
Sester, Christian, 15, 23
burial of, 41–42, *43*
contract, *27*, 28
early training and experience, 28–29
gardens at Çırağan Palace Palace, 31–34, *32–33*

gardens in Constantinople, 29, 36–37
influence of German philosophy on, 30–31
meeting with Frankl, 36–37
in the Ottoman Empire, 35
Ottoman seal of, 36
as palace informant, 40
plan for Ottoman gardens, 29–30
residence in Constantinople, 37–39
work for German community in Istanbul, 41
Sester, Rosa (Askerian), 37, 41
  burial of, 42, *43*
Sharon, Smadar, 191
Shiber, Saba George, 242, 245
Shiber, Victor, 242
Shiber Consultants, 242, 250, *251–52*, 256, *257*
Shoked, Moshe, 192, 201, 205
SHTT. *See* Société des Hôtels Tunisiens Touristiques (Tunisian Hotel and Tourism Society; SHTT)
Silsilat-al-Muluk (Syed Ahmad), 71
Singh, R., 250
Six-Day War, 184
Skidmore, Owings and Merrill (SOM), 239
Smith, Robert, 65
Smithson, Alison, 250
Smithson, Peter, 250
social capital, 54
socialist internationalism, 240
socialization, linguistic, 88–89
Société des Hôtels Tunisiens Touristiques (Tunisian Hotel and Tourism Society; SHTT), 161, *161*, 164, 174
  brochure, *162*
Société Zin, 165
Solpol department store (Wrocław), 264
Sopon Bezirdjian, undated sketches, *114*
Spitta, Max, 7–9
Spridd, 275–77, 283–84
St Esprit Cathedral, 41
  catacombs, 42, *42*

St Mary Queen of Peace church (Wrocław-Popowice), 243
Stäck, Josef M., 282
Staniek, Ewa, 243
Staniek, Rudolf, 243
Steffel (assistant to Sester), 43–44
Steinitz, Carl, 227–228
Stirling, James, 247
Stock Exchange (Kuwait), 261
Stockholm Large Mosque Organization, 275–76, 282
Strojexport, 244
Sturm und Drang, 31
Sublime Porte, 15
Sultan, Ghazi, 245, 249
Sultan al-Mansur Qala'un complex
  Coste's drafting of ground plan, *135*
  Coste's drafting of street façade, *136*, 136
  modern floor plan of funerary and madrasa wing, *135*
  street façade, *137*
Sultan al-Zahir Baybars, madrasa of, 138
Sultan Hasan mosque, 132
Suq Al-Kuwait, 250
Suq Dawliyah, 250, *253*, 256
Suz Al-Wataniya, 250
Sweden, mosque design in, 18, 273, *274*, 275–84
Syed Ahmad Khan, 53–54, 77, 78n7
  architectural expertise of, 59, 69
  See also Āṣār-us-Ṣanādīd (Traces of Noblemen)

T
TAHAL (Water Planning for Israel), 189, 192
Talmon, Micha, 185
Tange, Kenzo, 239
tapestry production, 165–66
Taragan, Hana, 11
Tavernier, Jean-Baptiste, 56
Technical Assistance Administration (TAA), 206n5

technicalism, 4–6
Technoexportstroy, 243
technological zones, 263
technology, in context, 259–63
Tefen Model, 17, 217–19, 221–24
    Brand's plan for, *223*
    production buildings, *224*
    regional argument for, 225–27
Tekeli-Sisa Architecture Partnership, 230
Tengbom Group, 275–76, 284
Tensta, 282
Teutonia Club, 41
tourism, in Tunisia, 158–66, 174–75
transmutation, 4–5
transnational funding, 215
transnational planning, 183, 189, 191, 231
triumphal gates, 91, 93
trompe l'oeil, 98, 110, 113
tuğra, 93–95, *96*, 97–98
Tunisia
    1 per cent law, 164, 177n32
    map of, *162*
    religious reform in 157–58
    Ten-Year Plan, 159, 164, 174
    tourism industry in, 17, 158–66, 174–75
tunisianité, 153, 161, 165–66, 168, 174
Turkey
    economic development in, 230–31, 232n7
    See also Istanbul
Turki, Yahia, 164
Turki, Zoubeïr
    articles in *Faïza*, 166–68
    commission for murals, 164
    illustrations for *Faïza*, 166–68, *167*
    mural in Radiodiffusion Télévision Tunisienne, *168*, 169
    murals by, 17, 153, *154–55*, 156, 165, *173*, 174–75
    and *tunisianité*, 166, 168

U
Union Inženjering, 244
United Nations Educational, Scientific and Cultural Organization (UNESCO), 186
United Nations International Children's Emergency Fund (UNICEF), 186
United Nations Technical Assistance (UNTA) programme, 181, 187, 189
    Qazvin project, 191–92
United States, relationship with Israel and Iran, 183
University of Tehran, 187
Uppsala Mosque, 277
urban renewal, 218
urban renovation, in Stockholm, 273
urban typologies, 249–50
urbanization
    in Kuwait, 18, 244–49
    post-oil, 245–46, 260
Urbanowicz, Jan, 242
Usul-u Mimari-i Osmani (the Rules of Ottoman Architecture), 88, 110
utopian living, 273
Utzon, Jørn, 239

V
Valide Mosque. *See* Pertevniyal Valide Sultan Mosque (Aksaray)
Vaudoyer, Antoine-Laurent-Thomas, 91
Vaudoyer, Léon, 113
Venturi, Robert, 247
village design, *195*, 196
Viollet-le-Duc, Eugène Emmanuel, 109, 113, 116, 120n103, 138

W
Water Towers (Kuwait), 244
Weissmann, Ernest, 187
Weitz, Raanan, 189, 191
Wentzel, Fritz, 43–44
Wertheimer, Stef, 17, 215, 217

Aqaba International Industrial Estate, 228, 230
Gebze industrial garden, 230–31
Israeli-Palestinian industrial gardens project, 227–29, *228–29*
Tefen Model, 217–19, 221–24
Wessel, Ola Broms, 276
Westernization, in Iran, 183–84
White Revolution (Iran), 181, 186, 206n3
Wickström, Johanna, 279
Wilhelm (Kaiser), 7–9
Wiśniowska, Anna, 243, 256, *258*
Wiśnowski, Krzysztof, 241–42, 250, *251–52*, 256, *256*, *258*
World Council of Churches, 187
World Health Organization (WHO), 186
World Monuments Fund, 10
Wrocław Polytechnic, 241

Y

Yıldız Palace, 23, 38
gardens, 34, *35*, 37, *39*, 44, *45*
Yıldız Pavilion, 38–39, *40*

Z

Żabiński, Marian, 243
Zaera-Polo, Alejandro, 223
Zaituna Mosqua-University, 157
Zarhy, Moshe, 222, 224–25
Zarhy Architects, 227
Israeli-Palestinian industrial gardens project, *229*
production buildings in Tefen, *224*
Zionism, 215, 219, 221
Eurocentric, 226
liberal, *220*, 221–22
Ziya, Halid, 38
zoning, 196